BERAKOTH

TRANSLATED INTO ENGLISH WITH NOTES,
GLOSSARY AND INDICES

All rights reserved.

No part of this publication may be reproduced, stored in a retrieval system, or transmitted in any form or by any means, electronic, mechanical, photocopying or otherwise, without the prior permission of the copyright owner.

© Copyright 2006 – BN Publishing

www.bnpublishing.com

info@bnpublishing.com

INTRODUCTION

The Tractate Berakoth ('Benedictions') consists of nine chapters of which only the last four are concerned with benedictions proper. The first three contain the rules for the recital of the shema' (Chapter one, Chapter two, Chapter three), the next two those for the recital of the tefillah (Chapter four, Chapter five). The Tractate first lays down the hours within which the shema' must be recited first in the evening and then in the morning — preferably in the synagogue — and then specifies a number of conditions for its recital and the persons who are exempt from reciting it. Incidentally the conditions under which the Torah may be studied and the tefillin worn are also discussed. The recital of the tefillah is then dealt with on similar lines and its wording is discussed. Chapter six first enunciates the principle that before partaking of any kind of food one must recite a benediction, and then lays down the form of blessing for various kinds of foodstuffs. Chapter seven deals specifically with grace before and after meals, and table etiquette generally, particularly zimmun or the invitation to join in the grace. Chapter eight lays down the rules for the washing of the hands in connection with a meal, grace over the wine-cup, and the habdalah on the termination of the Sabbath. Chapter nine formulates the benedictions to be uttered on a large number of special occasions.

Berakoth contains more Aggada in proportion to its length than any other tractate. The long Chapter nine is mostly aggadic, and is notable for a lenghty excursus on the interpretation of dreams. Another striking piece of Aggada is the account of the quarrel between Rabban Gamaliel and R. Joshua in Chapter four. Chapter six throws great light on the dietary of the Jews in Babylon, while Chapter eight shows that the table customs of Jews in Palestine were largely modelled on those of the Romans.

For some reason which is not obvious Berakoth is included in the 'Order' of Zera'im, or Seeds. In complete editions of the Talmud it has always been placed first in the sequence of tractates. The reason for this is no doubt — as suggested by Maimonides — that the precepts with which it deals — the recital of the shema' and the tefillah and the benedictions — are among the first which claim the attention of the Jew in his daily life, and are also among the first taught to the Jewish child. Containing as it does few passages of legal casuistry, Berakoth is among the easiest of the tractates, and on this account and because of its wealth of Aggada it is perhaps the most suitable with which to commence the study of the Talmud.

MAURICE SIMON

PREFATORY NOTE BY THE EDITOR

The Editor desires to state that the translation of the several Tractates, and the notes thereon, are the work of the individual contributors and that he has not attempted to secure general uniformity in style or mode of rendering. He has, nevertheless, revised and supplemented, at his own discretion, their interpretation and elucidation of the original text, and has himself added the notes in square brackets containing alternative explanations and matter of historical and geographical interest.

ISIDORE EPSTEIN

Folio 2a

CHAPTER I

MISHNAH. FROM WHAT TIME MAY ONE RECITE THE SHEMA' IN THE EVENING? FROM THE TIME THAT THE PRIESTS ENTER [THEIR HOUSES] IN ORDER TO EAT THEIR TERUMAH[1] UNTIL THE END OF THE FIRST WATCH.[2] THESE ARE THE WORDS OF R. ELIEZER. THE SAGES SAY: UNTIL MIDNIGHT. R. GAMALIEL SAYS: UNTIL THE DAWN COMES UP.[3] ONCE IT HAPPENED THAT HIS[4] SONS CAME HOME [LATE] FROM A WEDDING FEAST AND THEY SAID TO HIM: WE HAVE NOT YET RECITED THE [EVENING] SHEMA'. HE SAID TO THEM: IF THE DAWN HAS NOT YET COME UP YOU ARE STILL BOUND TO RECITE. AND NOT IN RESPECT TO THIS ALONE DID THEY SO DECIDE, BUT WHEREVER THE SAGES SAY UNTIL MIDNIGHT', THE PRECEPT MAY BE PERFORMED UNTIL THE DAWN COMES UP. THE PRECEPT OF BURNING THE FAT AND THE [SACRIFICIAL] PIECES, TOO, MAY BE PERFORMED TILL THE DAWN COMES UP.[5] SIMILARLY, ALL [THE OFFERINGS] THAT ARE TO BE EATEN WITHIN ONE DAY MAY LAWFULLY BE CONSUMED TILL THE COMING UP OF THE DAWN. WHY THEN DID THE SAGES SAY 'UNTIL MIDNIGHT'? IN ORDER TO KEEP A MAN FAR FROM TRANSGRESSION.

GEMARA. On what does the Tanna base himself that he commences: FROM WHAT TIME?[6] Furthermore, why does he deal first with the evening [Shema']? Let him begin with the morning [Shema']! — The Tanna bases himself on the Scripture, where it is written [And thou shalt recite them] ... when thou liest down and when thou risest up,[7] and he states [the oral law] thus: When does the time of the recital of the Shema' of lying down begin? When the priests enter to eat their terumah.[8] And if you like, I can answer: He learns [the precedence of the evening] from the account of the creation of the world, where it is written, And there was evening and there was morning, one day.[9] Why then does he teach in the sequel: THE MORNING [SHEMA'] IS PRECEDED BY TWO BENEDICTIONS AND FOLLOWED BY ONE. THE EVENING [SHEMA'] IS PRECEDED BY TWO BENEDICTIONS AND FOLLOWED BY TWO?[10] Let him there, too, mention the evening [Shema'] first? — The Tanna commences with the evening [Shema'], and proceeds then to the morning [Shema']. While dealing with the morning [Shema'], he expounds all the matters relating to it, and then he returns again to the matters relating to the evening [Shema'].

---

[1] If the priests have become ritually unclean, they are not permitted to eat terumah, to which a certain holiness attaches, till they have taken a bath and the sun has set.
[2] I.e., until either a fourth or a third of the night has passed. V. infra 3a.
[3] Maim: about one and one fifth hours before actual sunrise. V. Pes. 93b.
[4] R. Gamaliel's.
[5] This sentence is parenthetical. It is nowhere laid down that the burning of the fat etc. is permitted only till midnight. It is mentioned here in order to inform us that wherever the time fixed for the performance of a duty is the night, it expires at the rise of the dawn (Rashi).
[6] I.e., where is it stated in the Law that the recital of the Shema' is prescribed at all?
[7] Deut. VI, 7.
[8] This answers also the second question, as the Bible mentions first the recital of the evening time.
[9] Gen. I, 5.
[10] Infra 11a.

The Master said: FROM THE TIME THAT THE PRIESTS ENTER TO EAT THEIR 'TERUMAH'. When do the priests eat terumah? From the time of the appearance of the stars. Let him then say: 'From the time of the appearance of the stars'? — This very thing he wants to teach us, in passing, that the priests may eat terumah from the time of the appearance of the stars. And he also wants to teach us that the expiatory offering is not indispensable,[1] as it has been taught[2]: And when the sun sets we-taher[3], the setting of the sun is indispensable [as a condition of his fitness] to eat terumah, but the expiatory offering is not indispensable to enable him to eat terumah. But how do you know that these words 'and the sun sets' mean the setting of the sun, and this 'we-taher' means that the day clears away?

---

[1] For the eating of terumah even where it is necessary to complete the purification rites, v. Ker. II, 1.
[2] Sifra, Emor.
[3] Lev. XXII, 7. This can be rendered as E.V.: 'he (the man) is clean', or it (the day) is clean (clear), as understood now by the Gemara.

Berakoth 2b

It means perhaps: And when the sun [of the next morning] appears, and we-taher means the man becomes clean?[1] — Rabbah son of R. Shila explains: In that case, the text would have to read we-yithar.[2] What is the meaning of we-taher?[3] The day clears away, conformably to the common expression, The sun has set and the day has cleared away. This explanation of Rabbah son of R. Shila was unknown in the West[4], and they raised the question: This 'and the sun sets', does it mean the real setting of the sun, and 'we-taher' means the day clears away? Or does it perhaps mean the appearance of the sun, and we-taher means the man becomes clean? They solved it from a Baraitha, it being stated in a Baraitha: The sign of the thing is the appearance of the stars. Hence you learn that it is the setting of the sun [which makes him clean] and the meaning of we-taher is the clearing away of the day.

The Master said: FROM THE TIME THAT THE PRIESTS ENTER TO EAT THEIR 'TERUMAH'. They pointed to a contradiction [from the following]: From what time may one recite the Shema' in the evening? From the time that the poor man[5] comes [home] to eat his bread with salt till he rises from his meal. The last clause certainly contradicts the Mishnah. Does the first clause also contradict the Mishnah? — No. The poor man and the priest have one and the same time.

They pointed to a contradiction [from the following]: From what time may one begin to recite the Shema' in the evening? From the time that the people come [home] to eat their meal on a Sabbath eve. These are the words of R. Meir. But the Sages say: From the time that the priests are entitled to eat their terumah. A sign for the matter is the appearance of the stars. And though there is no real proof of it,[6] there is a hint for it. For it is written: So we wrought in the work: and half of them held the spears from the rise of the dawn till the appearance of the stars.[7] And it says further: That in the night they may be a guard to us, and may labour in the day.[8] (Why this second citation?[9] — If you object and say that the night really begins with the setting of the sun, but that they left late and came early, [I shall reply]: Come and hear [the other verse]: 'That in the night they may be a guard to us, and may labour in the day'). Now it is assumed that the 'poor man' and 'the people' have the same time [for their evening meal.][10] And if you say that the poor man and the priest also have the same time, then the Sages would be saying the same thing as R. Meir? Hence you must conclude that the poor man has one time and the priest has another time? — No; the 'poor man' and the priest have the same time, but the 'poor man' and the 'people' have not the same time.

But have the 'poor man' and the priest really the same time? They pointed to a contradiction [from the

---

[1] Through his sin-offering.
[2] The verb being in the future.
[3] Which may be taken as a past tense, the waw not being conversive.
[4] In the Palestinian schools.
[5] Who cannot afford an artificial light.
[6] That the day ends with the appearance of the stars.
[7] Neh. IV, 15.
[8] Ibid. 16.
[9] The first verse seems to afford ample proof.
[10] I.e., the time the 'poor man' mentioned in the first Baraitha comes home to take his evening meal is identical with that at which people generally come to eat their meals on Sabbath eve.

following]: From what time may one begin to recite the Shema' in the evening? From the time that the [Sabbath] day becomes hallowed on the Sabbath eve. These are the words of R. Eliezer. R. Joshua says: From the time that the priests are ritually clean to eat their terumah. R. Meir says: From the time that the priests take their ritual bath in order to eat their terumah. (Said R. Judah to him: When the priests take their ritual bath it is still day-time!)[1] R. Hanina says: From the time that the poor man comes [home] to eat his bread with salt. R. Ahai (some say: R. Aha). says: From the time that most people come home to sit down to their meal. Now, if you say that the poor man and the priest have the same time, then R. Hanina and R. Joshua would be saying the same thing? From this you must conclude, must you not, that the poor man has one time and the priest has another time. — Draw indeed that conclusion!

Which of them is later? — It is reasonable to conclude that the 'poor man' is later. For if you say that the 'poor man' is earlier, R. Hanina would be saying the same thing as R. Eliezer.[2] Hence you must conclude that the poor man is later, must you not? — Draw indeed that conclusion.

The Master said:[3] 'R. Judah said to him: When the priests take their ritual bath it is still daytime!' The objection of R. Judah to R. Meir seems well founded? — R. Meir may reply as follows: Do you think that I am referring to the twilight [as defined] by you?[4] I am referring to the twilight [as defined] by R. Jose. For R. Jose says: The twilight is like the twinkling of an eye. This[5] enters and that[6] departs — and one cannot exactly fix it.[7]

---

[1] And not even twilight, v. Shab. 35a.
[2] Tosef. points out that the ground for this statement is not clear.
[3] In the Baraitha just quoted.
[4] According to which definition it lasts as long as it takes to walk half a mil, v. Shab. 34b.
[5] The evening.
[6] The day.
[7] And consequently the priests may bathe at twilight as defined by R. Jose since it is still day, and one may also read at that time the Shema' since it is practically night.

Folio 3a

There is a contradiction between R. Meir [of one Baraitha][1] and R. Meir [of the last Baraitha]?[2] — Yes, two Tannaim transmit different versions of R. Meir's opinion. There is a contradiction between R. Eliezer [of the last Baraitha][3] and R. Eliezer [of the Mishnah]?[4] — Yes, two Tannaim[5] transmit two different versions of R. Eliezer's opinion. If you wish I can say: The first clause of the Mishnah[6] is not R. Eliezer's.[7]

UNTIL THE END OF THE FIRST WATCH. What opinion does R. Eliezer hold? If he holds that the night has three watches, let him say: Till four hours [in the night]. And if he holds that the night has four watches, let him say: Till three hours? — He holds indeed, that the night has three watches, but he wants to teach us that there are watches in heaven[8] as well as on earth. For it has been taught: R. Eliezer says: The night has three watches, and at each watch the Holy One, blessed be He, sits and roars like a lion. For it is written: The Lord does roar from on high, and raise His voice from His holy habitation; 'roaring He doth roar'[9] because of his fold. And the sign of the thing is:[10] In the first watch, the ass brays; in the second, the dogs bark; in the third, the child sucks from the breast of his mother, and the woman talks with her husband. What does R. Eliezer understand [by the word watch]? Does he mean the beginning of the watches? The beginning of the first watch needs no sign, it is the twilight! Does he mean the end of the watches? The end of the last watch needs no sign, it is the dawn of the day! He, therefore, must think of the end of the first watch, of the beginning of the last watch, and of the midst of the middle watch. If you like I can say: He refers to the end of all the watches. And if you object that the last watch needs no sign, [I reply] that it may be of use for the recital of the Shema', and for a man who sleeps in a dark room[11] and does not know when the time of the recital arrives. When the woman talks with her husband and the child sucks from the breast of the mother, let him rise and recite.

R. Isaac b. Samuel says in the name of Rab: The night has three watches, and at each watch the Holy One, blessed be He, sits and roars like a lion and says: Woe to the children, on account of whose sins I destroyed My house and burnt My temple and exiled them among the nations of the world.

It has been taught: R. Jose says, I was once travelling on the road, and I entered into one of the ruins of Jerusalem in order to pray. Elijah of blessed memory appeared and waited for me at the door till I finished my prayer.[12] After I finished my prayer, he said to me: Peace be with you, my master! and I replied: Peace be with you, my master and teacher! And he said to me: My son, why did you go into this ruin? I replied: To pray. He said to me: You ought to have prayed on the road. I replied: I feared

---

[1] Where he says: When people come home for their Sabbath-meal, which is after twilight.
[2] Which fixes a time which is before twilight.
[3] Which fixes sunset as the time-standard.
[4] Which fixes as time-standard, the appearance of the stars (when priests enter to eat terumah).
[5] V. Glos.
[6] Where the beginning of the time is fixed.
[7] 7R. Eliezer's ruling being merely with reference to the terminus ad quem.
[8] Among the ministering angels.
[9] So literally. Thus 'roaring' is mentioned three times in the text.
[10] I.e., of each watch.
[11] That has no windows to admit the daylight.
[12] The Tefillah, v. Glos.

lest passers-by might interrupt me. He said to me: You ought to have said an abbreviated prayer.[1] Thus I then learned from him three things: One must not go into a ruin; one may say the prayer on the road; and if one does say his prayer on the road, he recites an abbreviated prayer. He further said to me: My son, what sound did you hear in this ruin? I replied: I heard a divine voice, cooing like a dove, and saying: Woe to the children, on account of whose sins I destroyed My house and burnt My temple and exiled them among the nations of the world! And he said to me: By your life and by your head! Not in this moment alone does it so exclaim, but thrice each day does it exclaim thus! And more than that, whenever the Israelites go into the synagogues and schoolhouses and respond: 'May His great name be blessed!'[2] the Holy One, blessed be He, shakes His head and says: Happy is the king who is thus praised in this house! Woe[3] to the father who had to banish his children, and woe to the children who had to be banished from the table of their father!

Our Rabbis taught: there are three reasons why one must not go into a ruin: because of suspicion,[4] of falling debris and of demons. — [It states] 'Because of suspicion'.[5] It would be sufficient to say, because of falling debris'? —

---

[1] V. infra 29a.
[2] The principal congregational response in the doxology, the Kaddish v. P.B. p. 37.
[3] V. D.S. cur. edd.; what is there for the father.
[4] That a woman may be waiting for him there.
[5] The Gemara now proceeds to explain why all the three reasons must be mentioned.

Berakoth 3b

When the ruin is new.[1] But it would be sufficient to say: 'because of demons'? — When there are two people.[2] If there are two people, then there is no suspicion either? — When both are licentious [there is suspicion]. — [It states] 'Because of falling debris'. It would be sufficient to say: 'because of suspicion and demons'? — When there are two decent people. [It states] 'Because of demons'. It would be sufficient to say; 'because of suspicion and falling debris'? — When there are two decent people going into a new ruin. But if there are two, then there is no danger of demons either? — In their haunt there is danger. If you like I can say, indeed the reference is to one man and to a new ruin which was situated in the fields; in which case there is no suspicion, for a woman would not be found in the fields, but the danger of demons does exist.

Our Rabbis taught: The night has four watches. These are the words of Rabbi. R. Nathan says: Three. What is the reason of R. Nathan? — It is written: So Gideon, and the hundred men that were with him, came into the outermost part of the camp in the beginning of the middle watch.[3] And one taught: Under 'middle' is to be understood only something which is preceded by one and followed by one. And Rabbi?[4] — 'The middle' means: one of the middle ones. And R. Nathan? — Not 'one of the middle ones' is written, but 'the middle' is written. What is Rabbi's reason? — R. Zerika, in the name of R. Joshua b. Levi, says: One verse reads, At midnight do I rise to give thanks unto Thee because of Thy righteous ordinances.[5] And another verse reads: Mine eyes forestall the watches.[6] How is this?[7] — [This is possible only if] the night has four watches. And R. Nathan? — He is of the opinion of R. Joshua, as we have learnt: R. Joshua says: until the third hour, for such is the custom of kings, to rise in the third hour.[8] Six hours of the night and two hours of the day amount to two watches.[9] R. Ashi says: One watch and a half are also spoken of as 'watches'. (R. Zerika further said, in the name of R. Ammi in the name of R. Joshua b. Levi: One may discuss in the presence of a dead body only things relating to the dead. R. Abba b. Kahana says: This refers only to religious matters,[10] but as for worldly matter there is no harm. Another version is: R. Abba b. Kahana says: This refers even to religious matters. How much more so to worldly matters!)

But did David rise at midnight? [Surely] he rose with the evening dusk? For it is written: I rose with the neshef and cried.[11] And how do you know that this word neshef means the evening? It is written: In the neshef, in the evening of the day, in the blackness of night and the darkness![12] — R. Oshaia, in the name of R. Aha, replies: David said: Midnight never passed me by in my sleep. R. Zera says: Till

---

[1] So that there is no danger of falling debris.
[2] The assumption is that where two are together there is no danger of an attack by demons.
[3] Judg. VII, 19.
[4] How does he explain the term middle?
[5] Ps. CXIX, 62.
[6] Ibid. 148.
[7] That somebody may rise at midnight and still have two watches before him, the minimum of the plural 'watches' being two.
[8] V. infra 9b. With reference to the morning Shema'.
[9] Since the day for royal personages begins at eight a.m. that is with the third hour when they rise. David by rising at midnight forestalled them by eight hours, i.e., two watches each having four hours.
[10] Lit., 'words of the Torah'. It would show disrespect for the dead.
[11] Ibid. 147. E.V. 'dawn'.
[12] Prov. VII, 9.

midnight he used to slumber like a horse,[1] from thence on he rose with the energy of a lion. R. Ashi says: Till midnight he studied the Torah, from thence on he recited songs and praises. But does neshef mean the evening? Surely neshef means the morning? For it is written: And David slew them from the 'neshef' to the evening 'ereb of the next day,[2] and does not this mean, from the 'morning dawn' to the evening? — No. [It means:] from the [one] eventide to the [next] eventide. If so, let him write: From neshef to neshef, or from 'ereb to 'ereb? — Rather, said Raba: There are two kinds of neshef: [the morning neshef], when the evening disappears [nashaf] and the morning arrives,[3] [and the evening neshef], when the day disappears [nashaf] and the evening arrives.[4]

But did David know the exact time of midnight? Even our teacher Moses did not know it! For it is written: About midnight I will go out into the midst of Egypt.[5] Why 'about midnight'? Shall we say that the Holy One, blessed be He, said to him: 'About midnight'? Can there be any doubt in the mind of God?[6] Hence we must say that God told him 'at midnight', and he came and said: 'About midnight'. Hence he [Moses] was in doubt; can David then have known it? — David had a sign. For so said R. Aha b. Bizana in the name of R. Simeon the Pious: A harp was hanging above David's bed. As soon as midnight arrived, a North wind came and blew upon it and it played of itself. He arose immediately and studied the Torah till the break of dawn. After the break of dawn the wise men of Israel came in to see him and said to him: Our lord, the King, Israel your people require sustenance! He said to them: Let them go out and make a living one from the other.[7] They said to him: A handful cannot satisfy a lion, nor can a pit be filled up with its own clods.[8] He said to them: Then go out in troops and attack [the enemy for plunder]. They at once took counsel with Ahithofel and consulted the Sanhedrin and questioned the Urim and Tummim.[9] R. Joseph says: What verse [may be cited in support of this]? And after Ahithofel was Jehoiada, the son of Benaiah,[10] and Abiathar; and the captain of the King's host was Joab.[11] 'Ahithofel', this was the counsellor. And so it is said: Now the counsel of Ahithofel, which he counselled in those days, was as if a man inquired of the word of God.

---

[1] That has a very light sleep, v. Suk. 26a.
[2] I Sam. XXX, 17.
[3] Neshef in this case denoting 'dawn'.
[4] Neshef in this case denoting 'dusk'.
[5] Ex. XI, 4.
[6] Lit., 'heaven'.
[7] Let the rich support the poor.
[8] We cannot be self-supporting to supply all our needs, any more than a handful can satisfy a lion, or the soil taken out of a pit fill its cavity.
[9] The divine oracle of the High-Priest's breast-plate.
1.22. The text here has 'Benaiah, the son of Jehoiada', who is mentioned in II Sam. XX, 2.23.
[10] I Chron. XXVII, 34.
[11] II Sam. XVI, 23.

Folio 4a

'Benaiah the son of Jehoiada', this means the Sanhedrin. 'And Abiathar',[1] these are the Urim and Tummim. And so it says: And Benaiah the son of Jehoiada was over the Kerethi and Pelethi.[2] Why are they[3] called 'Kerethi' and 'Pelethi'? Kerethi, because their words are decisive [korethim]; Pelethi, because they are distinguished [mufla'im] through their words. And then it comes 'the captain of the King's host Joab'. R. Isaac b. Adda says: (Some say, R. Isaac the son of Addi says) Which verse?[4] Awake, my glory; awake, psaltery and harp; I will awake the dawn.[5]

R. Zera says:[6] Moses certainly knew and David, too, knew [the exact time of midnight]. Since David knew, why did he need the harp? That he might wake from his sleep. Since Moses knew, why did he say 'about midnight'? — Moses thought that the astrologers of Pharaoh might make a mistake, and then they would say that Moses was a liar. For so a Master said: Let thy tongue acquire the habit of saying, 'I know not', lest thou be led to falsehoods [lying]. R. Ashi says: It[7] was at midnight of the night of the thirteenth passing into the fourteenth [of Nisan], and thus said Moses to Israel: The Holy One, blessed be He, said: Tomorrow [at the hour] like[8] the midnight of to-night, I will go out into the midst of Egypt.

A prayer of David … Keep my soul, for I am pious.[9] Levi and R. Isaac:[10] The one says, Thus spoke David before the Holy One, blessed be He; Master of the world, am I not pious? All the kings of the East and the West sleep to the third hour [of the day], but I, at midnight I rise to give thanks unto Thee.[11] The other one says: Thus spoke David before the Holy One, blessed be He: Master of the world, am I not pious? All the kings of the East and the West sit with all their pomp among their company, whereas my hands are soiled with the blood [of menstruation], with the foetus and the placenta, in order to declare a woman clean for her husband.[12] And what is more, in all that I do I consult my teacher, Mephibosheth, and I say to him: My teacher Mephibosheth, is my decision right? Did I correctly convict, correctly acquit, correctly declare clean, correctly declare unclean? And I am not ashamed [to ask]. R. Joshua, the son of R. Iddi, says Which verse [may be cited in support]? And I recite Thy testimonies before kings and am not ashamed.[13] A Tanna taught: His name was not Mephibosheth. And why then was he called Mephibosheth? Because he humiliated[14] David in the

---

[1] He was the High Priest of David.
[2] II Sam. XX, 23.
[3] The Sanhedrin (Rashi). The Tosafists, however, refer this to the Urim and Tummim.
[4] May be cited in support of the story of David's harp.
[5] Ps. LVII 9.
[6] Here the Gemara resumes the discussion of the question raised above as to how it is possible that David knew something which Moses did not know.
[7] The incident of Ex. XI, 4.
[8] The particle ka being rendered 'like' and not 'about'.
[9] Ps. LXXXVI, 1-2.
[10] Offer different homiletical interpretations.
[11] Ibid. CXIX, 62.
[12] The restrictions of Lev. XII, 2ff do not apply to all cases of abortion nor is all discharge treated as menstrual, and David is represented as occupying himself with deciding such questions instead of with feasting. MS.M. omits 'blood'.
[13] Ps. CXIX, 46.
[14] The homiletical interpretation of the name is, Out of my mouth humiliation.

Halachah. Therefore was David worthy of the privilege that Kileab[1] should issue from him. R. Johanan said: His name was not Kileab but Daniel. Why then was he called Kileab? Because he humiliated [maklim] Mephibosheth [ab][2] in the Halachah. And concerning him Solomon said in his wisdom: My son, if thy heart be wise, my heart will be glad, even mine.[3] And he said further: My son, be wise, and make my heart glad, that I may answer him that taunteth me.[4]

But how could David call himself pious? It is not written: I am not sure [lule] to see the good reward of the Lord in the land of the living;[5] and a Tanna taught in the name of R. Jose: Why are there dots upon the world 'lule'?[6] David spoke before the Holy One, blessed be He: 'Master of the world, I am sure that you will pay a good reward to the righteous in the world to come, but I do not know whether I shall have a share in it'?[7] [He was afraid that] some sin might cause [his exclusion].[8] This conforms to the following saying of R. Jacob b. Iddi. For R. Jacob b. Iddi pointed to a contradiction. One verse reads: And behold, I am with thee, and will keep thee whithersoever thou goest,[9] and the other verse reads: Then Jacob was greatly afraid![10] [The answer is that] he thought that some sin might cause [God's promise not to be fulfilled]. Similarly it has been taught: Till Thy people pass over, O Lord, till the people pass over that Thou hast gotten.[11] 'Till Thy people pass over, O Lord': this is the first entry [into the Land]. 'Till the people pass over that Thou hast gotten': this is the second entry. Hence the Sages say: The intention was to perform a miracle for Israel[12] in the days of Ezra, even as it was performed for them in the days of Joshua bin Nun,[13] but sin caused [the miracle to be withheld].[14]

THE SAGES SAY: UNTIL MIDNIGHT. Whose view did the Sages adopt?[15] If it is R. Eliezer's view, then let them express themselves in the same way as R. Eliezer?

R. Gamaliel understands them to mean, when you sleep; hence he fixes the whole night as the time of the recital.

---

[1] Cf. II Sam. III, 3.
[2] Lit., 'father', a teacher.
[3] Prov. XXIII, 15.
[4] Ibid. XXVII, II.
[5] Ps. XXVII, 13.
[6] The dots are interpreted as meaning he was not quite sure.
[7] Hence you see that he was not so sure of his piety.
[8] This is the reply to the question. David was quite sure of his general pious character, but he feared that his sins might exclude him from the reward etc.
[9] Gen. XXVIII, 15.
[10] Ibid. XXXII, 8. The contradiction lies in the fact that Jacob was afraid in spite of having God's promise.
[11] Ex. XV, 16.
[12] Lit. 'the Israelites were worthy to have a miracle performed for them'.
[13] When they entered victoriously.
[14] And they entered only as subjects of Cyrus.
[15] According to the Gemara, R. Eliezer and R. Gamaliel differ in the interpretation of the Bible words, 'And when thou liest down'. R. Eliezer explains them to mean, when you go to bed; hence he says that the time expires at the end of the first watch.

Berakoth 4b

If it is R. Gamaliel's view, let them express themselves in the same way as R. Gamaliel? — In reality it is R. Gamaliel's view that they adopted, and their reason for saying, UNTIL MIDNIGHT is to keep a man far from transgression. For so it has been taught: The Sages made a fence for their words so that a man, on returning home from the field in the evening, should not say: I shall go home, eat a little, drink a little, sleep a little, and then I shall recite the Shema' and the Tefillah, and meanwhile, sleep may overpower him, and as a result he will sleep the whole night. Rather should a man, when returning home from the field in the evening, go to the synagogue. If he is used to read the Bible, let him read the Bible, and if he is used to repeat the Mishnah, let him repeat the Mishnah, and then let him recite the Shema' and say the Tefillah, [go home] and eat his meal and say the Grace. And whosoever transgresses the words of the Sages deserves to die. Why this difference that, in other cases, they do not say 'he deserves to die', and here they do say 'he deserves to die'? — If you wish, I can say because here there is danger of sleep overpowering him. Or, if you wish, I can say because they want to exclude the opinion of those who say that the evening prayer is only voluntary.[1] Therefore they teach us that it is obligatory.

The Master said:[2] 'Let him recite Shema' and say the Tefillah'. This accords with the view of R. Johanan.[3] For R. Johanan says: Who inherits the world to come? The one who follows the Ge'ullah[4] immediately with the evening Tefillah. R. Joshua b. Levi says: The Tefilloth were arranged to be said in the middle.[5] What is the ground of their difference? — If you like, I can say it is [the interpretation of] a verse, and if you like, I can say that they reason differently. For R. Johanan argues: Though the complete deliverance from Egypt took place in the morning time only,[6] there was also some kind of deliverance in the evening;[7] whereas R. Joshua b. Levi argues that since the real deliverance happened in the morning [that of the evening] was no proper deliverance.[8] 'Or if you like, I can say it is [the interpretation of] a verse'. And both interpret one and the same verse, [viz.,] When thou liest down and when thou risest up.[9] R. Johanan argues: There is here an analogy between lying down and rising. Just as [at the time of] rising, recital of Shema' precedes Tefillah, so also [at the time of] lying down, recital of Shema' precedes Tefillah. R. Joshua b. Levi argues [differently]: There is here an analogy between lying down and rising. Just as [at the time of] rising, the recital of Shema' is next to [rising from] bed,[10] so also [at the time of] lying down, recital of Shema' must be next to [getting into] bed.[11]

---

[1] V. infra 27b.
[2] In the Baraitha just quoted.
[3] That in the evening, too, the Shema' has to precede the Tefillah.
[4] The benediction for the deliverance from Egypt (v. P. B. p. 99). It follows the Shema' and precedes the Tefillah.
[5] Between the two Shema' recitals. In the morning the Tefillah follows, and in the evening it precedes the Shema'.
[6] As it says, On the morrow of the Passover the children of Israel went forth (Num. XXXIII, 3).
[7] Hence even in the evening Ge'ullah must be joined closely to Tefillah.
[8] Hence in the evening the Ge'ullah must not be joined closely to Tefillah.
[9] Deut. VI, 7.
[10] I.e., it is the first prayer said on rising from the bed.
[11] I.e., it is the last prayer said before going to bed.

Mar b. Rabina raised an objection. In the evening, two benedictions precede and two benedictions follow the Shema'.[1] Now, if you say he has to join Ge'ullah with Tefillah, behold he does not do so, for he has to say [in between], 'Let us rest'?[2] — I reply: Since the Rabbis ordained the benediction, 'Let us rest', it is as if it were a long Ge'ullah. For, if you do not admit that, how can he join in the morning, seeing that R. Johanan says: In the beginning [of the Tefillah] one has to say: O Lord, open Thou my lips [etc.],[3] and at the end one has to say: Let the words of my mouth be acceptable?[4] [The only explanation] there [is that] since the Rabbis ordained that O Lord, open Thou my lips should be said, it is like a long Tefillah.[5] Here, too, since the Rabbis ordained that 'Let us rest' should be said, it is like a long Ge'ullah.

R. Eleazar b. Abina says: Whoever recites [the psalm] Praise of David[6] three times daily, is sure to inherit[7] the world to come. What is the reason? Shall I say it is because it has an alphabetical arrangement? Then let him recite, Happy are they that are upright in the way,[8] which has an eightfold alphabetical arrangement. Again, is it because it contains [the verse], Thou openest Thy hand [and satisfiest every living thing with favour]?[9] Then let him recite the great Hallel,[10] where it is written: Who giveth food to all flesh![11] — Rather, [the reason is] because it contains both.[12] R. Johanan says: Why is there no nun in Ashre?[13] Because the fall of Israel's enemies[14] begins with it. For it is written: Fallen is[15] the virgin of Israel, she shall no more rise.[16] (In the West[17] this verse is thus interpreted: She is fallen, but she shall no more fall. Rise, O virgin of Israel). R. Nahman b. Isaac says: Even so, David refers to it by inspiration[18] and promises them an uplifting. For it is written: The Lord upholdeth all that fall.[19]

R. Eleazar b. Abina said furthermore: Greater is [the achievement] ascribed to Michael than that ascribed to Gabriel. For of Michael it is written: Then flew unto me one of the Seraphim,[20] whereas

---

[1] V. infra 11a.
[2] This is the second benediction, to be said in the evening between Ge'ullah and Tefillah, v. P.B. p. 99. The prayer, 'Blessed be the Lord for evermore' that follows the second benediction is a later addition.
[3] Ps. LI, 17. This verse said in introduction to the Tefillah ought to be considered an interruption.
[4] Ps. XIX, 15.
[5] I.e., part of the Tefillah.
[6] I.e., Ps. CXLV.
[7] Lit., 'that he is a son of'.
[8] Ps. CXIX.
[9] Ibid. CXLV, 16.
[10] I.e., Ibid. CXXXVI. On Hallel, v. Glos.
[11] Ibid. v. 25.
[12] The alphabetical arrangement and the sixteenth verse, dealing with God's merciful provision for all living things.
[13] This is Psalm CXLV, which is arranged alphabetically, save that the verse beginning with the letter nun (N) is missing.
[14] Euphemistic for Israel.
[15] Heb.
[16] Amos V, 2.
[17] Palestine. V. supra p. 3, n. 4.
[18] Lit., 'the Holy Spirit'. The meaning is, David knew by inspiration that Amos was going to prophesy the downfall of Israel, and he refers to that verse and prophesies their being raised up again, though their downfall is not mentioned by David.
[19] Ps. CXLV, 14.
[20] Isa. VI, 6.

of Gabriel it is written: The man Gabriel whom I had seen in the vision at the beginning, being caused to
fly in a flight etc.¹ How do you know that this [word] 'one' [of the Seraphim] means Michael? — R. Johanan says: By an analogy from [the words] 'one', 'one'. Here it is written: Then flew unto me one of the Seraphim; and in another place it is written: But, lo, Michael, one of the chief princes, came to help me.² A Tanna taught: Michael [reaches his goal] in one [flight], Gabriel in two, Elijah in four, and the Angel of Death in eight. In the time of plague, however, [the Angel of Death, too, reaches his goal] in one.

R. Joshua b. Levi says: Though a man has recited the Shema' in the synagogue, it is a religious act to recite it again upon his bed. R. Assi says: Which verse [may be cited in support]? Tremble and sin not; commune with your own heart upon your bed, and be still, Selah.³ R. Nahman, however, says:

---

¹ Dan. IX, 21. The meaning is: Michael covered the distance in one flight, without any stop, whereas Gabriel had to make two flights, resting in between. This is inferred from the fact that the word fly occurs twice.
² Ibid. X, 13.
³ Ps. IV, 5.

Folio 5a

If he is a scholar, then it is not necessary. Abaye says: Even a scholar should recite one verse of supplication, as for instance: Into Thy hand I commit my spirit. Thou hast redeemed me, O Lord, Thou God of truth.[1]

R. Levi b. Hama says in the name of R. Simeon b. Lakish: A man should always incite the good impulse [in his soul][2] to fight against the evil impulse. For it is written: Tremble and sin not.[3] If he subdues it, well and good. If not, let him study the Torah. For it is written: 'Commune with your own heart'.[4] If he subdues it, well and good. If not, let him recite the Shema'. For it is written: 'Upon your bed'. If he subdues it, well and good. If not, let him remind himself of the day of death. For it is written: 'And be still, Selah'.

R. Levi b. Hama says further in the name of R. Simeon b. Lakish: What is the meaning of the verse: And I will give thee the tables of stone, and the law and the commandment, which I have written that thou mayest teach them?[5] 'Tables of stone': these are the ten commandments; 'the law': this is the Pentateuch; 'the commandment': this is the Mishnah; 'which I have written': these are the Prophets and the Hagiographa; 'that thou mayest teach them': this is the Gemara.[6] It teaches [us] that all these things were given to Moses on Sinai.

R. Isaac says: If one recites the Shema' upon his bed, it is as though he held a two-edged sword in his hand.[7] For it is said: Let the high praises of God be in their mouth, and a two-edged sword in their hand.[8] How does it indicate this? — Mar Zutra, (some say, R. Ashi) says: [The lesson is] from the preceding verse. For it is written: Let the saints exult in glory, let them sing for joy upon their beds,[9] and then it is written: Let the high praises of God be in their mouth, and a two-edged sword in their hand. R. Isaac says further: If] one recites the Shema' upon his bed, the demons keep away from him. For it is said: And the sons of reshef[10] fly ['uf] upward.[11] The word 'uf refers only to the Torah, as it is written: Wilt thou cause thine eyes to close [hata'if][12] upon it? It is gone.[13] And 'reshef' refers only to the demons, as it is said: The wasting of hunger, and the devouring of the reshef [fiery bolt] and bitter destruction.[14] R. Simeon b. Lakish says: If one studies the Torah, painful sufferings are kept away

---

[1] Ibid. XXXI, 6.
[2] In the Talmud the good impulses and evil impulses of a man are personified as two genii or spirits dwelling in his soul, the one prompting him to do good things and the other one to do wicked things. The meaning of this saying here is that a man has always to make an effort and to fight against the evil instincts.
[3] Ibid. IV, 5. The word uzdr is translated, not as tremble, but as fight, incite to fight.
[4] Ibid.
[5] Ex. XXIV, 12.
[6] MS.M. Talmud, v. B.M., Sonc. ed., p. 206, n. 6.
[7] To protect him against the demons.
[8] Ps. CXLIX, 6.
[9] Ibid. v. 5.
[10] E.V. 'sparks'.
[11] Job V, 7.
[12] I.e., if thou neglect it (the Torah). E.V. 'Wilt thou set thine eyes etc.'.
[13] Prov. XXIII, 5.
[14] Deut. XXXII, 24.

from him. For it is said: And the sons of reshef fly upward. The word 'uf refers only to the Torah, as it is written: 'Wilt thou cause thine eyes to close upon it? It is gone'. And 'reshef' refers only to painful sufferings, as it is said: 'The wasting of hunger, and the devouring of the reshef [fiery bolt]. R. Johanan said to him: This[1] is known even to school children.[2] For it is said: And He said: If thou wilt diligently hearken to the voice of the Lord thy God, and wilt do that which is right in His eyes, and wilt give ear to His commandments, and keep all His statutes, I will put none of the diseases upon thee which I have put upon the Egyptians; for I am the Lord that healeth thee.[3] Rather [should you say]: If one has the opportunity to study the Torah and does not study it, the Holy One, blessed be He, visits him with ugly and painful sufferings which stir him up. For it is said: I was dumb with silence, I kept silence from the good thing, and my pain was stirred up.[4] 'The good thing' refers only to the Torah, as it is said: For I give you good doctrine; forsake ye not My teaching.[5]

R. Zera (some say, R. Hanina b. Papa) says: Come and see how the way of human beings differs from the way of the Holy One, blessed be He. It is the way of human beings that when a man sells[6] a valuable object to his fellow, the seller grieves and the buyer rejoices. The Holy One, blessed be He, however, is different. He gave the Torah to Israel and rejoiced. For it is said: For I give you good doctrine; forsake ye not My teaching.

Raba (some say, R. Hisda) says: If a man sees that painful sufferings visit him, let him examine his conduct. For it is said: Let us search and try our ways, and return unto the Lord.[7] If he examines and finds nothing [objectionable], let him attribute it to the neglect of the study of the Torah. For it is said: Happy is the man whom Thou chastenest, O Lord, and teachest out of Thy law.[8] If he did attribute it [thus], and still did not find [this to be the cause], let him be sure that these are chastenings of love. For it is said: For whom the Lord loveth He correcteth.[9]

Raba, in the name of R. Sahorah, in the name of R. Huna, says: If the Holy One, blessed be He, is pleased with a man, he crushes him with painful sufferings. For it is said: And the Lord was pleased with [him, hence] he crushed him by disease.[10] Now, you might think that this is so even if he did not accept them with love. Therefore it is said: To see if his soul would offer itself in restitution.[11] Even as the trespass-offering must be brought by consent, so also the sufferings must be endured with consent. And if he did accept them, what is his reward? He will see his seed, prolong his days.[12] And more than that, his knowledge [of the Torah] will endure with him. For it is said: The purpose of the Lord will prosper in his hand.[13]

R. Jacob b. Idi and R. Aha b. Hanina differ with regard to the following: The one says: Chastenings

---

[1] That the Torah is a protection against painful disease.
[2] Who study the Pentateuch, where it is plainly said.
[3] Ex. XV, 26.
[4] Ps. XXXIX, 3. E.V. 'I held my peace, had no comfort, and my pain was held in check'.
[5] Prov. IV, 2.
[6] Out of poverty and not for business.
[7] Lam. III, 40.
[8] Ps. XCIV, 12.
[9] Prov. III, 12.
[10] Isa. LIII, 10.
[11] Ibid. The Hebrew word for 'restitution' is asham which means also 'trespass-offering'.
[12] Ibid.
[13] Ibid.

of love are such as do not involve the intermission of study of the Torah. For it is said: Happy is the man whom Thou chastenest, O Lord, and teachest out of Thy law.[1] And the other one says: Chastenings of love are such as do not involve the intermission of prayer. For it is said: Blessed be God, Who hath not turned away my prayer, nor His mercy from me.[2] R. Abba the son of R. Hiyya b. Abba said to them: Thus said R. Hiyya b. Abba in the name of R. Johanan: Both of them are chastenings of love. For it is said: For whom the Lord loveth He correcteth.[3] Why then does it say: 'And teachest him out of Thy law'? Do not read telammedennu, [Thou teachest him] but telammedenu, [Thou teachest us]. Thou teachest us this thing out of Thy law as a conclusion a fortiori from the law concerning tooth and eye.[4] Tooth and eye are only one limb of the man, and still [if they are hurt], the slave obtains thereby his freedom. How much more so with painful sufferings which torment the whole body of a man! And this agrees with a saying of R. Simeon b. Lakish. For R. Simeon b. Lakish said: The word 'covenant' is mentioned in connection with salt, and the word 'covenant' is mentioned in connection with sufferings: the word 'covenant' is mentioned in connection with salt, as it is written: Neither shalt thou suffer the salt of the covenant of thy God to be lacking.[5] And the word 'covenant' is mentioned in connection with sufferings, as it is written: These are the words of the covenant.[6] Even as in the covenant mentioned in connection with salt, the salt lends a sweet taste to the meat, so also in the covenant mentioned in connection with sufferings, the sufferings wash away all the sins of a man.

It has been taught: R. Simeon b. Yohai says: The Holy One, blessed be He, gave Israel three precious gifts, and all of them were given only through sufferings. These are: The Torah, the Land of Israel and the world to come. Whence do we know this of the Torah? — Because it is said: Happy is the man whom Thou chastenest, o Lord, and teachest him out of Thy law.[7] Whence of the Land of Israel? — Because it is written: As a man chasteneth his son, so the Lord thy God chasteneth thee,[8] and after that it is written: For the Lord thy God bringeth thee into a good land.[9] Whence of the world to come? — Because it is written: For the commandment is a lamp, and the teaching is light, and reproofs of sufferings are the way of life.[10]

A Tanna recited before R. Johanan the following: If a man busies himself in the study of the Torah and in acts of charity

---

[1] Ps. XCIV, 12.
[2] Ps. LXVI, 20.
[3] Prov. III 12.
[4] V. Ex. XXI, 26, 27. If the master knocks out the tooth or eye of his slave, then the slave has to be set free.
[5] Lev. II, 13.
[6] Deut. XXVIII, 69. These words refer to the chapter dealing with the sufferings of Israel.
[7] Ps. XCIV, 12.
[8] Deut. VIII, 5.
[9] Ibid. v. 7.
[10] Prov. VI, 23.

Berakoth 5b

and [nonetheless] buries his children,[1] all his sins are forgiven him. R. Johanan said to him: I grant you Torah and acts of charity, for it is written: By mercy and truth iniquity is expiated.[2] 'Mercy' is acts of charity, for it is said: He that followeth after righteousness and mercy findeth life, prosperity and honour.[3] 'Truth' is Torah, for it is said: Buy the truth and sell it not.[4] But how do you know [what you say about] the one who buries his children? — A certain Elder [thereupon] recited to him in the name of R. Simeon b. Yohai: It is concluded from the analogy in the use of the word 'iniquity'. Here it is written: By mercy and truth iniquity is expiated. And elsewhere it is written: And who recompenseth the iniquity of the fathers into the bosom of their children.[5]

R. Johanan says: Leprosy and [the lack of] children are not chastisements of love. But is leprosy not a chastisement of love? Is it not taught: If a man has one of these four symptoms of leprosy,[6] it is nothing else but an altar of atonement? — They are an altar of atonement, but they are not chastisements of love. If you like, I can say: This [teaching of the Baraitha] is ours [in Babylonia], and that [saying of R. Johanan] is theirs [in Palestine].[7] If you like, I can say: This [teaching of the Baraitha] refers to hidden [leprosy], that [saying of R. Johanan] refers to a case of visible [leprosy]. But is [the lack of] children not a chastisement of love? How is this to be understood? Shall I say that he had children and they died? Did not R. Johanan himself say: This is the bone of my tenth son?[8] — Rather [say then] that the former saying refers to one who never had children, the latter to one who had children and lost them.

R. Hiyya b. Abba fell ill and R. Johanan went in to visit him. He said to him: Are your sufferings welcome to you? He replied: Neither they nor their reward.[9] He said to him: Give me your hand. He gave him his hand and he[10] raised him.

R. Johanan once fell ill and R. Hanina went in to visit him. He said to him: Are your sufferings welcome to you? He replied: Neither they nor their reward. He said to him: Give me your hand. He gave him his hand and he raised him. Why could not R. Johanan raise himself?[11] — They replied:

---

[1] An allusion to R. Johanan himself, who was a great scholar and a charitable man, and was bereft of his children.
[2] Ibid. XVI, 6.
[3] Ibid. XXI, 21.
[4] Ibid. XXIII, 23.
[5] Jer. XXXII, 18.
[6] Which are enumerated in Mishnah Nega'im I, I.
[7] In Palestine where a leprous person had to be isolated outside the city (cf. Lev. XIII, 46), leprosy was not regarded as 'chastisements of love' owing to the severity of the treatment involved.
[8] Who died in his lifetime. The Gemara deduces from that saying that he regarded the death of children as a chastisement of love. Aruch understands this to have been a tooth of the last of his sons which he preserved and used to show to people who suffered bereavement in order to induce in them a spirit of resignation such as he himself had in his successive bereavements.
[9] The implication is that if one lovingly acquiesces in his sufferings, his reward in the world to come is very great.
[10] R. Johanan. He cured him by the touch of his hand.
[11] If he could cure R. Hiyya b. Abba, why could not he cure himself?

The prisoner cannot free himself from jail.¹

R. Eleazar fell ill and R. Johanan went in to visit him. He noticed that he was lying in a dark room,² and he bared his arm and light radiated from it.³ Thereupon he noticed that R. Eleazar was weeping, and he said to him: Why do you weep? Is it because you did not study enough Torah? Surely we learnt: The one who sacrifices much and the one who sacrifices little have the same merit, provided that the heart is directed to heaven.⁴ Is it perhaps lack of sustenance? Not everybody has the privilege to enjoy two tables.⁵ Is it perhaps because of [the lack of] children? This is the bone of my tenth son! — He replied to him: I am weeping on account of this beauty⁶ that is going to rot in the earth. He said to him: On that account you surely have a reason to weep; and they both wept. In the meanwhile he said to him: Are your sufferings welcome to you? — He replied: Neither they nor their reward. He said to him: Give me your hand, and he gave him his hand and he raised him.

Once four hundred jars of wine belonging to R. Huna turned sour. Rab Judah, the brother of R. Sala the Pious, and the other scholars (some say: R. Adda b. Ahaba and the other scholars) went in to visit him and said to him: The master ought to examine his actions.⁷ He said to them: Am I suspect in your eyes? They replied: Is the Holy One, blessed be He, suspect of punishing without justice? — He said to them: If somebody has heard of anything against me, let him speak out. They replied: We have heard that the master does not give his tenant his [lawful share in the] vine twigs. He replied: Does he leave me any? He steals them all! They said to him: That is exactly what the proverb says.⁸ If you steal from a thief you also have a taste of it!⁹ He said to them: I pledge myself to give it to him [in the future]. Some report that thereupon the vinegar became wine again; others that the vinegar went up so high that it was sold for the same price as wine.

It has been taught: Abba Benjamin says, All my life I took great pains about two things: that my prayer should be before my bed and that my bed should be placed north and south. 'That my prayer should be before my bed'. What is the meaning of 'before my bed'? Is it perhaps literally in front of my bed? Has not Rab Judah said in the name of Rab (some say, in the name of R. Joshua b. Levi): How do you know that when one prays there should be nothing interposing between him and the wall? Because it says: Then Hezekiah turned his face to the wall and prayed?¹⁰ — Do not read 'before my bed', but 'near¹¹ my bed'. 'And that my bed should be placed north and south'. For R. Hama b. R. Hanina said in the name of R. Isaac: Whosoever places his bed north and south will have male children, as it says: And whose belly Thou fillest with Thy treasure,¹² who have sons in plenty.¹³ R.

---

¹ And the patient cannot cure himself.
² R. Eleazar was a poor man and lived in a room without windows.
  1.14. R. Johanan was supposed to be so beautiful that a light radiated from his body, v.
  2.B.M. 84a.
³ Men. 110b.
⁴ Learning and wealth. Or perhaps, this world and the next.
⁵ I.e., the beautiful body of yours.
⁶ You may perhaps have deserved your misfortune through some sin.
⁷ Lit., 'what people say'.
⁸ Even if your tenant is a thief this does not free you from giving him his lawful share.
⁹ Isa. XXXVIII, 2.
¹⁰ Near in time. He used to pray immediately after rising.
¹¹ The word may mean treasure and also north.
¹² Ps. XVII, 14.
¹³ Gen. XXV, 24.

Nahman b. Isaac says: His wife also will not miscarry. Here it is written: And whose belly Thou fillest with Thy treasure, and elsewhere it is written: And when her days to be delivered were fulfilled, behold there were twins in her womb.[1]

It has been taught: Abba Benjamin says, When two people enter [a Synagogue] to pray, and one of them finishes his prayer first and does not wait for the other but leaves,[2] his prayer is torn up before his face.[3] For it is written: Thou that tearest thyself in thine anger, shall the earth be forsaken for thee?[4] And more than that, he causes the Divine Presence to remove itself from Israel. For it says Or shall the rock be removed out of its place?[5] And 'rock' is nothing else than the Holy One, blessed be He, as it says: Of the Rock that begot thee thou wast unmindful. And if he does wait, what is his reward? —

---

[1] The synagogues were outside the town and it was dangerous to remain alone.
[2] I.e., rejected.
[3] Job. XVIII, 4. The homiletical interpretation of the verse is: 'Your prayer will be thrown into your face, if on your account the earth or synagogue is forsaken'.
[4] Ibid.
[5] Deut. XXXII, 18.

Folio 6a

R. Jose b. R. Hanina says: He is rewarded with the blessings enumerated in the following verse: Oh that thou wouldest hearken to My commandments! Then would thy peace be as a river, and thy righteousness as the waves of the sea; Thy seed also would be as the sand, and the offspring of thy body like the grains thereof etc.[1]

It has been taught: Abba Benjamin says, If the eye had the power to see them, no creature could endure the demons. Abaye says: They are more numerous than we are and they surround us like the ridge round a field. R. Huna says: Every one among us has a thousand on his left hand and ten thousand on his right hand.[2] Raba says: The crushing in the Kallah[3] lectures comes from them.[4] Fatigue in the knees comes from them. The wearing out of the clothes of the scholars is due to their rubbing against them. The bruising of the feet comes from them. If one wants to discover them,[5] let him take sifted ashes and sprinkle around his bed, and in the morning he will see something like the footprints of a cock. If one wishes to see them, let him take the after-birth of a black she-cat, the offspring of a black she-cat, the first-born of a first-born, let him roast it in fire and grind it to powder, and then let him put some into his eye, and he will see them. Let him also pour it into an iron tube and seal it with an iron signet that they[6] should not steal it from him. Let him also close his mouth, lest he come to harm. R. Bibi b. Abaye did so,[7] saw them and came to harm. The scholars, however, prayed for him and he recovered.

It has been taught: Abba Benjamin says: A man's prayer is heard [by God] only in the Synagogue. For it is said: To hearken unto the song and to the prayer.[8] The prayer is to be recited where there is song.[9] Rabin b. R. Adda says in the name of R. Isaac: How do you know that the Holy One, blessed be He, is to be found in the Synagogue? For it is said: God standeth in the congregation of God.[10] And how do you know that if ten people pray together the Divine presence is with them? For it is said: 'God standeth in the congregation of God'.[11] And how do you know that if three are sitting as a court of judges the Divine Presence is with them? For it is said: In the midst of the judges He judgeth.[12] And how do you know that if two are sitting and studying the Torah together the Divine Presence is with them? For it is said: Then they that feared the Lord spoke one with another;[13] and the Lord hearkened and heard, and a book of remembrance was written before Him, for them that feared the Lord and that thought upon His name.[14] (What does it mean: 'And that thought upon His name'?

---

[1] Isa. XLVIII, 18, 19.
[2] Cf. Ps. XCI, 7 which verse is quoted in some editions.
[3] The Assemblies of Babylonian students during the months of Elul and Adar, v. Glos.
[4] For really the lectures are not overcrowded.
[5] MS.M.: their footprints.
[6] The demons.
[7] He put the powder into his eye.
[8] I Kings VIII, 28.
[9] The song of the community and of the officiating Cantor.
[10] Ps. LXXXII, I.
[11] And a congregation consists of not less than ten, v. Sanh. 2b.
[12] Ibid. A Beth din consists of three.
[13] A phrase denoting two.
[14] Mal. III, 16.

— R. Ashi[1] says: If a man thought to fulfill a commandment and he did not do it, because he was prevented by force or accident, then the Scripture credits it to him as if he had performed it.) And how do you know that even if one man sits and studies the Torah the Divine Presence is with him? For it is said: In every place where I cause My name to be mentioned I will come unto thee and bless thee.[2] Now, since [the Divine presence is] even with one man, why is it necessary to mention two?[3] — The words of two are written down in the book of remembrance, the words of one are not written down in the book of remembrance. Since this is the case with two, why mention three? — I might think [the dispensing of] justice is only for making peace, and the Divine Presence does not come [to participate]. Therefore he teaches us that justice also is Torah. Since it is the case with three, why mention ten? — To [a gathering of] ten the Divine Presence comes first, to three, it comes only after they sit down.

R. Abin[4] son of R. Ada in the name of R. Isaac says [further]: How do you know that the Holy One, blessed be He, puts on tefillin?[5] For it is said: The Lord hath sworn by His right hand, and by the arm of His strength.[6] 'By His right hand': this is the Torah; for it is said: At His right hand was a fiery law unto them.[7] 'And by the arm of his strength': this is the tefillin; as it is said: The Lord will give strength unto His people.[8] And how do you know that the tefillin are a strength to Israel? For it is written: And all the peoples of the earth shall see that the name of the Lord is called upon thee, and they shall be afraid of thee,[9] and it has been taught: R. Eliezer the Great says: This refers to the tefillin of the head.[10]

R. Nahman b. Isaac said to R. Hiyya b. Abin: What is written in the tefillin of the Lord of the Universe? — He replied to him: And who is like Thy people Israel, a nation one in the earth.[11] Does, then, the Holy One, blessed be He, sing the praises of Israel? — Yes, for it is written: Thou hast avouched the Lord this day ... and the Lord hath avouched thee this day.[12] The Holy One, blessed be He, said to Israel: You have made me a unique entity[13] in the world, and I shall make you a unique entity in the world. 'You have made me a unique entity in the world', as it is said: Hear, O Israel, the Lord our God, the Lord is one.[14] 'And I shall make you a unique entity in the world', as it is said: And who is like Thy people Israel, a nation one in the earth.[15] R. Aha b. Raba said to R. Ashi: This accounts for one case, what about the other cases?[16] — He replied to him: [They contain the following verses]: For what great nation is there, etc.; And what great nation is there, etc.;[17] Happy

---

[1] MS.M.: R. Assi. This remark is made in passing by the editor of the Gemara, R. Ashi. Hence the reading 'R. Ashi' as given by the editions, seems to be correct.
[2] Ex. XX, 21. The lesson is derived from the use of the singular 'thee'.
[3] This question is asked by the Gemara apropos of Rabin's statement.
[4] The same as the Rabin mentioned above.
[5] Phylacteries, v. Glos.
[6] Isa. LXII, 8.
[7] Deut. XXXIII, 2.
[8] Ps. XXIX, 11.
[9] Deut. XXVIII, 10.
[10] The tefillin of the arm are covered by the sleeves.
[11] I Chron. XVII, 21.
[12] Deut. XXVI, 17, 18.
[13] So the Aruch. Jastrow, however, translates 'the only object of your love'.
[14] Deut. VI, 4.
[15] I Chron. XVII, 21.
[16] The tefillin of the head has four cases.
[17] Deut. IV, 7, 8.

art thou, O Israel, etc.;[1] Or hath God assayed, etc.;[2] and To make thee high above all nations.[3] If so, there would be too many cases? — Hence [you must say]: For what great nation is there, and And what great nation is there, which are similar, are in one case; Happy art thou, O Israel, and Who is like Thy people, in one case; Or hath God assayed, in one case; and To make thee high, in one case.

---

[1] Ibid. XXXIII, 29.
[2] Ibid. IV, 34.
[3] Ibid. XXVI, 19.

Berakoth 6b

And all these verses are written on [the tefillin of] His arm.

Rabin son of R. Adda in the name of R. Isaac says [further]: If a man is accustomed to attend Synagogue [daily] and one day does not go, the Holy One, blessed be He, makes inquiry about him. For it is said: Who is among you that feareth the Lord, that obeyeth the voice of His servant, and now walketh in darkness and hath no light?[1] [And still] if he absented himself on account of some religious purpose, he shall have light. But if he absented himself on account of a worldly purpose, he shall have no light. Let him trust in the name of the Lord.[2] Why?[3] Because he ought to have trusted in the name of the Lord and he did not trust.

R. Johanan says: Whenever the Holy One, blessed be He, comes into a Synagogue and does not find ten persons there,[4] He becomes angry at once.[5] For it is said: Wherefore, when I came, was there no man? When I called, was there no answer?[6]

R. Helbo, in the name of R. Huna, says: Whosoever has a fixed place for his prayer has the God of Abraham as his helper. And when he dies, people will say of him: Where is the pious man,[7] where is the humble man,[8] one of the disciples of our father Abraham! — How do we know that our father Abraham had a fixed place [for his prayer]? For it is written: And Abraham got up early in the morning to the place where he had stood.[9] And 'standing' means nothing else but prayer. For it is said: Then stood up Phinehas and prayed.[10]

R. Helbo, in the name of R. Huna, says [further]: When a man leaves the Synagogue, he should not take large steps. Abaye says: This is only when one goes from the Synagogue, but when one goes to the Synagogue, it is a pious deed to run. For it is said: Let us run to know the Lord.[11] R. Zera says: At first when I saw the scholars running to the lecture on a Sabbath day, I thought that they were desecrating the Sabbath.[12] But since I have heard the saying of R. Tanhum in the name of R. Joshua b. Levi: A man should always, even on a Sabbath, run to listen to the word of Halachah, as it is said: They shall walk after the Lord, who shall roar like a lion,[13] I also run. R. Zera says: The merit of attending a lecture lies in the running. Abaye says: The merit of attending the Kallah sessions[14] lies in the crush. Raba says: The merit of repeating a tradition lies in [improving] the understanding of it. R. Papa says: The merit of attending a house of mourning lies in the silence observed. Mar Zutra says:

---

[1] Isa. L, 10.
[2] Ibid.
[3] Has he no light.
[4] The number required for a public service.
[5] In the absence of a quorum of ten, a number of important features in the service are omitted.
[6] Sc. the congregational responses. Isa. L, 2.
[7] Aliter: Alas, the pious man (is no more)!
[8] Cf. previous note.
[9] Gen. XIX, 27.
[10] Ps. CVI, 30.
[11] Hos. VI, 3.
[12] It is forbidden to take large steps on the Sabbath, v. Shab. 113b.
[13] Hos. XI, 10. The text continues: For he shall roar, and the children shall come hurrying (E.V. 'trembling').
[14] V. Glos.

The merit of a fast day lies in the charity dispensed. R. Shesheth says: The merit of a funeral oration lies in raising the voice.[1] R. Ashi says: The merit of attending a wedding lies in the words [of congratulation addressed to the bride and bridegroom].[2]

R. Huna says: Whosoever prays at the rear of a Synagogue is called wicked. For it is said: The wicked walk round about.[3] Abaye says: This only applies where he does not turn his face towards the Synagogue, but if he does turn his face towards the Synagogue there is no objection to it. There was once a man who prayed at the rear of a Synagogue and did not turn his face towards the Synagogue. Elijah passed by and appeared to him in the guise of an Arabian[4] merchant. He said to him: Are you standing with your back to your Master?[5] and drew his sword and slew him.

One of the scholars said to R. Bibi b. Abaye (some say: R. Bibi said to R. Nahman b. Isaac): What is the meaning of: When vileness is exalted among the sons of men?[6] He replied to him: These are the things of supreme importance[7] which nevertheless people neglect.[8] R. Johanan and R. Eliezer both interpret: As soon as a man needs the support of his fellow-creatures his face changes colour like the kerum, as it is said: 'As the kerum is to be reviled among the sons of men'. What is the 'kerum'? When R. Dimi came [from Palestine] he said: There is a bird in the coast towns[9] whose name is kerum, and as soon as the sun shines upon it it changes into several colours.[10] R. Ammi and R. Assi both say: [When a man needs the support of his fellow-beings] it is as if he were punished with two [opposite] punishments, with fire and water. For it is said: When Thou hast caused men to ride over our heads, we went through fire and through water.[11]

R. Helbo further said in the name of R. Huna: A man should always take special care about the afternoon-prayer. For even Elijah was favourably heard only while offering his afternoon-prayer. For it is said: And it came to pass at the time of the offering of the evening offering, that Elijah the prophet came near and said … Hear me, O Lord, hear me.[12] 'Hear me', that the fire may descend from heaven, and 'hear me', that they may not say it is the work of sorcery. R. Johanan says: [Special care should be taken] also about the evening-prayer. For it is said: Let my prayer be set forth as incense before Thee, the lifting up of my hands as the evening sacrifice.[13] R. Nahman b. Isaac says: [Special care should be taken] also about the morning.prayer. For it is said: O Lord, in the morning shalt Thou hear my voice; in the morning will I order my prayer unto Thee, and will look forward.[14]

---

[1] I.e., in the loud lamentation of the listeners.
[2] These aphorisms are intended to bring home the lesson that the real merit of doing certain things lies not in themselves, but in their concomitants. For instance, the people running to the lectures do not benefit by the lectures, as they do not understand them. However they will be rewarded for enduring the rush and crush. The mechanical repetition of a tradition has no value if you do not try to understand it better. The merit of a fast day lies not in the fasting but in giving charity to the poor people, that they may have something to eat, etc.
[3] Ps. XII, 9.
[4] MS.M.: An Arab passed by and saw him.
[5] V. Jast. Rashi: 'As if there were two powers'.
[6] Ibid.
[7] Lit., 'standing on the highest point of the world'.
[8] He interprets, 'When the exalted things (kerum) are reviled among the sons of men'. The reference is to Prayer.
[9] The meaning is: In the distant countries lying across the sea.
[10] Lewysohn, Zoologie, p. 183 identifies the bird with the 'bird of Paradise'.
[11] Ps. LXVI, 12.
[12] I Kings XVIII, 36, 37.
[13] Ps. CXLI, 2.
[14] Ibid. V, 4.

R. Helbo further said in the name of R. Huna: Whosoever partakes of the wedding meal of a bridegroom and does not felicitate him does violence to 'the five voices' mentioned in the verse: The voice of joy and the voice of gladness, the voice of the bridegroom and the voice of the bride, the voice of them that say, Give thanks to the Lord of Hosts.[1] And if he does gladden him what is his reward? — R. Joshua b. Levi said: He is privileged to acquire [the knowledge of] the Torah which was given with five voices. For it is said: And it came to pass on the third day, when it was morning, that there were thunders[2] and lightnings and a thick cloud upon the mount, and the voice of a horn ... and when the voice of the horn waxed louder ... Moses spoke and God answered him by a voice.[3] (This is not so![4] For it is written: And all the people perceived the thunderings?[5] — These voices were before the revelation of the Torah.) R. Abbahu says: It is as if he[6] had sacrificed a thanksgiving offering. For it is said: Even of them that bring offerings of thanksgiving into the house of the Lord.[7] R. Nahman b. Isaac says: It is as if he had restored one of the ruins of Jerusalem. For it is said: For I will cause the captivity of the land to return as at the first, saith the Lord.[8]

R. Helbo further said in the name of R. Huna: If one is filled with the fear of God his words are listened to. For it is said: The end of the matter, all having been heard: fear God, and keep his commandments, for this is the whole man.[9] What means, 'For this is the whole man'? — R. Eleazar says: The Holy One, blessed be He, says: The whole world was created for his sake only. R. Abba b. Kahana says: He is equal in value to the whole world. R. Simeon b. 'Azzai says (some say, R. Simon b. Zoma says): The whole world was created as a satellite for him.

R. Helbo further said in the name of R. Huna: If one knows that his friend is used to greet him, let him greet him first.[10] For it is said: Seek peace and pursue it.[11] And if his friend greets him and he does not return the greeting he is called a robber. For it is said: It is ye that have eaten up the vineyard; the spoil of the poor is in your houses.[12]

---

[1] Jer. XXXIII, II.

[2] Lit., 'voices'. The plural is counted as two.

[3] Ex. XIX, 16, 19.

[4] There were not only five, but seven voices.

[5] Ibid. XX, 15. Cf. n. 5.

[6] One who felicitates the bridegroom.

[7] Jer. XXXIII, II.

[8] Ibid.

[9] Eccl. XII, 13. He interprets: 'Everything is heard, if you fear God'.

[10] [MS.M.: If one is used to greet his neighbour and fails to do so a single day, he transgresses the injunction 'Seek peace, etc.']

[11] Ps. XXXIV, 15.

[12] Isa. III, 14.

Folio 7a

R. Johanan says in the name of R. Jose: How do we know that the Holy One, blessed be He, says prayers? Because it says: Even them will I bring to My holy mountain and make them joyful in My house of prayer.[1] It is not said, 'their prayer', but 'My prayer'; hence [you learn] that the Holy One, blessed be He, says prayers. What does He pray? — R. Zutra
b. Tobi said in the name of Rab: 'May it be My will that My mercy may suppress My anger, and that My mercy may prevail over My [other] attributes, so that I may deal with My children in the attribute of mercy and, on their behalf, stop short of the limit of strict justice'.[2] It was taught: R. Ishmael b. Elisha says: I once entered into the innermost part [of the Sanctuary] to offer incense and saw Akathriel Jah,[3] the Lord of Hosts, seated upon a high and exalted throne. He said to me: Ishmael, My son, bless Me! I replied: May it be Thy will that Thy mercy may suppress Thy anger and Thy mercy may prevail over Thy other attributes, so that Thou mayest deal with Thy children according to the attribute of mercy and mayest, on their behalf, stop short of the limit of strict justice! And He nodded to me with His head. Here we learn [incidentally] that the blessing of an ordinary man must not be considered lightly in your eyes.
R. Johanan further said in the name of R. Jose: How do you know that we must not try to placate a man in the time of his anger? For it is written: My face will go and I will give thee rest.[4] The Holy One, blessed be He, said to Moses: Wait till My countenance of wrath shall have passed away and then I shall give thee rest. But is anger then a mood of the Holy One, blessed be He? — Yes. For it has been taught:[5] A God that hath indignation every day.[6] And how long does this indignation last? One moment. And how long is one moment? One fifty-eight thousand eight hundred and eighty-eighth part of an hour. And no creature has ever been able to fix precisely this moment except the wicked Balaam, of whom it is written: He knoweth the knowledge of the Most High.[7] Now, he did not even know the mind of his animal; how then could he know the mind of the Most High? The meaning is, therefore, only that he knew how to fix precisely this moment in which the Holy One, blessed be He, is angry. And this is just what the prophet said to Israel: O my people, remember now what Balak king of Moab devised, and what Balaam the son of Beor answered him ... that ye may know the righteous acts of the Lord.[8] What means 'That ye may know the righteous acts of the Lord'? — R. Eleazar says: The Holy One, blessed be He, said to Israel: See now, how many righteous acts I performed for you in not being angry in the days of the wicked Balaam. For had I been angry, not one remnant would have been left of the enemies of Israel.[9] And this too is the meaning of what Balaam said to Balak: How shall I curse, whom God hath not cursed? And how shall I execrate, whom the Lord hath not execrated?[10] This teaches us that He was not angry all these days. And how long does His anger last? One moment. And how long is one moment? R. Abin (some say R. Abina) says: As long as it takes to say Rega'.[11] And how do you know that He is angry one moment? For it is said: For

---

[1] Ibid. LVI, 7. 'In the house of My prayer'.
[2] I.e., not exact the full penalty from them.
[3] Lit., 'crown of God'.
[4] Ex. XXXIII, 14.
[5] V. A.Z. 4a.
[6] Ps. VII, 12.
[7] Num. XXIV, 16.
[8] Micah VI, 5.
[9] Euphemism for Israel.
[10] Num. XXIII, 8.
[11] 'A moment'.

His anger is but for a moment [rega'], His favor is for a lifetime.[1] Or if you prefer you may infer it from the following verse: Hide thyself for a little moment until the indignation be overpast.[2] And when is He angry? — Abaye says: In [one moment of] those first three hours of the day, when the comb of the cock is white and it stands on one foot. Why, in each hour it stands thus [on one foot]?[3] — In each other hour it has red streaks, but in this moment it has no red streaks at all.

In the neighbourhood of R. Joshua b. Levi there was a Sadducee[4] who used to annoy him very much with [his interpretations of] texts. One day the Rabbi took a cock, placed it between the legs of his bed and watched it. He thought: When this moment arrives I shall curse him. When the moment arrived he was dozing [On waking up][5] he said: We learn from this that it is not proper to act in such a way. It is written: And His tender mercies are over all His works.[6] And it is further written: Neither is it good for the righteous to punish.[7] It was taught in the name of R. Meir: At the time when the sun rises and all the kings of the East and West put their crowns upon their heads and bow down to the sun, the Holy One, blessed be He, becomes at once angry.

R. Johanan further said in the name of R. Jose: Better is one self-reproach in the heart of a man than many stripes, for it is said: And she shall run after her lovers ... then shall she say,[8] I shall go and return to my first husband; for then was it better with me than now.[9] R. Simon b. Lakish says: It is better than a hundred stripes, for it is said: A rebuke entereth deeper into a man of understanding than a hundred stripes into a fool.[10]

R. Johanan further said in the name of R. Jose: Three things did Moses ask of the Holy One, blessed be He, and they were granted to him. He asked that the Divine Presence should rest upon Israel, and it was granted to him. For it is said: Is it not in that Thou goest with us [so that we are distinguished, I and Thy people, from all the people that are upon the face of the earth].[11] He asked that the Divine Presence should not rest upon the idolaters, and it was granted to him. For it is said: 'So that we are distinguished, I and Thy people'. He asked that He should show him the ways of the Holy One, blessed be He, and it was granted to him. For it is said: Show me now Thy ways.[12] Moses said before Him: Lord of the Universe, why is it that some righteous men prosper and others are in adversity, some wicked men prosper and others are in adversity? He replied to him: Moses, the righteous man who prospers is the righteous man the son of a righteous man; the righteous man who is in adversity is a righteous man the son of a wicked man. The wicked man who prospers is a wicked man son of a righteous man; the wicked man who is in adversity is a wicked man son of a wicked man.

The Master said above: 'The righteous man who prospers is a righteous man son of a righteous man; the righteous man who is in adversity is a righteous man son of a wicked man'. But this is not so! For,

---

[1] Ps. XXX, 6.
[2] Isa. XXVI, 20.
[3] A better reading is. 'its comb is thus (viz., white)'.
[4] Var. lec. Min. v. Glos.
[5] Added with MS.M.
[6] Ps. CXLV, 9.
[7] Prov. XVII, 26.
[8] In her heart.
[9] Hos. II, 9.
[10] Prov. XVII, 10.
[11] Ex. XXXIII, 16.
[12] Ex. XXXIII, 13.

lo, one verse says: Visiting the iniquity of the fathers upon the children,[1] and another verse says: Neither shall the children be put to death for the fathers.[2] And a contradiction was pointed out between these two verses, and the answer was given that there is no contradiction. The one verse deals with children who continue in the same course as their fathers, and the other verse with children who do not continue in the course of their fathers! — [You must] therefore [say that] the Lord said thus to Moses: A righteous man who prospers is a perfectly righteous man; the righteous man who is in adversity is not a perfectly righteous man. The wicked man who prospers is not a perfectly wicked man; the wicked man who is in adversity is a perfectly wicked man. Now this [saying of R. Johanan][3] is in opposition to the saying of R. Meir. For R. Meir said: only two [requests] were granted to him, and one was not granted to him. For it is said: And I will be gracious to whom I will be gracious, although he may not deserve it, And I will show mercy on whom I will show mercy,[4] although he may not deserve it.[5]

And He said, Thou canst not see My face.[6] A Tanna taught in the name of R. Joshua b. Korhah: The Holy One, blessed be He, spoke thus to Moses: When I wanted, you did not want [to see My face][7] now that you want, I do not want. — This is in opposition to [the interpretation of this verse by] R. Samuel b. Nahmani in the name of R. Jonathan. For
R. Samuel b. Nahmani said in the name of R. Jonathan: As a reward of three [pious acts][8] Moses was privileged to obtain three [favours]. In reward of 'And Moses hid his face', he obtained the brightness of his face.[9] In reward of 'For he was afraid', he obtained the privilege that They were afraid to come nigh him.[10] In reward of 'To look upon God', he obtained The similitude of the Lord doth he behold.[11]

And I will take away My hand, and thou shalt see My back.[12] R. Hama b. Bizana said in the name of R. Simon the Pious: This teaches us that the Holy One, blessed be He, showed Moses the knot of the tefillin.[13]

R. Johanan further said in the name of R. Jose: No word of blessing that issued from the mouth of the Holy One, blessed be He, even if based upon a condition, was ever withdrawn by Him. How do we know this? From our teacher Moses. For it is said: Let me alone, that I may destroy them, and blot out their name from under heaven; and I will make of thee a nation mightier and greater than they.[14] Though Moses prayed that this might be mercifully averted and it was cancelled, [the blessing] was nevertheless fulfilled towards his children. For it is said: The sons of Moses: Gershom and Eliezer ... And the sons of Eliezer were Rehabia the chief ... and the sons of Rehabiah were very many.[15] And

---

[1] Ibid. XXXIV, 7.
[2] Deut. XXIV, 16.
[3] That all the three requests of Moses were granted.
[4] Ex. XXXIII, 19.
[5] And God's ways therefore cannot be known.
[6] Ibid. v. 20.
[7] At the burning bush, Ex. III, 6.
[8] Mentioned in Ex. III, 6; (i) And Moses hid his face; (ii) for he was afraid; (iii) to look upon God.
[9] Cf. Ex. XXXIV, 29-30.
[10] Ibid. v. 30.
[11] Num. XII, 8.
[12] Ex. XXXIII, 23.
[13] Worn at the back of the head.
[14] Deut. IX, 14. This verse contains a curse and a blessing, the blessing being conditional upon the realization of the curse.
[15] I Chron. XXIII, 15-17.

R. Joseph learnt: They were more than sixty myriads. This is to be learnt from two occurrences of the term 'manifold'. Here it is written: were very many, and elsewhere It is written: And the children of Israel were very fruitful and increased abundantly, and became very many.[1]

---
[1] Ex. I, 7. And we know that they were about sixty myriads when leaving Egypt.

Berakoth 7b

R. Johanan said [further] in the name of R. Simeon b. Yohai: From the day that the Holy One, blessed be He, created the world there was no man that called the Holy One, blessed be He, Lord,[1] until Abraham came and called Him Lord. For it is said: And he said, O Lord [Adonai] God, whereby shall I know that I shall inherit it?[2] Rab said: Even Daniel was heard [in his prayer] only for the sake of Abraham. For it says: Now therefore, O our God, hearken unto the prayer of Thy servant, and to his supplications, and cause Thy face to shine upon Thy sanctuary that is desolate, for the Lord's sake.[3] He ought to have said: 'For Thy sake', but [he means]: For the sake of Abraham, who called Thee Lord.

R. Johanan further said in the name of R. Simeon b. Yohai: How do you know that we must not try to placate a man in the time of his anger? Because it is said: My face will go and I will give thee rest.[4]

R. Johanan further said in the name of R. Simeon b. Yohai: From the day that the Holy One, blessed be He, created His world there was no man that praised the Holy One, blessed be He, until Leah came and praised Him. For it is said: This time will I praise the Lord.[5]

Reuben. [What is the meaning of 'Reuben'?][6] — R. Eleazar said: Leah said: See the difference between[7] my son and the son of my father-in-law. The son of my father-in-law voluntarily sold his birthright, for it is written: And he sold his birthright unto Jacob.[8] And, nonetheless, behold, it is written of him: And Esau hated Jacob,[9] and it is also written: And he said, is not he rightly named Jacob? for he hath supplanted me these two times.[10] My son, however, although Joseph took his birthright from him against his will — as it is written: But, for as much as he defiled his father's couch, his birthright was given unto the sons of Joseph,[11] — was not jealous of him. For it is written: And Reuben heard it, and delivered him out of their hand.[12]

Ruth. What is the meaning of Ruth? — R. Johanan said: Because she was privileged to be the ancestress of David, who saturated[13] the Holy One, blessed be He, with songs and hymns. How do we know that the name [of a person] has an effect [upon his life]?[14] —
R. Eleazar said: Scripture says: Come, behold the works of the Lord, who hath made desolations in the earth.[15] Read not shammoth, ['desolations'], but shemoth, [names].

---
[1] In Hebrew: Adon.
[2] Gen. XV, 8.
[3] Dan. IX, 17.
[4] Ex. XXXIII, 14. Cf. also supra 7a.
[5] Gen. XXIX, 35. She implied that this had never been done before.
[6] Words in brackets added from MS.M. This passage is suggested by the mention of Leah.
[7] Reuben is explained as ihc utr, 'See the difference between'.
[8] Ibid. XXV, 33.
[9] Ibid. XXVII, 41.
[10] Ibid. XXVII, 36.
[11] I Chron. V, I.
[12] Gen. XXXVII, 21.
[13] is derived from to saturate.
[14] Lit., 'causes', 'determines (one's destiny)'.
[15] Ps. XLVI, 9.

R. Johanan further said in the name of R. Simeon b. Yohai: A bad son[1] in a man's house is worse than the war of Gog and Magog. For it is said: A Psalm of David, when he fled from Absalom his son,[2] and it is written after that: Lord, how many are mine adversaries become! Many are they that rise up against me.[3] But in regard to the war of Gog and Magog it is written: Why are the nations in an uproar? And why do the peoples mutter in vain,[4] but, it is not written: 'How many are mine adversaries become!'

'A Psalm of David, when he fled from Absalom his son'. 'A Psalm of David'? He ought to have said: 'A Lamentation of David'! R. Simeon b. Abishalom said: A parable: To what is this to be compared? To a man who has a bond outstanding against him; until he pays it he worries[5] but after he has paid it, he rejoices. So was it with David. When the Holy One, blessed be He, said to him: Behold, I will raise up evil against thee out of thine own house,[6] he began worrying. He thought: it may be a slave or a bastard who will have no pity on me. When he saw that it was Absalom, he was glad, and therefore he said: 'A Psalm'.

R. Johanan further said in the name of R. Simeon b. Yohai: It is permitted to contend with the wicked in this world. For it is said: They that forsake the law praise the wicked, but such as keep the law contend with them.[7] It has been taught to the same effect: R. Dosthai son of R. Mattun says: It is permitted to contend with the wicked in this world. For it is said: 'They that forsake the law praise the wicked, etc.' — Should somebody whisper to you: But is it not written: Contend not with evil-doers, neither be thou envious against them that work unrighteousness,[8] then you may tell him: Only one whose conscience smites[9] him says so. In fact, 'Contend not with evil-doers', means, to be like them; 'neither be thou envious against them that work unrighteousness', means, to be like them. And so it is said: Let not thy heart envy sinners, but be in the fear of the Lord all the day.[10] But this is not so! For R. Isaac said: If you see a wicked man upon whom fortune[11] is smiling, do not attack him. For it is said: His ways prosper at all times.[12] And more than that, he is victorious in the court of judgment; for it is said: Thy judgments are far above out of his sight.[13] And still more than that, he sees the discomfiture of his enemies; for it is said: As for all his adversaries, he puffeth at them.[14] There is no contradiction. The one [R. Isaac] speaks of his private affairs, the other one [R. Johanan] of matters of religion.[15] If you wish I can say: both speak of matters of religion, and still there is no contradiction. The one [R. Isaac] speaks of a wicked man upon whom fortune is smiling, the other one speaks of a wicked man upon whom fortune is not smiling. Or if you wish, I can say, both speak of a wicked man upon whom fortune is smiling, and still there is no contradiction. The one [R.

---

[1] Lit., 'training', 'upbringing'.

[2] Ibid. III, I.

[3] Ibid. 2.

[4] Ibid, II, I.

[5] MS.M.: To a man to whom it is said tomorrow a bill will be issued against you until he sees it … after he sees it etc.

[6] II Sam. XII, II.

[7] Prov. XXVIII, 4.

[8] Ps. XXXVII, I. E.V. 'Fret not thyself'.

[9] Lit., 'whose heart knocks him'.

[10] Prov. XXIII, 17.

[11] Lit., 'the hour'.

[12] Ps. X, 5.

[13] Ibid.

[14] Ibid.

[15] You may fight him with regard to religious affairs, but not with regard to his private affairs.

Johanan] speaks of a perfectly righteous man, the other one of a man who is not perfectly righteous. For R. Huna said: What is the meaning of the verse: Wherefore lookest Thou, when they deal treacherously, and holdest Thy peace, when the wicked swalloweth up the man that is more righteous than he?[1] Can then the wicked swallow up the righteous? Is it not written: The Lord will not leave him in his hand?[2] And is it not written further: There shall no mischief befall the righteous?[3] [You must] therefore [say]: He swallows up the one who is only 'more righteous than he', but he cannot swallow up the perfectly righteous man. If you wish I can say: It is different when fortune is smiling upon him.

R. Johanan further said in the name of R. Simeon b. Yohai: If a man has a fixed place for his prayer, his enemies succumb to him. For it is said: And I will appoint a place for My people Israel, and will plant them, that they may dwell in their own place, and be disquieted no more; neither shall the children of wickedness afflict them any more as at the first.[4]
R. Huna pointed to a contradiction. [Here] it is written: 'To afflict them', and [elsewhere]: To exterminate them?[5] [The answer is]: First to afflict them and then to exterminate them.

R. Johanan further said in the name of R. Simeon b. Yohai: The service of the Torah is greater than the study thereof.[6] For it is said: Here is Elisha the son of Shaphat, who poured water on the hands of Elijah.[7] It is not said, who learned, but who poured water. This teaches that the service of the Torah is greater than the study thereof.

R. Isaac said to R. Nahman: Why does the Master not come to the Synagogue in order to pray?[8] — He said to him: I cannot.[9] He asked him: Let the Master gather ten people and pray with them [in his house]? — He answered: It is too much of a trouble for me. [He then said]: Let the Master ask the messenger of the congregation[10] to inform him of the time when the congregation prays?[11] He answered: Why all this [trouble]? — He said to him: For R. Johanan said in the name of R. Simeon b. Yohai:

---

[1] Hab. I, 13.
[2] Ps. XXXVII, 33.
[3] Prov. XII, 21.
[4] II Sam. VII, 10.
[5] I Chron. XVII, 9. The Gemara read there . Our masoretic text, however, reads . The meaning is the same.
[6] To act as the famulus of the teacher is even more meritorious than being his disciple.
[7] II Kings III, II.
[8] Why does he not pray publicly with the congregation?
[9] For physical reasons.
[10] The Reader.
[11] So that R. Nahman might say his prayers at the same time as the congregation.

Folio 8a

What is the meaning of the verse: But as for me, let my prayer be made unto Thee, O Lord, in an acceptable time?[1] When is the time acceptable? When the congregation prays. R. Jose b. R. Hanina says: [You learn it] from here: Thus saith the Lord, In an acceptable time have I answered thee.[2] R. Aha son of R. Hanina says: [You learn it] from here: Behold, God despiseth not the mighty.[3] And it is further written: He hath redeemed my soul in peace so that none came nigh me; for they were many with me.[4] It has been taught also to the same effect; R. Nathan says: How do we know that the Holy One, blessed be He, does not despise the prayer of the congregation? For it is said: 'Behold, God despiseth not the mighty'. And it is further written: 'He hath redeemed my soul in peace so that none came nigh me, etc.'. The Holy One, blessed be He, says: If a man occupies himself with the study of the Torah and with works of charity and prays with the congregation, I account it to him as if he had redeemed Me and My children from among the nations of the world.

Resh Lakish said: Whosoever has a Synagogue in his town and does not go there in order to pray, is called an evil neighbour. For it is said: Thus saith the Lord, as for all Mine evil neighbours, that touch the inheritance which I have caused My people Israel to inherit.[5] And more than that, he brings exile upon himself and his children. For it is said: Behold, I will pluck them up from off their land, and will pluck up the house of Judah from among them.[6]

When they told R. Johanan[7] that there were old men in Babylon, he showed astonishment and said: Why, it is written: That your days may be multiplied, and the days of your children, upon the land;[8] but not outside the land [of Israel]! When they told him that they came early to the Synagogue and left it late, he said: That is what helps them. Even as R. Joshua b. Levi said to his children: Come early to the Synagogue and leave it late that you may live long. R. Aha son of R. Hanina says: Which verse [may be quoted in support of this]? Happy is the man that hearkeneth to Me, watching daily at My gates, waiting at the posts of My doors,[9] after which it is written: For whoso findeth me findeth life.[10] R. Hisda says: A man should always enter two doors into the Synagogue.[11] What is the meaning of 'two doors'? Say: The distance of two doors, and then pray.[12]

For this let every one that is godly pray unto Thee in the time of finding.[13] R. Hanina says: 'In the time of finding' refers to [the finding of] a wife. For it is said: Whoso findeth a wife findeth a great

---

[1] Ps. LXIX, 14.
[2] Isa. XLIX, 8.
[3] Job. XXXVI, 5. I.e., the mighty and numerous people that pray to Him. E.V. God is mighty and despiseth not any.
[4] Joining me in prayer. Ps. LV, 19. (E.V. 'for there were many that strove with me'.)
[5] Jer. XII, 14.
[6] Ibid.
[7] Who was a Palestinian.
[8] Deut. XI, 21.
[9] Prov. VIII, 34.
[10] Ibid. 35.
[11] MS.M. adds: 'and then pray, for it is written: "Waiting at the posts of My doors".'
[12] Were he to remain at the entrance, near the door, it would look as if he was anxious to leave.
[13] Ps. XXXII, 6.

good.¹ In the West they used to ask a man who married a wife thus: Maza or Moze?² 'Maza', for it is written: Whoso findeth [maza] a wife findeth a great good. 'Moze', for it is written: And I find [moze] more bitter than death the woman.³ R. Nathan says: 'In the time of finding' refers to the [finding of] Torah. For it is said: For whoso findeth me findeth life, etc.⁴ R. Nahman b. Isaac said: 'In the time of finding' refers to the [finding of] death. For it is said: The issues of death.⁵ Similarly it has been taught: Nine hundred and three species of death were created in this world. For it is said: The issues of death, and the numerical value of Toza'oth is so. The worst of them is the croup, and the easiest of them is the kiss.⁶ Croup is like a thorn in a ball of wool pulled out backwards.⁷ Some people say: It is like [pulling] a rope through the loop-holes [of a ship].⁸ [Death by a] kiss is like drawing a hair out of milk. R. Johanan said: 'In the time of finding' refers to the [finding of a] grave. R. Hanina said: Which verse [may be quoted in support]? Who rejoice unto exultation and are glad, when they can find the grave.⁹ Rabbah son of R. Shila said: Hence the proverb: A man should pray for peace even to the last clod of earth [thrown upon his grave]. Mar Zutra said: 'In the time of finding', refers to the [finding of a] privy.¹⁰ They said in the West: This [interpretation] of Mar Zutra is the best of all.

Raba said to Rafram b. Papa: Let the master please tell us some of those fine things that you said in the name of R. Hisda on matters relating to the Synagogue! — He replied: Thus said R. Hisda: What is the meaning of the verse: The Lord loveth the gates of Zion [Ziyyon] more than all the dwellings of Jacob?¹¹ The Lord loves the gates that are distinguished [me-zuyanim] through Halachah more than the Synagogues and Houses of study.¹² And this conforms with the following saying of R. Hiyya b. Ammi in the name of 'Ulla: Since the day that the Temple was destroyed, the Holy One, blessed be He, has nothing in this world but the four cubits of Halachah alone. So said also Abaye: At first I used to study in my house and pray in the Synagogue. Since I heard the saying of R. Hiyya
b. Ammi in the name of 'Ulla: 'Since the day that the Temple was destroyed, the Holy One, blessed be He, has nothing in His world but the four cubits of Halachah alone', I pray only in the place where I study. R. Ammi and R. Assi, though they had thirteen Synagogues in Tiberias, prayed only between the pillars where they used to study.¹³
R. Hiyya b. Ammi further said in the name of 'Ulla: A man who lives from the labour [of his hands] is greater than the one who fears heaven.¹⁴ For with regard to the one who fears heaven it is written: Happy is the man that feareth the Lord,¹⁵ while with regard to the man who lives from his own work

---

¹ Prov. XVIII, 22.
² Whereas the word maza is used in the Bible in connection with a good wife, the word moze is used in connection with a bad wife.
³ Eccl. VII, 26.
⁴ Prov. VIII, 35.
⁵ Ps. LXVIII, 21. is translated 'findings'.
⁶ The Talmud refers to an easy death as the 'death by a kiss'.
⁷ And drawing the wool with it.
⁸ The' friction being very great (Rashi). Jast.: Like the whirling waters at the entrance of a canal (when the sluicebars are raised).
⁹ Job. III, 22.
¹⁰ In Babylon, owing to the marshy character of the soil, privies were for the most part outside the town at some distance from the dwellings.
¹¹ Ps. LXXXVII, 2.
¹² Beth Midrash is here understood as the house of popular, aggadic lectures which, however, was not devoted to the study of Halachah.
¹³ In the Beth-hamidrash.
¹⁴ But for his living relies upon the support of other people.
¹⁵ Ps. CXII, I.

it is written: When thou eatest the labour of thy hands, happy shalt thou be, and it shall be well with thee.[1] 'Happy shalt thou be', in this world, 'and it shall be well with thee', in the world to come. But of the man that fears heaven it is not written: 'and it shall be well with thee'.

R. Hiyya b. Ammi further said in the name of 'Ulla: A man should always live in the same town as his teacher. For as long as Shimei the son of Gera was alive Solomon did not marry the daughter of Pharaoh.[2] — But it has been taught that he should not live [in the same place]? — There is no contradiction. The former [speaks of a disciple] who is submissive to him, the other [of a disciple] who is not submissive.

R. Huna b. Judah in the name of R. Menahem in the name of R. Ammi said: What is the meaning of the verse: And they that forsake the Lord shall be consumed?[3] This refers to people who leave the Scroll of the Law [while it is being read from] and go out [from the Synagogue]. R. Abbahu used to go out between one reader and the next.[4] R. Papa raised the question: What of going out between verse and verse? It remains unanswered. — R. Shesheth used to turn his face to another side and study. He said: We [are busy] with ours, and they [are busy] with theirs.[5]

R. Huna b. Judah says in the name of R. Ammi: A man should always complete his Parashoth together with the congregation,[6] [reading] twice the Hebrew text and once the [Aramaic] Targum,

---

[1] Ibid. CXXVIII, 2.
[2] The assumption is that he forbore to do so out of respect for his teacher.
[3] Isa. I, 28.
[4] I.e., when one portion was finished and before the next had commenced.
[5] They are engaged in listening to the public reading and we, more profitably, with more advanced study.
[6] I.e., recite (at home) the same weekly portion (parashah) from the Pentateuch.

Berakoth 8b

and even [such verses as] Ataroth and Dibon,[1] for if one completes his Parashoth together with the congregation, his days and years are prolonged. R. Bibi b. Abaye wanted to finish all the Parashoth of the whole year on the eve of the Day of Atonement. But Hiyya
b. Rab of Difti[2] recited to him [the following Baraitha]: It is written: And ye shall afflict your souls, in the ninth day of the month at even.[3] Now, do we fast on the ninth? Why, we fast on the tenth! But this teaches you that if one eats and drinks on the ninth, Scripture accounts it to him as if he fasted on the ninth and tenth.[4] Thereupon he wanted to finish them in advance. But a certain Elder recited to him a Baraitha teaching: However, he should not read them in advance of nor later [than the congregation]. Even so did R. Joshua
b. Levi say to his children: Complete your Parashoth together with the congregation, twice the Hebrew text and once Targum; be careful with the jugular veins to follow [the teaching of] R. Judah, as we have learnt: R. Judah says: He must cut through the jugular veins; and be careful [to respect] an old man who has forgotten his knowledge through no fault of his own,[5] for it was said: Both the whole tables and the fragments of the tables were placed in the Ark.[6]

Raba said to his children: When you are cutting meat, do not cut it upon your hand. (Some people say on account of danger;[7] and some in order not to spoil the meal.)[8] Do not sit upon the bed of an Aramaean woman, and do not pass behind a Synagogue when the congregation is praying. 'Do not sit upon the bed of an Aramaean woman'; some say that this means: Do not go to bed before reciting the Shema';[9] some say it means: Do not marry a proselyte woman; and some say it means literally [the bed of] an Aramaean woman, and this rule was laid down because of what happened to R. Papa. For R. Papa once visited an Aramaean woman. She brought out a bed and said: Sit down. He said to her: I will not sit down until you raise the cover of the bed. She raised the cover and they found there a dead baby. Hence said the scholars: It is not permitted to sit down upon the bed of an Aramaean woman. 'And do not pass behind a Synagogue when the congregation is praying'; this supports the teaching of R. Joshua b. Levi. For R. Joshua b. Levi said: It is not permitted for a man to pass behind a Synagogue when the congregation is praying. Abaye said: This applies only when there is no other door, but when there is another door,[10] there is no objection. Furthermore, this applies only when there is no other Synagogue, but when there is another Synagogues there is no objection. And furthermore, this applies only when he does not carry a burden, and does not run, and does not wear tefillin. But where one of these conditions is present there is no objection.

---

[1] Num. XXXII, 3. Even strings of names which are left untranslated in the Targum should be recited in Hebrew and in the Aramaic version.
[2] Dibtha on the Tigris.
[3] Lev. XXIII, 32.
[4] Therefore he should not devote the whole day to study.
[5] I.e., as a result of illness or struggle for a livelihood.
[6] V. B.B. 14b.
[7] Lest he should cut his hand.
[8] With the blood that will ooze from the meat.
[9] So that your bed should not be like that of an Aramaean.
[10] By which he can enter and join in the prayers.

It has been taught: R. Akiba says: For three things I like the Medes: When they cut meat, they cut it only on the table; when they kiss, they kiss only the hand; and when they hold counsel, they do so only in the field. R. Adda b. Ahabah says: Which verse [may be quoted in support of the last]? *And Jacob sent and called Rachel and Leah to the field unto his flock.*[1] It has been taught: R. Gamaliel says: For three things do I like the Persians: They are temperate in their eating, modest in the privy, and chaste in another matter.[2] *I have commanded My consecrated ones.*[3] R. Joseph learnt: This refers to the Persians who are consecrated and destined for Gehinnom.[4]

R. GAMALIEL SAYS: UNTIL THE DAWN RISES. Rab Judah says in the name of Samuel: The Halachah is as laid down by R. Gamaliel. It was taught, R. Simeon b. Yohai says: Sometimes a man may recite the Shema' twice in the night, once before the dawn breaks and once after the dawn breaks, and thereby fulfil his duty once for the day and once for the night.

Now this is self-contradictory. You say: 'A man may sometimes recite the Shema' twice in the night', which shows that it is still night after the dawn breaks. And then you say: 'He thereby fulfils his duty once for the day and once for the night', which shows that it is daytime? — No! It is in reality night, but he calls it day because some people rise at that time. R. Aha b. Hanina said in the name of R. Joshua b. Levi: The Halachah is as stated by

R. Simeon b. Yohai. Some people refer this [statement] of R. Aha b. Hanina to the following lesson,[5] which has been taught: R. Simeon b. Yohai says in the name of R. Akiba: Sometimes a man may recite the Shema' twice in the day-time, once before sunrise and once after sunrise, and thereby fulfill his duty once for the day and once for the night. Now this is self-contradictory. You say: 'A man may sometimes recite the Shema' twice in the daytime', which shows that before sunrise it is daytime, and then you state: 'He thereby fulfills his duty once for the day and once for the night', which shows that it is night? —

---

[1] Gen. XXXI, 4.
[2] In sexual matters.
[3] Isa. XIII, 3.
[4] R. Joseph experienced the Persecution under Shapor II.
[5] Which is most probably only another version of the previous one.

Folio 9a

No! It is in reality day, but he calls it night because some people go to bed at that time. R. Aha b. Hanina said in the name of R. Joshua b. Levi: The Halachah is as stated by R. Simeon who said in the name of R. Akiba. R. Zera says: However, he must not say [the prayer]: 'cause us to lie down'.[1] When R. Isaac b. Joseph came [from Palestine], he said: This [tradition] of R. Aha b. Hanina in the name of R. Joshua b. Levi was not expressly said [by R. Joshua], but it was said [by R. Aha] by inference.[2] For it happened that a couple of scholars became drunk at the wedding feast of the son of R. Joshua b. Levi, and they came before R. Joshua b. Levi [before the rise of the sun] and he said: R. Simeon is a great enough authority to be relied on in a case of emergency.

IT ONCE HAPPENED THAT HIS SONS CAME HOME [LATE], etc. How is it that they had not heard before of this opinion of R. Gamaliel? — [They had heard], but they asked thus: Do the Rabbis join issue with you? For if so, where there is a controversy between an individual and a group, the Halachah follows the group. Or do the Rabbis agree with you [in substance], but they say: UNTIL MIDNIGHT, in order to keep a man far away from transgression? — He replied: The Rabbis do agree with me, and it is your duty [to recite the Shema']. But they say, UNTIL MIDNIGHT, in order to keep a man far from transgression.

AND NOT IN RESPECT TO THIS ALONE DID THEY SO DECIDE, etc. But does R. Gamaliel say 'until midnight', that he should continue AND NOT IN RESPECT TO THIS ALONE DID THEY SO DECIDE? — That is what R. Gamaliel said to his sons: Even according to the Rabbis who say, 'UNTIL MIDNIGHT', the obligation continues until the dawn breaks, but the reason they said, 'UNTIL MIDNIGHT', was in order to keep a man far away from transgression.

THE BURNING OF THE FAT, etc. But [the Mishnah] does not mention the eating of the Passover offering. This would point to a contradiction [with the following Baraitha]: The duty of the recital of the Shema' in the evening, and of the Hallel[3] on the night of the Passover, and of the eating of the Passover sacrifice can be performed until the break of the dawn? — R. Joseph says: There is no contradiction. One statement [the Mishnah] conforms with the view of R. Eleazar b. Azariah, and the other with the view of R. Akiba. For it has been taught: And they shall eat of the flesh in that night.[4] R. Eleazar b. Azariah says: Here it is said: 'in that night', and further on it is said: For I will go through the land of Egypt in that night.[5] Just as the latter verse means until midnight, so also here it means until midnight. R. Akiba said to him: But it is also said: Ye shall eat it in haste,[6] which means: until the time of haste?[7] [Until the break of the dawn]. [Said R. Eleazar to him,][8] If that is so, why does it say: in the night? [R. Akiba answered,][9] Because I might think that it may be eaten in the

---

[1] V. P.B. p. 99. This is essentially a night prayer.
[2] From a decision of R. Joshua.
[3] V. Glos.
[4] Ex. XII, 8.
[5] Ibid. 12.
[6] Ibid. 11.
[7] The hour of the break of dawn, when they hastened out of Egypt, v. Ex. XII, 22.
[8] Inserted with MS.M.
[9] Inserted with MS.M.

daytime¹ like the sacrifices; therefore it is said: 'in the night', indicating that only in the night is it eaten and not in the day. We can understand why according to R. Eleazar b. Azariah, whose opinion is based on the Gezerah shawah,² the word 'that' is necessary. But according to R. Akiba what is the purpose of this word 'that'?³ — It is there to exclude another night. For, since the Passover sacrifice is a sacrifice of minor sanctity and peace-offerings are sacrifices of minor sanctity, I might think that just as the peace-offerings are eaten for two days and one night so is also the Passover-offering eaten for two nights instead of the two days, and therefore it might be eaten for two nights and one day! Therefore it is said: 'in that night'; in that night it is eaten, but it is not eaten in another night. And R. Eleazar b. Azariah?⁴ He deduces it from the verse: And ye shall let nothing of it remain until the morning.⁵ R. Akiba? — If [you deduced it] from there, I could say that 'morning' refers to the second morning. And R. Eleazar? — He answers you: 'Morning' generally means the first morning.

And [the controversy of] these Tannaim is like [the controversy of] the other Tannaim in the following Baraitha: There thou shalt sacrifice the passover-offering at even, at the going down of the sun, at the season that thou camest forth out of Egypt.⁶ R. Eliezer says: 'At even',⁷ you sacrifice; 'at sunset', you eat; and 'at the season that thou camest out of Egypt',⁸ you must burn [the remainder]. R. Joshua says: 'At even', you sacrifice; 'at sunset', you eat; a and how long do you continue to eat? Till 'the season that thou camest out of Egypt'.

R. Abba said: All agree that when Israel was redeemed⁹ from Egypt they were redeemed in the evening. For it is said: The Lord thy God brought thee forth out of Egypt by night.¹⁰ But they did not actually leave Egypt till the daytime. For it is said: On the morrow after the passover the children of Israel went out with a high hand.¹¹ About what do they disagree? — About the time of the haste.¹² R. Eleazar b. Azariah says: What is meant by 'haste'? The haste of the Egyptians.¹³ And R. Akiba says: It is the haste of Israel.¹⁴ It has also been taught likewise: 'The Lord thy God brought thee forth out of Egypt by night.' But did they leave in the night? Did not they in fact leave only in the morning, as it says: 'On the morrow after the passover the children of Israel went out with a high hand? But this teaches that the redemption had already begun in the evening.

Speak now [na] in the ears of the people, etc.¹⁵ In the school of R. Jannai they said: The word 'na' means: I pray. The Holy One, blessed be He, said to Moses: I pray of thee, go and tell Israel, I pray of you to borrow from the Egyptians vessels of silver and vessels of gold, so that

---

¹ I.e., during the very day on which it was slaughtered.
² V. Glos.
³ The text should have simply stated 'in the night'.
⁴ How does he deduce this latter ruling?
⁵ Ibid. XII, 10.
⁶ Deut. XVI, 6.
⁷ In the afternoon.
⁸ At the break of dawn. Hence according to R. Eliezer, the time of eating extends only till midnight.
⁹ I.e., obtained permission to leave.
¹⁰ Ibid. XVI, 1.
¹¹ Num. XXXIII, 3.
¹² Which is the termination of the time when it is permitted to eat; v. Ex. XII, 11 and the Gemara above.
¹³ At midnight the Egyptians hastened to urge Israel to leave Egypt.
¹⁴ I.e., in the morning when the Israelites hastened to go out.
¹⁵ Ex. XI, 2.

Berakoth 9b

this righteous man [Abraham] may not say: And they shall serve them, and they shall afflict them[1] He did fulfill for them, but And afterward shall they come out with great substance[2] He did not fulfill for them. They said to him: If only we could get out with our lives! A parable: [They were] like a man who was kept in prison and people told him: To-morrow, they will release you from the prison and give you plenty of money. And he answered them: I pray of you, let me go free today and I shall ask nothing more!

And they let them have what they asked.[3] R. Ammi says: This teaches that they let them have it against their will. Some say, against the will of the Egyptians, and some say, against the will of the Israelites. Those that say 'against the will of the Egyptians' cite the verse: And she that tarrieth at home divideth the spoil.[4] Those that say: 'against the will of the Israelites', say it was because of the burden [of carrying it]. And they despoiled Egypt.[5]
R. Ammi says: This teaches that they made it like a snare[6] without corn. Resh Lakish said: They made it like a pond without fish.

I am that I am.[7] The Holy One, blessed be He, said to Moses: Go and say to Israel: I was with you in this servitude, and I shall be with you in the servitude of the [other] kingdoms.[8] He said to Him: Lord of the Universe, sufficient is the evil in the time thereof! Thereupon the Holy One, blessed be He, said to him: Go and tell them: I AM has sent me unto you.[9]

Hear me, O Lord, hear me.[10] R. Abbahu said: Why did Elijah say twice: 'Hear me'? This teaches that Elijah said before the Holy One, blessed be He: Lord of the Universe, 'hear me', that the fire may descend from heaven and consume everything that is upon the altar; and 'hear me', that Thou mayest turn their mind that they may not say that it was the work of sorcery. For it is said: For Thou didst turn their heart backward.[11]

MISHNAH. FROM WHAT TIME MAY ONE RECITE THE SHEMA IN THE MORNING? FROM THE TIME THAT ONE CAN DISTINGUISH BETWEEN BLUE AND WHITE. R. ELIEZER SAYS: BETWEEN BLUE AND GREEN. AND HE HAS TIME TO FINISH UNTIL SUNRISE. R. JOSHUA SAYS: UNTIL THE THIRD HOUR OF THE DAY, FOR SUCH IS THE CUSTOM OF KINGS, TO RISE AT THE THIRD HOUR. IF ONE RECITES THE SHEMA' LATER HE LOSES NOTHING, BEING LIKE ONE WHO READS IN THE TORAH.[12]

---

[1] Gen. XV, 14.
[2] Ibid.
[3] Ex. XII, 36.
[4] Ps. LXVIII, 13.
[5] Ex. XII, 36.
[6] For birds with corn for a lure. Var. lec.: like husks without grain, like a net without fish.
[7] Ibid. III, 14.
[8] Babylon and Rome.
[9] Ibid.
[10] I Kings XVIII, 37.
[11] Ibid. Sc., from such a thought.
[12] It is not a transgression. On the contrary, he has the ordinary merit of one who reads in the Torah, though he

GEMARA. What is the meaning of BETWEEN BLUE AND WHITE? Shall I say: between a lump of white wool and a lump of blue wool? This one may also distinguish in the night! It means rather: between the blue in it and the white in it.[1] It has been taught: R. Meir says: [The morning Shema' is read] from the time that one can distinguish between a wolf and a dog; R. Akiba says: Between an ass and a wild ass. Others say: From the time that one can distinguish his friend at a distance of four cubits. R. Huna says: The halachah is as stated by the 'Others'. Abaye says: In regard to the tefillin,[2] the halachah is as stated by the 'Others'; in regard to [the recital of] the Shema', as practised by the watikin.[3] For R. Johanan said: The watikin used to finish it [the recital of the Shema'] with sunrise, in order to join the ge'ullah with the tefillah,[4] and say the tefillah in the daytime. R. Zera says: What text can be cited in support of this? They shall fear Thee with the sun,[5] and so long as the moon throughout all generations.[6] R. Jose b. Eliakim testified[7] in the name of the holy community of Jerusalem:[8] If one joins the ge'ullah to the tefillah, he will not meet with any mishap for the whole of the day. Said R. Zera: This is not so! For I did join, and did meet with a mishap. They asked him: What was your mishap? That you had to carry a myrtle branch into the king's palace?[9] That was no mishap, for in any case you would have had to pay something in order to see the king! For R. Johanan said: A man should always be eager to run to see the kings of Israel. And not only to see the kings of Israel, but also to see the kings of the Gentiles, so that, if he is found worthy,[10] he may be able to distinguish between the kings of Israel and the kings of the Gentiles.

R. Ela said to 'Ulla: When you go up there,[11] give my greeting to my brother R. Berona in the presence of the whole college, for he is a great man and rejoices to perform a precept [in the correct manner]. Once he succeeded in joining ge'ullah with tefillah,[12] and a smile did not leave his lips the whole day. How is it possible to join the two, seeing that R. Johanan has said:[13] At the beginning of the tefillah one has to say, O, Lord, open Thou my lips,[14] and at the end he has to say, Let the words of my mouth be acceptable etc.?[15] — R. Eleazar replied: This[16] must then refer to the tefillah of the evening. But has not R. Johanan said: Who is it that is destined for the world to come? One who joins the ge'ullah of the evening with the tefillah of the evening? — Rather said R. Eleazar: This must then refer to the tefillah of the afternoon. R. Ashi said: You may also say that it refers to all the tefillahs,

---

has not fulfilled the obligation of reading the Shema'.
[1] In one and the same lump of wool which was dyed blue but had some white spots in it. J. T. refers it to the 'fringes' which contain a thread of blue and which are used when reading the Shema'.
[2] I.e., the time for putting them on. MS.M. reads Tefillah (v. Glos.).
[3] Lit., strong' (sc., in piety), a title probably applied to certain men who, in the time of the Hasmonean kingdom, set an example of exceptional piety. Some identify them with the Essenes.
[4] V. supra 4b.
[5] I.e., when the sun rises. E.V. 'While the sun endureth'.
[6] Ps. LXXII, 5.
[7] I.e., transmitted a tradition.
[8] V. J.E. p. 226.
[9] He was compelled to do some forced labour. V. T.J.
[10] To live to the time of the restoration of the Jewish kingdom and to see the Jewish kings.
[11] To Palestine.
[12] Apparently this means, having read the Shema' after the manner of the watikin. V. Tosaf. ad loc.
[13] V. supra, 4b.
[14] Ps. LI, 17.
[15] Ps. XIX, 15.
[16] The recital of these extra verses at the beginning and end of the tefillah.

but since the Rabbis instituted [these words][1] in the tefillah, the whole is considered one long tefillah. For if you do not admit this, how can he join in the evening, seeing that he has to say the benediction of 'Let us rest'?[2] You must say then that, since the Rabbis ordained the saying of 'Let us rest', it is considered one long ge'ullah.[3] So here, since the Rabbis instituted these words in the tefillah, the whole is considered one long tefillah.

Seeing that this verse, 'Let the words of my mouth be acceptable etc.' is suitable for recital either at the end or the beginning [of the tefillah], why did the Rabbis institute it at the end of the eighteen benedictions? Let it be recited at the beginning? — R. Judah the son of R. Simeon b. Pazzi said: Since David said it only after eighteen chapters [of the Psalms],[4] the Rabbis too enacted that it should be said after eighteen blessings. But those eighteen Psalms are really nineteen? — 'Happy is the man' and 'Why are the nations in an uproar'[5] form one chapter. For R. Judah the son of R. Simeon b. Pazzi said: David composed a hundred and three chapters [of psalms], and he did not say 'Hallelujah' until he saw the downfall of the wicked, as it says, Let sinners cease out of the earth, and let the wicked be no more. Bless the Lord, O my soul. Hallelujah.[6] Now are these a hundred and three? Are they not a hundred and four? You must assume therefore that 'Happy is the man' and 'Why are the nations in an uproar' form one chapter. For R. Samuel b. Nahmani said in the name of R. Johanan:

---

[1] The recital of these extra verses at the beginning and end of the tefillah.
[2] V. supra, 4b.
[3] The benediction of 'Let us rest' also comes between ge'ullah and tefillah.
[4] It comes at the end of Ps. XIX
[5] The opening verses of Pss. I and II.
[6] Ibid. CIV, 35.

Folio 10a

Every chapter that was particularly dear to David he commenced with 'Happy' and terminated with 'Happy'.[1] He began with 'Happy', as it is written, 'Happy is the man', and he terminated with 'Happy', as it is written, 'happy are all they that take refuge in Him'.[2]

There were once some highwaymen[3] in the neighbourhood of R. Meir who caused him a great deal of trouble. R. Meir accordingly prayed that they should die. His wife Beruria[4] said to him: How do you make out [that such a prayer should be permitted]? Because it is written Let hatta'im cease? Is it written hot'im?[5] It is written hatta'im![6] Further, look at the end of the verse: and let the wicked men be no more. Since the sins will cease, there will be no more wicked men! Rather pray for them that they should repent, and there will be no more wicked. He did pray for them, and they repented.

A certain Min[7] said to Beruria: it is written: Sing, O barren, thou that didst not bear.[8] Because she did not bear is she to sing? She replied to him: You fool! Look at the end of the verse, where it is written, For the children of the desolate shall be more than the children of the married wife, saith the Lord.[9] But what then is the meaning of 'a barren that did not bear'? Sing, O community of Israel, who resemblest a barren woman, for not having born children like you for Gehenna.

A certain Min said to R. Abbahu: It is written: A Psalm of David when he fled from Absalom his son.[10] And it is also written, A mihtam of David when he fled from Saul in the cave.[11] Which event happened first? Did not the event of Saul happen first? Then let him write it first? He replied to him: For you who do not derive interpretations from juxtaposition, there is a difficulty, but for us who do derive interpretations from juxtaposition there is no difficulty. For R. Johanan said: How do we know from the Torah that juxtaposition counts? Because it says, They are joined[12] for ever and ever, they are done in truth and uprightness.[13] Why is the chapter of Absalom juxtaposed to the chapter of Gog and Magog?[14] So that if one should say to you, is it possible that a slave should rebel against his master,[15] you can reply to him: Is it possible that a son should rebel against his father? Yet this happened; and so this too [will happen].

---

[1] In point of fact this is the only one. V. Tosaf. a.l.
[2] The last verse of Ps. II, which shows that according to R. Johanan Pss. I and II formed one Psalm.
[3] Baryone, a word of doubtful meaning.
[4] Valeria.
[5] Pres. part. of the verb hata, to sin. Hence meaning sinners.
[6] Which can be read sins. M.T. vocalizes (sinners).
[7] So MS.M. (v. Glos.) curr. edd.: Sadducee.
[8] Isa. LIV, 1.
[9] Apparently the point is that at present she is barren, but in the future she shall have many children. Probably Beruria was thinking of Rome as 'the married wife' and Jerusalem as 'the desolate'.
[10] Ps. III, 1.
[11] Ibid. LVII, 1.
[12] Heb. semukim, the same word as for juxtaposed. E.V. 'established'.
[13] Ibid. CXI, 8.
[14] Ps. II, which is supposed by the Rabbis to refer to the rebellion of Gog and Magog against God and the Messiah.
[15] Sc. the nations against God.

R. Johanan said in the name of R. Simeon b. Yohai: What is the meaning of the verse, She openeth her mouth with wisdom, and the law of kindness is on her tongue?[1] To whom was Solomon alluding in this verse? He was alluding only to his father David who dwelt in five worlds and composed a psalm [for each of them]. He abode in his mother's womb, and broke into song, as it says, Bless the Lord, O my soul, and all my inwards[2] bless His holy name.[3] He came out into the open air and looked upon the stars and constellations and broke into song, as it says, Bless the Lord, ye angels of His, ye mighty in strength that fulfil His word, hearkening unto the voice of His word. Bless the Lord, all ye His hosts[4] etc. He sucked from his mother's bosom and looked on her breasts and broke into song, as it says, Bless the Lord, O my soul, and forget not all His benefits.[5] What means 'all His benefits'? — R. Abbahu said: That He placed her breasts at the source of understanding.[6] For what reason is this? — Rab Judah said: So that he should not look upon the place of shame; R. Mattena said: So that he should not suck from a place that is foul. He saw the downfall of the wicked and broke into song, as it says, Let sinners cease out of the earth and let the wicked be no more. Bless the Lord, O my soul, Hallelujah.[7] He looked upon the day of death and broke into song, as it says, Bless the Lord, O my soul. O Lord my God, Thou art very great, Thou art clothed with glory and majesty.[8] How does this verse refer to the day of death? — Rabbah son of R. Shila said: We learn it from the end of the passage, where it is written: Thou hidest Thy face, they vanish, Thou withdrawest their breath, they perish etc.[9]

R. Shimi b. 'Ukba (others say, Mar 'Ukba) was often in the company of R. Simeon b. Pazzi, who[10] used to arrange aggadahs [and recite them] before R. Johanan. He[11] said to him: What is the meaning of the verse, Bless the Lord, O my soul, and all that is within me bless His holy name?[12] — He replied: Come and observe how the capacity of human beings falls short of the capacity of the Holy One, blessed be He. It is in the capacity of a human being to draw a figure on a wall, but he cannot invest it with breath and spirit, bowels and intestines. But the Holy One, blessed be He, is not so; He shapes one form in the midst of another, and invests it with breath and spirit, bowels and intestines. And that is what Hannah said: There is none holy as the Lord, for there is none beside Thee, neither is there any zur [rock] like our God.[13] What means, neither is there any zur like our God'? There is no artist [zayyar] like our God. What means, 'For there is none beside Thee'? R. Judah b. Menasiah said: Read not, There is none bilteka, but, There is none lebalotheka [to consume Thee]. For the nature of flesh and blood is not like that of the Holy One, blessed be He. It is the nature of flesh and blood to be outlived by its works, but the Holy One, blessed be He, outlives His works. He said to him:[14] What I meant to tell you is this: To whom did David refer in these five verses beginning with 'Bless the Lord, O my soul'? He was alluding only to the Holy One, blessed be He, and to the soul. Just as the

---

[1] Prov. XXXI, 26.
[2] I.e., his mother's womb. E.V. 'all that is within me'.
[3] Ps. CIII, 1.
[4] Ps. CIII, 20, 21.
[5] Ibid. 2.
[6] I.e., the heart, (the seat of understanding). R. Abbahu connects the word gemulaw (his benefits) with gamal (weaned).
[7] Ibid. CIV, 35.
[8] Ibid. I.
[9] Ibid. 29.
[10] Reading with MS.M.
[11] R. Shimi or Mar 'Ukba.
[12] Ibid. CIII, 1.
[13] I Sam. II, 2.
[14] R. Shimi to R. Simeon b. Pazzi.

Holy One, blessed be He, fills the whole world, so the soul fills the body. Just as the Holy One, blessed be He, sees, but is not seen, so the soul sees but is not itself seen. Just as the Holy One, blessed be He, feeds the whole world, so the soul feeds the whole body. Just as the Holy One, blessed be He, is pure, so the soul is pure. Just as the Holy One, blessed be He, abides in the innermost precincts, so the soul abides in the innermost precincts. Let that which has these five qualities come and praise Him who has these five qualities.

R. Hamnuna said: What is the meaning of the verse, Who is as the wise man? And who knoweth the interpretation [pesher] of a thing?[1] Who is like the Holy One, blessed be He, who knew how to effect a reconciliation [pesharah] between two righteous men, Hezekiah and Isaiah? Hezekiah said: Let Isaiah come to me, for so we find that Elijah went to Ahab,[2] as it says, And Elijah went to show himself unto Ahab.[3] Isaiah said: Let Hezekiah come to me, for so we find that Jehoram son of Ahab went to Elisha.[4] What did the Holy One, blessed be He, do? He brought sufferings upon Hezekiah and then said to Isaiah, Go visit the sick. For so it says, In those days was Hezekiah sick unto death. And Isaiah the prophet, son of Amoz, came to him and said unto him, Thus saith the Lord, Set thy house in order, for thou shalt die and not live[5] etc. What is the meaning of 'thou shalt die and not live'? Thou shalt die in this world and not live in the world to come. He said to him: Why so bad? He replied: Because you did not try to have children. He said: The reason was because I saw by the holy spirit that the children issuing from me would not be virtuous. He said to him: What have you to do with the secrets of the All-Merciful? You should have done what you were commanded, and let the Holy One, blessed be He, do that which pleases Him. He said to him: Then give me now your daughter; perhaps through your merit and mine combined virtuous children will issue from me. He replied:[6] The doom has already been decreed. Said the other: Son of Amoz, finish your prophecy and go. This tradition I have from the house of my ancestor:[7] Even if a sharp sword rests upon a man's neck he should not desist from prayer.[8] This saying is also recorded in the names of R. Johanan and R. Eleazar: Even if a sharp sword rests on a man's neck, he should not desist from prayer, as it says, Though He slay me, yet will I trust in Him.[9]

---

[1] Eccl. VIII, 1.
[2] The prophet went to the king.
[3] 1 Kings XVIII, 2.
[4] V. II Kings III, 12.
[5] Isa. XXXVIII, 1.
[6] Insert with MS.M. Behold I say to you 'Set thy house in order', and you say to me 'Give me now your daughter'.
[7] David.
[8] Cf. II Sam. XXIV, 17.
[9] Job XIII, 15.

Berakoth 10b

[Similarly] R. Hanan said: Even if the master of dreams[1] says to a man that on the morrow he will die, he should not desist from prayer, for so it says, For in the multitude of dreams are vanities and also many words, but fear thou God.[2] Thereupon straightway, Hezekiah turned his face to the kir [wall] and prayed unto the Lord.[3] What is the meaning of 'kir'? — R. Simeon b. Lakish said: [He prayed] from the innermost cham bers [kiroth] of his heart, as it says, My bowels, my bowels, I writhe in pain! Kiroth [The chambers] of my heart etc.[4] R. Levi said: [He prayed] with reference to [another] 'kir'. He said before Him: Sovereign of the Universe! The Shunammite woman made only one little chamber [on the roof] and Thou didst restore her son to life.[5] How much more so then me whose ancestor[6] overlaid the Temple with silver and gold! Remember now, O Lord, I beseech Thee, how I have walked before Thee in truth and with a whole heart, and have done that which is good in Thy sight.[7] What means, 'I have done that which is good in Thy sight'? — Rab Judah says in the name of Rab: He joined the ge'ullah with the tefillah.[8] R. Levi said: He hid away the Book of Cures.[9]

Our Rabbis taught:[10] King Hezekiah did six things; of three of them they [the Rabbis] approved and of three they did not approve. Of three they approved: he hid away the Book of Cures; and they approved of it; he broke into pieces the brazen serpent,[11] and they approved of it; and he dragged the bones of his father [to the grave] on a bed of ropes,[12] and they approved of it.[13] Of three they did not approve: He stopped up the waters of Gihon,[14] and they did not approve of it; he cut off [the gold] from the doors of the Temple and sent it to the King of Assyria,[15] and they did not approve of it; and he intercalated the month of Nisan during Nisan,[16] and they did not approve of it. But did not

---

[1] This seems to be simply a periphrasis for 'if a man is told in a dream'. Two explanations are then possible of what follows. (i) If he dreams and the dream so far comes true that a sword is placed on his neck, still he should pray. (ii) Even if he only dreams this, he should still pray etc. (R. Bezalel of Regensburg.)
[2] Eccl. V, 6. Apparently this is how R. Hanan understands the verse. E.V. Through the multitude and vanities there are also many words.
[3] Isa. XXXVIII, 2. MS.M. adds: Finally he gave him his daughter (in marriage) and there issued from him Menasseh and Rabshakeh. One day he (Hezekiah) carried them on his shoulder to the Synagogue (Var. lec. to the house of learning) and one of them said, 'Father's bald head is good for breaking nuts on', while the other said, 'it is good for roasting fish on. He thereupon threw them both on the ground and Rabshakeh was killed, but not Menasseh. He then applied to them the verse, The instruments also of the churl are evil; he deviseth wicked devices. (Isa. XXXII, 7).
[4] Jer. IV, 19.
[5] V. II Kings IV, 10.
[6] King Solomon.
[7] Isa. XXXVIII, 3. This comes in the prayer of Hezekiah.
[8] V. supra, 9b.
[9] A book containing remedies for various illnesses which Hezekiah hid from the public in order that people might pray for healing to God; v. infra.
[10] V. Pes. 56a.
[11] V. II Kings XVIII, 4.
[12] Instead of giving him a royal burial.
[13] Because Ahaz was a wicked man.
[14] V. II Chron. XXXII, 30.
[15] V. II Kings XVIII, 16.
[16] V. II Chron. XXX, 2.

Hezekiah accept the teaching: This month shall be unto you the beginning of months:[1] [this means] that this is Nisan and no other month shall be Nisan?[2] — He went wrong over the teaching enunciated by Samuel. For Samuel said: The year must not be declared a prolonged year on the thirtieth of Adar, since this day may possibly belong to Nisan;[3] and he thought: We do not pay heed to this possibility.[4]

R. Johanan said in the name of R. Jose b. Zimra: If a man makes his petition depend on his own merit, heaven makes it depend on the merit of others; and if he makes it depend on the merit of others, heaven makes it depend on his own merit. Moses made his petition depend on the merit of others, as it says, Remember Abraham, Isaac and Israel Thy servants![5] and Scripture made it depend on his own merit, as it says, Therefore He said that He would destroy them, had not Moses His chosen stood before Him in the breach to turn back His wrath, lest He should destroy them.[6] Hezekiah made his petition depend on his own merit, as it is written: Remember now, O Lord, I beseech Thee, how I have walked before Thee,[7] and God made it depend on the merit of others, as it says, For I will defend this city to save it, for Mine own sake and for My servant David's sake.[8] And this agrees with R. Joshua b. Levi. For R. Joshua b. Levi said: What is the meaning of the verse, Behold for my peace I had great bitterness?[9] Even when the Holy One, blessed be He, sent him [the message of] peace it was bitter for him.[10]

Let us make, I pray thee, a little chamber on the roof.[11] Rab and Samuel differ.[12] One says: It was an open upper chamber, and they put a roof on it. The other says: It was a large verandah, and they divided it into two.[13] For him who says that it was a verandah, there is a good reason why the text says kir [wall]. But how does he who says that it was an upper chamber account for the word kir? — [It is used] because they put a roof on it [kiruah]. For him who says it was an upper chamber there is a good reason why the text uses the word 'aliyath [upper chamber]. But how does he who says it was a verandah account for the word 'aliyath? — It was the best [me'ulla][14] of the rooms.

And let us set for him there a bed, and a table, and a stool and a candlestick.[15] Abaye (or as some say, R. Isaac) said: If one wants to benefit from the hospitality of another, he may benefit, as Elisha did;[16] and if he does not desire to benefit, he may refuse to do so, as Samuel the Ramathite did,[17] of whom we read, And his return was to Ramah, for there was his house;[18] and R. Johanan said: [This teaches

---

[1] Ex. XII, 2.
[2] I.e., a second Nisan must not be intercalated.
[3] If the new moon is observed on it.
[4] And he declared the month Adar Sheni (Second Adar).
[5] Ex. XXXII, 13. .
[6] Ps. CVI, 23.
[7] Isa. XXXVIII, 3.
[8] Ibid. XXXVII 35.
[9] Ibid. XXXVIII, 17.
[10] Because it was not made to depend on his own merit.
[11] II Kings IV, 10.
[12] In the explanation of which means literally 'an upper chamber of (with) a wall'.
[13] By means of a wall.
[14] Lit., 'elevated'
[15] II Kings IV, 10.
[16] There is no prohibition against this.
[17] And this is not to be taken as a sign of pride or enmity.
[18] I Sam. VII, 17.

that] wherever he travelled, his house was with him.[1]

And she said unto her husband: Behold now, I perceive that he is a holy man of God.[2]
R. Jose b. Hanina said: You learn from this that a woman recognizes the character of a guest better than a man. 'A holy man'. How did she know this? — Rab and Samuel gave different answers. One said: Because she never saw a fly pass by his table. The other said: She spread a sheet of linen over his bed, and she never saw a nocturnal pollution on it. He is a holy [man]. R. Jose son of R. Hanina said: He is holy, but his attendant is not holy. For so it says: And Gehazi came near to thrust her away;[3] R. Jose son of Hanina said: He seized her by the breast.[4]

That passeth by us continually.[5] R. Jose son of R. Hanina said in the name of R. Eliezer b. Jacob: If a man entertains a scholar in his house and lets him enjoy his possessions, Scripture accounts it to him as if he had sacrificed the daily burnt-offering.[6]
R. Jose son of Hanina further said in the name of R. Eliezer b. Jacob: A man should not stand on a high place when he prays, but he should pray in a lowly place, as it says; Out of the depths have I called Thee, O Lord.[7] It has been taught to the same effect: A man should not stand on a chair or on a footstool or on a high place to pray, but he should pray in a lowly place, since there is no elevation before God, and so it says, 'Out of the depths have I called Thee, O Lord', and it also says, A prayer of the afflicted, when he fainteth.[8]
R. Jose son of R. Hanina also said in the name of R. Eliezer b. Jacob: When one prays, he should place his feet in proper position,[9] as it says, And their feet were straight feet.[10]
R. Jose son of R. Hanina also said in the name of R. Eliezer b. Jacob: What is the meaning of the verse, Ye shall not eat with the blood?[11] Do not eat before ye have prayed for your blood.[12] R. Isaac said in the name of R. Johanan, who had it from R. Jose son of R. Hanina in the name of R. Eliezer b. Jacob: If one eats and drinks and then says his prayers, of him the Scripture says, And hast cast Me behind thy back.[13] Read not gaweka [thy back], but geeka [thy pride]. Says the Holy One, blessed be He: After[14] this one has exalted himself, he comes and accepts the kingdom of heaven![15]
R. JOSHUA SAYS: UNTIL THE THIRD HOUR. Rab Judah said in the name of Samuel: The halachah is as stated by R. Joshua.

HE WHO RECITES THE SHEMA' LATER LOSES NOTHING. R. Hisda said in the name of Mar 'Ukba: Provided he does not say the benediction of 'Who formest the light'.[16] An objection was raised

---

[1] I.e., he did not accept the hospitality of the people. R. Johanan takes the word 'there' to refer to all the places mentioned above.
[2] II Kings IV, 9.
[3] Ibid. 27.
[4] Lit., 'the pride of her beauty', a play on the word 'to thrust her away'.
[5] Ibid. 9.
[6] Which is also called tamid, lit., 'continually'.
[7] Ps. CXXX, 1.
[8] Ibid. CII, 1.
[9] I.e., close together and level.
[10] Ezek. I, 7.
[11] Lev. XIX, 26.
[12] I.e., life.
[13] I Kings XIV, 9.
[14] The same Hebrew word may be translated 'behind' and 'after'.
[15] The technical term for reciting the Shema'.
[16] The first of the two introductory benedictions to the Shema'. V. P. B. p. 37.

from the statement: He who recites the Shema' later loses nothing; he is like one reading in the Torah, but he says two blessings before it and one after. Is not this a refutation of R. Hisda? It is [indeed] a refutation. Some there are who say: R. Hisda said in the name of Mar 'Ukba: What is the meaning of HE LOSES NOTHING? He does not lose the benedictions. It has been taught to the same effect: He who says the Shema' later loses nothing, being like one who reads from the Torah, but he says two blessings before and one after.

R. Mani said: He who recites the Shema' in its proper time is greater than he who studies the Torah.[1] For since it says, HE WHO SAYS LATER LOSES NOTHING, BEING LIKE A MAN WHO READS IN THE TORAH, we may conclude that one who recites the Shema' at its proper time is superior.

MISHNAH. BETH SHAMMAI SAY: IN THE EVENING EVERY MAN SHOULD RECLINE AND RECITE [THE SHEMA'], AND IN THE MORNING HE SHOULD STAND, AS IT SAYS, AND WHEN THOU LIEST DOWN AND WHEN THOU RISEST UP.[2] BETH HILLEL, HOWEVER, SAY THAT EVERY MAN SHOULD RECITE IN HIS OWN WAY, AS IT SAYS, AND WHEN THOU WALKEST BY THE WAY.[3] WHY THEN IS IT SAID, AND WHEN THOU LIEST DOWN AND WHEN THOU RISEST UP? [THIS MEANS], AT THE TIME WHEN PEOPLE LIE DOWN AND AT THE TIME WHEN PEOPLE RISE UP. R. TARFON SAID: I WAS ONCE WALKING BY THE WAY AND I RECLINED TO RECITE THE SHEMA' IN THE MANNER PRESCRIBED BY BETH SHAMMAI, AND I INCURRED DANGER FROM ROBBERS. THEY SAID TO HIM: YOU DESERVED TO COME TO HARM, BECAUSE YOU ACTED AGAINST THE OPINION OF BETH HILLEL.

---

[1] If he who says later is as good, he who says at the proper time must be better.
[2] Deut. VI, 7.
[3] Ibid.

Folio 11a

GEMARA. Beth Hillel cause no difficulty; they explain their own reason and the reason [why they reject the opinion] of Beth Shammai. But why do not Beth Shammai accept the view of Beth Hillel? — Beth Shammai can reply: If this is so,[1] let the text say, 'In the morning and in the evening'. Why does it say, 'When thou liest down and when thou risest up'? To show that in the time of lying down there must be actual lying down, and in the time of rising up there must be actual rising up. And how do Beth Shammai explain the words 'And when thou walkest by the way'? — They need it for the following, as has been taught: 'When thou sittest in thy house':[2] this excludes a bridegroom. 'And when thou walkest by the way': this excludes one who is occupied with the performance of a religious duty.[3] Hence they laid down that one who marries a virgin is free [from the obligation to say the Shema' in the evening] while one who marries a widow is bound.[4] How is the lesson[5] derived? — R. Papa said: [The circumstances must be] like a 'way'. As a 'way' [journey] is optional, so whatever is optional [does not exempt from the obligation]. But does not the text treat [also] of one who is going to perform a religious duty, and even so the All Merciful said that he should recite? — If that were so, the All Merciful should have written [simply], 'While sitting and while walking'. What is the implication of when thou sittest and when thou walkest? — In the case of thy sitting and thy walking thou art under the obligation, but in the case of performing a religious duty thou art exempt. If that is so, one who marries a widow should also be exempt? — The one[6] is agitated, the other not. If a state of agitation is the ground, it would apply also the the case of his ship sinking at sea! And should you say, Quite so, why did R. Abba b. Zabda say in the name of Rab: A mourner is under obligation to perform all the precepts laid down in the Torah except that of the tefillin, because the term 'headtire' is applied to them, as it says, Bind thy headtire upon thee?[7] — In that case the agitation is over a religious duty, here it is over an optional matter.

And Beth Shammai?[8] — They require it to exclude persons on a religious mission.[9] And Beth Hillel?[10] — They reply: Incidentally it tells you that one recites also by the way.[11]

Our Rabbis taught: Beth Hillel say that one may recite the Shema' standing, one may recite it sitting, one may recite it reclining, one may recite it walking on the road, one may recite it at one's work. Once R. Ishmael and R. Eleazar b. Azariah were dining at the same place, and R. Ishmael was

---

[1] That only the time of the recital is meant.
[2] Ibid.
[3] This is the reading of MS.M., and this is the version found in Tosaf. Suk. 25a a.v. and elsewhere. Cur. edd. reverse the positions of 'bridegroom' and 'one who is occupied, etc.'
[4] V. infra.
[5] Relating to one who is occupied with the performance.
[6] The one who marries a virgin is worried as to whether he shall find her really such.
[7] Ezek. XXIV, 17. Ezekiel, though a mourner, was commanded exceptionally to wear his headtire, i.e., (as the Rabbis understand) tefillin, from which it is deduced that ordinarily a mourner does not do so. But the fact remains that worry as a rule does not exempt from the precepts.
[8] How do they interpret the words 'and when thou walkest by the way'? V. next note.
[9] This seems to be a repetition of the question and answer given above and is best left out with MS.M.
[10] How can they infer their view from this verse, seeing that it is required to exempt one who is occupied in performing a religious duty.
[11] I.e., in his own way, as explained above.

reclining while R. Eleazar was standing upright. When the time came for reciting the Shema', R. Eleazar reclined and R. Ishmael stood upright. Said R. Eleazar b. Azariah to R. Ishmael: Brother Ishmael, I will tell you a parable. To what is this [our conduct] like? It is like that of a man to whom people say, You have a fine beard, and he replies, Let this go to meet the destroyers.[1] So now, with you: as long as I was upright you were reclining, and now that I recline you stand upright![2] He replied: I have acted according to the rule of Beth Hillel and you have acted according to the rule of Beth Shammai. And what Is more, [I had to act thus], lest the disciples should see and fix the halachah so for future generations. What did he mean by 'what is more'? He meant: Should you argue that Beth Hillel also allow reclining, [I reply that] this is the case only where one was reclining from the first. Here, however, since at first you were upright and now you recline, they may say, This shows that they [both] are of the opinion of Beth Shammai, and perhaps the disciples will see and fix the halachah so for future generations.

R. Ezekiel learnt: If one follows the rule of Beth Shammai he does right, if one follows the rule of Beth Hillel he does right. R. Joseph said: If he follows the rule of Beth Shammai, his action is worthless, as we have learnt: If a man has his head and the greater part of his body in the sukkah[3] while the table is in the house, Beth Shammai declare his action void, while Beth Hillel declare it valid. Said Beth Hillel to Beth Shammai: Once the Elders of Beth Shammai and the Elders of Beth Hillel went to visit R. Johanan b. Ha-horanith, and they found him with his head and the greater part of his body in the sukkah while the table was in the house, and they made no objection. They replied: Do you bring a proof from this?[4] [The fact is that] they also said to him: If such has been your regular custom, you have never performed the precept of the sukkah in your lifetime.[5] R. Nahman b. Isaac said: One who follows the rule of Beth Shammai makes his life forfeit, as we have learnt:

R. TARFON SAID: I WAS ONCE WALKING BY THE WAY AND I RECLINED TO RECITE THE SHEMA' IN THE MANNER PRESCRIBED BY BETH SHAMMAI, AND I INCURRED DANGER FROM ROBBERS. THEY SAID TO HIM: YOU DESERVED TO COME TO HARM, BECAUSE YOU ACTED AGAINST THE OPINION OF BETH HILLEL.

MISHNAH. IN THE MORNING TWO BLESSINGS ARE TO BE SAID BEFORE IT[6] AND ONE AFTER IT. IN THE EVENING TWO ARE SAID BEFORE IT AND TWO AFTER IT, ONE LONG AND ONE SHORT.[7] WHERE THEY [THE SAGES] LAID DOWN THAT A LONG ONE SHOULD BE SAID, IT IS NOT PERMITTED TO SAY A SHORT ONE. WHERE THEY ORDAINED A SHORT ONE A LONG ONE IS NOT PERMITTED. [A PRAYER] WHICH THEY ORDERED TO BE CONCLUDED [WITH A BENEDICTION][8] MUST NOT BE LEFT WITHOUT SUCH A CONCLUSION; ONE WHICH THEY ORDERED TO BE LEFT WITHOUT SUCH A CONCLUSION MUST NOT BE SO CONCLUDED.

GEMARA. What benedictions does one say [in the morning]? R. Jacob said in the name of

---

[1] As much as to say, I will have it cut off just to spite you.
[2] As if to spite me.
[3] V. Glos.
[4] In respect of fulfilling the precept of the sukkah, v. Suk. 28a.
[5] And since Beth Shammai invalidated action according to Beth Hillel, similarly Beth Hillel declared invalid action according to Beth Shammai.
[6] Sc. the Shema'.
[7] The reference is to the two that follow the evening Shema'.
[8] I.e., with the words, Blessed art Thou, O Lord, etc.

R. Oshaia:

Berakoth 11b

'[Blessed art Thou] who formest light and createst darkness'.[1] Let him say rather: 'Who formest light and createst brightness'? — We keep the language of the Scripture.[2] If that is so, [what of the next words in the text], Who makest peace and createst evil: do we repeat them as they are written? It is written 'evil' and we say 'all things' as a euphemism. Then here too let us say 'brightness' as a euphemism! — In fact, replied Raba, it is in order to mention the distinctive feature of the day in the night-time and the distinctive feature of the night in the day-time. It is correct that we mention the distinctive feature of the night in the day-time, as we say, 'Who formest light and createst darkness'.[3] But where do you find the distinctive feature of the day mentioned in the night-time? — Abaye replied: [In the words,] 'Thou rollest away the light from before the darkness and the darkness from before the light'.[4]

Which is the other [benediction]?[5] — Rab Judah said in the name of Samuel: 'With abounding love'.[6] So also did R. Eleazar instruct his son R. Pedath [to say]: 'With abounding love'. It has been taught to the same effect: We do not say, 'With everlasting love', but 'With abounding love'. The Rabbis, however, say that 'With everlasting love'[7] is said; and so it is also said, Yea, I have loved thee with an everlasting love; therefore with affection I have drawn thee.[8]

Rab Judah said in the name of Samuel: If one rose early to study [the Torah] before he had recited the Shema', he must say a benediction [over the study]. But if he had already recited the Shema', he need not say a benediction, because he has already become quit by saying 'With abounding love'.[9]

R. Huna said: For the reading of Scripture it is necessary to say a benediction,[10] but for the study of the Midrash[11] no benediction is required. R. Eleazar, however, says that for both Scripture and Midrash a benediction is required, but not for the Mishnah. R. Johanan says that for the Mishnah also a benediction is required, [but not for the Talmud]. Raba said: For the Talmud also it is necessary to say a blessing. R. Hiyya b. Ashi said:[12] Many times did I stand before Rab to repeat our section in the Sifra of the School of Rab,[13] and he used first to wash his hands and say a blessing, and then go over our section with us.[14]

---

[1] V. P.B. P. 37.
[2] The words are a quotation from Isa. XLV, 7.
[3] This formula is said only in the morning prayer.
[4] V. P.B. p. 96.
[5] Said before the morning Shema'.
[6] V. P.B. p. 39.
[7] In fact this blessing is now said in the evening. V. P.B. p. 96.
[8] Jer. XXXI, 3.
[9] This blessing contains a benediction over the Torah, v. P.B. p. 39.
[10] In the morning, v. P. B. p. 4.
[11] The exegetical midrashim of the Torah (Sifra, Sifre and Mekilta) are referred to.
[12] So MS.M. Curr. edd., 'For R. Hiyya b. Ashi, etc.'.
[13] Sifra debe Rab, an halachic Midrash on Leviticus, v. J.E. XI, p. 330.
[14] This proves that over Midrash a benediction is required.

What benediction is said [before the study of the Torah]? — Rab Judah said in the name of Samuel: [Blessed art Thou …] who hast sanctified us by Thy commandments, and commanded us to study the Torah.[1] R. Johanan used to conclude as follows:[2] 'Make pleasant, therefore, we beseech Thee, O Lord our God, the words of Thy Torah in our mouth and in the mouth of Thy people the house of Israel, so that we with our offspring and the offspring of Thy people the house of Israel may all know Thy name and study Thy Torah. Blessed art Thou, O Lord, who teachest Torah to Thy people Israel'.[3] R. Hamnuna said: '[Blessed art Thou …] who hast chosen us from all the nations and given us Thy Torah. Blessed art Thou, O Lord, who givest the Torah'.[4] R. Hamnuna said: This is the finest of the benedictions. Therefore let us say all of them.[5]

We have learnt elsewhere:[6] The deputy high priest[7] said to them [the priests], Say one benediction, and they said the benediction and recited the Ten Commandments, the Shema', the section 'And it shall come to pass if ye hearken diligently', and 'And the Lord said',[8] and recited with the people three benedictions, viz., 'True and firm',[9] the benediction of the 'Abodah,[10] and the priestly benediction.[11] On Sabbath they said an additional benediction for the outgoing watch. Which is the 'one benediction' referred to above? The following will show. R. Abba and R. Jose came to a certain place the people of which asked them what was the 'one benediction' [referred to], and they could not tell them. They went and asked R. Mattena, and he also did not know. They then went and asked Rab Judah, who said to them: Thus did Samuel say: It means, 'With abounding love'.
R. Zerika in the name of R. Ammi, who had it from R. Simeon b. Lakish said: It is, 'Who formest light'. When R. Isaac b. Joseph came [from Palestine] he said: This statement of R. Zerika was not made explicitly [by R. Simeon b. Lakish], but was inferred by him [from another statement]. For R. Zerika said in the name of R. Ammi, who had it from R. Simeon
b. Lakish: This shows that the recital of one blessing is not indispensable for that of the other. Now if you say that they used to recite 'Who formest the light', it is correct to infer that the recital of one blessing is not indispensable for that of the other, since they did not say, 'With abounding love'.

---

[1] V. P.B. p. 4.
[2] In order both to open and close with a benediction.
[3] P.B. p. 4.
[4] Ibid.
[5] Alfasi and R. Asher have before these last words: R. Papa says.
[6] Tamid 32b.
[7] Memuneh; lit., 'the appointed one'; v. Yoma, Sonc. ed., p. 97, n. 3.
22. The second and third sections of the Shema', Deut. XI, 13ff. and Num. XV, 37ff. V. P.B. p. 40ff.
[8] V. P.B. p. 42.
24. The benediction commencing 'Accept, O Lord our God' in the Amidah. V. P.B. p. 50.
[9] V. P.B. P. 53.
[10] The priestly watches in the Temple (which were twenty-four in number) were changed every week.
[11] The fact that they said one blessing only.

Folio 12a

But if you say that they used to say, 'With abounding love', how can you infer that one blessing is not indispensable for the recital of the other? Perhaps the reason why they did not say, Who formest the light' was because the time for it had not yet arrived,[1] but when the time for it did arrive, they used to say it! And if this statement was made only as an inference, what does it matter? — If it was made only as an inference [I might refute it as follows]: In fact, they said, 'With abounding love', and when the time came for 'Who formest the light', they said that too. What then is the meaning of 'One blessing is not indispensable for the other'? The order of the blessings is not indispensable.

'They recited the Ten Commandments, the Shema', the sections "And it shall come to pass if ye diligently hearken", and "And the Lord said", "True and firm", the 'Abodah, and the priestly benediction'. Rab Judah said in the name of Samuel: Outside the Temple also people wanted to do the same,[2] but they were stopped on account of the insinuations of the Minim.[3] Similarly it has been taught: R. Nathan says, They sought to do the same outside the Temple,[4] but it had long been abolished on account of the insinuations of the Minim. Rabbah b. Bar Hanah[5] had an idea of instituting this in Sura,[6] but R. Hisda said to him, It had long been abolished on account of the insinuations of the Minim. Amemar had an idea of instituting it in Nehardea, but R. Ashi said to him, It had long been abolished on account of the insinuations of the Minim.

'On Sabbath they said an additional blessing on account of the outgoing watch'. What was this benediction? — R. Helbo said: The outgoing watch said to the incoming one, May He who has caused His name to dwell in this house cause to dwell among you love and brotherhood and peace and friendship.

WHERE THEY ORDAINED THAT A LONG BENEDICTION SHOULD BE SAID. There is no question that where a man took up a cup of wine thinking that it was beer and commenced [with the intention to say the benediction] for beer but finished with that of wine, he has fulfilled his obligation. For even had he said the benediction, 'By whose word all things exist',[7] he would have fulfilled his duty, as we have learnt: 'In the case of all of them,[8] if he says, "By whose word all things exist", he has performed his obligation'.[9] But where he took up a cup of beer thinking it was wine and began [with the intention to say the benediction] for wine and finished with the benediction for beer, the question arises, do we judge his benediction according to its beginning or according to its ending?

Come and hear: 'In the morning, if one commenced with [the intention to say] "Who formest light" and finished with "Who bringest on the evening twilight",[10] he has not performed his obligation; if he commences [with the intention to say] "Who bringest on the evening twilight" and finished with

---

[1] The priests of the watch used to say the Shema' before daybreak. V. infra.
[2] To say the Ten Commandments before the Shema'.
[3] That the Ten Commandments were the only valid part of the Torah. V. Glos. s.v. Min.
[4] Lit., 'in the borders', 'outlying districts'.
[5] MS.M. reads: 'Rabbah b. R. Huna', which is more correct; v. D.S. a.l.
[6] In Babylon, the seat of the famous School founded by Rab.
[7] The blessing over all liquors except wine. V. P.B. p. 290.
[8] Even wine.
[9] V. infra 40a.
[10] Instead of the morning formula 'Who formest light' he employed the evening formula, P.B. p. 96.

"Who formest the light", he has performed his obligation. In the evening, if one commenced [with the intention to say] "Who bringest on the evening twilight" and finished with "Who formest the light", he has not performed his obligation; if he begins with [the intention to say] "Who formest the light" and closes with "Who bringest on the evening twilight", he has performed his obligation. The principle is that the final form is decisive'. — It is different there because [at the end] he says, 'Blessed art Thou who formest the luminaries'.[1] This would be a good argument for Rab who said that any blessing that does not contain the mention of God's name is no blessing.[2] But if we accept the view of R. Johanan who said that any blessing that does not contain a mention of the divine kingship is no blessing, what can be said?[3] Rather [we must reply]: Since Rabbah b. 'Ulla has said: So as to mention the distinctive quality of the day in the night-time and the distinctive feature of the night in the day-time,[4] [we may assume that] when he said a blessing [with the divine name] and with the kingship[5] in the beginning, he refers to both of them.[6]

Come and hear from the concluding clause: 'The principle is that the final form is decisive'. What further case is included by the words 'the principle is'? Is it not the one we have mentioned?[7] — No; it is to include bread and dates. How are we to understand this? Shall I say that he ate bread thinking that he was eating dates,[8] and commenced [with the intention of saying the benediction] for dates and finished [with the blessing for] bread? This is just the same thing! — No, this is required [for the case where] he ate dates thinking that he was eating bread, and he began with [the intention to say the blessing] for bread and finished with that of dates. In this case he has fulfilled his obligation; for even if he had concluded with the blessing for bread, he would also have fulfilled it. What is the reason? — Because dates also give sustenance.[9]

Raba b. Hinena the elder said in the name of Rab: If one omits to say True and firm'[10] in the morning and 'True and trustworthy'[11] in the evening, he has not performed his obligation; for it is said, To declare Thy lovingkindness in the morning and Thy faithfulness in the night seasons.[12]

Raba b. Hinena the elder also said in the name of Rab: In saying the Tefillah, when one bows,[13] one should bow at [the word] 'Blessed' and when returning to the upright position one should return at

---

[1] Which is the concluding formula of the morning benediction and is a complete blessing by itself. Hence we can disregard the beginning. The same is not the case with wine and beer where there was no benediction to rectify the error made at the beginning.
[2] Which implies that if this condition is fulfilled, it is a blessing.
[3] According to R. Johanan, since the concluding formula does not contain the words 'King of the Universe', it cannot be considered a complete benediction.
[4] V. supra 11b.
[5] The reference is to the introductory words 'who createst darkness' in the morning benediction and 'who rollest away light' in the evening benediction, which makes either of them appropriate for either morning or evening. These in turn are introduced by the formula making mention of Divine Kingship.
[6] Hence in this case the beginning too was in order, but not in the case of wine and beer.
[7] Of wine and beer.
[8] The benediction after which is different from that after bread. V. P. B. p. 287 for the former and p. 280 for the latter.
[9] Like bread, which is regarded as food par excellence.
[10] V. P.B. p. 42.
[11] V. ibid. P.
[12] Ps. XCII, 3.
[13] One has to bow four times in the course of the Tefillah: at the beginning and end of the first benediction (v. P. B. p. 44) and at 'We give thanks unto Thee' (p. 51) and at the close of the last but one benediction (p. 53).

[the mention of] the Divine Name. Samuel said: What is Rab's reason for this? — Because it is written: The Lord raiseth up them that are bowed down.[14] An objection was raised from the verse, And was bowed before My name?[15]

— Is it written, 'At My name'? It is written, 'Before My Name'.[4] Samuel said to Hiyya the son of Rab: O, Son of the Law, come and I will tell you a fine saying enunciated by your father.[5] Thus said your father: When one bows, one should bow at 'Blessed', and when returning to the upright position, one should return at [the mention of] the Divine Name.

---

[14] Ps. CXLVI, 8.
[15] Mal. II, 5. E.V. 'And was afraid of My name'.
[4] I.e., before the mention of the name.
[5] Samuel outlived Rab.

Berakoth 12b

R. Shesheth, when he bowed, used to bend like a reed,[1] and when he raised himself, used to raise himself like a serpent.[2]

Raba b. Hinena the elder also said in the name of Rab: Throughout the year one says in the Tefillah, 'The holy God', and 'King who lovest righteousness and judgment',[3] except during the ten days between New Year and the Day of Atonement, when he says, 'The holy King' and 'The King of judgment'. R. Eleazar says: Even during these days, if he said, 'The holy God', he has performed his obligation, since it says, But the Lord of Hosts is exalted through justice, and the holy God is sanctified through righteousness:[4] When is the Lord of Hosts exalted through justice? In these ten days from New Year to the Day of Atonement; and none-the-less it says, 'the holy God'. What do we decide?[5] — R. Joseph said: 'The holy God' and 'The King who loves righteousness and judgment'; Rabbah said: 'The holy King' and 'The King of judgment'. The law is as laid down by Rabbah.

Raba b. Hinena the elder said further in the name of Rab: If one is in a position to pray on behalf of his fellow and does not do so, he is called a sinner, as it says, Moreover as for me, far be it from me that I should sin against the Lord in ceasing to pray for you.[6] Raba said: If [his fellow] is a scholar, he must pray for him even to the point of making himself ill. What is the ground for this? Shall I say, because it is written, There is none of you that is sick for me or discloseth unto me?[7] Perhaps the case of a king is different. It is in fact derived from here: But as for me, when they[8] were sick, my clothing was sackcloth, I afflicted my soul with fasting.[9]

Raba b. Hinena the elder further said in the name of Rab: If one commits a sin and is ashamed of it,[10] all his sins are forgiven him, as it says, That thou mayest remember and be confounded, and never open thy mouth any more, because of thy shame; when I have forgiven thee all that thou hast done, saith the Lord God.[11] Perhaps with a whole congregation the case is different? — Rather [we derive it] from here: And Samuel said to Saul, Why hast thou disquieted me to bring me up? And Saul answered, I am sore distressed; for the Philistines make war against me, and God is departed from me, and answereth me no more, neither by prophets nor by dreams; therefore I called thee that thou mayest make known unto me what I shall do.[12] But he does not mention the Urim and Thummim[13] because he had killed all [the people of] Nob, the city of the priests.[14] And how do we know that Heaven had forgiven him? — Because it says, And Samuel said ... Tomorrow shalt thou and thy sons

---

[1] I.e., sharply, all at once.
[2] Slowly and with effort.
[3] In the third and twelfth benedictions respectively, v. P.B. pp. 45 and 48.
[4] Isa. V, 16.
[5] What should be said on the ten days of penitence.
[6] I Sam. XII, 23.
[7] With reference to Saul. I Sam. XXII, 8. E.V. 'that is sorry for me'.
[8] This is said to refer to Doeg and Ahitophel, who were scholars.
[9] Ps. XXXV, 13.
[10] I.e., conscience-stricken.
[11] Ezek. XVI, 63.
[12] I Sam. XXVIII, 15.
[13] Though from v. 6 of this chapter it appears that he did consult the Urim.
[14] And his silence shows that he was conscience-stricken.

be with me,¹ and R. Johanan said: 'With me means, in my compartment [in Paradise]. The Rabbis say [we learn it] from here: We will hang them up unto the Lord in Gibeah of Saul, the chosen of the Lord.² A divine voice came forth and proclaimed: The chosen of the Lord.³

R. Abbahu b. Zutrathi said in the name of R. Judah b. Zebida: They wanted to include the section of Balak⁴ in the Shema', but they did not do so because it would have meant too great a burden for the congregation.⁵ Why [did they want to insert it]? — Because it contains the words, God who brought them forth out of Egypt.⁶ Then let us say the section of usury⁷ or of weights⁸ in which the going forth from Egypt is mentioned?
— Rather, said R. Jose b. Abin, [the reason is] because it contains the verse, He couched, he lay down as a lion, and as a lioness; who shall rouse him up?⁹ Let us then say this one verse and no more? — We have a tradition that every section which our master, Moses, has divided off we may divide off, but that which our master, Moses, has not divided off, we may not divide off. Why did they include the section of fringes?¹⁰ — R. Judah b. Habiba said: Because it makes reference to five¹¹ things — the precept of fringes, the exodus from Egypt, the yoke of the commandments, [a warning against] the opinions of the Minim, and the hankering after sexual immorality and the hankering after idolatry. The first three we grant you are obvious: the yoke of the commandments, as it is written: That ye may look upon it and remember all the commandments of the Lord;¹² the fringes, as it is written: That they make for themselves fringes;¹³ the exodus from Egypt, as it is written: Who brought you out of the land of Egypt.¹⁴ But where do we find [warnings against] the opinions of the heretics, and the hankering after immorality and idolatry? — It has been taught: After your own heart:¹⁵ this refers to heresy; and so it says, The fool hath said in his heart, There is no God.¹⁶ After your own eyes:¹⁷ this refers to the hankering after immorality; and so it says, And Samson said to his father, Get her for me, for she is pleasing in my eyes.¹⁸ After which ye use to go astray:¹⁹ this refers to the hankering after idolatry; and so it says, And they went astray after the Baalim.²⁰

MISHNAH. THE EXODUS FROM EGYPT IS TO BE MENTIONED [IN THE SHEMA'] AT NIGHT-TIME. SAID R. ELEAZAR B. AZARIAH: BEHOLD I AM ABOUT²¹ SEVENTY YEARS

---

¹ I Sam. XXVIII, 16 and 19.
² II Sam. XXI, 6.
³ And it was not the Gibeonites who said, this.
⁴ Num. XXII-XXIV.
⁵ On account of its length.
⁶ Ibid. XXIII, 22.
⁷ Lev. XXV, 35-38.
⁸ Ibid. XIX, 36.
⁹ Num. XXIV, 9. The reason is that it mentions 'lying down' and 'rising up'. Tanhuma substitutes XXIII, 24.
¹⁰ Ibid. XV, 37-41.
¹¹ Var. lec.: 'six', which seems more correct.
¹² Ibid. XV, 39.
¹³ Num. XV, 38.
¹⁴ Ibid. 41.
¹⁵ Ibid. 39.
¹⁶ Ps. XIV, 1.
¹⁷ Ibid. 39.
¹⁸ Judg. XIV, 3.
¹⁹ Ibid. 39.
²⁰ Ibid. VIII, 33.
²¹ Or, 'like one'. V. infra, 28a.

OLD,[1] AND I HAVE NEVER BEEN WORTHY TO [FIND A REASON] WHY THE EXODUS FROM EGYPT SHOULD BE MENTIONED AT NIGHTTIME UNTIL BEN ZOMA EXPOUNDED IT: FOR IT SAYS: THAT THOU MAYEST REMEMBER THE DAY WHEN THOU CAMEST FORTH OUT OF THE LAND OF EGYPT ALL THE DAYS OF THY LIFE.[2] [HAD THE TEXT SAID,] 'THE DAYS OF THY LIFE' IT WOULD HAVE MEANT [ONLY] THE DAYS; BUT 'ALL THE DAYS OF THY LIFE' INCLUDES THE NIGHTS AS WELL. THE SAGES, HOWEVER, SAY: 'THE DAYS OF THY LIFE REFERS TO THIS WORLD; ALL THE DAYS OF THY LIFE' IS TO ADD THE DAYS OF THE MESSIAH.

GEMARA. It has been taught: Ben Zoma said to the Sages: Will the Exodus from Egypt be mentioned in the days of the Messiah? Was it not long ago said: Therefore behold the days come, saith the Lord, that they shall no more say: As the Lord liveth that brought up the children of Israel out of the land of Egypt; but, As the Lord liveth that brought up and that led the seed of the house of Israel out of the north country and from all the countries whither I had driven them?[3] They replied: This does not mean that the mention of the exodus from Egypt shall be obliterated, but that the [deliverance from] subjection to the other kingdoms shall take the first place and the exodus from Egypt shall become secondary. Similarly you read: Thy name shall not be called any more Jacob, but Israel shall be thy name.[4]

---

[1] Or, 'like one'. V. infra, 28a.
[2] Deut. XVI, 3.
[3] Jer. XXIII, 7. 8.
[4] Gen. XXXV, 10.

Folio 13a

This does not mean that the name Jacob shall be obliterated, but that Israel shall be the principal name and Jacob a secondary one. And so it says: Remember ye not the former things, neither consider the things of old.[1] 'Remember ye not the former things': this refers to the subjections to the other nations; 'Neither consider the things of old': this refers to the exodus from Egypt.

Behold I shall do a new thing; now shall it spring forth.[2] R. Joseph learnt: This refers to the war of Gog and Magog. A parable: To what is this like? To a man who was travelling on the road when he encountered a wolf and escaped from it, and he went along relating the affair of the wolf. He then encountered a lion and escaped from it, and went along relating the affair of the lion. He then encountered a snake and escaped from it, whereupon he forgot the two previous incidents and went along relating the affair of the snake. So with Israel: the later troubles make them forget the earlier ones.

Abram the same is Abraham.[3] At first he became a father to Aram [Ab-Aram] only, but in the end he became a father to the whole world.[4] [Similarly] Sarai is the same as Sarah. At first she became a princess to her own people, but later she became a princess to all the world.[5] Bar Kappara taught: Whoever calls Abraham Abram transgresses a positive precept, since it says, Thy name shall be Abraham.[6] R. Eliezer says: He transgresses a negative command,[7] since it says, Neither shall thy name any more be called Abram.[8] But if that is so, then the same should apply to one who calls Sarah Sarai? — In her case the Holy One, blessed be He, said to Abraham, As for Sarai thy wife, thou shalt not call her Sarai, but Sarah shall her name be.[9] But if that is so, the same should apply to one who calls Jacob Jacob? — There is a difference in his case, because Scripture restored it [the name Jacob] to him, as it is written: And God spoke unto Israel in the visions of the night, and said, Jacob, Jacob.[10] R. Jose b. Abin (or, as some say, R. Jose b. Zebida) cited in objection the following: Thou art the Lord, the God who didst choose Abram![11] — The answer was given: There the prophet[12] is recounting the noble deeds of the All Merciful [and relates] that that was the case originally.

---

[1] Isa. XLIII, 18.
[2] Ibid. 29.
[3] I Chron. I, 27.
[4] As it says, Behold I have made thee a father of a multitude of nations, Gen. XVII, 5.
[5] 'Sarai' means literally 'my princess', Sarah 'princess' simply.
[6] Ibid.
[7] Which is more serious.
[8] Ibid.
[9] Sc. for you but not necessarily for others. Gen. XVII, 15.
[10] Ibid. XLVI, 2.
[11] Neh. IX, 7.
[12] Nehemiah, so called because he was here speaking under the guidance of the holy spirit.

CHAPTER II

MISHNAH. IF ONE WAS READING IN THE TORAH [THE SECTION OF THE SHEMA'] WHEN THE TIME FOR ITS RECITAL ARRIVED, IF HE HAD THE INTENTION[1] HE HAS PERFORMED HIS OBLIGATION. IN THE BREAKS[2] ONE MAY GIVE GREETING OUT OF RESPECT[3] AND RETURN GREETING; IN THE MIDDLE [OF A SECTION] ONE MAY GIVE GREETING OUT OF FEAR[4] AND RETURN IT. SO R. MEIR. RABBI JUDAH SAYS: IN THE MIDDLE ONE MAY GIVE GREETING OUT OF FEAR AND RETURN IT OUT OF RESPECT, IN THE BREAKS ONE MAY GIVE GREETING OUT OF RESPECT AND RETURN GREETING TO ANYONE. THE BREAKS ARE AS FOLLOWS: BETWEEN THE FIRST BLESSING AND THE SECOND,[5] BETWEEN THE SECOND AND 'HEAR', BETWEEN 'HEAR' AND 'AND IT SHALL COME TO PASS', BETWEEN AND IT SHALL COME TO PASS' AND 'AND THE LORD SAID AND BETWEEN AND THE LORD SAID' AND 'TRUE AND FIRM'.[6] RABBI JUDAH SAYS: BETWEEN 'AND THE LORD SAID' AND 'TRUE AND FIRM' ONE SHOULD NOT INTERRUPT.
R. JOSHUA B. KORHAH SAID: WHY WAS THE SECTION OF 'HEAR' PLACED BEFORE THAT OF 'AND IT SHALL COME TO PASS'? SO THAT ONE SHOULD FIRST ACCEPT UPON HIMSELF THE YOKE OF THE KINGDOM OF HEAVEN[7] AND THEN TAKE UPON HIMSELF THE YOKE OF THE COMMANDMENTS.[8] WHY DOES THE SECTION OF 'AND IT SHALL COME TO PASS' COME BEFORE THAT OF 'AND THE LORD SAID'? BECAUSE [THE SECTION] 'AND IT SHALL COME TO PASS' IS APPLICABLE BOTH TO THE DAY AND TO THE NIGHT,[9] WHEREAS [THE SECTION] 'AND THE LORD SAID' IS APPLICABLE ONLY TO THE DAY.[10]

GEMARA. This[11] proves that precepts must be performed with intent.[12] [No, perhaps] what IF HE HAD THE INTENTION means is, if it was his intention to read the Scripture? 'To read'? But surely he is reading! — [The Mishnah may refer] to one who is reading [a scroll] in order to revise it.[13]

Our Rabbis taught: The Shema' must be recited as it is written.[14] So Rabbi. The Sages, however, say that it may be recited in any language. What is Rabbi's reason? — Scripture says: and they shall be,[15]

---

[1] This is explained in the Gemara. Lit., 'he directed his heart'.
[2] Between the sections, as presently explained.
[3] E.g., to a teacher.
[4] To one who he is afraid will harm him if he does not give greeting, but not merely out of respect.
[5] V. P.B. p. 39.
[6] Ibid. p. 42.
[7] By proclaiming the unity of God.
[8] By saying the words, if ye shall diligently hearken to all My commandments.
[9] Since it mentions all the commandments.
[10] Since it mentions only the precept of fringes, which is not obligatory by night.
[11] The words IF HE HAD INTENTION.
[12] And not, as it were, accidentally.
[13] And is not attending to the sense.
[14] I.e., in the original language.
[15] Deut. VI, 6.

implying, as they are they shall remain.[1] What is the reason of the Rabbis? — Scripture says 'hear',[2] implying, in any language that you understand.[3] Rabbi also must see that 'hear' is written? — He requires it [for the lesson]: Make your ear hear what your mouth utters.[4] The Rabbis, however, concur with the authority who says that even if he did not say it audibly he has performed his obligation. The Rabbis too must see that 'and they shall be' is written? — They require this to teach that he must not say the words out of order. Whence does Rabbi derive the rule that he must not say the words out of order? — He derives it from the fact that the [text says] 'ha-debarim' [the words] when it might have said simply debarim [words]. And the Rabbis? — They derive no lesson from the substitution of ha-debarim for debarim.

May we assume that Rabbi was of opinion that the whole Torah is allowed to be read in any language, since if you assume that it is allowed to be read only in the holy tongue, why the 'and they shall be' written by the All-Merciful? — This was necessary, because 'hear' is written.[5] May we assume that the Rabbis were of opinion that the whole Torah is allowed to be read only in the holy tongue. since if you assume that it is allowed to be read only in any language. why the 'hear' written by the All-Merciful? — It is necessary because 'and they shall be' is written.[6]

Our Rabbis taught: 'And they shall be'.[7] This teaches that they must not be read backwards. 'These words upon thy heart'.[8] Am I to say that the whole [first] section requires kawanah?[9] Therefore the text says 'these': up to this point kawanah is necessary, from this point kawanah is not necessary. So R. Eliezer. Said R. Akiba to him: Behold it says.

---

[1] Lit., 'in their being they shall be'.
[2] Ibid. 4.
[3] The Hebrew verb shema', like the French entendre, means both 'hear' and 'understand'.
[4] I.e., say it audibly.
[5] And otherwise I might take this to imply, in any language.
[6] Which otherwise I might take to imply, in the original only.
[7] Deut. VI, 6.
[8] Deut. VI, 6.
[9] The Hebrew word kawanah combines the meanings of attention and intention-attention to what is being said, intention to perform the commandment.

Berakoth 13b

Which I command thee this day upon thy heart. From this you learn that the whole section requires to be said with kawanah. Rabbah b. Hanah said in the name of R. Johanan: The halachah is as laid down by R. Akiba. Some refer this statement[1] to the following. as it has been taught: One who reads the Shema' must pay proper attention[2] to what he says.
R. Aha said in the name of R. Judah: If he has paid proper attention to the first section, he need not do so for the rest. Rabba b. Bar Hanah said in the name of R. Johanan: The halachah is as stated by R. Aha in the name of R. Judah.

Another [Baraitha] taught: 'And they shall be': this teaches that they must not be said backwards. 'upon thy heart': R. Zutra says: Up to this point extends the command of kawanah,[3] from this point only the command of reciting applies. R. Josiah says: Up to this point extends the command of reciting; from this point the command of kawanah applies. Why this difference in the application from this point of the command of reciting? [presumably] because it is written 'to speak of them';[4] here too [in the first] also it is written, 'and thou shalt speak of them'![5] What he means is this: Up to this point applies the command both of kawanah and reciting; from this point onwards applies the command of reciting [even] without kawanah.[6] And why this difference in the application up to the point of the command both of reciting and kawanah? [presumably] because it is written, upon thy heart and thou shalt speak of them?[7] [In the second section] there too it is written, 'upon thy hearts to speak of them.[8] That text was required for the lesson enunciated by R. Isaac, who said: 'Ye shall put these my words [upon your hearts]';[9] it is requisite that the placing [of the tefillin] should be opposite the heart.

The Master stated [above]: 'R. Josiah said: Up to this point extends the command of reciting; from this point onwards the command of kawanah applies'. Why this difference in the application from this point onward of the command of kawanah? [Presumably] because it is written, 'upon your heart'? There too [in the first section] also it is written upon thy heart? — What he meant is this: Up to this point applies the command of reciting and kawanah, from this point onwards applies that of kawanah [even] without reciting.[10] Why this difference in the application up to this point of the command of reciting and kawanah? [Presumably] because it is written, 'upon thy heart and thou shalt speak of them?' There too [in the second section] also it is written, 'upon your heart to speak. of them'! These words have reference to words of Torah, and what the All-Merciful meant is this: Teach your children Torah, so that they may be fluent in them.

---

[1] Of Rabbah b. Bar Hanah's statement of the halachah.
[2] Lit., 'direct his heart'. I.e., have kawanah.
[3] Presumably kawanah here means concentration without reciting. i.e., reading with the eyes.
[4] Ibid. VI; XI. This is the command of reciting.
[5] Deut. VI.
[6] I.e., attention is optional.
[7] Ibid. 6.
[8] Ibid. XI, 18. E.V. 'lay up in your heart'.
[9] Ibid. XI, 18. E.V. 'lay up in your heart'.
[10] I.e., it is permitted to read with the eyes.

Our Rabbis taught: Hear, O Israel, the Lord our God, the Lord is one.[1] Up to this point concentration[2] is required. So says R. Meir. Raba said: The halachah is as stated by R. Meir.

It has been taught: Symmachus says: Whoever prolongs the word ehad [one]. has his days and years prolonged. R. Aha b. Jacob said: [He must dwell] on the daleth.[3] R. Ashi said: Provided he does not slur over the heth.[4] R. Jeremiah was once sitting before R. Hiyya b. Abba, and the latter saw that he was prolonging [the word ehad] very much. He said to him: Once you have declared Him king[5] over [all that is] above and below and over the four quarters of the 'heaven, no more is required.

R. Nathan b. Mar 'Ukba said in the name of Rab Judah: 'upon thy heart' must be said standing. [Only] 'Upon thy heart'? How can you assume this? Rather say: Up to 'upon thy heart' must be said standing; from there onwards not [necessarily]. R. Johanan, however, said: The whole [first] section must be said standing. And R. Johanan in this is consistent; for Rabbah b. Bar Hanah said in the name of R. Johanan: The halachah is as stated by R. Aha in the name of R. Judah.[6]

Our Rabbis taught: 'Hear, O Israel, the Lord our God, the Lord is one': this was R. Judah the Prince's recital of the Shema'.[7] Rab said once to R. Hiyya: I do not see Rabbi accept upon himself the yoke of the kingdom of heaven.[8] He replied to him: Son of Princes![9] In the moment when he passes his hand over his eyes, he accepts upon himself the yoke of the kingdom of heaven. Does he finish it afterwards or does he not finish it afterwards?[10] Bar Kappara said: He does not finish it afterwards; R. Simeon son of Rabbi said, He does finish it afterwards. Said Bar Kappara to R. Simeon the son of Rabbi: On my view that he does not finish it afterwards, there is a good reason why Rabbi always is anxious to take a lesson in which there is mention of the exodus from Egypt.[11] But on your view that he does finish it afterwards, why is he anxious to take such a lesson?
— So as to mention the going forth from Egypt at the proper time.[12]
R. Ela the son of R. Samuel b. Martha said in the name of Rab: If one said 'Hear, O Israel, the Lord our God, the Lord is one', and was then overpowered by sleep, he has performed his obligation. R. Nahman said to his slave Daru: For the first verse prod me,[13] but do not prod me for any more. R. Joseph said to R. Joseph the son of Rabbah: How did your father use to do? He replied: For the first verse he used to take pains [to keep awake], for the rest he did not use to take pains.
R. Joseph said: A man lying on his back should not recite the Shema'. [This implies] that he may not read [the Shema' lying on his back], but there is no objection to his sleeping in this posture. But did not R. Joshua b. Levi curse anyone who slept lying on his back?[14] In reply it was said: To sleeping

---

[1] Ibid. VI, 4.

[2] Lit., 'direction of the heart'.
[3] Because the word does not mean 'one' till he comes to this letter.
[4] Omitting its vowel and so make the word meaningless.
[5] I.e., in your thoughts while saying the word.
[6] Supra, that the first section requires kawanah.
[7] I.e., he said only this verse and no more.
[8] V. supra, p. 75 n. 7. Rabbi commenced studying with his disciples before daybreak and did not break off when the time came for reciting the Shema'
[9] I.e., of great scholars; Rab was a nephew of R. Hiyya.
[10] After he dismisses his disciples.
[11] As a substitute for this, the third section, which deals with the exodus.
[12] I.e., when the Shema' is to be recited.
[13] Lit., 'worry me so that I may be wide awake'.
[14] V. infra 15a.

thus if he turns over a little on his side there is no objection, but to read the Shema' thus is forbidden even if he turns over somewhat. But R. Johanan turned over a little and read the Scripture? — R. Johanan was an exception, because he was very corpulent.

IN THE BREAKS HE MAY GIVE GREETING etc. For what may he RETURN GREETING? Shall I say, out of respect? But seeing that he may give greeting, is there any question that he may return it? Rather [what I must say is]: He gives greeting out of respect and returns greeting to anyone. [But then] read the next clause: IN THE MIDDLE HE GIVES GREETING OUT OF FEAR AND RETURNS IT. Returns it for what reason? Shall I say, out of fear? But seeing that he may give greeting, is there any question that he may return it? Rather [what we must say is], out of respect. But then this is the view of R. Judah,[2] as we learn, R. JUDAH SAYS: IN THE MIDDLE HE GIVES GREETING OUT OF FEAR AND RETURNS IT OUT OF RESPECT, AND IN THE BREAKS HE GIVES GREETING OUT OF RESPECT AND RETURNS GREETING TO ANYONE? — There is a lacuna, and [our Mishnah] should read as follows: IN THE BREAKS HE GIVES GREETING OUT OF RESPECT, and needless to say he may return it, AND IN THE MIDDLE HE GIVES GREETING OUT OF FEAR and needless to say he may return it. So
R. Meir. R. Judah says: IN THE MIDDLE HE GIVES GREETING OUT OF FEAR AND RETURNS IT OUT OF RESPECT,

---

[2] Who is supposed to differ from R. Meir, whose views we have been stating so far.

Folio 14a

AND IN THE BREAKS HE GIVES GREETING OUT OF RESPECT AND RETURNS IT TO ANYONE. It has been taught similarly: If one was reciting the Shema' and his teacher or superior meets him in the breaks, he may give greeting out of respect, and needless to say he may return it, and in the middle he may give greeting out of fear and needless to say he may return it. So R. Meir. R. Judah said: In the middle he may give greeting out of fear and return it out of respect, and in the breaks he may give greeting out of respect and return it to anyone.

Ahi the Tanna[1] of the school of R. Hiyya put a question to R. Hiyya: What of interrupting [to give greeting] during the recital of Hallel[2] and the reading of the Megillah?[3] Do we argue a fortiori that if he may interrupt during the recital of the Shema' which is a Biblical precept, there is no question that he may do so during the recital of Hallel, which is a Rabbinical precept, or do we say that the proclaiming of the miracle[4] is more important? — He replied: He may interrupt, and there is no objection. Rabbah said: On the days on which the individual says the complete Hallel,[5] he may interrupt between one section and another but not in the middle of a section; on the days on which the individual does not say the complete Hallel[6] he may interrupt even in the middle of a section. But that is not so. For surely Rab b. Shaba once happened to visit Rabina on one of the days on which the individual does not say the complete Hallel and he [Rabina] did not break off to greet him? — It is different with Rab b. Shaba, because Rabina had no great respect for him.

Ashian the Tanna[7] of the school of R. Ammi enquired of R. Ammi: May one who is keeping a [voluntary][8] fast take a taste?[9] Has he undertaken to abstain from eating and drinking, and this is really not such, or has he undertaken not to have any enjoyment, and this he obtains? — He replied: He may taste, and there is no objection. It has been taught similarly: A mere taste does not require a blessing, and one who is keeping a [voluntary] fast may take a taste, and there is no objection. How much may he taste? — R. Ammi and
R. Assi used to taste as much as a rebi'ith.[10]

Rab said: If one gives greeting to his fellow before he has said his prayers[11] it is as if he made him a high place, as it says, Cease ye from man in whose nostrils is a breath, for how little is he to be accounted![12] Read not bammeh [how little], but bammah [high place].[13] Samuel interpreted: How

---

[1] The one who repeated the section of the Mishnah for the teacher to expound. V. Glos. s.v. (b).
[2] V. Glos.
[3] V. Glos.
[4] The Hallel proclaims the exodus on Passover, and the Megillah the miraculous deliverance from Haman.
[5] E.g., Tabernacles and Hanukah. V. 'Ar. 10b.
[6] Viz., New Moon and the last six days of passover.
[7] The one who repeated the section of the Mishnah for the teacher to expound. V. Glos. s.v. (b).
[8] V. Tosaf s.v.
[9] To see if food is cooked properly.
[10] A fourth of a log, i.e., about an egg and a half.
[11] I.e., before he recites the tefillah.
[12] Isa. II, 22.
[13] And render, if he is esteemed he becomes a high place.

come you to esteem this man and not God?[1] R. Shesheth raised an objection: IN THE BREAKS HE GIVES GREETING OUT OF RESPECT AND RETURNS IT![2] — R. Abba explains the dictum to refer to one who rises early to visit another.[3] R. Jonah said in the name of R. Zera: If a man does his own business before he says his prayers, it is as if he had built a high p]ace. He said to him: A high place, do you say? No, he replied; I only mean that it is forbidden.[4] R. Idi b. Abin said in the name of R. Isaac b. Ashian:[5] It is forbidden to a man to do his own business before he says his prayers, as it says, Righteousness shall go before him and then he shall set his steps on his own way.[6]

R. Jonah further said in the name of R. Zera: Whoever goes seven days without a dream is called evil, as it says, And he that hath it shall abide satisfied; he shall not be visited with evil.[7] Read not sabea', [satisfied] but sheba' [seven].[8] R. Aha the son of R. Hiyya b. Abba said to him: Thus said R. Hiyya in the name of R. Johanan: Whoever sates himself with words of Torah before he retires will receive no evil tidings, as it says, And if he abides sated he shall not be visited with evil.

THE BREAKS ARE AS FOLLOWS etc. R. Abbahu said in the name of R. Johanan: The halachah follows R. Judah, who says that one should not interrupt between 'your God' and 'True and firm'. R. Abbahu said in the name of R. Johanan: What is R. Judah's reason? Because we find in Scripture the words,

---

[1] Samuel draws a similar lesson without altering the text.

[2] Though the Shema' is said before the tefillah.

[3] After the manner of the Roman clientes with their patrons. But if one meets his neighbour he may greet him.

[4] But it is not so bad as idolatry.

[5] This is the reading of Rashi. Cur. edd. have: This agrees with the dictum of R. Idi b. Abin etc., which is obviously a contradiction.

[6] Ps. LXXXV, 14. 'Righteousness' here is taken to mean justification by prayer. E.V., 'Righteousness shall go before Him and shall make His footsteps a way'.

[7] Prov. XIX, 23.

[8] And render, 'if he abides seven nights without and is not visited (with a dream, this shows that) he is evil'.

Berakoth 14b

The Lord God is truth.[1] Does he repeat the word 'true'[2] or does he not repeat the word 'true'? — R. Abbahu said in the name of R. Johanan: He repeats the word 'true'; Rabbah says: He does not repeat the word 'true'. A certain man went down to act as reader before Rabbah, and Rabbah heard him say 'truth, truth', twice; whereupon he remarked: The whole of truth has got hold of this man.[3]

R. Joseph said: How fine was the statement which was brought by R. Samuel b. Judah when he reported that in the West [Palestine] they say [in the evening], Speak unto the children of Israel and thou shalt say unto them, I am the Lord your God, True.[4] Said Abaye to him: What is there so fine about it, seeing that R. Kahana has said in the name of Rab: [In the evening] one need not begin [this third section of the Shema'] but if he does begin, he should go through with it? And should you say that the words, 'and thou shalt say unto them' do not constitute a beginning, has not R. Samuel b. Isaac said in the name of Rab, 'Speak unto the children of Israel' is no beginning, but 'and thou shalt say unto them' is a beginning? — R. Papa said: In the West they hold that 'and thou shalt say unto them' also is no beginning, until one says, 'and they shall make unto themselves fringes'. Abaye said: Therefore we [in Babylon] begin [the section], because they begin it in the West; and since we begin we go through with it, because R. Kahana has said in the name of Rab: One need not begin, but if he begins he should go through with it.

Hiyya b. Rab said: If one has said [in the evening] 'I am the Lord your God,' he must say also, 'True [etc.]'; if he has not said 'I am the Lord your God', he need not say 'True'. But one has to mention the going forth from Egypt?[5] — He can say thus: We give thanks to Thee O Lord our God, that Thou hast brought us forth from the land of Egypt and redeemed us from the house of servitude and wrought for us miracles and mighty deeds, by the [Red] Sea, and we did sing unto Thee.[6]

R. JOSHUA B. KORHAH SAID: WHY IS THE SECTION OF 'HEAR' SAID BEFORE etc. It has been taught: R. Simeon b. Yohai says: It is right that 'Hear' should come before 'And it shall come to pass because the former prescribes learning[7] and the latter teaching,[8] and that 'and it shall come to pass' should precede 'And the Lord said' because the former prescribes teaching and the latter performance. But does then 'hear' speak only of learning and not also of teaching and doing? Is it not written therein, 'And thou shalt teach diligently, and thou shalt bind them and thou shalt write them'? Also, does 'and it shall come to pass' speak only of teaching and not also of performance? Is it not written therein, 'and ye shall bind and ye shall write'? — Rather this is what he means to say: It is

---

[1] Jer. X, 10. E.V. 'the true God'.
[2] After concluding the Shema' with the word true, does he have to repeat the word which is really the beginning of the next paragraph in the prayers?
[3] Sc., he cannot stop saying 'truth'.
[4] I.e., the opening and closing words of the third section, omitting the middle part which deals with the fringes since the law of fringes does not apply at night.
[5] And if he omits both the third section and 'True and faithful' where does he mention it?
1.6.   And he then continues, 'Who is like unto Thee' and 'Cause us to lie down'. P.B., p.
2.99.
[6] As it says, and thou shalt speak.
[7] As it says, and ye shall teach them to your children.
[8] Viz., say the Shema' before putting on tefillin.

right that 'hear' should precede 'and it shall come to pass', because the former mentions both learning, teaching, and doing; and that 'and it shall come to pass' should precede 'and the Lord said', because the former mentions both teaching and doing, whereas the latter mentions doing only. But is not the reason given by R. Joshua b. Korhah sufficient? — He
[R. Simeon b. Yohai] gave an additional reason. One is that he should first accept Upon himself the yoke of the kingdom of heaven and then accept the yoke of the commandments. A further reason is that it [the first section] has these other features.

Rab once washed his hands and recited the Shema' and put on tefillin and said the tefillah. But how could he act in this way,[3] seeing that it has been taught: 'One who digs a niche in a grave for a corpse is exempt from reciting Shema' and tefillah and from tefillin and from all the commandments prescribed in the Torah. When the hour for reciting the Shema' arrives, he goes up and washes his hands and puts on tefillin and recites the Shema' and says the tefillah?' Now this statement itself contains a contradiction. First it says that he is exempt and then it says that he is under obligation? — This is no difficulty; the latter clause speaks of where there are two,[4] the former of where there is only one. In any case this seems to contradict Rab? — Rab held with R. Joshua b. Korhah, who said that first he accepts the yoke of the kingdom of heaven and then he accepts the yoke of the commandments.[5] I will grant you that R. Joshua b. Korhah meant that the recital [of one section] should precede that of the other. But can you understand him to mean that the recital should precede the act [of putting on the tefillin]? And further, did Rab really adopt the view of R. Joshua b. Korhah? Did not R. Hiyya b. Ashi say: On many occasions I stood before Rab when he rose early and said a blessing and taught us our section and put on phylacteries and then recited the Shema'?[6] And should you say, he did this only when the hour for reciting the Shema' had not yet arrived — if that is so what is the value of the testimony of R. Hiyya b. Ashi? — To refute the one who says that a blessing need not be said for the study of the Mishnah;[7] he teaches us that for the Mishnah also a blessing must be said. All the same there is a contradiction of Rab?[8] — His messenger was at fault.[9]

'Ulla said: If one recites the Shema' without tefillin it is as if he bore false witness against himself. (16) R. Hiyya b. Abba said in the name of R. Johanan: It is as if he offered a burnt-offering without a meal-offering and a sacrifice without drink-offering.

R. Johanan also said: If one desires to accept upon himself the yoke of the kingdom of heaven in the most complete manner,

---

[3] And one prays while the other goes on digging.
[4] By putting on tefillin.
[5] 'Teaching' is here regarded as equivalent to accepting the yoke of thecommandments.
[6] V. supra 11b.
[7] The original contradiction has not yet been solved.
[8] And brought him his tefillin late, so he said the Shema' first.
[9] Rather, he accuses himself of falsehood, i.e., inconsistency.

Folio 15a

he should consult nature and wash his hands and put on tefillin and recite the Shema' and say the tefillah: this is the complete acknowledgment of the kingdom of heaven. R. Hiyya
b. Abba said in the name of R. Johanan: If one consults nature and washes his hands and puts on tefillin and recites the Shema' and says the tefillah, Scripture accounts it to him as if he had built an altar and offered a sacrifice upon it, as it is written, I will wash my hands in innocency and I will compass Thine altar, O Lord.[1] Said Raba to him: Does not your honour think that it is as if he had bathed himself, since it is written, I will wash in purity and it is not written, 'I will wash my hands'?[2]

Rabina said to Raba: Sir, pray look at this student who has come from the West [Palestine] and who says: If one has no water for washing his hands, he can rub[3] his hands with earth or with a pebble or with sawdust. He replied: He is quite correct. Is it written, I will wash in water? It is written: In cleanliness — with anything which cleans. For R. Hisda cursed anyone who went looking for water at the time of prayer.[4] This applies to the recital of the Shema', but for the tefillah one may go looking. How far? — As far as a parasang. This is the case in front of him, but in the rear, he may not go back even a mil. [From which is to be deduced], A mil he may not go back; but less than a mil he may go back.

MISHNAH. IF ONE RECITES THE SHEMA' WITHOUT HEARING WHAT HE SAYS, HE HAS PERFORMED HIS OBLIGATION. R. JOSE SAYS: HE HAS NOT PERFORMED HIS OBLIGATION. IF HE RECITES IT WITHOUT PRONOUNCING THE LETTERS CORRECTLY, R. JOSE SAYS THAT HE HAS PERFORMED HIS OBLIGATION, R. JUDAH SAYS THAT HE HAS NOT PERFORMED HIS OBLIGATION. IF HE RECITES IT BACKWARD,[5] HE HAS NOT PERFORMED HIS OBLIGATION. IF HE RECITES IT AND MAKES A MISTAKE HE GOES BACK TO THE PLACE WHERE HE MADE THE MISTAKE.

GEMARA. What is R. Jose's reason? — Because it is written, 'Hear' which implies, let your ear hear what you utter with your mouth. The first Tanna, however, maintains that 'hear' means, in any language that you understand. But R. Jose derives both lessons from the word.

We have learnt elsewhere: A deaf person who can speak but not hear should not set aside terumah;[6] if, however, he does set aside, his action is valid. Who is it that teaches that the action of a deaf man who can speak but not hear in setting aside terumah is valid if done, but should not be done in the first instance? — Said R. Hisda: It is R. Jose, as we have learnt: IF ONE RECITES THE SHEMA' WITHOUT HEARING WHAT HE SAYS, HE HAS PERFORMED HIS OBLIGATION. R. JOSE SAYS: HE HAS NOT PERFORMED HIS OBLIGATION. Now R. Jose holds that he has not performed his obligation only in the case of the recital of the Shema', which is Scriptural, but the setting aside of terumah, [is forbidden] only on account of the blessing, and blessings are an

---

[1] Ps. XXVI, 6.
[2] Raba apparently stresses the order of the words in the original, and renders: I will (do the equivalent) of bathing in purity [by washing] my hands.
[3] Lit., 'wipe'.
[4] And so delayed to say his prayers.
[5] I.e., with the sections in the wrong order.
[6] Because he cannot hear the blessing which he has to say over the action.

ordinance of the Rabbis,[1] and the validity of the act does not depend upon the blessing. But why should you say that this[2] is R. Jose's opinion? Perhaps it is R. Judah's opinion, and he holds that in the case of the recital of the Shema' also, it is valid only if the act is done, but it should not be done in the first instance, and the proof of this is that he states, IF ONE RECITES, which implies, if done, it is done, but it should not be done in the first instance? — The answer is: The reason why it says, IF ONE RECITES, is to show you how far R. Jose is prepared to go, since he says that even if it is done it is not valid. For as to R. Judah, he holds that even if he does it in the first instance he has performed his obligation. Now what is your conclusion? That it is the opinion of R. Jose. What then of this which we have learnt: A man should not say the grace after meals mentally, but if he does so he has performed his obligation. Whose opinion is this? It is neither R. Jose's nor R. Judah's. For it cannot be R. Judah's, since he said that even if he does so in the first instance he has performed his obligation; nor can it be R. Jose's, since he says that even if done it is not valid![3] What must we say then? That it is R. Judah's opinion' and he holds that it is valid only if done but it should not be done in the first instance. But what of this which was taught by R. Judah the son of R. Simeon b. Pazzi: A deaf man who can speak but not hear may set aside terumah in the first instance. Whose view does this follow? It can be neither
R. Judah's nor R. Jose's. For as for R. Judah, he says that it is valid only if done but it should not be done in the first instance; while R. Jose says that even if done it is not valid! In fact it follows R. Judah's view, and he holds that it may be done even in the first instance, and there is no contradiction [between the two views attributed to him], one being his own and the other that of his teacher, as we have learnt: R. Judah said in the name of R. Eleazar b. Azariah: When one recites the Shema', he must let himself hear what he says,[4] as it says, 'Hear, O Israel, the Lord our God, the Lord is one'. Said R. Meir to him: Behold it says, 'Which I command thee this day upon thy heart': on the intention of the heart depends the validity of the words.[5] If you come so far, you may even say that R. Judah agreed with his teacher, and there is no contradiction: one statement[6] gives R. Meir's view, the other R. Judah's.

We have learnt elsewhere:[7] All are qualified to read the Megillah[8] except a deaf-mute, an imbecile and a minor; R. Judah declares a minor qualified. Who is it that declares the act of a deaf-mute, even if done, to be invalid?[9] R. Mattena says: It is R. Jose, as we have learnt: IF ONE RECITES THE SHEMA' WITHOUT HEARING WHAT HE SAYS, HE HAS PERFORMED HIS OBLIGATION. SO R. JUDAH. R. JOSE SAYS: HE HAS NOT PERFORMED HIS OBLIGATION. But why should we say that the above statement [regarding a deaf-mute] follows R. Jose, and that the act even if done is invalid?

---

[1] V. Pes. 7.
[2] That a deaf man should not set aside terumah.
[3] Since grace after meals is a Scriptural injunction.
[4] I.e., in the first instance, but the act if done is valid.
[5] Hence even in the first instance the act is valid.
[6] That of R. Judah son of R. Simeon b. Pazzi.
[7] Meg. 1b.
[8] V. Glos.
[9] The questioner assumes this to be the intention of the statement just quoted.

Berakoth 15b

Perhaps it follows R. Judah, and while the act may not be done [only] in the first instance, yet if done it is valid? — Do not imagine such a thing. For the statement puts a deaf-mute on the same level as an imbecile and a minor, [implying that] just as in the case of an imbecile and a minor the act if done is not valid,[1] so in the case of a deaf-mute the act if done is not valid. But perhaps each case has its own rule?[2] — But [even if so] can you construe this statement as following R. Judah? Since the later clause[3] says that 'R. Judah declares it valid', may we not conclude that the earlier clause does not follow R. Judah? — Perhaps the whole statement follows R. Judah, and two kinds of minor are referred to, and there is a lacuna, and the whole should read thus: All are qualified to read the Megillah except a deaf-mute, an imbecile and a minor. This applies only to one who is not old enough to be trained [in the performance of the precepts].[4] But one who is old enough to be trained may perform the act even in the first instance. This is the ruling of R. Judah: for
R. Judah declares a minor qualified. How have you construed the statement? As following
R. Judah, and that the act is valid only if done but should not be done in the first instance. But then what of that which R. Judah the son of R. Simeon b. Pazzi taught, that a deaf person who can speak but not hear may set aside terumah in the first instance-which authority does this follow? It is neither R. Judah nor R. Jose! For if it is R. Judah, he says that the act is valid only if done, but it may not be done in the first instance; and if R. Jose, he says that even if done it is not valid! — What then do you say, that the authority is R. Judah and that the act may be done even in the first instance? What then of this which has been taught: A man should not say the grace after meals mentally, but if he does so he has performed his obligation? Whose opinion is this? It can be neither R. Judah's nor R. Jose's. For as to R. Judah, he has said that it may be done even in the first instance, and as to R. Jose, he has said that even if done it is not valid! — In truth it is the opinion of R. Judah, and the act may be done even in the first instance, and there is no contradiction between his two statements; in one case he is giving his own view, in the other that of his teacher, as it has been taught: R. Judah said in the name of R. Eleazar b. Azariah: One who recites the Shema' must let his ear hear what he says, as it says, 'Hear, O Israel'. Said R. Meir to him: 'Which I command thee this day upon thy heart', indicating that the words derive their validity from the attention of the heart. Now that you have come so far, you may even say that R. Judah was of the same opinion as his teacher, and still there is no contradiction: one statement gives the view of R. Judah, the other that of R. Meir.

R. Hisda said in the name of R. Shila: The halachah is as laid down by R. Judah in the name of R. Eleazar b. Azariah, and the halachah is as laid down by R. Judah. Both these statements are necessary. For if we had been told only that the halachah is as stated by R. Judah I might have thought that the act may be done even in the first instance. We are therefore informed that the halachah is as laid down by R. Judah in the name of R. Eleazar
b. Azariah. And if we had been told that the halachah is as laid down by R. Judah in the name of R. Eleazar b. Azariah, I might have thought that the act must [be performed thus] and if not there is no remedy.[5] We are therefore informed that the halachah is as stated by R. Judah.

---

[1] This is deduced in respect of a minor from the fact that he is mentioned inconjunction with an imbecile.
[2] I.e., we do not put a deaf-mute on the same footing as an imbecile, although they are mentioned in conjunction.
[3] In the passage cited from Meg.
[4] I.e., up to nine or ten years old; v. Yoma 82a.
[5] I.e., even if done, it is not valid

R. Joseph said: The difference of opinion relates only to the recital of the Shema', but in the case of other religious acts all agree that he has not performed his obligation [if he says the formula inaudibly], as it is written, attend and hear, O Israel.[1] An objection was raised: A man should not say grace after meals mentally, but if he does he has performed his obligation! — Rather, if this statement was made it was as follows: R. Joseph said: The difference of opinion relates only to the Shema', since it is written, 'Hear O Israel'; but in regard to all the other religious acts, all are agreed that he performs his obligation. But it is written, 'Attend and hear, O Israel'? — That [text] applies only to words of Torah.[2]

IF ONE RECITED WITHOUT PRONOUNCING THE LETTERS DISTINCTLY. R. Tabi said in the name of R. Josiah: The halachah in both cases follows the more lenient authority.[3]

R. Tabi further said in the name of R. Josiah: What is meant by the text, There are three things which are never satisfied, … the grave and the barren womb?[4] How comes the grave next to the womb? It is to teach you that just as the womb takes in and gives forth again, so the grave takes in and will give forth again. And have we not here a conclusion a fortiori: if the womb which takes in silently gives forth with loud noise,[5] does it not stand to reason that the grave which takes in with loud noise[6] will give forth with loud noise? Here is a refutation of those who deny that resurrection is taught in the Torah.[7]

R. Oshaia taught in the presence of Raba: And thou shalt write them:[8] the whole section must be written [in the mezuzah[9] and tefillin], even the commands.[10] He said to him: From whom do you learn this?[11] This is the opinion of R. Judah, who said with reference to the sotah:[12] He writes the imprecation but not the commands. [And you argue that] this is the rule in that case, since it is written, And he shall write these curses,[13] but here, since it is written, 'and thou shalt write them', even the commands are included. But is R. Judah's reason because it is written, 'and he shall write'? [Surely] R. Judah's reason is because it is written, 'curses', which implies, curses he is to write but not commands![14] — It was still necessary.[15] You might have thought that we should draw an analogy between the 'writing' mentioned here and the 'writing' mentioned there, and that just as there he writes curses but not commands, so here he should not write commands. Therefore the All-Merciful wrote 'and thou shalt write them', implying, commands also.

---

[1] Deut. XXVII, 9. E.V. 'Keep silence and hear'.
[2] As explained infra 63b.
[3] I.e., R. Judah in the matter of audibility, and R. Jose in the matter of pronouncing distinctly.
[4] Prov. XXX, 15, 16.
[5] The crying of the child.
[6] The wailing of the mourners.
[7] V. Sanh. 92a.
[8] Deut. VI, 9.
[9] V. Glos.
[10] I.e., the words 'and thou shalt write them, and thou shalt bind them'. This is derived from being interpreted as, a complete writing.
[11] That o special text is required to include the writing of the commands.
[12] The woman suspected of adultery, v. Num. V, 11ff.
[13] Num. V, 23.
[14] And but for that implied limitation the expression 'he shall write' by itself would have included commands.
[15] To appeal to the exposition based on.

R. Obadiah recited in the presence of Raba: 'And ye shall teach them':[16] as much as to say thy teaching must be faultless[17] by making a pause 'between the joints'.[18] For instance, said Raba, supplementing his words 'Al lebabeka [upon thy heart], 'al lebabekem [upon your heart], Bekol lebabeka [with all thy heart], bekol lebabekem [with all your heart], 'eseb be-sadeka [grass in thy field], wa-'abaddetem meherah [and ye shall perish speedily], ha-kanaf pesil [the corner a thread], etthkem me-erez [you from the land]. R. Hama b. Hanina said: If one in reciting the Shema' pronounces the letters distinctly, hell is cooled for him, as it says, When the Almighty scattereth kings therein, it snoweth in Zalmon.[19] Read not be-fares [when he scattereth] but befaresh [when one pronounces distinctly], and read not be-zalmon [in Zalmon] but be-zalmaweth [in the shadow of death].

R. Hama b. Hanina further said: Why are 'tents' mentioned

---

[16] Deut. XI, 19.

[17] We-limmadetem (and you shall train them) is read as we-limmud tam (and the teaching shall be perfect); cf. p. 91, n. 10.

[18] I.e., not running together two words of which the first ends and the second begins with the same letter. The expression is from 1 Kings XXII, 34.

[19] Ps. LXVIII, 15.

Folio 16a

alongside of 'streams' as it says, [How goodly are thy tents, O Jacob ...][1] as streams[2] stretched out, as gardens by the river side, as aloes planted[3] etc.? To tell you that, just as streams bring a man up from a state of uncleanness to one of cleanness, so tents[4] bring a man up from the scale of guilt to the scale of merit.

IF ONE RECITES IT BACKWARD, HE HAS NOT PERFORMED HIS OBLIGATION etc. R. Ammi and R. Assi were once decorating the bridal chamber for R. Eleazar. He said to them: In the meantime I will go and pick up something from the House of Study and come back and tell you. He went and found a Tanna reciting before R. Johanan: If [reciting the Shema'] one [recollects that] he made a mistake but does not know where, if he is in the middle of a section he should go back to the beginning; if he is in doubt which section he has said, he should go back to the first break;[5] if he is in doubt which writing[6] he is on, he goes back to the first one. Said R. Johanan to him: This rule applies only where he has not yet got to 'In order that your days may be prolonged', but if he has got to 'In order that your days may be prolonged', then [he can assume that] force of habit has kept him right.[7] He came and told them, and they said to him, If we had come only to hear this, it would have been worth our while.

MISHNAH. WORKMEN MAY RECITE [THE SHEMA'] ON THE TOP OF A TREE OR THE TOP OF A SCAFFOLDING, A THING THEY ARE NOT ALLOWED TO DO IN THE CASE OF THE TEFILLAH. A BRIDEGROOM IS EXEMPT FROM THE RECITAL OF THE SHEMA' FROM THE FIRST NIGHT UNTIL THE END OF THE SABBATH, IF HE HAS NOT CONSUMMATED THE MARRIAGE.[8] IT HAPPENED WITH R. GAMALIEL THAT WHEN HE MARRIED HE RECITED THE SHEMA ON THE FIRST NIGHT: SO HIS DISCIPLES SAID TO HIM: OUR MASTER, YOU HAVE TAUGHT US THAT A BRIDEGROOM IS EXEMPT FROM THE RECITAL OF THE SHEMA'. HE REPLIED TO THEM: I WILL NOT LISTEN TO YOU TO REMOVE FROM MYSELF THE KINGSHIP OF HEAVEN EVEN FOR A MOMENT.

GEMARA. Our Rabbis taught: Workmen may recite [the Shema'] on the top of a tree or on the top of a scaffolding, and they may say the tefillah, on the top of an olive tree and the top of a fig tree,[9] but from all other trees they must come down to the ground before saying the tefillah, and the employer must in any case come down before saying the tefillah,[10] the reason in all cases being that their mind is not clear.[11] R. Mari the son of the daughter of Samuel[12] pointed out to Rab a contradiction. We

---

[1] V. Tosaf., s.v.
[2] E.V. 'valleys'.
[3] Num. XXIV, 5, 6.
[4] Where the Torah is studied.
[5] I.e., to 'and it shall come to pass'.
[6] I.e., 'and thou shalt write them' in the first section or 'and ye shall write' in the second.
[7] Lit., 'he has taken his usual course'.
[8] Lit., 'performed the act'.
[9] These trees have thick branches which afford a firm foothold.
[10] Seeing that he is not bound to work.
[11] To concentrate on their prayers, from anxiety lest they may fall.
[12] His mother was carried away captive and he was not born in lawful wedlock, and therefore his father's name is

have learnt, he said: WORKMEN MAY RECITE [THE SHEMA'] ON THE TOP OF A TREE OR THE TOP OF A SCAFFOLDING which would show that the recital does not require kawanah.[1] Contrast with this: When one recites the Shema', it is incumbent that he should concentrate his attention[2] on it, since it says, 'Hear, O Israel', and in another place it says, Pay attention and hear, O Israel,[3] showing that just as in the latter 'hearing' must be accompanied by attention, so here it must be accompanied by attention. He gave no reply. Then he said to him: Have you heard any statement on this point? — He replied: Thus said

R. Shesheth: This is the case only if they stop from their work to recite. But it has been taught: Beth Hillel say that they may go on with their work while reciting? — There is no contradiction. The former statement refers to the first section, the latter to the second section [of the Shema'].

Our Rabbis taught: Labourers working for an employer recite the Shema' and say blessings before it and after it and eat their crust and say blessings before it and after it, and say the tefillah of eighteen benedictions, but they do not go down before the ark[4] nor do they raise their hands [to give the priestly benediction].[5] But it has been taught: [They say] a resume of the eighteen benedictions?[6] — Said R. Shesheth: There is no contradiction: one statement gives the view of R. Gamaliel, the other of R. Joshua.[7] But if R. Joshua is the authority, why does it say 'labourers'? The same applies to anyone! — In fact, both statements represent the view of R. Gamaliel, and still there is no contradiction: one refers to [labourers] working for a wage, and the other to [those] working for their keep;[8] and so it has been taught: Labourers working for an employer recite the Shema' and say the tefillah and eat their crust without saying a blessing before it, but they say two blessings after it, namely, [he says] the first blessing[9] right through[10] and the second blessing he begins with the blessing for the land, including 'who buildest Jerusalem' in the blessing[11] for the land. When does this hold good? For those who work for a wage. But those who work for their keep or who eat in the company of the employer say the grace right through.[12]

A BRIDEGROOM IS EXEMPT FROM RECITING THE SHEMA'. Our Rabbis taught: 'When thou sittest in thy house': this excludes one engaged in the performance of a religious duty. 'And when thou walkest by the way': this excludes a bridegroom. Hence they deduced the rule that one who marries a virgin is exempt, while one who marries a widow is not exempt. How is this derived? — R. Papa said: [The sitting in the house] is compared to the way: just as the way is optional, so here it must be optional. But are we not dealing [in the words 'walkest by the way'] with one who goes to

---

not mentioned. (Rashi). V. Keth. 23a.

[1] V. Glos.

[2] Lit., 'direct his heart'.

[3] V. supra, p. 91 n. 1.

[4] I.e., act as reader to a congregation.

[5] Because this would rob their employer of too much of their time

[6] V. P.B. p. 55.

[7] Infra, 28b.

[8] Those who work for a wage have less time to spare.

[9] V. P. B. p. 280.

[10] Lit., 'as arranged'.
   1. 23. The benedictions beginning with 'We thank thee' (ibid.) and 'And rebuild Jerusalem'
   2. (p. 282) are condensed into one.

[11] For notes on this passage, v. supra p. 60.

[12] V. P. B. p. 280.

perform a religious duty, and even so the All-Merciful said that he should recite? — If that were so, the text should say, 'in going'. What is meant by 'in thy going'? This teaches that it is in thy going that thou art under obligation, and in the going for a religious duty thou art exempt.

Berakoth 16b

If that is the case, why does it say, 'One who marries a virgin'? The same would apply to one who marries a widow! — In the former case he is agitated, in the latter case he is not agitated. If his agitation is the ground, then even if his ship has sunk in the sea he should also be exempt? [And if this is so], why then has R. Abba b. Zabda said in the name of Rab: A mourner is under obligation to perform all the precepts laid down in the Torah except that of tefillin, because they are called 'headtire', as it says, 'Thy headtire bound upon thy head' etc.? — The reply is: There the agitation is over an optional matter, here it is over a religious duty.

MISHNAH. [RABBAN GAMALIEL] BATHED ON THE FIRST NIGHT AFTER THE DEATH OF HIS WIFE. HIS DISCIPLES SAID TO HIM: YOU HAVE TAUGHT US, SIR, THAT A MOURNER IS FORBIDDEN TO BATHE. HE REPLIED TO THEM: I AM NOT LIKE OTHER MEN, BEING VERY DELICATE. WHEN TABI HIS SLAVE DIED HE ACCEPTED CONDOLENCES FOR HIM. HIS DISCIPLES SAID TO HIM: YOU HAVE TAUGHT US, SIR, THAT CONDOLENCES ARE NOT ACCEPTED FOR SLAVES? HE REPLIED TO THEM: MY SLAVE TABI WAS NOT LIKE OTHER SLAVES: HE WAS A GOOD MAN. IF A BRIDEGROOM DESIRES TO RECITE THE SHEMA ON THE FIRST NIGHT, HE MAY DO SO. RABBAN SIMEON B. GAMALIEL SAYS: NOT EVERYONE WHO DESIRES TO PASS AS A SCHOLAR MAY DO SO.

GEMARA. How did Rabban Gamaliel[2] justify his action?[3] — He held that the observance of aninuth[4] by night is only an ordinance of the Rabbis, as it is written, [And I will make it as the mourning for an only son,] and the end thereof as a bitter day,[5] and where it concerns a delicate person the Rabbis did not mean their ordinance to apply.

WHEN TABI HIS SLAVE DIED etc. Our Rabbis taught: For male and female slaves no row [of comforters][6] is formed, nor is the blessing of mourners[7] said, nor is condolence offered. When the bondwoman of R. Eliezer died, his disciples went in to condole with him. When he saw them he went up to an upper chamber, but they went up after him. He then went into an ante-room and they followed him there. He then went into the dining hall and they followed him there. He said to them: I thought that you would be scalded with warm water; I see you are not scalded even with boiling hot water.[8] Have I not taught you that a row of comforters is not made for male and female slaves, and that a blessing of mourners is not said for them, nor is condolence offered for them? What then do

---

[1] Lit., 'to take the name', viz., of a scholar.
[2] Cur. edd.: R. Simeon b. Gamaliel, which can hardly be justified.
[3] In bathing while onan.
[4] The name given to the mourning of the first day, or the whole period before the burial.
[5] Amos VIII, 10. This shows that according to Scripture mourning is to be observed only by day.
[6] It was customary for those returning from a burial to the mourner's house to stand in a row before him to comfort him.
[7] Said after the first meal taken by the mourner after the funeral, v. Keth. 8a.
[8] As much as to say: I thought you would take the first hint, and you do not even take the last!

they say for them? The same as they say to a man for his ox and his ass: 'May the Almighty replenish your loss'. So for his male and female slave they say to him: 'May the Almighty replenish your loss'. It has been taught elsewhere: For male and female slaves no funeral oration is said. R. Jose said: If he was a good slave, they can say over him, Alas for a good and faithful man, who worked for his living! They said to him: If you do that, what do you leave for free-born?

Our Rabbis taught: The term 'patriarchs' is applied only to three,[1] and the term 'matriarchs' only to four.[2] What is the reason? Shall we say because we do not know if we are descended from Reuben or from Simeon? But neither do we know in the case of the matriarchs whether we are descended from Rachel or from Leah! — [Rather the reason is] because up to this point they were particularly esteemed, from this point they were not so particularly esteemed. It has been taught elsewhere: Male and female slaves are not called 'Father so-and so' or 'Mother so-and so'; those of Rabban Gamaliel, however, were called 'Father so-and-so' and 'Mother so-and-so'. The example [cited] contradicts your rule? It was because they were particularly esteemed.

R. Eleazar said: What is the meaning of the verse, So will I bless Thee as long as I live; in Thy name will I lift up my hands?[3] 'I will bless Thee as long as I live' refers to the Shema'; 'in Thy name I will lift up my hands' refers to the tefillah. And if he does this, Scripture says of him, My soul is satisfied as with marrow and fatness.[4] Nay more, he inherits two worlds, this world and the next, as it says, And my mouth doth praise Thee with joyful lips.[5]

R. Eleazar on concluding his prayer[6] used to say the following: May it be Thy will, O Lord our God, to cause to dwell in our lot love and brotherhood and peace and friendship, and mayest Thou make our borders rich in disciples and prosper our latter end with good prospect and hope, and set our portion in Paradise, and confirm us[7] with a good companion and a good impulse in Thy world, and may we rise early and obtain the yearning of our heart to fear Thy name,[8] and mayest Thou be pleased to grant the satisfaction of our desires![9]

R. Johanan on concluding his prayer added the following: May it be Thy will, O Lord our God, to look upon our shame, and behold our evil plight, and clothe Thyself in Thy mercies, and cover Thyself in Thy strength, and wrap Thyself in Thy lovingkindness, and gird Thyself with Thy graciousness, and may the attribute of Thy kindness and gentleness come before Thee!

R. Zera on concluding his prayer added the following: May it be Thy will, O Lord our God, that we sin not nor bring upon ourselves shame or disgrace before our fathers![10]

R. Hiyya on concluding his prayer added the following: May it be Thy will, O Lord our God, that our Torah may be our occupation, and that our heart may not be sick nor our eyes darkened!

---

[1] Abraham, Isaac and Jacob.
[2] Sarah, Rebeccah, Rachel and Leah.
[3] Ps. LXIII, 5.
[4] Ibid. 6.
[5] Ibid. Lit., 'lips of songs', i.e., two songs.
[6] I.e., after the last benediction of the Amidah.
[7] Or perhaps, cause us to obtain.
[8] I.e., may we be filled with pious thoughts on waking.
[9] Lit., may the coolness of our soul come before Thee for good'.
[10] 'Aruch: more than our fathers.

Rab on concluding his prayer added the following: May it be Thy will, O Lord our God, to grant us long life, a life of peace, a life of good, a life of blessing, a life of sustenance, a life of bodily vigour,[1] a life in which there is fear of sin, a life free from shame and confusion, a life of riches and honour, a life in which we may be filled with the love of Torah and the fear of heaven, a life in which Thou shalt fulfil all the desires of our heart for good![2]

Rabbi on concluding his prayer added the following: May it be Thy will, O Lord our God, and God of our fathers, to deliver us from the impudent and from impudence, from an evil man, from evil hap, from the evil impulse, from an evil companion, from an evil neighbour, and from the destructive Accuser, from a hard lawsuit and from a hard opponent, whether he is a son of the covenant or not a son of the covenant![3] [Thus did he pray] although guards[4] were appointed to protect Rabbi.

R. Safra on concluding his prayer added the following: May it be Thy will, O Lord our God, to establish peace

---

[1] Lit., 'vigour of the bones'.
1.20. This prayer is now said on the Sabbath on which the New Moon is announced. V.
2.P.B. p. 154.
[2] I.e., a Jew or non-Jew. This now forms part of the daily prayers. V. P. B. p. 7
[3] Lit., eunuchs'.
[4] By the Roman Government.

Folio 17a

among the celestial family,[1] and among the earthly family,[2] and among the disciples who occupy themselves with Thy Torah whether for its own sake or for other motives; and may it please Thee that all who do so for other motives may come to study it for its own sake!

R. Alexandri on concluding his prayer added the following: May it be Thy will, O Lord our God, to station us in an illumined corner and do not station us in a darkened corner, and let not our heart be sick nor our eyes darkened! According to some this was the prayer of R. Hamnuna, and R. Alexandri on concluding his prayer used to add the following: Sovereign of the Universe, it is known full well to Thee that our will is to perform Thy will, and what prevents us? The yeast in the dough[3] and the subjection to the foreign Powers. May it be Thy will to deliver us from their hand, so that we may return to perform the statutes of Thy will with a perfect heart!

Raba on concluding his prayer added the following: My God, before I was formed I was not worthy [to be formed], and now that I have been formed I am as if I had not been formed. I am dust in my lifetime, all the more in my death. Behold I am before Thee like a vessel full of shame and confusion. May it be Thy will, O Lord my God, that I sin no more, and the sins I have committed before Thee wipe out in Thy great mercies, but not through evil chastisements and diseases! This was the confession of R. Hamnuna Zuti on the Day of Atonement.[4]

Mar the son of Rabina on concluding his prayer added the following: My God, keep my tongue from evil and my lips from speaking guile. May my soul be silent to them that curse me and may my soul be as the dust to all. Open Thou my heart in Thy law, and may my soul pursue Thy commandments, and deliver me from evil hap, from the evil impulse and from an evil woman and from all evils that threaten to come upon the world. As for all that design evil against me, speedily annul their counsel and frustrate their designs![5] May the words of my mouth and the meditation of my heart be acceptable before Thee, O Lord, my rock and my redeemer![6]

---

[1] The Guardian Angels of the various nations.
[2] From the context this would seem to refer to the nations of the earth. Rashi, however, takes it to mean the assembly of the wise men.
[3] I.e., the evil impulse, which causes a ferment in the heart.
[4] It occupies the same place in the present day liturgy. V. P.B. p. 263.
[5] MS.M adds: Pay them their recompense upon their heads; destroy them and humble them before me, and deliver me from all calamities which are threatening to issue and break forth upon the world!
[6] In the present day liturgy this prayer is also added (in a slightly altered form) at the end of every Amidah. V. P.B. p. 54. The last sentence is from Ps. XIX, 15.

When R. Shesheth kept a fast, on concluding his prayer he added the following: Sovereign of the Universe, Thou knowest full well that in the time when the Temple was standing, if a man sinned he used to bring a sacrifice, and though all that was offered of it was its fat and blood, atonement was made for him therewith. Now I have kept a fast and my fat and blood have diminished. May it be Thy will to account my fat and blood which have been diminished as if I had offered them before Thee on the altar, and do Thou favour me.[1]

When R. Johanan finished the Book of Job,[2] he used to say the following: The end of man is to die, and the end of a beast is to be slaughtered, and all are doomed to die. Happy he who was brought up in the Torah and whose labour was in the Torah and who has given pleasure to his Creator and who grew up with a good name and departed the world with a good name; and of him Solomon said: A good name is better than precious oil, and the day of death than the day of one's birth.[3]

A favourite saying of R. Meir was: Study with all thy heart and with all thy soul to know My ways and to watch at the doors of My law. Keep My law in thy heart and let My fear be before thy eyes. Keep thy mouth from all sin and purify and sanctify thyself from all trespass and iniquity, and I will be with thee in every place.
A favourite saying of the Rabbis of Jabneh was: I am God's creature and my fellow[4] is God's creature. My work is in the town and his work is in the country. I rise early for my work and he rises early for his work. Just as he does not presume to do my work, so I do not presume to do his work. Will you say, I do much[5] and he does little? We have learnt:[6] One may do much or one may do little; it is all one, provided he directs his heart to heaven.

A favourite saying of Abaye was: A man should always be subtle in the fear of heaven.[7] A soft answer turneth away wrath,[8] and one should always strive to be on the best terms with his brethren and his relatives and with all men and even with the heathen in the street, in order that he may be beloved above and well-liked below and be acceptable to his fellow creatures. It was related of R. Johanan b. Zakkai that no man ever gave him greeting first, even a heathen in the street.

A favourite saying of Raba was: The goal of wisdom is repentance and good deeds, so that a man should not study Torah and Mishnah and then despise[9] his father and mother and teacher and his superior in wisdom and rank, as it says, The fear of the Lord is the beginning of wisdom, a good understanding have all they that do thereafter.[10] It does not say, 'that do',[11] but 'that do thereafter',

---

[1] MS.M. adds: A certain disciple after he prayed used to say: 'Close mine eyes from evil, and my ears from hearing idle words, and my heart from reflecting on unchaste thoughts, and my veins from thinking of transgression, and guide my feet to (walk in) Thy commandments and Thy righteous ways, and may Thy mercies be turned upon me to be of those spared and preserved for life in Jerusalem'!
[2] M. reads: R. Johanan said: When R. Meir finished etc.
[3] Eccl. VII, 1. R. Johanan was prompted to this reflection by the fact that Job departed with a good name.
[4] I.e., the 'am ha-arez, or nonstudent.
[5] In the way of Torah.
[6] Men. 110a.
[7] I.e., in finding out new ways of fearing heaven.
[8] Prov. XV, I.
[9] Lit., 'kick at'.
[10] Ps. CXI, 10.
[11] Another reading is, that learn them.

which implies, that do them for their own sake and not for other motives.[1] If one does them for other motives, it were better that he had not been created.

A favourite saying of Rab was: [The future world is not like this world.][2] In the future world there is no eating nor drinking nor propagation nor business nor jealousy nor hatred nor competition, but the righteous sit with their crowns on their heads feasting on the brightness of the divine presence, as it says, And they beheld God, and did eat and drink.[3]

[Our Rabbis taught]:[4] Greater is the promise made by the Holy One, blessed be He, to the women than to the men; for it says, Rise up, ye women that are at ease; ye confident daughters, give ear unto my speech.[5] Rab said to R. Hiyya: Whereby do women earn merit? By making their children go to the synagogue[6] to learn Scripture and their husbands to the Beth Hamidrash to learn Mishnah, and waiting for their husbands till they return from the Beth Hamidrash. When the Rabbis[7] took leave from the school of R. Ammi — some say, of R. Hanina — they said to him: May you see your requirements provided[8] in your lifetime, and may your latter end be for the future world and your hope for many generations; may your heart meditate understanding, your mouth speak wisdom and your tongue indite song; may your eyelids look straight before you,[9] may your eyes be enlightened by the light of the Torah and your face shine like the brightness of the firmament; may your lips utter knowledge, your reins rejoice in uprightness[10] and your steps run to hear the words of the Ancient of Days. When the Rabbis took leave from the school of R. Hisda — others Say, of R. Samuel b. Nahmani — they said to him: We are instructed, we are well laden[11] etc. 'We are instructed, we are well laden'. Rab and Samuel — according to others, R. Johanan and R. Eleazar — give different explanations of this. One Says: 'We are instructed' — in Torah, 'and well laden' — with precepts. The other says: 'We are instructed' — in Torah and precepts; 'we are well laden' — with chastisements.

---

[1] I.e., to criticise and quarrel. V. Rashi and Tosaf. ad loc.
[2] These words are bracketed in the text.
[3] Ex. XXIV, 11. These words are interpreted to mean that the vision of God seen by the young men was like food and drink to them.
[4] These words are missing in cur. edd., but occur in MS.M.
[5] Isa. XXXII, 9. The women are said to be 'at ease' and 'confident', which is more than is said of the men.
[6] Where children were usually taught.
[7] Who had left home to study with R. Ammi.
[8] Lit., 'see your world'.
[9] The expression is taken from Prov. IV, 25. The meaning here seems to be, may you have a correct insight into the meaning of the Torah'.
[10] The reins were supposed to act as counsellors.
[11] Ps. CXLIV, 14. E.V. Our oxen are well laden.

Berakoth 17b

There is no breach: [that is], may our company not be like that of David from which issued Ahitophel.[1] And no going forth: [that is] may our company not be like that of Saul from which issued Doeg the Edomite.[2] And no outcry: may our company not be like that of Elisha, from which issued Gehazi.[3] In our broad places: may we produce no son or pupil who disgraces himself[4] in public.[5]

Hearken unto Me, ye stout-hearted, who are far from righteousness.[6] Rab and Samuel — according to others, R. Johanan and R. Eleazar — interpret this differently. One says: The whole world is sustained by [God's] charity, and they[7] are sustained by their own force.[8] The other says: All the world is sustained by their merit, and they are not sustained even by their own merit. This accords with the saying of Rab Judah in the name of Rab. For Rab Judah said in the name of Rab: Every day a divine voice goes forth from Mount Horeb and proclaims: The whole world is sustained for the sake of My son Hanina, and Hanina My son has to subsist on a kab of carobs from one week end to the next. This [explanation] conflicts with that of Rab Judah. For Rab Judah said: Who are the 'stout-hearted'? The stupid Gubaeans.[9] R. Joseph said: The proof is that they have never produced a proselyte. R. Ashi said: The people of Mata Mehasia[10] are 'stout-hearted', for they see the glory of the Torah twice a year,[11] and never has one of them been converted.

A BRIDEGROOM IF HE DESIRES TO RECITE etc. May we conclude from this that Rabban Simeon b. Gamaliel deprecates showing off[12] and the Rabbis do not deprecate it? But do we not understand them to hold the opposite views, as we have learnt: In places where people are accustomed to work in the month of Ab they may work, and in places where it is the custom not to work they may not work; but in all places Rabbinical students abstain from study. R. Simeon b. Gamaliel says: A man should always conduct himself as if he were a scholar.[13] We have here a contradiction between two sayings of the Rabbis, and between two sayings of R. Simeon b. Gamaliel! — R. Johanan said: Reverse the names; R. Shisha the son of R. Idi said: There is no need to reverse. There is no contradiction between the two sayings of the Rabbis. In the case of the recital of the Shema', since everybody else recites, and he also recites, it does not look like showing off on his part; but in the case of the month of Ab, since everybody else does work and he does no work, it looks like showing off. Nor is there a contradiction between the two sayings of
R. Simeon b. Gamaliel. In the case of the Shema', the validity of the act depends on the mental

---

[1] Who made a 'breach' in the kingdom of David. V. Sanh. 106b.
[2] Who went forth to evil ways (ibid.).
[3] Who became a leper and had to cry 'unclean, unclean'.
[4] Lit., 'spoils his food', by addition of too much salt. A metaphor for the open acceptance of heretical teachings.
[5] MS.M. adds: like the Nazarene.
[6] Isa. XLVI, 12. Heb. zedakah, which is taken by the Rabbis in the sense of 'charity'.
[7] The 'stout-hearted', i.e., righteous.
[8] Lit., 'arm'. I.e., the force of their own good deeds.
[9] A tribe in the neighbourhood of Babylon.
[10] A suburb of Sura, where one of the great Academies was situated.
[11] At the 'kallahs' (v. Glos). In Adar and Elul.
[12] I.e., show of superior piety or learning.
[13] V. Pes. 55a.

concentration and we are witnesses that he is unable to concentrate. Here, however, anyone who sees will say, He has no work; go and see how many unemployed there are in the market place![1]

CHAPTER III

MISHNAH. ONE WHOSE DEAD [RELATIVE] LIES BEFORE HIM[2] IS EXEMPT FROM THE RECITAL OF THE SHEMA' AND FROM THE TEFILLAH AND FROM TEFILLIN AND FROM ALL THE PRECEPTS LAID DOWN IN THE TORAH. WITH REGARD TO THE BEARERS OF THE BIER AND THOSE WHO RELIEVE THEM AND THOSE WHO RELIEVE THEM AGAIN,[3] WHETHER IN FRONT OF THE BIER OR BEHIND THE BIER[4] — THOSE IN FRONT OF THE BIER, IF THEY ARE STILL REQUIRED, ARE EXEMPT; BUT THOSE BEHIND THE BIER EVEN IF STILL REQUIRED, ARE NOT EXEMPT.[5] BOTH, HOWEVER, ARE EXEMPT FROM [SAYING] THE TEFILLAH. WHEN THEY HAVE BURIED THE DEAD AND RETURNED [FROM THE GRAVE], IF THEY HAVE TIME TO BEGIN AND FINISH [THE SHEMA'] BEFORE FORMING A ROW,[6] THEY SHOULD BEGIN, BUT IF NOT THEY SHOULD NOT BEGIN. AS FOR THOSE WHO STAND IN THE ROW, THOSE ON THE INSIDE ARE EXEMPT, BUT THOSE ON THE OUTSIDE ARE NOT EXEMPT.[7] [WOMEN, SLAVES AND MINORS ARE EXEMPT FROM RECITING THE SHEMA' AND PUTTING ON TEFILLIN, BUT ARE SUBJECT TO THE OBLIGATIONS OF TEFILLAH, MEZUZAH, AND GRACE AFTER MEALS].[8]

GEMARA. [If the dead] LIES BEFORE HIM, he is exempt.[9] [implying] if it does not lie before him,[10] he is not exempt.[11] This statement is contradicted by the following:[12] One whose dead lies before him eats in another room. If he has not another room, he eats in his fellow's room. If he has no fellow to whose room he can go, he makes a partition and eats [behind it]. If he has nothing with which to make a partition, he turns his face away and eats. He may not eat reclining, nor may he eat flesh or drink wine; he does not say a blessing [over food] nor grace after meals,[13]

---

[1] Even on working days.
[2] I.e., is not yet buried.
[3] In carrying the bier to the grave.
[4] Those in front of the bier have still to carry; those behind have already carried.
[5] Since they have already carried once.
[6] To comfort the mourners. v. p. 97, n. 2.
[7] If they stand two or more deep.
[8] Words in brackets belong properly to the next Mishnah, v. infra 20a.
[9] Lit., 'yes'.
[10] This phrase is now understood literally and thus to include the case where he is in a different room.
[11] Lit., 'No'.
[12] M.K. 23b.
[13] So Rashi. V. however M.K., Sonc. ed., p. 147, n. 2.

Folio 18a

nor do others say a blessing for him nor is he invited to join in the grace. He is exempt from reciting the Shema', from saying the tefillah, from putting on tefillin and from all the precepts laid down in the Torah. On Sabbath, however, he may recline and eat meat and drink wine, and he says a blessing, and others may say the blessing for him and invite him to join in grace, [and he is subject to the obligation of reading the Shema' and tefillah],[1] and he is subject to all the precepts laid down in the Torah. R. Simeon b. Gamaliel says: Since he is subject to these, he is subject to all of them; and R. Johanan said: Where do they differ in practice? In regard to marital intercourse.[2] At any rate it states that he is exempt from the recital of the Shema' and from saying the tefillah and putting on tefillin and all the precepts laid down in the Torah?[3] — Said R. Papa: Explain this [Baraitha] as applying only to one who turns his face away and eats.[4] R. Ashi, however, said: Since the obligation of burial devolves on him, it is as if the corpse was before him,[5] as it says: And Abraham rose up from before his dead,[6] and it says. That I may bury my dead out of my sight:[7] this implies that so long as the obligation to bury devolves upon him, it is as if the corpse were lying before him.[8]

[I infer from our Mishnah] that this is the rule for a dead relative but not for one whom he is merely watching.[9] But it has been taught: One who watches a dead [body] even if it is not his dead [relative], is exempt from reciting the Shema' and saying the tefillah and putting on tefillin and all the precepts laid down in the Torah? — [We interpret therefore]: He who watches the dead, even if it is not his dead [relative], [is exempt], and [likewise in the case of] his dead relative, even if he is not watching it, he is [exempt], but if he is walking in the cemetery, he is not. But it has been taught: A man should not walk in a cemetery with tefillin on his head or a scroll of the Law in his arm, and recite the Shema',[10] and if he does so, he comes under the heading of 'He that mocketh the poor[11] blasphemeth his Maker'?[12] — In that case the act is forbidden within four cubits of the dead, but beyond four cubits the obligation [to say Shema' etc.] devolves. For a Master has said: A dead body affects four cubits in respect of the recital of the Shema'. But in this case he is exempt even beyond four cubits.

[To turn to] the above text: One who watches a dead [body], even though it is not his own dead [relative], is exempt from the recital of the Shema' and from saying the tefillah and from putting on tefillin and from all the precepts laid down in the Torah. If there were two [watching], one goes on watching while the other recites, and then the other watches while this one recites. Ben 'Azzai says: If

---

[1] Inserted with MS.M.
[2] At a time when it is a duty. Rabban Simeon declares the mourner subject to this duty on the Sabbath, though it is otherwise forbidden during the week of mourning.
[3] Apparently even if he eats in a neighbour's house, contra the implied ruling of our Mishnah.
[4] I.e., has no other room and so it does not contradict our Mishnah.
[5] And this is the case mentioned n the Baraitha.
[6] Gen. XXIII, 3.
[7] Ibid. 4.
[8] Even if he is in another room. The phrase 'lying before him' is not to be understood literally, and consequently there is no contradiction between the Baraitha and our Mishnah.
[9] And which he is not under obligation to bury. A dead body, according to Jewish law, must be watched to protect it from mice, v. infra.
[10] And the same applies even if he is not carrying a scroll.
[11] I.e., the dead, who are 'poor' in precepts.
[12] Prov. XVII, 5.

they were bringing it in a ship, they put it in a corner and both say their prayers in another corner. Why this difference? — Rabina said: They differ on the question whether there is any fear of mice¹ [on board ship]. One held that there is a fear of mice and the other held that there is no fear of mice.

Our Rabbis taught: A man who is carrying bones from place to place should not put them in a saddle-bag and place them on his ass and sit on them, because this is a disrespectful way of treating them. But if he was afraid of heathens and robbers, it is permitted. And the rule which they laid down for bones applies also to a scroll of the Law. To what does this last statement refer? Shall I say to the first clause?² This is self-evident: Is a scroll of the Law inferior to bones? — Rather; it refers to the second clause.³

Rehaba said in the name of Rab Judah: Whoever sees a corpse [on the way to burial] and does not accompany it⁴ comes under the head of 'He that mocketh the poor blasphemeth his Maker'. And if he accompanies it, what is his reward? R. Assi says: To him apply the texts: He that is gracious unto the poor lendeth unto the Lord,⁵ and he that is gracious unto the needy honoureth Him.⁶

R. Hiyya and R. Jonathan were once walking about in a cemetery, and the blue fringe of R. Jonathan was trailing on the ground. Said R. Hiyya to him: Lift it up, so that they [the dead] should not say: Tomorrow they are coming to join us and now they are insulting us! He said to him: Do they know so much? Is it not written, But the dead know not anything?⁷ He replied to him: If you have read once, you have not repeated; if you have repeated, you have not gone over a third time; if you have gone over a third time, you have not had it explained to you. For the living know that they shall die:⁸ these are the righteous who in their death are called living as it says. And Benaiah the son of Jehoiada, the son of a living⁹ man from Kabzeel, who had done mighty deeds, he smote the two altar-hearths of Moab; he went down and also slew a lion in the midst of a pit in the time of snow.¹⁰

---

¹ The reason why a corpse has to be watched is to protect it from mice.
² That it must not be ridden upon.
³ That in time of danger it is permitted.
⁴ MS.M. adds, for four cubits.
⁵ Prov. XIX, 17.
⁶ Ibid. XIV, 31.
⁷ Eccl. IX, 5.
⁸ Ibid.
⁹ So the kethib. E.V., following the keri, 'valiant'.
¹⁰ II Sam XXIII, 20.

Berakoth 18b

'The son of a living man': are all other people then the sons of dead men? Rather 'the son of a living man' means that even in his death he was called living. 'From Kabzeel, who had done mighty deeds': this indicates that he gathered [kibbez] numerous workers for the Torah. 'He smote two altar-hearths of Moab'; this indicates that he did not leave his like either in the first Temple or in the second Temple.[1] 'He went down and also slew a lion in the midst of a pit in the time of snow': some say that this indicates that he broke blocks of ice and went down and bathed;[2] others say that he went through the Sifra of the School of Rab[3] on a winter's day. 'But the dead know nothing': These are the wicked who in their lifetime are called dead, as it says. And thou, O wicked one, that art slain, the prince of Israel.[4] Or if you prefer. I can derive it from here: At the mouth of two witnesses shall the dead be put to death.[5] He is still alive! What it means is, he is already counted as dead.

The sons of R. Hiyya went out to cultivate their property,[6] and they began to forget their learning.[7] They tried very hard to recall it. Said one to the other: Does our father know of our trouble? How should he know, replied the other, seeing that it is written, His sons come to honour and he knoweth it not?[8] Said the other to him: But does he not know? Is it not written: But his flesh grieveth for him, and his soul mourneth over him?[9] And R. Isaac said [commenting on this]: The worm is as painful to the dead as a needle in the flesh of the living? [He replied]: It is explained that they know their own pain, they do not know the pain of others. Is that so? Has it not been taught: It is related that a certain pious man gave a denar to a poor man on the eve of New Year in a year of drought, and his wife scolded him, and he went and passed the night in the cemetery, and he heard two spirits conversing with one another. Said one to her companion: My dear, come and let us wander about the world and let us hear from behind the curtain[10] what suffering is coming on the world.[11] Said her companion to her: I am not able, because I am buried in a matting of reeds.[12] But do you go, and whatever you hear tell me. So the other went and wandered about and returned. Said her companion to her: My dear, what have you heard from behind the curtain? She replied: I heard that whoever sows after the first rainfall[13] will have his crop smitten by hail. So the man went and did not sow till after the second rainfall,[14] with the result that everyone else's crop was smitten and his was not smitten.[15] The next year he again went and passed the night in the cemetery, and heard the two spirits conversing with

---

[1] 'Altar-hearths of Moab' are taken by the Rabbis to refer to the two Temples, on account of David's descent from Ruth the Moabitess.
[2] To cleanse himself of pollution in order to study the Torah in cleanliness.
[3] The halachic midrash on Leviticus. Lion-like he mastered in a short time (a winter's day) all the intricacies of this midrash.
[4] Ezek. XXI, 30. E.V. 'that art to be slain'.
[5] Deut. XVII, 6. E.V. 'he that is to die'.
[6] Lit., 'to the villages'.
[7] Lit., 'their learning grew heavy for them'.
[8] Job XIV, 21.
[9] Ibid. 22.
[10] Screening the Divine Presence.
[11] Sc., in the divine judgment pronounced on New Year.
[12] And not in a linen shroud.
[13] The first fall of the former rains, which would be about the seventeenth of Heshvan (Rashi).
[14] Which would be about six days after the first.
[15] Being not yet sufficiently grown.

one another. Said one to her companion: Come and let us wander about the world and hear from behind the curtain what punishment is coming upon the world. Said the other to her: My dear, did I not tell you that I am not able because I am buried in a matting of reeds? But do you go, and whatever you hear, come and tell me. So the other one went and wandered about the world and returned. She said to her: My dear, what have you heard from behind the curtain? She replied: I heard that whoever sows after the later rain will have his crop smitten with blight. So the man went and sowed after the first rain with the result that everyone else's crop was blighted and his was not blighted.[1] Said his wife to him: How is it that last year everyone else's crop was smitten and yours was not smitten, and this year everyone else's crop is blighted and yours is not blighted? So he related to her all his experiences. The story goes that shortly afterwards a quarrel broke out between the wife of that pious man and the mother of the child,[2] and the former said to the latter, Come and I will show you your daughter buried in a matting of reeds. The next year the man again went and spent the night in the cemetery and heard those conversing together. One said: My dear, come and let us wander about the world and hear from behind the curtain what suffering is coming upon the world. Said the other: My dear, leave me alone; our conversation has already been heard among the living. This would prove that they know? — Perhaps some other man after his decease went and told them. Come and hear; for Ze'iri deposited some money with his landlady, and while he was away visiting Rab[3] she died. So he went after her to the cemetery[4] and said to her, Where is my money? She replied to him: Go and take it from under the ground, in the hole of the doorpost, in such and such a place, and tell my mother to send me my comb and my tube of eye-paint by the hand of So-and-so who is coming here tomorrow. Does not this[5] show that they know? — Perhaps Dumah[6] announces to them beforehand.[7] Come and hear: The father of Samuel had some money belonging to orphans deposited with him. When he died, Samuel was not with him, and they called him, 'The son who consumes the money of orphans'. So he went after his father to the cemetery, and said to them [the dead]. I am looking for Abba.[8] They said to him: There are many Abbas here. I want Abba b. Abba, he said. They replied: There are also several Abbas b. Abba here. He then said to them: I Want Abba b. Abba the father of Samuel; where is he? They replied: He has gone up to the Academy of the Sky.[9] Meanwhile he saw Levi sitting outside.[10] He said to him: Why are you sitting outside? Why have you not gone up [to heaven]? He replied: Because they said to me: For as many years as you did not go up to the academy of R. Efes and hurt his feelings,[11] we will not let you go up to the Academy of the Sky. Meanwhile his father came. Samuel observed that he was both weeping and laughing. He said to him: Why are you weeping? He replied: Because you are coming here soon. And why are you laughing? Because you are highly esteemed in this world. He thereupon said to him: If I am esteemed, let them take up Levi; and they did take up Levi. He then said to him: Where is the money of the orphans? He replied: Go and you will find it in the case of the millstones. The money at the top and the bottom is mine, that in the middle is the orphans' He said to him: Why did you do like that? He replied: So that if thieves

---

[1] Being by now strong enough to resist.
[2] Whose spirit the pious man had heard conversing
[3] Or 'the school house'.
[4] Lit., 'court of death'.
[5] That she knew someone else was going to die.
[6] Lit., 'Silence'. The angel presiding over the dead.
[7] That So-and-so will die, but they know nothing else.
[8] This was his father's name.
[9] Where the souls of the pious learned foregathered.
[10] Apart from the other dead.
[11] v. Keth. 113b.

came, they should take mine, and if the earth destroyed any, it should destroy mine. Does not this[1] show that they know? — Perhaps Samuel was exceptional: as he was esteemed, they proclaimed beforehand, Make way [for him]!

R. Jonathan also retracted his opinion. For R. Samuel b. Nahmani said in the name of R. Jonathan: Whence do we know that the dead converse with one another? Because it says: And the Lord said unto him: This is the land which I swore unto Abraham, unto Isaac, and unto Jacob, saying.[2] What is the meaning of 'saying'?[3] The Holy One, blessed be He, said to Moses: Say to Abraham, Isaac and Jacob: The oath which I swore to you I have already carried out for your descendants.

---

[1] His knowing that Samuel would soon die.
[2] Deut. XXXIV, 4.
[3] Lit., 'to say'.

Folio 19a

Now if you maintain that the dead do not know, what would be the use of his telling them? — You infer then that they do know. In that case, why should he need to tell them? — So that they might be grateful to Moses. R. Isaac said: If one makes remarks about the dead, it is like making remarks about a stone. Some say [the reason is that] they do not know, others that they know but do not care. Can that be so? Has not R. Papa said: A certain man made[1] derogatory remarks about Mar Samuel and a log fell from the roof and broke his skull?[2] — A Rabbinical student is different, because the Holy One, blessed be He, avenges his insult.[3]

R. Joshua b. Levi said: Whoever makes derogatory remarks about scholars after their death[4] is cast into Gehinnom, as it says, But as for such as turn aside[5] unto their crooked ways, the Lord will lead them away with the workers of iniquity. Peace be upon Israel:[6] even at a time when there is peace upon Israel, the Lord will lead them away with the workers of iniquity.[7] It was taught in the school of R. Ishmael: If you see a scholar who has committed an offence by night, do not cavil at him by day, for perhaps he has done penance. 'Perhaps', say you? — Nay, rather, he has certainly done penance. This applies only to bodily [sexual] offences, but if he has misappropriated money, [he may be criticised] until he restores it to its owner.

R. Joshua b. Levi further said: In twenty-four places we find that the Beth din inflicted excommunication for an insult to a teacher, and they are all recorded in the Mishnah.[8] R. Eleazar asked him, Where? He replied: See if you can find them. He went and examined and found three cases: one of a scholar who threw contempt on the bashing of the hands, another of one who made derogatory remarks about scholars after their death, and a third of one who made himself too familiar towards heaven. What is the case of making derogatory remarks about scholars after their death? — As we have learnt:[9] He[10] used to say: The water [of the sotah][11] is not administered either to a proselyte or to an emancipated woman; the Sages, however say that it is. They said to him: There is the case of Karkemith an emancipated bondwoman in Jerusalem to whom Shemaiah and Abtalyon administered the water? He replied: They administered it to one like themselves.[12] They thereupon excommunicated him, and he died in excommunication, and the Beth din stoned his coffin.[13] What is the case of treating with contempt the washing of the hands? — As we have learnt: R. Judah said: Far be it from us to think that Akabiah b. Mahalalel was excommunicated, for the doors of the Temple

---

[1] MS.M.: Did not R. Papa make etc.; cf. next note.
[2] MS.M.: and nearly broke (lit., 'wished to break') his skull. This suits better the reading of MS.M. mentioned in previous note.
[3] Lit., 'his honour'.
[4] Lit., 'Speaks after the bier of scholars'.
[5] Heb. mattim, connected by R. Joshua with mittathan (their bier) above.
[6] Ps. CXXV, 5.
[7] To Gehinnom.
[8] I.e., the Mishnah as a whole.
[9] 'Ed. V, 6.
[10] Akabiah b. Mahalalel.
[11] A woman suspected of infidelity. V. Num. V, 11ff.
[12] They were supposed to be descended from Sennacherib and so from a family of proselytes. Others render: they only pretended to administer it.
[13] V. 'Ed. V. 6 (Sonc. ed.) notes.

hall did not close on any man in Israel[1] the equal of Akabiah b. Mahalalel in wisdom, in purity and in fear of sin. Whom did they in fact excommunicate? It was Eleazar b. Hanoch, who raised doubts about washing the hands, and when he died the Beth din sent and had a large stone placed on his coffin, to teach you that if a man is excommunicated and dies in his excommunication, the Beth din stone his coffin.[2]

What is the case of one behaving familiarly with heaven? — As we have learnt: Simeon b. Shetah sent to Honi ha-Me'aggel:[3] You deserve to be excommunicated, and were you not Honi, I would pronounce excommunication against you. But what can I do seeing that you ingratiate yourself[4] with the Omnipresent and He performs your desires, and you are like a son who ingratiates himself with his father and he performs his desires; and to you applies the verse: Let thy father and thy mother be glad, and let her that bore thee rejoice.[5]

But are there no more [instances of excommunication]? Is not there the case learnt by R. Joseph: Thaddeus a man of Rome accustomed the Roman [Jews] to eat kids roasted whole[6] on the eve of Passover. Simeon b. Shetah sent to him and said: Were you not Thaddeus, I would pronounce sentence of excommunication on you, because you make Israel [appear to] eat holy things outside the precincts.[7] — We say, in our Mishnah. and this is in a Baraitha. But is there no other in our Mishnah? Is there not this one, as we have learnt: If he cuts it[8] up into rings and puts sand between the rings.[9] R. Eliezer declares that it is [permanently] clean, while the Rabbis declare that it is unclean; and this is the stove of Akna'i. Why Akna'i? Rab Judah said in the name of Samuel: Because they surrounded it with halachoth like a serpent [akna'i] and declared it unclean. And it has been taught: On that day they brought all the things that R. Eliezer had declared clean[10] and burnt them before him, and in the end they blessed[11] him.[12] — Even so we do not find excommunication stated in our Mishnah.[13] How then do you find the twenty-four places? — R. Joshua b. Levi compares one thing to another,[14] R. Eleazar does not compare one thing to another.

THOSE WHO CARRY THE BIER AND THOSE WHO RELIEVE THEM. Our Rabbis taught: A dead body is not taken out shortly before the time for the Shema', but if they began to take it they do not desist. Is that so? Was not the body of R. Joseph taken out shortly before the time for the Shema'? — An exception can be made for a distinguished man.

BEFORE THE BIER AND BEHIND THE BIER. Our Rabbis taught: Those who are occupied with

---

[1] When they all assembled there to kill their paschal lambs.
[2] Pes. 64b.
[3] The word Me'aggel probably means 'circle-drawer'; v. Ta'an. 19a.
[4] Aliter: 'take liberties with'.
[5] Prov. XXIII, 25. V. Ta'an 19a.
[6] Lit., 'Helmeted goats' — goats roasted whole with their entrails and legs placed on the head, like a helmet. This was how the Passover sacrifice was roasted.
[7] V. Pes. (Sonc. ed.) p. 260 notes.
[8] An earthenware stove which has been declared unclean, and cannot be used till it has been broken up and remade.
[9] To cement them.
[10] After contact with such a stove.
[11] Euphemism for 'excommunicated'.
[12] V. B.M. (Sonc. ed.) 59b notes.
[13] The last statement being from a Baraitha.
[14] I.e., he takes count of all the cases where the ruling of the Rabbis was disregarded by an individual, and excommunication should have been incurred, even if this is not mentioned.

the funeral speeches, if the dead body is still before them, slip out one by one and recite the Shema'; if the body is not before them, they sit and recite it, and he [the mourner] sits silent; they stand up and say the tefillah and he stands up and accepts God's judgement and says: Sovereign of the Universe, I have sinned much before Thee and Thou didst not punish me one thousandth part. May it be Thy will, O Lord our God, to close up our breaches and the breaches of all Thy people the house of Israel in mercy! Abaye said: A man should not speak thus,[1] since R. Simeon b. Lakish said, and so it was taught in the name of R. Jose: A man should never speak in such a way as to give an opening to Satan. And R. Joseph said: What text proves this? Because it says: We were almost like Sodom.[2] What did the prophet reply to them? Hear the word of the Lord, ye rulers of Sodom.[3]

WHEN THEY HAVE BURIED THE DEAD BODY AND RETURNED, etc. [I understand]: If they are able to begin and go through all of it, yes, but if they have only time for one section or one verse, no. This statement was contradicted by the following: When they have buried the body and returned, if they are able to begin and complete even one section or one verse, [they do so]! — That is just what he says: If they are able to begin and go through even one section or one verse before they form a row, they should begin, but otherwise they should not begin.

---

[1] Saying, 'Thou didst not punish me', which is like a hint to punish.
[2] Isa. I, 9. E.V. '... a little. We were like etc.'
[3] Ibid. 10.

Berakoth 19b

THOSE WHO STAND IN A ROW etc. Our Rabbis taught: The row which can see inside[1] is exempt, but one which cannot see inside is not exempt. R. Judah said: Those who come on account of the mourner are exempt, but those who come for their own purposes[2] are not exempt.

R. Judah said in the name of Rab: If one finds mixed kinds[3] in his garment, he takes it off even in the street. What is the reason? [It says]: There is no wisdom nor understanding nor counsel against the Lord;[4] wherever a profanation of God's name is involved no respect is paid to a teacher.

An objection was raised: If they have buried the body and are returning, and there are two ways open to them, one clean and the other unclean,[5] if [the mourner] goes by the clean one they go with him by the clean one, and if he goes by the unclean one they go with him by the unclean one, out of respect for him. Why so? Let us say, There is no wisdom nor understanding against the Lord? — R. Abba explained the statement to refer to a beth ha-peras,[6] which is declared unclean only by the Rabbis;[7] for Rab Judah has said in the name of Samuel: A man may blow in front of him[8] in a beth ha-peras and proceed. And Rab Judah b. Ashi also said in the name of Rab: A beth ha-peras which has been well trodden is clean.[9] — Come and hear; for R. Eleazar b. Zadok[10] said: We used to leap over coffins containing bodies to see the Israelite kings.[11] Nor did they mean this to apply only to Israelite kings, but also to heathen kings, so that if he should be privileged [to live to the time of the Messiah], he should be able to distinguish between the Israelite and the heathen kings. Why so? Let us say, 'There is no wisdom and no understanding and no counsel before the Lord'? — [It is in accord with the dictum of Raba; for Raba said: It is a rule of the Torah[12] that a 'tent'[13] which has a hollow space of a handbreadth[14] forms a partition against uncleanness, but if it has not a hollow space of a handbreadth it forms no partition against uncleanness.[15] Now most coffins have a space of a handbreadth, and [the Rabbis] decreed that those which had such a space [should form no partition] for fear they should be confused with those which had no space, but where respect to kings was involved they did not enforce the decree.

Come and hear. 'Great is human dignity, since it overrides a negative precept of the Torah'.[16] Why should it? Let us apply the rule, 'There is no wisdom nor understanding nor counsel against the Lord? — Rab b. Shaba explained the dictum in the presence of R. Kahana to refer to the negative precept of

---

[1] I.e., which can see the mourner, if they stand several deep.
[2] To see the crowd.
[3] Linen and wool.
[4] Prov. XXI, 30.
[5] Because there is a grave in it.
[6] A field in which there was once a grave which has been ploughed up, so that bones may be scattered about.
[7] But not by the Scripture.
[8] To blow the small bones away.
[9] V. Pes. (Sonc. ed.) p. 492-4 notes.
[10] He was a priest.
[11] Which proves that showing respect overrides the rules of uncleanness.
[12] I.e., a 'law of Moses from Sinai'.
[13] I.e., anything which overshadows, v. Num. XIX, 14.
[14] Between its outside and what it contains.
[15] The uncleanness which it overshadows breaks through and extends beyond its confines.
[16] Men. 37b.

'thou shalt not turn aside'.[1] They laughed at him. The negative precept of 'thou shalt not turn aside' is also from the Torah![2] Said R. Kahana: If a great man makes a statement, you should not laugh at him. All the ordinances of the Rabbis were based by them on the prohibition of 'thou shalt not turn aside'[3] but where the question of [human] dignity is concerned the Rabbis allowed the act.[4]

Come and hear.[5] And hide thyself from them.[6] There are times when thou mayest hide thyself from them and times when thou mayest not hide thyself from them. How so? If the man [who sees the animal] is a priest and it [the animal] is in a graveyard, or if he is an elder and it is not in accordance with his dignity [to raise it], or if his own work was of more importance than that of his fellow.[7] Therefore it is said, And thou shalt hide. But why so? Let us apply the rule, 'There is no wisdom nor understanding nor counsel against the Lord'? — The case is different there, because it says expressly, And thou shalt hide thyself from them. Let us then derive from this [the rule for mixed kinds]?[8] — We do not derive a ritual ruling from a ruling relating to property.[9] Come and hear:[10] Or for his sister.[11] What does this teach us? Suppose he[12] was going to kill his paschal lamb or to circumcise his son, and he heard that a near relative of his had died, am I to say that he should go back and defile himself? You say, he should not defile himself.[13] Shall I say that just as he does not defile himself for them, so he should not defile himself for a meth mizwah?[14] It says significantly, 'And for his sister': for his sister he does not defile himself,

---

[1] Deut. XVII, 11, and not to negative precepts in general.
[2] And the objection still remains.
[3] They based on these words their authority to make rules equally binding with those laid down in the Torah, and Rab b. Shaba interprets the words 'negative precept of the Torah' in the passage quoted to mean, 'Rabbinical ordinances deriving their sanction from this negative precept of their Torah'.
[4] V. Shab. 81b.
[5] For notes V. B.M. (Sonc. ed.) 30a.
[6] Deut. XXII, 1, 4.
[7] I.e., if he stood to lose more from neglecting his own work than the other from the loss of his animal.
[8] Of which it was said supra that he takes off the garment even in the street.
[9] Lit., 'money'. To override a ritual rule is more serious.
[10] Nazir 48b.
[11] Num. VI, 7.
[12] A Nazirite who is also a priest.
[13] Because those things must be done at a fixed time, and cannot be postponed.
[14] Lit., '(the burial of) a dead, which is a religious obligation'. V. Glos.

Folio 20a

but he does defile himself for a meth mizwah. But why should this be? Let us apply the rule, 'There is no wisdom nor understanding nor counsel against the Lord?'[1] — The case is different there, because it is written, 'And for his sister'. Let us then derive a ruling from this [for mixed kinds]? — Where it is a case of 'sit still and do nothing', it is different.[2]

Said R. Papa to Abaye: How is it that for the former generations miracles were performed and for us miracles are not performed? It cannot be because of their [superiority in] study, because in the years of Rab Judah the whole of their studies was confined to Nezikin, and we study all six Orders, and when Rab Judah came in [the tractate] 'Ukzin [to the law], 'If a woman presses vegetables in a pot'[3] (or, according to others, 'olives pressed with their leaves are clean'),[4] he used to say, I see all the difficulties of Rab and Samuel here.[5] and we have thirteen versions of Ukzin.[6] And yet when Rab Judah drew off one shoe,[7] rain used to come, whereas we torment ourselves and cry loudly, and no notice is taken of us![8] He replied: The former generations used to be ready to sacrifice their lives for the sanctity of [God's] name; we do not sacrifice our lives for the sanctity of [God's] name. There was the case of R. Adda b. Ahaba who saw a heathen woman wearing a red head-dress[9] in the street, and thinking that she was an Israelite woman, he rose and tore it from her. It turned out that she was a heathen woman, and they fined him four hundred zuz. He said to her: What is your name. She replied: Mathun. Mathun, he said to her: that makes four hundred zuz.[10]

R. Giddal was accustomed to go and sit at the gates of the bathing-place.[11] He used to say to the women [who came to bathe]: Bathe thus, or bathe thus. The Rabbis said to him: Is not the Master afraid lest his passion get the better of him? — He replied: They look to me like so many white geese. R. Johanan was accustomed to go and sit at the gates of the bathing place. He said: When the daughters of Israel come up from bathing they look at me and they have children as handsome as I am.[12] Said the Rabbis to him: Is not the Master afraid of the evil eye? — He replied: I come from the seed of Joseph, over whom the evil eye has no power, as it is written, Joseph is a fruitful vine, a fruitful vine above the eye,[13] and R. Abbahu said with regard to this, do not read 'ale 'ayin, but 'ole 'ayin'.[14]

---

[1] For notes V. Sanh. (Sonc. ed.) 35a.
[2] Wearing mixed kinds is certainly an active breaking of a rule, but it is not clear how attending to a meth mizwah comes under the head of 'sit and do nothing'. V. Rashi and Tosaf. ad loc.
[3] 'Ukzin, II, 1.
[4] Ibid.
[5] I.e., this Mishnah itself presents as many difficulties to me as all the rest of the Gemara.
[6] I.e., the Mishnah and the various Baraithas and Toseftas. Aliter: We have thirteen colleges which are well versed in it.
[7] In preparation for fasting.
[8] For fuller notes on the passage, v. Sanh. (Sonc. ed.) p. 728.
[9] Aliter: 'mantle'.
[10] The Aramaic for two hundred is mathan. Mathun also means 'deliberate'; had he been less rash he would have saved himself 400 zuz; there is here a double play on words.
[11] Where the women took their ritual bath.
[12] R. Johanan was famous for his beauty. V. supra 5b.
[13] Gen. XLIX, 22.
[14] Lit., 'rising above the (power of the) eye'. I.e., superior to the evil eye.

R. Judah son of R. Hanina derived it from this text: And let them multiply like fishes [we-yidgu] in the midst of the earth.[1] Just as the fishes [dagim] in the sea are covered by water and the evil eye has no power over them, so the evil eye has no power over the seed of Joseph. Or, if you prefer I can say: The evil eye has no power over the eye which refused to feed itself on what did not belong to it.[2]

MISHNAH. WOMEN, SLAVES AND MINORS ARE EXEMPT FROM RECITING THE SHEMA'

---

[1] So lit. E.V. 'grow into a multitude'. Ibid. XLVIII, 16.
[2] Sc. Potiphar's wife.

Berakoth 20b

AND FROM PUTTING ON TEFILLIN. BUT THEY ARE SUBJECT TO THE OBLIGATIONS OF TEFILLAH AND MEZUZAH[1] AND GRACE AFTER MEALS.

GEMARA. That they are exempt from the Shema' is self-evident — It is a positive precept for which there is a fixed time?[2] You might say that because it mentions the kingship of heaven it is different. We are therefore told that this is not so.

AND FROM PUTTING ON THE TEFILLIN. This also is self-evident?[3] You might say that because it is put on a level with the mezuzah[4] [therefore women should be subject to it]. Therefore we are told that this is not so.

THEY ARE SUBJECT TO THE OBLIGATION OF TEFILLAH. Because this [is supplication for Divine] mercy. You might [however] think that because it is written in connection therewith, Evening and morning and at noonday,[5] therefore it is like a positive precept for which there is a fixed time. Therefore we are told [that this is not so].

AND MEZUZAH. This is self-evident?[6] You might say that because it is put on a level with the study of the Torah,[7] [therefore women are exempt]. Therefore it tells us [that this is not so].

AND GRACE AFTER MEALS. This is self-evident? — You might think that because it is written, When the Lord shall give you in the evening flesh to eat and in the morning bread to the full,[8] therefore it is like a positive precept for which there is a definite time. Therefore it tells us [that this is not so].

R. Adda b. Ahabah said: Women are under obligation to sanctify the [Sabbath] day[9] by ordinance of the Torah. But why should this be? It is a positive precept for which there is a definite time, and women are exempt from all positive precepts for which there is a definite time? — Abaye said: The obligation is only Rabbinical. Said Raba to him: But it says, 'By an ordinance of the Torah'? And further, on this ground we could subject them to all positive precepts by Rabbinical authority? Rather, said Raba. The text says Remember and Observe.[10] Whoever has to 'observe' has to 'remember'; and since these women have to 'observe',[11] they also have to 'remember'.[12]

---

[1] V. Glos.
[2] And women are exempt from such precepts. V. infra.
[3] For the same reason.
[4] Since it is written, and thou shalt bind them, and thou shalt write them.
[5] Ps. LV, 18.
[6] For what reason is there for exempting them?
[7] As it says, And ye shall teach them to your sons, and ye shall write them; and the obligation of teaching applies only to the males.
[8] Ex. XVI, 8.
[9] Over wine. V. P.B. p. 124.
[10] In the two versions of the Fourth Commandment, viz., Ex. XX, 8 and Deut. V, 12 respectively.
[11] I.e., abstain from work.
[12] I.e., say sanctification. (Kiddush). V. Glos.

Rabina said to Raba: Is the obligation of women to say grace after meals Rabbinical or Scriptural? — What difference does it make in practice which it is? — For deciding whether they can perform the duty on behalf of others. If you say the obligation is Scriptural, then one who is bound by Scripture can come and perform the duty on behalf of another who is bound by Scripture. But if you say the obligation is only Rabbinical, then [a woman] is not strictly bound to do this, and whoever is not strictly bound to do a thing cannot perform the obligation on behalf of others. What [do we decide]? — Come and hear: 'In truth they did say: A son[1] may say grace on behalf of his father and a slave may say grace on behalf of his master and a woman may say grace on behalf of her husband. But the Sages said: A curse light on the man whose wife or children have to say grace for him.'[2] If now you say that [the obligation of these others] is Scriptural, then there is no difficulty: one who is bound by the Scripture comes and performs the duty on behalf of one who is bound by the Scripture. But if you say that the obligation is Rabbinic, can one who is bound only Rabbinically come and perform the duty on behalf of one who is bound Scripturally?
— But even accepting your reasoning, is a minor subject to obligation [Scripturally]?[3]
Nay. With what case are we dealing here? If, for instance, he ate a quantity for which he is only Rabbinically bound [to say grace],[4] in which case one who is Rabbinically bound[5] comes and performs the duty on behalf of one who is only Rabbinically bound.[6]

R. 'Awira discoursed — sometimes in the name of R. Ammi, and sometimes in the name of R. Assi — as follows: The ministering angels said before the Holy One, blessed be He: Sovereign of the Universe, it is written in Thy law, Who regardeth not persons[7] nor taketh reward,[8] and dost Thou not regard the person of Israel, as it is written, The Lord lift up His countenance upon thee?[9] He replied to them: And shall I not lift up My countenance for Israel, seeing that I wrote for them in the Torah, And thou shalt eat and be satisfied and bless the Lord thy God,[10] and they are particular [to say the grace] if the quantity is but an olive or an egg.[11]

---

[1] I.e., a minor.
[2] Because he cannot say it himself; v. Suk. 38a.
[3] As would be presupposed in your argument.
[4] Viz., the quantity of an olive according to R. Meir and an egg according to R. Judah. Infra 45a.
[5] A minor.
[6] The father who had less than the minimum quantity. And it is only in such a case that a woman may say grace on behalf of her husband.
[7] Lit., 'Who lifteth not up the countenance'.
[8] Deut. X, 17.
[9] Num. VI, 26.
[10] Deut. VIII, 10.
[11] Cf. supra n. 2.

MISHNAH. A BA'AL KERI[1] SAYS THE WORDS [OF THE SHEMA'][2] MENTALLY[3] WITHOUT SAYING A BLESSING EITHER BEFORE OR AFTER. AT MEALS HE SAYS THE GRACE AFTER, BUT NOT THE GRACE BEFORE. R. JUDAH SAYS: HE SAYS THE GRACE BOTH BEFORE AND AFTER.

GEMARA. Said Rabina: This would show that saying mentally is equivalent to actual saying.[4] For if you assume that it is not equivalent to actual saying, why should he say mentally?[5] What then? [You say that] saying mentally is equivalent to actual saying. Then let him utter the words with his lips! — We do as we find it was done at Sinai.[6] R. Hisda said: Saying mentally is not equivalent to actual saying. For if you assume that saying mentally is equivalent to actual saying, then let him utter the words with his lips! What then? [You say that] saying mentally is not equivalent to actual saying? Why then should he say mentally? — R. Eleazar replied: So that he should not have to sit saying nothing while everyone else is engaged saying the Shema'. Then let him read some other section? — R. Adda b. Ahaba said: [He must attend to that] with which the congregation is engaged.

---

[1] V. Glos.
[2] When the hour arrives for reciting it.
[3] Lit., 'in his heart'.
[4] Lit., 'thinking is like speech'.
[5] What religious act does he perform thereby?
[6] Moses ordered the Israelites to keep away from woman before receiving the Torah, but those who were unclean could still accept mentally.

Folio 21a

But what of tefillah which is a thing with which the congregation is engaged, and yet we have learnt: If he was standing reciting the tefillah and he suddenly remembered that he was a ba'al keri he should not break off, but he should shorten [each blessing]. Now the reason is that he had commenced; but if he had not yet commenced, he should not do so?
— Tefillah is different because it does not mention the kingdom of heaven.[1] But what of the grace after meals in which there is no mention of the sovereignty of heaven, and yet we have learnt: AT MEALS HE SAYS GRACE AFTER, BUT NOT THE GRACE BEFORE?
— [Rather the answer is that] the recital of the Shema' and grace after food are Scriptural ordinances, whereas tefillah is only a Rabbinical ordinance.[2]

Rab Judah said: Where do we find that the grace after meals is ordained in the Torah? Because it says: And thou shalt eat and be satisfied and bless.[3] Where do we find that a blessing before studying the Torah is ordained in the Torah? Because it says: When I proclaim the name of the Lord, ascribe ye greatness to our God.[4] R. Johanan said: We learn that a blessing should be said after studying the Torah by an argument a fortiori from grace after food; and we learn that grace should be said before food by an argument a fortiori from the blessing over the Torah. The blessing after the Torah is learnt a fortiori from the grace after food as follows: Seeing that food which requires no grace before it[5] requires a grace after it, does it not stand to reason that the study of the Torah which requires a grace before it should require one after it? The blessing before food is learnt a fortiori from the blessing over the Torah as follows: Seeing that the Torah which requires no blessing after it[6] requires one before it, does it not stand to reason that food which requires one after it should require one before it? A flaw can be pointed out in both arguments. How can you reason from food [to the Torah], seeing that from the former he derives physical benefit? And how can you reason from the Torah [to food], seeing that from the former he obtains everlasting life? Further, we have learnt: AT MEALS HE SAYS THE GRACE AFTER BUT NOT THE GRACE BEFORE?[7] — This is a refutation.

Rab Judah said: If a man is in doubt whether he has recited the Shema', he need not recite it again. If he is in doubt whether he has said 'True and firm', or not, he should say it again. What is the reason?
— The recital of the Shema' is ordained only by the Rabbis, the saying of 'True and firm' is a Scriptural ordinance.[8] R. Joseph raised an objection to this,[9] 'And when thou liest down, and when thou risest up'. — Said Abaye to him: That was written with reference to words of Torah.[10]

We have learnt: A BA'AL KERI SAYS MENTALLY, AND SAYS NO BLESSING EITHER BEFORE OR AFTER. AT MEALS HE SAYS THE GRACE AFTER BUT NOT THE GRACE

---

[1] The words 'King of the Universe' are not used in the Eighteen Benedictions.
[2] And therefore he need not say it even mentally.
[3] Deut. VIII, 10.
[4] Ibid. XXXII, 3. E.V. 'for I will proclaim etc.'. V. Yoma 37a.
[5] I.e., no such grace is distinctly prescribed in the Torah.
[6] I.e., no such grace is distinctly prescribed in the Torah.
[7] Which proves that the grace before food is not Biblical.
[8] Because it mentions the going forth from Egypt, as prescribed in Deut. XVI, 3.
[9] That the Shema' is not Scriptural.
[10] And it is applied to the Shema' only as an allusion.

BEFORE. Now if you assume that 'True and firm' is a Scriptural regulation, let him say the blessing after the Shema'? — Why should he say [the blessing after]? If it is in order to mention the going forth from Egypt, that is already mentioned in the Shema'! But then let him say the former, and he need not say the latter?[1] — The recital of Shema' is preferable, because it has two points.[2] R. Eleazar says: If one is in doubt whether he has recited the Shema' or not, he says the Shema' again. If he is in doubt whether he has said the Tefillah or not, he does not say it again. R. Johanan, however, said: Would that a man would go on praying the whole day!

Rab Judah also said in the name of Samuel: If a man was standing saying the Tefillah and he suddenly remembered that he had already said it, he breaks off even in the middle of a benediction. Is that so? Has not R. Nahman said: When we were with Rabbah b. Abbuha, we asked him with reference to disciples who made a mistake and began the weekday benediction on a Sabbath, whether they should finish it, and he said to us that they should finish that blessing! — Are these cases parallel? In that case one[3] is in reality under obligation,[4] and it is the Rabbis who did not trouble him out of respect for the Sabbath, but in this case he has already said the prayer.

Rab Judah further said in the name of Samuel: If a man had already said the Tefillah and went into a synagogue and found the congregation saying the Tefillah, if he can add something fresh, he should say the Tefillah again, but otherwise he should not say it again. And both these rulings are required.[5] For if I had been told only the first, I should have said, This applies only to [a case where he said the Tefillah] alone and [is repeating it] alone

---

[1] I.e., let him say the blessing openly, and not the Shema' mentally.
[2] It mentions both the Kingdom of Heaven and the going forth from Egypt.
[3] Lit., 'the man'.
[4] To say the weekday Tefillah.
[5] This latter ruling and the case where one remembered whilst praying that he had already prayed.

Berakoth 21b

, or [where he said it] with a congregation and [is repeating it] with a congregation,[1] but when [one who has prayed] alone goes into a congregation, it is as if he had not prayed at all. Hence we are told that this is not so. And if we had been told only the second case, I might think that this ruling applies only because he had not commenced, but where he had commenced I might say that he should not [break off]. Therefore both are necessary.

R. Huna said: If a man goes into a synagogue and finds the congregation saying the Tefillah, if he can commence and finish before the reader[2] reaches 'We give thanks',[3] he may say the Tefillah,[4] but otherwise he should not say it. R. Joshua b. Levi says: If he can commence and finish before the reader reaches the Sanctification,[5] he should say the Tefillah, but otherwise he should not say it. What is the ground of their difference? One authority held that a man praying by himself does say the Sanctification, while the other holds that he does not. So, too, R. Adda b. Abahah said: Whence do we know that a man praying by himself does not say the Sanctification? Because it says: I will be hallowed among the children of Israel;[6] for any manifestation of sanctification not less than ten are required. How is this derived? Rabinai the brother of R. Hiyya b. Abba taught: We draw an analogy between two occurrences of the word 'among'. It is written here, I will be hallowed among the children of Israel, and it is written elsewhere. Separate yourselves from among this congregation.[7] Just as in that case ten are implied,[8] so here ten are implied. Both authorities, however, agree that he does not interrupt [the Tefillah].[9]

The question was asked: What is the rule about interrupting [the Tefillah] to respond. May His great name be blessed?[10] — When R. Dimi came from Palestine, he said that R. Judah and R. Simeon[11] the disciples of R. Johanan say that one interrupts for nothing except 'May His great name be blessed', for even if he is engaged in studying the section of the work of [the Divine] Chariot,[12] he must interrupt [to make this response]. But the law is not in accordance with their view.[13]

R. JUDAH SAYS: HE SAYS THE GRACE BOTH BEFORE AND, AFTER. This would imply that R. Judah was of opinion that a ba'al keri is permitted to [occupy himself] with the words of the Torah.

---

[1] I.e., after having prayed with one congregation, he goes in to another.
[2] Lit., 'the messenger of the congregation'.
[3] The seventeenth benediction, v. P.B. p. 51.
[4] In order that he may be able to bow at this point with the congregation.
[5] Recited in the third benediction. In this also the congregation joins in, v. P.B. p. 45.
[6] Lev. XXII, 32.
[7] Num. XVI, 21.
1.8. The 'congregation' referred to being the ten spies, Joshua and Caleb being excluded.
2.V. Meg. 23b.
[8] If he has commenced his Tefillah he does not interrupt in order to say theSanctification with the congregation or to bow down with them.
[9] In the Kaddish, v. Glos.
[10] I.e., Judah b. Pazzi and Simeon b. Abba.
[11] V. Hag. 11b.
[12] So MS.M. Cur. edd., 'with him'.
[13] Deut. IV, 9.

But has not R. Joshua b. Levi said: How do we know that a ba'al keri is forbidden to study the Torah? Because it says, Make them known unto thy children and thy children's children,[1] and immediately afterwards, The day that thou stoodest [before the Lord thy God in Horeb],[2] implying that just as on that occasion those who had a seminal issue were forbidden,[3] so here too those who have a seminal issue are forbidden? And should you say that R. Judah does not derive lessons from the juxtaposition of texts, [this does not matter] since R. Joseph has said: Even those who do not derive lessons from the juxtaposition of texts in all the rest of the Torah, do so in Deuteronomy; for R. Judah does not derive such lessons in all the rest of the Torah, and in Deuteronomy he does. And how do we know that in all the rest of the Torah he does not derive such lessons? — As it has been taught; Ben 'Azzai says: Thou shalt not suffer a sorceress to live.[4] and it says [immediately afterwards], Whosoever lieth with a beast shall surely be put to death.[5] The two statements were juxtaposed to tell you that just as one that lieth with a beast is put to death by stoning, so a sorceress also is put to death by stoning. Said R. Judah to him: Because the two statements are juxtaposed, are we to take this one out to be stoned? Rather [we learn it as follows]: They that divine by a ghost or a familiar spirit come under the head of sorceress. Why then were they mentioned separately?[6] To serve as a basis for comparison: just as they that divine by a ghost or familiar spirit are to be stoned, so a sorceress is to be stoned. And how do we know that he derives lessons from juxtaposition in Deuteronomy? — As it has been taught: R. Eliezer said, A man may marry a woman who has been raped by his father or seduced by his father, one who has been raped by his son, or one who has been seduced by his son. R. Judah prohibits one who has been raped by his father or seduced by his father. And R. Giddal said with reference to this: What is the reason of R. Judah? Because it is written: A man shall not take his father's wife and shall not uncover his father's skirt;[7] which implies, he shall not uncover the skirt which his father saw. And how do we know that the text is speaking of one raped by his father? — Because just before it are the words, Then the man that lay with her shall give unto the father, etc.![8] — They replied: Yes, in Deuteronomy he does draw such lessons, but this juxtaposition he requires for the other statement of R. Joshua b. Levi. For R. Joshua
b. Levi said: If any man teaches his son Torah, the Scripture accounts it to him as if he had received it from Mount Horeb, as it says, 'And thou shalt make them known unto thy children and thy children's children', and immediately afterwards it is written, 'The day that thou stoodest before the Lord thy God in Horeb.'[9]

We have learnt: A sufferer from gonorrhoea who had an emission, a niddah from whom semen has escaped and a woman who became niddah during sexual intercourse require ritual ablution;[10] R. Judah, however, exempts them.[11] Now R. Judah's exemption extends only to a gonorrhoeic person

---

[1] Ibid. 10.
[2] V. supra p. 124 n. 1.
[3] Ex. XXII, 27.
[4] Ibid. 18.
[5] In Lev. XX, 27. 'A man also … that divineth by a ghost or a familiar spirit shall surely be put to death; they shall stone them with stones'.
[6] Deut. XXIII, 1.
[7] Ibid. XXII, 29. This shows that R. Judah derives lessons from juxtaposed texts in Deuteronomy. How then does he permit a ba'al keri to occupy himself with Torah in view of Deut. IV, 9 and 10?
[8] Ibid. IV, 9 and 10.
[9] In order to be able to read Shema' or other words of the Torah.
[10] V. infra 26a.
[11] I.e., before he experienced the emission.

who had an emission, because ritual ablution in his first condition[1] is useless for him,[2] but an ordinary person who has an emission requires ritual ablution![3] And should you maintain that R. Judah exempts an ordinary ba'al keri also, and the reason why he and the Rabbis joined issue over the gonorrhoeic person was to show how far the Rabbis are prepared to go, then look then at the next clause: 'A woman who became niddah during sexual intercourse requires a ritual ablution'. Whose opinion is here stated? Shall I say it is the Rabbis? Surely this is self-evident! Seeing that a gonorrhoeic person who has an emission, although a ritual ablution is useless in his first condition, was yet required by the Rabbis to take one, how much more so a woman who becomes niddah during sexual intercourse, for whom in her first condition a ritual ablution was efficacious! We must say therefore that it states the opinion of R. Judah, and he meant exemption to apply only to this case.

---

[1] He has to wait seven days before he is clean.
[2] 6Contra his own ruling in our Mishnah.
[3] To cleanse her from the seminal issue that took place before the niddah.

Folio 22a

so that a woman who becomes niddah during sexual intercourse does not require a ritual ablution, but an ordinary ba'al keri does require ritual ablution! — Read [in the Mishnah] not: [R. JUDAH SAYS,] HE SAYS THE BLESSING, but 'He says mentally'. But does R. Judah [in any case] prescribe saying mentally? Has it not been taught: A ba'al keri who has no water for a ritual ablution recites the Shema' without saying a blessing either before or after, and he eats bread and says a blessing after it. He does not, however, say a blessing before it, but says it mentally without uttering it with his lips. So R. Meir. R. Judah says: In either case he utters it with his lips? — Said R. Nahman b. Isaac: R. Judah put it on the same footing as the halachoth of Derek Erez,[1] as it has been taught: 'And thou shalt make them known to thy children and thy children's children', and it is written immediately afterwards, 'The day on which thou didst stand before the Lord thy God in Horeb'. Just as there it was in dread and fear and trembling and quaking, so in this case too[2] it must be in dread and fear and trembling and quaking. On the basis of this they laid down that sufferers from gonorrhoea, lepers, and those who had intercourse with niddoth are permitted to read the Torah, the Prophets and the Hagiographa, and to study the Mishnah, [Midrash][3] the Talmud,[4] halachoth and haggadoth, but a ba'al keri is forbidden.[5] R. Jose said: He may repeat those with which he is familiar, so long as he does not expound the Mishnah. R. Jonathan b. Joseph said: He may expound the Mishnah but he must not expound the Talmud.[6] R. Nathan b. Abishalom says: He may expound the Talmud also, provided only he does not mention the divine names that occur[7] in it. R. Johanan the sandal-maker, the disciple of R. Akiba, said in the name of R. Akiba: He should not enter upon the Midrash at all. (Some read, he should not enter the Beth Ha-midrash at all.) R. Judah says: He may repeat the laws of Derek Erez.[8] Once R. Judah after having had a seminal issue was walking along a river bank, and his disciples said to him, Master repeat to us a section from the laws of Derek Erez, and he went down and bathed and then repeated to them. They said to him: Have you not taught us, Master, 'He may repeat the laws of Derek Erez'? He replied: Although I make concessions to others, I am strict with myself.

It has been taught: R. Judah b. Bathyra used to say: Words of Torah are not susceptible of uncleanness. Once a certain disciple was mumbling over against R. Judah b. Bathyra.[9] He said to him: My son, open thy mouth and let thy words be clear, for words of Torah are not susceptible to uncleanness, as it says, Is not My word like as fire.[10] Just as fire is not susceptible of uncleanness, so words of Torah are not susceptible of uncleanness.

The Master said: He may expound the Mishnah, but he must not expound the Talmud. This supports

---

[1] Lit., 'Good Behaviour', two small tractates which did not enjoy the same authority as the rest of the Mishnah.
[2] Viz., the study of the Torah.
[3] Inserted with MS.M.
[4] So MS.M.; cur. edd. Gemara, v. supra p. 64, n. 9.
[5] Because the seminal issue is a sign of frivolity.
[6] Rashi reads 'Midrash'.
[7] In the Biblical verses which it expounds (Rashi).
[8] V. M.K. 15a.
[9] He had had an issue and was afraid to say the words distinctly.
[10] Jer. XXIII, 29.

R. Ila'i; for R. Ila'i said in the name of R. Aha b. Jacob, who gave it in the name of our Master:[1] The halachah is that he may expound the Mishnah but he must not expound the Talmud. The same difference of opinion is found among Tannaim. 'He may expound the Mishnah but he must not expound the Talmud'. So R. Meir. R. Judah b. Gamaliel says in the name of R. Hanina b. Gamaliel: Both are forbidden. Others report him as having said: Both are permitted. The one who reports 'Both are forbidden' concurs with R. Johanan the sandal-maker; the one who reports, 'both are permitted' concurs with R. Judah b. Bathyra.

R. Nahman b. Isaac said: It has become the custom[2] to follow these three elders, R. Ila'i in the matter of the first shearing,[3] R. Josiah in the matter of mixed kinds, and R. Judah b. Bathyra in the matter of words of Torah. 'R. Ila'i in the matter of the first shearing', as it has been taught: R. Ila'i says: The rule of the first shearing applies only in Palestine. 'R. Josiah in the matter of mixed kinds', as it is written, Thou shalt not sow thy vineyard with two kinds of seeds.[4] R. Josiah says: The law has not been broken until one sows wheat, barley and grape kernels with one throw.[5] 'R. Judah b. Bathyra in the matter of words of Torah,' as it has been taught: R. Judah b. Bathyra says: Words of Torah are not susceptible of uncleanness. When Ze'iri came [from Palestine]. he said: They have abolished the ritual ablution. Some report him to have said: They have abolished the washing of hands. The one who reports 'they have abolished the ritual ablution' concurs with R. Judah b. Bathyra. The one who reports 'they have abolished the washing of hands' is in accord with R. Hisda, who cursed anyone who went looking for water at the hour of prayer.[6]

Our Rabbis taught: A ba'al keri on whom nine kabs[7] of water have been thrown is clean. Nahum a man of Gimzu[8] whispered it to R. Akiba, and R. Akiba whispered it to Ben 'Azzai, and Ben 'Azzai went forth and repeated it to the disciples in public. Two Amoraim in the West differed in regard to this, R. Jose b. Abin and R. Jose b. Zebida. One stated: He repeated it, and one taught, He whispered it. The one who taught 'he repeated it' held that the reason [for the concession] was to prevent neglect of the Torah and of procreation. The one who taught 'he whispered it' thought that the reason was in order that scholars might not always be with their wives like cocks.[9]

R. Jannai said: I have heard of some who are lenient in this matter,[10] and I have heard of some who are strict in it;[11] and if anyone is strict with himself in regard to it, his days and years are prolonged.

R. Joshua b. Levi said: What is the sense of those who bathe in the morning? [He asks], What is the sense! Why, it was he himself who said that a ba'al keri is forbidden [to occupy himself] with the words of the Torah! What he meant is this: What is the sense of bathing in forty se'ahs[12] when one can make shift with nine kabs? What is the sense of going right in when throwing the water over one

---

[1] Rab.
[2] Lit., 'the world is accustomed'.
[3] V. Deut. XVIII, 4.
[4] Deut. XXII, 9.
[5] Wheat and barley being mixed seeds, and grape kernels mixed seeds of thevineyard.
[6] V. supra 15a.
[7] A kab is four logs of twenty-four eggs.
[8] V. Ta'an. 21a.
[9] And therefore he did not want it to be too well known among the scholars.
[10] Of using only nine kabs, or not bathing at all.
[11] Insisting on forty se'ahs.
[12] The minimum quantity of water required for ritual ablution.

is sufficient? R. Hanina said: They put up a very valuable fence by this,[1] as it has been taught: Once a man enticed a woman to commit an offence and she said to him: Vagabond,[2] have you forty se'ahs to bathe in, and he at once desisted. Said R. Huna to the disciples: My masters, why do you make so light of this bathing? Is it because of the cold? You can use the baths! Said R. Hisda to him: Can ablution be performed in hot baths? — He replied: R. Adda b. Ahabah is of the same opinion as you. R. Ze'ira used to sit in a tub of water in the baths and say to his servant, Go and fetch nine kabs and throw over me. R. Hiyya b. Abba said to him: Why, sir, do you take this trouble, seeing that you are sitting in [that quantity of] water? — He replied: The nine kabs must be like the forty se'ahs: just as the forty se'ahs are for immersion and not for throwing, so the nine kabs are for throwing and not for immersion. R. Nahman prepared an ewer holding nine kabs.[3] When R. Dimi came, he reported that R. Akiba and R. Judah Glostera[4] had said: The rule,[5] was laid down only for a sick person who has an emission involuntarily, but for a sick person who has a voluntary emission[6] forty se'ahs [are required]. Said R. Joseph: R. Nahman's ewer was broken.[7] When Rabin came, he said: The thing took place in Usha

---

[1] Insisting on forty se'ahs.

[2] Rekah (Raka) 'empty one', 'good for nothing'.

[3] For the use of the disciples.

[4] According to some, this word means 'locksmith'.

[5] That nine kabs are sufficient.

[6] Lit., 'a sick person who induces it'. I.e., after marital intercourse.

[7] I.e., rendered useless, because in view of his teaching nine kabs can rarely be of effect.

Berakoth 22b

in the anteroom of R. Oshaia. They came and asked R. Assi, and he said to them, This rule was laid down only for a sick person whose emission is voluntary, but a sick person whose emission is involuntary requires nothing at all. Said R. Joseph: R. Nahman's ewer has been repaired again.[1]

Let us see! The dispute between all these Tannaim and Amoraim is as to the ordinance of Ezra. Let us see then what Ezra did ordain! Abaye said: Ezra ordained that a healthy man whose emission is voluntary must immerse in forty se'ahs, and a healthy man whose emission is involuntary must use nine kabs, and the Amoraim came and differed over the sick person.[2] One held that a sick person whose emission is voluntary is on the same footing as a healthy person whose emission is voluntary, and a sick person whose emission is involuntary as a healthy person whose emission is involuntary; while the other held that a sick person whose emission is voluntary is on the same footing as a healthy person whose emission is involuntary and a sick person whose emission is involuntary requires nothing at all. Raba said: Granted that Ezra ordained immersion, did he ordain throwing? Has not a master said: Ezra ordained immersion for persons who have had a seminal emission? Rather, said Raba, Ezra ordained for a healthy person whose emission is voluntary forty se'ahs, and the Rabbis [after Ezra] came and ordained for a healthy person whose emission is involuntary nine kabs. and the [Tannaim and][3] Amoraim came and differed with regard to a sick person,[4] one holding that a sick person whose emission is voluntary is on the same footing as a healthy person whose emission is voluntary and a sick person whose emission is involuntary as a healthy person whose emission is involuntary, while the other held that a healthy person whose emission is voluntary requires forty se'ahs and a sick person whose emission is voluntary is on the same footing as a healthy person whose emission is involuntary and requires nine kabs, while a sick person whose emission is involuntary requires nothing at all. Raba said: The law is that a healthy person whose emission is voluntary and a sick person whose emission is voluntary require forty se'ahs, a healthy person whose emission is involuntary requires nine kabs, and a sick person whose emission is involuntary requires nothing at all.[5]

Our Rabbis taught: A ba'al keri over whom nine kabs of water have been thrown is clean. When is this the case? When it is for himself;[6] but when it is for others,[7] he requires forty se'ahs. R. Judah says: Forty se'ahs in all cases. R. Johanan and R. Joshua b. Levi and R. Eleazar and R. Jose son of R. Hanina [made pronouncements]. One of the first pair and one of the second pair dealt with the first clause of this statement. One said: This statement of yours, 'When is this the case? When it is for himself, but for others he requires forty se'ahs', was meant to apply only to a sick person whose emission is voluntary, but for a sick person whose emission is involuntary nine kabs are enough. The other said: Wherever it is for others, even if he is a sick person whose emission is involuntary, there

---

[1] I.e., the disciples can still make use of it.
[2] Inserted with D.S.
[3] Inserted with MS.M.
[4] Cf. n. 1.
[5] This ruling was previous to, and therefore superseded by, that of R. Nahman, that the law follows R. Judah b. Bathyra.
[6] E.g., if he wants to study.
[7] E.g., if he has to teach.

must be forty se'ahs. One of the first pair and one of the second pair differed as to the second clause of the statement. One said: When R. Judah said that 'forty se'ahs are required in all cases', he was speaking only of water in the ground,[1] but not in vessels. The other said: Even in vessels.

On the view of the one who says 'even in vessels', there is no difficulty, that is why R. Judah taught: 'Forty se'ahs in all cases'. But on the view of the one who says 'in the ground, yes, in vessels, no', what is added by the words 'in all cases'? — They add drawn water.[2]

R. Papa and R. Huna the son of R. Joshua and Raba b. Samuel were taking a meal together. Said R. Papa to them: Allow me to say the grace [on your behalf] because nine kabs of water have been thrown on me. Said Raba b. Samuel to them: We have learnt: When is this the case? When it is for himself; but if it is for others, forty se'ahs are required. Rather let me say the grace, since forty se'ahs have been thrown on me. Said R. Huna to them: Let me say the grace since I have had neither the one nor the other on me.[3] R. Hama bathed on the eve of Passover in order [that he might be qualified] to do duty on behalf of the public,[4] but the law is not as stated by him.[5]

MISHNAH. IF A MAN WAS STANDING SAYING THE TEFILLAH AND HE REMEMBERS THAT HE IS A BA'AL KERI, HE SHOULD NOT BREAK OFF BUT HE SHOULD SHORTEN [THE BENEDICTIONS].[6] IF HE WENT DOWN TO IMMERSE HIMSELF, IF HE IS ABLE TO COME UP AND COVER HIMSELF AND RECITE THE SHEMA' BEFORE THE RISING OF THE SUN, HE SHOULD GO UP AND COVER HIMSELF AND RECITE, BUT IF NOT HE SHOULD COVER HIMSELF WITH THE WATER AND RECITE. HE SHOULD, HOWEVER, NOT COVER HIMSELF EITHER WITH FOUL WATER[7] OR WITH WATER IN WHICH SOMETHING[8] HAS BEEN STEEPED UNTIL HE POURS FRESH WATER INTO IT. HOW FAR SHOULD HE REMOVE HIMSELF FROM IT[9] AND FROM EXCREMENT? FOUR CUBITS.

GEMARA. Our Rabbis taught: If a man was standing saying the Tefillah and he remembered that he was a ba'al keri, he should not break off but shorten the benedictions. If a man was reading the Torah and remembered that he was a ba'al keri, he should not break off and leave it but should go on reading in a mumbling tone. R. Meir said: A ba'al keri is not permitted to read more than three verses in the Torah. Another [Baraitha] taught: If a man was standing saying the Tefillah and he saw excrement in front of him, he should go forward until he has it four cubits behind him. But it has been taught: He should move to the side? — There is no contradiction; one statement speaks of where it is possible for him [to go forward], the other of where it is not possible.[10] If he was praying and he discovered some excrement where he was standing, Rabbah says, even though he has sinned,[11] his prayer is a valid one. Raba demurred to this, citing the text, The sacrifice of the wicked is an abomination?[12] No, said Raba: Since he has sinned, although he said the Tefillah, his prayer is an abomination.

---

[1] E.g., in a cistern, river or well.
[2] I.e., water not directly from a spring.
[3] I.e., I have required neither the one nor the other.
[4] Say grace on their behalf.
[5] That immersion is required to qualify for acting on behalf of others. Or it may mean that the law follows R. Judah b. Bathyra.
[6] I.e., say a shorter form of each one.
[7] I.e., urine, as explained below.
[8] E.g., flax.
[9] I.e., urine, as explained below.
[10] E.g., if there is a river in the way.
[11] I.e., is himself responsible, v. Tosaf.
[12] Prov. XXI, 27.

Our Rabbis taught: If a man was standing saying the Tefillah and water drips over his knees, he should break off until the water stops and then resume his Tefillah. At what point should he resume? — R. Hisda and R. Hamnuna gave different replies. One said that he should go back to the beginning, the other said, to the place where he halted. May we say that the ground of their difference is this,

Folio 23a

that one authority holds that if one stops long enough to finish the whole he goes back to the beginning, while the other holds that he goes back [in any event] to the place where he stopped?[1] Said R. Ashi: In that case the statement should distinguish between whether he stopped [long enough] or did not stop.[2] We must therefore say that both are agreed that if he stopped long enough to finish the whole of it he goes back to the beginning, and here they differ in regard to the case where he did not stop [so long], one holding that the man was unfit[3] [to have commenced his prayers] and hence his prayer is no prayer, while the other holds that the man was [nevertheless] in a fit state [to pray] and his prayer is a valid one.

Our Rabbis taught: If a man needs to consult nature he should not say the Tefillah, and if he does, his prayer is an abomination. R. Zebid — or as some say Rab Judah — said: They meant this to apply only if he is not able to hold himself in, but if he is able to hold himself in, his prayer is a valid one. How much must he be able to hold himself in? — R. Shesheth said: Long enough to go a parasang. Some teach this statement as part of the Baraitha [just quoted], thus: When is this the case [that his prayer is an abomination]? When he cannot hold himself in; but if he can hold himself in, his prayer is valid. And how long must he be able to do so? — R. Zebid said: Long enough for him to walk a parasang.

R. Samuel b. Nahmani said in the name of R. Jonathan: One who needs to ease himself should not say the Tefillah, as it says, Prepare to meet thy God, O Israel.[4] R. Samuel b. Nahmani also said in the name of R. Jonathan: What is the meaning of the verse, Guard thy foot when thou goest to the house of God?[5] Guard thyself so that thou shouldst not sin, and if thou dost sin, bring an offering before Me. And be ready to hearken.[6] Raba said. Be ready to hearken to the words of the wise who, if they sin, bring an offering and repent. It is better than when the fools give![7] Do not be like the fools who sin and bring an offering and do not repent. For they know not to do evil,[8] — if that is the case, they are righteous? — What it means is: Do not be like the fools who sin and bring an offering and do not know whether they bring it for a good action or a bad action. Says the Holy One, blessed be He: They do not distinguish between good and evil, and they bring an offering before Me. R. Ashi, — or, as

---

[1] V. infra 24b.
[2] I.e., the two Rabbis should have stated their views on this case also.
[3] Since he could not contain himself till he finished. Lit., 'rejected'. Cur. edd. add 'and he is unfit', which is omitted in MS.M.
[4] Amos. IV, 12. Interpreted to mean, Put thyself in a fit state to meet etc.
[5] Eccl. IV, 17.
[6] Eccl. IV, 17.
[7] Ibid.
[8] Ibid. This is the literal rendering; E.V. 'for they know not that they do evil'.

some say, R. Hanina b. Papa — said: Guard thy orifices[1] at the time when thou art standing in prayer before Me.

Our Rabbis taught: One who is about to enter a privy should take off his tefillin at a distance of four cubits and then enter. R. Aha son of R. Huna said in the name of R. Shesheth: This was meant to apply only to a regular privy,[2] but if it is made for the occasion, he takes them off and eases himself at once, and when he comes out he goes a distance of four cubits and puts them on, because he has now made it a regular privy. The question was asked, What is the rule about a man going in to a regular privy with his tefillin to make water? Rabina allowed it; R. Adda b. Mattena forbade it. They went and asked Raba and he said to them: It is forbidden, since we are afraid that he may ease himself in them, or, as some report, lest he may break wind in them. Another [Baraitha] taught: One who enters a regular privy takes off his tefillin at a distance of four cubits and puts them in the window on the side of the public way[3] and enters, and when he comes out he goes a distance of four cubits and puts them on. So Beth Shammai. Beth Hillel say: He keeps them in his hand and enters. R. Akiba said: He holds them in his garment and enters. 'In his garment', do you say? Sometimes they may slip out[4] and fall! — Say rather, he holds them in his hand and in his garment, and enters, and he puts them in a hole on the side of the privy, but he should not put them in a hole on the side of the public way, lest they should be taken by passers-by, and he should render himself suspect. For a certain student once left his tefillin in a hole adjoining the public way, and a harlot passed by and took them, and she came to the Beth ha-Midrash and said: See what So-and-so gave me for my hire, and when the student heard it, he went to the top of a roof and threw himself down and killed himself. Thereupon they ordained that a man should hold them in his garment and in his hand and then go in.

The Rabbis taught: Originally they used to leave tefillin in holes on the side of the privy, and mice used to come and take them. They therefore ordained that they should be put in the windows on the side of the public way. Then passers-by came and took them. So they ordained that a man should hold them in his hand and enter. R. Meyasha the son of R. Joshua b. Levi said: The halachah is that he should roll them up like a scroll[5] and keep them in his right hand, opposite his heart. R. Joseph b. Manyumi said in the name of R. Nahman: He must see that not a handbreadth of strap hangs loose from his hand. R. Jacob
b. Aha said in the name of R. Zera: This is the rule only if there is still time left in the day to put them on[6] but if there is no time left in the day, he makes a kind of bag for them of the size of a handbreadth and puts them there.[7] Rabbah b. Bar Hanah said in the name of R. Johanan: In the daytime [when he enters a privy] he rolls them up like a scroll and keeps them in his hand opposite his heart, and for the night he makes a kind of bag for them of the size of a handbreadth, and puts them there. Abaye said: This rule was meant to apply only to a bag which is meant for them, but if the bag is not meant for them, even less than a handbreadth is sufficient. Mar Zutra — or as some say R. Ashi — said: The

---

[1] This is an alternative rendering of the word ragleka (thy foot) which is taken in the same sense as in I Sam. XXIV, 4.

[2] Where there is already excrement.
[3] The privies in Babylon were out in the fields.
[4] V. MS.M.
[5] I.e., wind the straps round them.
[6] It was customary to wear the tefillin the whole of the day and take them off at night-time.
[7] A bag of this size would protect them from uncleanness.

proof is that small vessels[1] protect [the contents from uncleanness] in a tent of the dead.[2]

Rabbah b. Bar Hanah further said: When we were following R. Johanan [as disciples], when he wanted to enter a privy, if he had a book of Aggada, he used to give it to us to hold, but if he was wearing tefillin he did not give them to us, saying, since the Rabbis have permitted them[3]

Berakoth 23b

they will protect me.[4] Raba said: When we were following R. Nahman, if he had a book of Aggada he used to give it to us, but if he was wearing tefillin he did not give them to us, saying, since the Rabbis have permitted them, they will guard me.

Our Rabbis taught: A man should not hold tefillin in his hand or a scroll of the Law in his arm while saying the Tefillah,[5] nor should he make water while wearing them, nor sleep in them, whether a regular sleep or a short snatch. Samuel says: A knife, money, a dish and a loaf of bread are on the same footing as tefillin.[6] Raba said in the name of R. Shesheth: The law is not in accordance with this Baraitha,[7] since it expresses the view of Beth Shammai. For seeing that Beth Hillel declare it permissible in a regular privy [to hold the tefillin] is there any question that they would permit it in an ad hoc privy?

An objection was raised: The things which I have permitted to you in the one place I have forbidden to you in the other. Presumably this refers to tefillin. Now if you say the Baraitha quoted follows Beth Hillel, there is no difficulty. 'I have permitted it to you in the one place'
— the regular privy, 'and I have forbidden it to you in the other' — the ad hoc privy. But if you say it is Beth Shammai, they do not permit anything! — That statement[8] refers to the baring of the handbreadth and two handbreadths, as one [Baraitha] taught: When a man eases himself, he may bare a hand breadth behind and two handbreadths in front, and another taught: a handbreadth behind and in front not at all. Is it not the case that both statements refer to a man, and there is no contradiction, the former referring to easing and the latter to making water? But do you think so? If for making water, why a handbreadth behind? Rather both refer to easing, and there is no contradiction, the one referring to a man and the other to a woman. If that is the case,[9] what of the succeeding statement, 'This is an a fortiori which cannot be rebutted'? What is the point of 'which cannot be rebutted'? This[10] is merely the natural way! We must say therefore that tefillin are referred to [in the Baraitha], and it is a refutation of what Raba said in the name of R. Shesheth. — It is a refutation. Still a difficulty

---

[1] With a tight fitting cover. V. Num. XIX, 15.
[2] Even if they are less than one handbreadth in size.
[3] To hold them to one's hand.
[4] From evil spirits. Var. lec.: we need not trouble (to take them off).
[5] The fear of dropping them will distract his attention.
[6] They also will distract his attention if he is holding them.
[7] That it is forbidden to make water in tefillin.
[8] 'The things I have forbidden to you, etc.'.
[9] If the Baraitha, 'The things which I have permitted to you in the one place' etc. refers to the difference between a man and a woman.
[10] Difference between man and woman.

remains: If it is permissible in a regular privy, how much more so in an ad hoc privy! — What it means is this: In a regular privy where there is no splashing, it is permitted; in an ad hoc privy where there is splashing,[1] it is forbidden. If that is the case, how can you say, 'which cannot be rebutted'? There is an excellent refutation? — What it means is this: This[2] rule is based upon a reason[3] and not upon an argument a fortiori; for if we were to employ here an argument a fortiori,[4] it would be one which could not be rebutted.

Our Rabbis taught: One who wishes to partake [in company] of a regular meal,[5] should walk four cubits ten times or ten cubits four times and ease himself and then go in. R. Isaac said: One who wishes to [partake of] a regular meal should take off his tefillin[6] and then go in. He differs from R. Hiyya; for R. Hiyya said: He places them on his table, and so it is becoming for him. How long does he leave them there? Until the time for grace.[7]

One [Baraitha] taught: A man may tie up his tefillin in his headgear[8] along with his money, while another teaches, He should not so tie them! — There is no contradiction; in the one case he sets it aside for this purpose, in the other he does not set it aside. For R. Hisda said: If a man has [mentally] set aside a cloth to tie up tefillin in, once he has tied up tefillin in it, it is forbidden to tie up in it money; if he has set it aside but not tied up the tefillin in it, or if he has tied them up in it without setting it aside for the purpose, he may tie up money in it. According to Abaye, however, who says that mere setting aside is operative,[9] once he has set it aside, even though he has not tied up tefillin in it, it is forbidden to tie up money, and if he has tied up tefillin in it, if he has set it aside it is forbidden to tie up money, but if he has not set it aside it is not forbidden.

R. Joseph the son of R. Nehunia asked Rab Judah: What is the rule about placing one's tefillin under one's pillow? About putting them under the place of his feet I have no need to ask, because that would be treating them contemptuously. What I do want to know is, what is the rule about putting them under his pillow? — He replied: Thus said Samuel: It is permitted, even if his wife is with him. An objection was raised. A man should not put his tefillin under the place of his feet, because this is treating them contemptuously, but he may place them under his pillow, but if his wife is with him this is forbidden. If, however, there is a place three handbreadths above his head or three handbreadths below,[10] he may put them there. Is not this a refutation of Samuel? It is. Raba said: Although it has been taught that this is a refutation of Samuel, the law follows his opinion. What is the reason?

---

[1] Since it is used for urine only.
[2] To permit in a regular privy and prohibit in an ad hoc one.
[3] The risk of soiling the hand.
[4] Viz., from a regular one to an ad hoc one.
[5] And is doubtful if he can contain himself, and to leave the company would be impolite. (Rashi.)
[6] As it would not be respectful to eat in them.
[7] When he puts them on again.
[8] Aparkesuth, a head-covering which flowed down over the body. Aliter: 'underwear', or 'sheet'.
[9] In the matter of weaving a sheet for a dead body, Sanh. 47b.
[10] Projecting from the bed.

Folio 24a

— Whatever conduces to their safe keeping[1] is of more importance.[2] Where should he put them? R. Jeremiah said: Between the coverlet and the pillow, not opposite to his head. But R. Hiyya taught: He puts them in a turban[3] under his pillow? — It must be in such a way as to make the top of the turban[4] project outside [the pillow]. Bar Kappara used to tie them in the bed-curtain and make them project outside.[5] R. Shesheth the son of R. Idi used to put them on a stool and spread a cloth over them. R. Hamnuna the son of R. Joseph said: Once when I was standing before Raba he said to me: Go and bring me my tefillin, and I found them between the coverlet and the pillow, not just opposite his head, and I knew that it was a day of ablution [for his wife],[6] and I perceived that he had sent me in order to impress upon me a practical lesson.

R. Joseph the son of R. Nehunia inquired of Rab Judah: If two persons are sleeping in one bed, how would it be for one to turn his face away and recite the Shema', and for the other to turn his face away and recite? — He replied: Thus said Samuel: [It is permitted] even if his wife is with him. R. Joseph demurred to this. [You imply, he said] 'His wife', and needless to say anyone else. On the contrary, [we should argue]: His wife is like himself,[7] another is not like himself! An objection was raised: If two persons are sleeping in one bed, one turns his face away and recites the Shema' and the other turns his face away and recites the Shema'. And it was taught in another [place]: If a man is in bed and his children and the members of his household[8] are at his side, he must not recite the Shema' unless there is a garment separating them, but if his children and the members of his household are minors, he may. Now I grant you that if we accept the ruling of R. Joseph there is no difficulty, as we can explain one [statement] to refer to his wife and the other to another person. But if we accept Samuel's view there is a difficulty? — Samuel can reply: And on R. Joseph's view is there no difficulty, seeing that it has been taught: If a man was in bed, and his sons[9] and the members of his household with him,[10] he should not recite the Shema' unless his garments separated them from him? What then must you say? That in R. Joseph's opinion there is a difference of opinion among Tannaim as to his wife. In my opinion also there is a difference among Tannaim.[11]

The Master has said: 'One turns his face away and recites the Shema'. But there is the contact of the buttocks? — This supports the opinion of R. Huna, who said: Contact of the buttocks is not sexual. May we say that it supports the following opinion of R. Huna: A woman may sit and separate her hallah[12] naked, because she can cover her nakedness in the ground[13] but not a man! — Said R.

---

[1] From mice or robbers.
[2] Than preserving them from disrespect.
[3] Which he uses as a bag.
[4] I.e., the side where the cases of the tefillin can be recognized.
[5] I.e., away from the bed.
[6] Which showed that he had slept with her.
[7] Lit., 'like his body'.
[8] I.e., slaves.
[9] BaH. omits this word.
[10] 'Members of the household' must here be understood to include the wife. This is a very unusual use of the expression, and Tosaf. emends, 'If he was in bed and his wife was by his side, etc.'.
[11] As to his wife or another person.
[12] V. Num. XV, 20. A blessing is prescribed for this rite.
[13] Although the posteriors are exposed.

Nahman b. Isaac: It means, if her nakedness was well covered by the ground!

The Master said: 'If his children and the members of his household were minors, it is permitted'. Up to what age? — R. Hisda said: A girl up to three years and one day, a boy up to nine years and one day. Some there are who say: A girl up to eleven years and a day, and a boy up to twelve years and a day; with both of them [it is] up to the time when Thy breasts were fashioned and thy hair was grown.[2] Said R. Kahana to R. Ashi: In the other case[3] Raba said that, although there was a refutation of Samuel, yet the law followed his ruling. What is the ruling here?[4] — He replied to him: Do we weave them all in the same web?[5] Where it has been stated [that the law follows him] it has been stated, and where it has not been stated it has not been stated.

R. Mari said to R. Papa: If a hair protrudes through a man's garment,[6] what is the rule?
— He exclaimed: 'Tis but a hair, a hair!'[7]

R. Isaac said: A handbreadth [exposed] in a [married] woman constitutes sexual incitement.[8] In which way? Shall I say, if one gazes at it? But has not R. Shesheth [already] said: Why did Scripture enumerate the ornaments worn outside the clothes with those worn inside?[9] To tell you that if one gazes at the little finger of a woman, it is as if he gazed at her secret place! — No, It means, in one's own wife, and when he recites the Shema'. R. Hisda said: A woman's leg is a sexual incitement, as it says. Uncover the leg, pass through the rivers,[10] and it says afterwards, Thy nakedness shall be uncovered, yea, thy shame shall be seen.[11] Samuel said: A woman's voice is a sexual incitement, as it says, For sweet is thy voice and thy countenance is comely.[12] R. Shesheth said: A woman's hair is a sexual incitement, as it says, Thy hair is as a flock of goats.[13]

R. Hanina said: I saw Rabbi hang up his tefillin. An objection was raised: If one hangs up his tefillin, his life will be suspended. The Dorshe hamuroth[14] said: And thy life shall hang in doubt before thee:[15] this refers to one who hangs up his tefillin! — This is no difficulty: the one statement refers to hanging by the strap, the other to hanging by the box. Or if you like, I can say that in either case, whether by the strap or by the box, it is forbidden, and when Rabbi hung his up it was in a bag. If so, what does this tell us? — You might think that they must be resting on something like a scroll of the Law. Therefore we are told that this is not necessary.

R. Hanina also said: I saw Rabbi [while Saying the Tefillah] belch and yawn and sneeze and spit

---

[1] So that even the posteriors are covered.
[2] Ezek. XVI, 7.
[3] Of putting the tefillin under the pillow, supra.
[4] In regard to reciting the Shema' in bed.
[5] I.e., adopt all his rulings indiscriminately.
[6] Is it regarded as indecent exposure?
[7] I.e., it does not matter.
[8] Lit. — 'nakedness'.
[9] Among the ornaments taken by the Israelites from the women of Midian (Num. XXXI, 50) was the kumaz (E.V. 'girdles') which the Rabbis supposed to have been worn inside under the garments, while the others were worn outside.
[10] Isa. XLVII, 2.
[11] Ibid. 3.
[12] Cant. II, 14.
[13] Ibid. IV, 1.
[14] Lit., 'Expounders of essentials', a school of early homiletical exegetes; v. Pes. (Sonc. ed.) p. 266, n. 9.
[15] Deut. XXVIII, 66.

Berakoth 24b

and adjust his garment,[1] but he did not pull it over him;[2] and when he belched, he would put his hand to his chin. The following objection was cited: 'One who says the Tefillah so that it can be heard is of the small of faith;[3] he who raises his voice in praying is of the false prophets;[4] he who belches and yawns is of the arrogant; if he sneezes during his prayer it is a bad sign for him — some say, it shows that he is a low fellow; one who spits during his prayer is like one who spits before a king'. Now in regard to belching and yawning there is no difficulty; in the one case it was involuntary, in the other case deliberate. But the sneezing in Rabbi's case does seem to contradict the sneezing in the other? — There is no contradiction between sneezing and sneezing either; in the one case it is above, in the other below.[5] For R. Zera said: This dictum was casually imparted to me in the school of R. Hamnuna, and it is worth all the rest of my learning: If one sneezes in his prayer it is a good sign for him, that as they give him relief below [on earth] so they give him relief above [in heaven]. But there is surely a contradiction between the spitting in the one case and the other? — There is no contradiction between the two cases of spitting either, since it can be done as suggested by Rab Judah. For Rab Judah said: If a man is standing saying the Tefillah, and spittle collects in his mouth, he covers it up in his robe, or, if it is a fine robe, in his scarf.[6] Rabina was once standing behind R. Ashi and he wanted to spit, so he spat out behind him. Said R. Ashi to him: Does not the Master accept the dictum of Rab Judah, that he covers it up in his scarf? He replied: I am rather squeamish.

'One who says the Tefillah so that it can be heard is of the small of faith'. R. Huna said: This was meant to apply only if he is able to concentrate his attention when speaking in a whisper, but if he cannot concentrate his attention when speaking in a whisper, it is allowed. And this is the case only when he is praying alone, but if he is with the congregation [he must not do so because] he may disturb the congregation.

R. Abba kept away from Rab Judah because he wanted to go up to Eretz Israel; for Rab Judah said, Whoever goes up from Babylon to Eretz Israel transgresses a positive precept, since it says, They shall be carried to Babylon and there shall they be, until the day that I remember them, saith the Lord.[7] He said: I will go and listen to what he is saying from outside[8] the Academy.[9] So he went and found the Tanna[10] reciting in the presence of Rab Judah: If a man was standing saying the Tefillah and he broke wind, he waits until the odour passes off and begins praying again. Some say: If he was standing saying the Tefillah and he wanted to break wind, he steps back four cubits and breaks wind and waits till the wind passes off and resumes his prayer, saying, Sovereign of the Universe, Thou hast formed us with various hollows and various vents. Well dost Thou know our shame and confusion, and that our latter end is worms and maggots! and he begins again from the place where

---

[1] Aliter: 'feel his garment', to remove insects.
[2] Because he imagines that otherwise God will not hear him.
[3] Cf. I Kings XVIII, 28.
[4] Euphemism.
[5] Aliter: underwear. V. supra p. 142, n. 1.
[6] Jer. XXVII, 22; v. Keth. 110b.
[7] V. Rashi.
[8] Lit., 'House of Meeting'.
[9] V. Glos. s.v. (b).
[10] Omitting 'to him' of cur. edd. V. BaH.

he stopped. He said:[1] Had I come only to hear this, it would have been worth my while.

Our Rabbis taught: If a man is sleeping in his garment and cannot put out his head on account of the cold, he folds his garment round his neck to make a partition[2] and recites the Shema'. Some say, round his heart. But how can the first Tanna [say thus]? His heart is surely in sight of the sexual organ! — He was of opinion that if the heart is in sight of the sexual organ, it is still permissible [to say the Shema'].

R. Huna said in the name of R. Johanan: If a man is walking in a dirty alley way, he puts his hand over his mouth and recites the Shema'. Said R. Hisda to him: By God, had R. Johanan said this to me with his own mouth, I would not have listened to him.[3] (Some report: Rabbah b. Bar Hanah said in the name of R. Joshua b. Levi: If a man is walking in a dirty alley way, he puts his hand over his mouth and recites the Shema'. Said R. Hisda to him: By God, had R. Joshua b. Levi said this to me with his own mouth, I would not have listened to him.) But could R. Huna have said this, seeing that R. Huna has said: A scholar is forbidden to stand in a place of filth, because he must not stand still without meditating on the Torah? — There is no contradiction: one statement speaks of standing, the other of walking. But could R. Johanan have said this, seeing that Rabbah b. Bar Hanah has said in the name of R. Johanan: In every place it is permitted to meditate on words of Torah except in the bath and in a privy? And should you reply, here also one statement speaks of standing and one of walking, can that be so, seeing that R. Abbahu was once walking behind R. Johanan and reciting the Shema', and when he came to a dirty alley way, he stopped; and [when they emerged] he said to R. Johanan, Where shall I commence again, and he replied: If you have stopped long enough to finish it, go back to the beginning? — What he meant to say to him was this: I do not hold [that you need have stopped]. But taking your view, that it was necessary, if you have stopped long enough to finish it, go back to the beginning. There is a teaching in accordance with R. Huna, and there is a teaching in accordance with R. Hisda. It has been taught in accordance with R. Huna: If one was walking in a dirty alley way, he puts his hand over his mouth and recites the Shema'. It has been taught in accordance with R. Hisda: If one was walking in a dirty alley way, he should not recite the Shema'; and what is more, if he was reciting and came to one, he should stop. Suppose he does not stop, what happens? R. Meyasha the grandson of R. Joshua b. Levi said: Of him Scripture says: Wherefore I gave them also statutes that were not good and ordinances whereby they should not live.[4] R. Assi said: Woe unto them that draw iniquity with cords of vanity.[5] R. Adda b. Ahabah said: Because he hath despised the word of the Lord.[6] And if he stops, what is his reward? — R. Abbahu said: Of him Scripture says: Through this word[7] ye shall prolong your days.

R. Huna said: If a man's garment is girded round his waist, he may recite the Shema'. It has been taught similarly: If his garment, whether of cloth or of leather or of sacking, is girded round his waist, he may recite the Shema',

---

[1] Between his face and the lower part of his body, if it was bare.

[2] I.e., he would not permit it.

[3] Ezek. XX, 25.

[4] Isa. V, 18.

[5] Num. XV, 31.

[6] E.V. 'thing'.

18. I.e., through being careful with regard to the utterance of the Torah. Deut. XXXII, 47.

[7] And hangs down from there, leaving his upper part uncovered.

Folio 25a

but the Tefillah he may not say until he covers his chest.[1] R. Huna further said: If a man forgot and entered a privy while wearing his tefillin, he places his hand over them till he finishes. 'Till he finishes'? How can this be assumed? Rather it is as R. Nahman b. Isaac said: Until he finishes the first discharge. But why should he not stop at once and get up?
— On account of the dictum of R. Simeon b. Gamaliel, as it has been taught: R. Simeon b. Gamaliel says: Keeping back the faeces brings on dropsy, keeping back urine brings on jaundice.

It has been stated: If there is some excrement on a man's flesh or if his hand is inside a privy,[2] R. Huna says that he is permitted to say the Shema', while R. Hisda says he is forbidden to say the Shema'. Raba said: What is the reason of R. Huna? — Because it is written, Let everything that hath breath praise the Lord.[3] R. Hisda says that it is forbidden to say the Shema'. What is the reason of R. Hisda? — Because it is written, All my bones shall say, Lord, who is like unto Thee.[4]

It has been stated: [If there is] an evil smell [proceeding] from some tangible source, R. Huna says that one removes [from the source of the smell] four cubits and recites the Shema'; R. Hisda says: He removes four cubits from the place where the smell ceases, and then recites the Shema'. It has been taught in accordance with R. Hisda: A man should not recite the Shema' either in front of human excrement or of the excrement of dogs or the excrement of pigs or the excrement of fowls or the filth of a dungheap which is giving off an evil smell. If, however, it is in a place ten handbreadths above him or ten handbreadths beneath him, he can sit at the side of it and recite the Shema'; otherwise he removes himself out of sight of it; and similarly for the Tefillah. [If there is] an evil smell [proceeding] from a tangible object, he removes four cubits from [the source of] the smell and recites the Shema'. Raba said: The law is not as stated in this Baraitha,[5] but it has been taught in the following: A man should not recite the Shema' in front either of human excrement or excrement of pigs or excrement of dogs when he puts skins in them.[6] They asked R. Shesheth: What of an evil smell which has no tangible source?[7] He said to them: Come and see these mats in the school house; some sleep on them[8] while others study. This, however, applies only to study,[9] but not to the Shema'. And even as regards study it applies only if the smell is made by another but not if it is made by himself.

It has been stated: If manure is being carried past one, Abaye says it is permitted to recite the Shema',[10] while Raba says it is forbidden to recite the Shema'. Said Abaye: Whence do I derive my opinion? Because we have learnt: If an unclean person is standing under a tree and a clean one passes by, he becomes unclean. If a clean person is standing under a tree and an unclean one passes by, he

---

[1] Because in the Tefillah he is like one standing before a king.
[2] I.e., he was standing outside with his hand inside the window.
[3] Ps. CL. 6. As much as to say, only the mouth and other breathing organs areconcerned with praise.
[4] Ibid. XXXV, 10.
[5] With reference to the excrement of dogs etc.
[6] The excrement of pigs and dogs was used for tanning.
[7] I.e., from the breaking of wind.
[8] And break wind.
[9] Rashi: lit., 'words of Torah'. He cannot study if he has to leave the school-house.
[10] And one need not break off.

remains clean, but if he [the unclean person] stands still, he becomes unclean. And similarly with a stone smitten with leprosy.[1] To which Raba can reply: In that case the deciding factor is the permanence,[2] as it is written, He shall dwell alone, without the camp shall his dwelling be.[3] But in this case, the All-Merciful has said, Therefore shall thy camp be holy,[4] and this condition is not fulfilled.

R. Papa said: The snout of a pig is like manure being carried past. This is obvious?[5] — It required to be stated, to show that it applies even if the animal is coming up from the river.

Rab Judah said: If there is a doubt about [the presence of] excrement, it is forbidden; if there is a doubt about urine, it is permitted. Some there are who say: Rab Judah said: If there is a doubt about excrement in the house, it is permitted,[6] in the dungheap it is forbidden. If there is a doubt about urine, it is permitted even in the dungheap. He adopted the view of R. Hamnuna; for R. Hamnuna said: The Torah forbade the recital of the Shema' only in face of the Stream [of urine]. And this is as taught by R. Jonathan; for R. Jonathan contrasted two texts. It is written: Thou shalt have a place also without the camp, whither thou shalt go forth abroad,[7] and it is also written, And thou shalt have a paddle … thou shalt cover that which cometh from thee.[8] How are these two statements to be reconciled? The one speaks of easing, the other of urine. This proves that urine was not forbidden by the Torah save in face of the stream only, and once it has fallen to the ground it is permitted, and it is the Rabbis who imposed a further prohibition, and when they did so, it was only in a case of certainty but not in a case of doubt. And in a case of certainty, how long is it forbidden? — Rab Judah said in the name of Samuel: So long as it moistens [the ground]. And so said Rabbah b. Hanah in the name of R. Johanan: So long as it moistens [the ground]. So too said 'Ulla: So long as it moistens [the ground]. Ganiba said in the name of Rab: So long as the mark is discernible. Said R. Joseph: May Ganiba be forgiven by his Master![9] Seeing that even of excrement Rab Judah has said in the name of Rab that as soon as it has dried on top it is permitted, is there any question about urine! Said Abaye to him: What reason have you for relying on this statement? Rely rather on this one which was made by Rabbah b. Bar Hanah in the name of Rab: Even if excrement is as a potsherd, it is forbidden [to recite the Shema' near it]. What is the test of its being as dry as a potsherd? — So long as one can throw it [on to the ground] and it does not break, [it is not so dry]. Some say: So long as one can roll it without breaking it.[10] Rabina said: I was once standing before Rab Judah of Difti, and he saw dung and said to me, Look if the top has dried, or not. Some say that what he said to him was this: Look if it has formed cracks. What is the ultimate decision?[11] It has been stated: When dung is like a potsherd, Amemar says it is forbidden and Mar Zutra says it is permitted [to say the Shema' near it]. Raba said: The law is that if dung is as dry as a potsherd it is forbidden, and in the case of urine as long as it is moistening [the ground]. An objection was raised: As long as urine is moistening [the ground] it is forbidden; if it has been absorbed [in the ground] or has dried up,[12] it is permitted. Now

---

[1] V. Kid. 33b. Neg. XIII, 7.
[2] I.e., the standing still of the unclean object.
[3] Lev. XIII, 46. This implies that the leper spreads uncleanness only if he remains in one place.
[4] Deut. XXIII, 15.
[5] That a pig's snout must always contain filth.
[6] Because excrement is not usually found in the house.
[7] Deut. XXIII, 13.
[8] Ibid. 14. Here 'covering' is mentioned.
[9] For reporting Rab wrongly.
[10] This is a more severe test.
[11] With regard to urine.
[12] On stones.

are we not to understand that 'absorption' here is compared to 'drying', and that just as after drying there is no mark left, so after absorption there must be no mark left, and that if there is still a mark it is forbidden, even though it no longer moistens? — But adopting your line of argument, let us see the first clause: 'As long [as urine] is moistening [the ground] it is forbidden', which implies that if there is a mark it is permitted.[1] — The fact is from this [Baraitha] we cannot infer [either way].

Shall we say that there is a difference of Tannaim [on this point]? [For it was taught:] If Urine has been poured out of a vessel, it is forbidden to recite the Shema' in front of that vessel. As for urine itself, if it has been absorbed in the ground it is permitted, if it has not been absorbed it is forbidden. R. Jose says: So long as it moistens the ground. Now what is meant by the 'absorbed' and 'not absorbed' mentioned by the first Tanna? Shall I say that 'absorbed' means that it does not moisten and that 'not absorbed' means that it still moistens, and R. Jose came and said that so long as it moistens it is forbidden, but if only the mark is discernible it is permitted? This is the same as the first Tanna says! We must say then that 'absorbed' means that the mark is not discernible and 'not absorbed' means that the mark is discernible, and R. Jose came and said that so long as it moistens it is forbidden, but if only the mark is discernible it is permitted? — No; both agree that so long as it moistens it is forbidden, and if only the mark is discernible it is permitted,

---

[1] Which is apparently in contradiction to the implication of the second clause.

Berakoth 25b

and here the difference between them is whether it must be wet enough to moisten something else?[1] (1)

IF HE WENT DOWN [TO IMMERSE HIMSELF], IF HE IS ABLE TO COME UP etc. May we say that the Mishnah teaches anonymously the same as R. Eliezer, who said that [the Shema' may be recited] until the rising of the sun?[2](2) You may even say that it is the same as R. Joshua,[3](3) and perhaps [the Mishnah] means this to apply to the wathikin, of whom R. Johanan said: The wathikin used to finish the recital with the rising of the sun.[4](4)

IF NOT, HE SHOULD COVER HIMSELF WITH WATER AND RECITE. But in this case his heart sees the sexual organs? — R. Eleazar said? — or as some also say, R. Aha b. Abba b. Aha said in the name of our teacher:[5](5) They meant this to apply to turbid water which is like solid earth, in order that his heart should not see his sexual organ.

Our Rabbis taught: If the water is clear, he may sit in it up to his neck and say the Shema'; some say, he should stir it up with his foot. On the ruling of the first Tanna, his heart sees his nakedness? — He held that if his heart sees the sexual organ it is permitted. But his heel sees his nakedness?[6](6) — He held that if his heel sees his nakedness it is permitted. It has been stated: If his heel sees his nakedness it is permitted [to read the Shema']; if it touches, Abaye says it is forbidden and Raba says it is permitted. This is the way in which R. Zebid taught this passage. R. Hinnena the son of R. Ika thus: If it touches, all agree that it is forbidden. If it sees, Abaye says it is forbidden and Raba says it is permitted; the Torah was not given to the ministering angels.[7](7) The law is that if it touches it is forbidden, but if it sees it is permitted.

Raba said: If one sees excrement through a glass,[8](8) he may recite the Shema' in face of it; if he sees nakedness through a glass, he must not recite the Shema' in face of it. 'If he sees excrement through a glass he may recite the Shema' in face of it', because [the permission or otherwise] in the case of excrement depends on whether it is covered.[9](9) 'If he sees nakedness through a glass it is forbidden to recite in face of it', because the All-Merciful said, that He see no unseemly thing in thee,[10](10) and here it is seen.

Abaye said: A little excrement may be neutralized with spittle; to which Raba added: It must be thick spittle. Raba said: If the excrement is in a hole, he may put his shoe over it and recite the Shema'. Mar the son of Rabina inquired: What is the rule if there is some dung sticking to his shoe? — This was

---

[1] Only in this case does the first Tanna forbid, but R. Jose is more stringent.
[2] V. supra 9b. And so the halachah is according to him.
[3] Who says that the time is up to the third hour, v. supra 9b.
[4] V. supra p. 49 n. 4.
[5] Rab.
[6] Since his knees are bent under him.
[7] As much as to say, too much must not be expected of human beings.
[8] Lit., 'a lantern' or 'anything transparent'.
[9] I.e., there is a partition between.
[10] Deut. XXIII, 15.

left unanswered.

Rab Judah said: It is forbidden to recite the Shema' in face of a naked heathen. Why do you say a heathen? The same applies even to an Israelite! — In the case of an Israelite there is no question to him that it is forbidden, but this had to be stated in the case of a heathen. For you might have thought that since Scripture says of them, Whose flesh is as the flesh of asses and whose issue is as the issue of horses,[1] therefore he is just like a mere ass. Hence we are told that their flesh also is called 'nakedness', as it says. And they saw not their father's nakedness.[2]

HE SHOULD NOT COVER HIMSELF EITHER WITH FOUL WATER OR WITH WATER IN WHICH SOMETHING HAS BEEN STEEPED UNTIL HE POURS WATER INTO IT. How much water must he go on pouring?[3] — What it means is this: He must not cover himself with foul water or with water used for steeping at all, nor [may he recite in face of] urine until he pours water into it.

Our Rabbis taught: How much water must he pour into it? A few drops [are enough]. R. Zakkai says: A rebi'ith.[4] R. Nahman said: Where they differ is when the water is poured in last, but if the water was there first, a few drops are sufficient.[5] R. Joseph, however, said: Where they differ is if the water was there first; but if the water was poured in afterwards both agree that there must be a rebi'ith. R. Joseph once said to his attendant: Bring me a rebi'ith of water, as prescribed by R. Zakkai.

Our Rabbis taught: It is forbidden to recite the Shema' in face of a chamber pot for excrement or urine even if there is nothing in it, or in face of urine itself [if it is in another vessel] until he pours water into it. How much must he pour? A few drops. R. Zakkai says: A Rebi'ith, whether it is in front of the bed or behind the bed.[6] R. Simeon b. Gamaliel says: If it is behind the bed, he may recite the Shema', if it is in front of the bed he may not recite, but he must remove four cubits and then recite. R. Simeon b. Eleazar says: Even if the room is a hundred cubits long he should not say the Shema' in it until he takes it away or places it under the bed. The question was asked: How did he [R. Simeon b. Gamaliel] mean? That if it is behind the bed he may recite at once and that if it is in front of the bed he must remove four cubits and then recite? Or did he perhaps mean it this way, that if it is behind the bed he removes to a distance of four cubits, but if it is in front of the bed he does not recite at al? — Come and hear, for it has been taught: R. Simeon b. Eleazar says: If it is behind the bed he may recite at once, if it is in front of the bed he removes four cubits. R. Simeon b. Gamaliel Says: Even in a room a hundred cubits long he should not recite until he takes it out or puts it under the bed. Our question has been answered, but there is a contradiction between the Baraitha? — Reverse the [names in] the second one. What reason have you for reversing the second one? Why not reverse the first? — Who is recorded to have said that the whole room is like four cubits? R. Simeon b. Eleazar.[7]

R. Joseph said: I asked R. Huna as follows: There is no question in my mind that a bed with legs less than three handbreadths long is reckoned as being attached to the soil.[8] What of one with legs four,

---

[1] Ezek. XXIII, 20.
[2] Gen. IX, 23 — of the sons of Noah.
[3] As much as to say, how can he hope to neutralize such a quantity?
[4] A quarter of a log.
[5] Because each drop of urine becomes neutralized as it falls in.
[6] I.e., whether the bed is between him and it or not.
[7] The source (If this dictum is not known (Rashi).
[8] Labud, v. Glos. And therefore anything placed under it is like being buried in the ground, (e.g., a chamber pot) and the Shema' may be recited.

five, six, seven, eight or nine handbreadths long? — He replied: I do not know. About ten I was certain and did not need to ask. Said Abaye: You did well not to ask; ten handbreadths constitutes a different domain.[1] Raba said: The law is that less than three is regarded as attached to the soil, ten constitutes a different domain, from ten to three is what R. Joseph asked R. Huna about and he did not decide it for him. Rab said: The halachah follows R. Simeon b. Eleazar. So too said Bali in the name of R. Jacob the son of the daughter of Samuel:[2] The halachah follows R. Simeon b. Eleazar. Raba, however, said: The halachah does not follow R. Simeon b. Eleazar.

R. Ahai contracted a match for his son with the house of R. Isaac b. Samuel b. Marta. He brought him into the bridal chamber but it was not a success.[3] He went in after him to look, and saw a scroll of the Torah lying there. He said to them:[4] Had I not come now, you would have endangered the life of my son, for it has been taught: It is forbidden to have marital intercourse in a room in which there is a scroll of the Law or tefillin, until they are taken out or placed in one receptacle inside of another. Abaye said: This rule applies only to a receptacle which is not meant for them, but if the receptacles are specially meant for them, ten are no better than one. Raba said: A covering

---

[1] And therefore it is no covering.
[2] V. supra p. 94. n. 4.
[3] Euphemism.
[4] To the relatives of his daughter-in-law.

Folio 26a

over a chest is like a receptacle within a receptacle.

R. Joshua b. Levi said: For a scroll of the Law it is necessary to make a partition of ten [handbreadths].[1] Mar Zutra was visiting R. Ashi, and he saw that in the place where Mar the son of R. Ashi slept there was a scroll of the Law and a partition of ten [handbreadths] was made for it. He said to him: Which authority are you following? R. Joshua b. Levi, is it not? I presume that R. Joshua b. Levi meant this to apply only where one had not another room, but your honour has another room! He replied: I had not thought of it.

HOW FAR SHOULD HE REMOVE FROM IT AND FROM EXCREMENT? FOUR CUBITS. Raba said in the name of R. Sehora reporting Rab: This was meant only if he leaves it behind him, but if he keeps it in front of him he must remove completely out of sight. The same rule applies to Tefillah. Is that so? Has not Rafram b. Papa said in the name of R. Hisda: A man can stand facing a privy [four cubits away] and say the Tefillah? What is referred to here?[2] A privy in which there is no excrement. Is that so? Has not R. Joseph b. Hanina said: When they spoke of a privy, they meant, even if there is no excrement in it, and when they spoke of a bath,[3] they meant even if there is no one in it! But in fact what is referred to here?[4] A new one. But surely this is the very thing about which Rabina asked a question: If a place has been set aside for a privy [but not yet used], what is the rule? Does setting aside count or does it not count?[5] — What Rabina wanted to know was whether one might stand in it to pray therein, but as to facing it [he was] not [in doubt].[6] Raba said: These Persian privies, although there is excrement in them, are counted as closed in.[7]

---

[1] To permit intercourse in the same room.
[2] In the ruling of R. Hisda.
[3] As being a forbidden place for meditating on words of Torah.
[4] In the ruling of R. Hisda.
[5] Shab. 10a; Ned. 7a.
[6] That it was permitted at a distance of four cubits.
[7] They were sloping and the excrement rolled into a deep hole out of sight.

MISHNAH. A GONORRHOEIC PERSON WHO HAS AN EMISSION AND A NIDDAH FROM WHOM SEMEN ESCAPES AND A WOMAN WHO BECOMES NIDDAH DURING INTERCOURSE REQUIRE A RITUAL BATH; R. JUDAH, HOWEVER EXEMPTS THEM![1]

GEMARA. The question was raised: What is R. Judah's opinion about a ba'al keri who has become gonorrhoeic? Are we to say that the case in which R. Judah exempted was that of a gonorrhoeic patient who had a seminal issue, because his first condition precludes him from ablution,[2] but he does not exempt a ba'al keri who becomes gonorrhoeic because in his first condition he does require ablution,[3] or are we to say that there is no difference? — Come and hear: A WOMAN WHO BECOMES NIDDAH DURING INTERCOURSE REQUIRES A RITUAL BATH: R. JUDAH, HOWEVER, EXEMPTS HER. Now a woman who becomes niddah during intercourse is on the same footing as a ba'al keri who becomes gonorrhoeic, and R. Judah exempts her. This proves [that there is no difference].

R. Hiyya taught expressly: A ba'al keri who has become gonorrhoeic requires ablution; R. Judah, however, exempts him.

---

[1] V. supra, p. 129, n. 4.
[2] A gonorrhoeic patient has to wait seven days.
1.10. Before being able to study the Torah, according to the ordinance of Ezra, supra. p.
2.134.
[3] Minhah, v. Glos.

CHAPTER IV

MISHNAH. THE MORNING TEFILLAH [CAN BE SAID] UNTIL MIDDAY; R. JUDAH SAYS TILL THE FOURTH HOUR. THE AFTERNOON PRAYER[1] [CAN BE SAID] TILL EVENING; R. JUDAH SAYS, UNTIL THE MIDDLE OF THE AFTERNOON.[2] THE EVENING PRAYER HAS NO FIXED LIMIT.[3] THE TIME FOR THE ADDITIONAL PRAYERS[4] IS THE WHOLE OF THE DAY; R. JUDAH SAYS, TILL THE SEVENTH HOUR.

GEMARA. [TILL MIDDAY]. This was contrasted with the following: The proper time for it [the Shema'] is at the rising of the sun, so that ge'ullah should be followed immediately by Tefillah, with the result that he would say the Tefillah in the day time![5] — That was taught in reference only to the wathikin; for R. Johanan said: The wathikin used to conclude it [the Shema'] as the sun rose.[6] And may other people delay till midday, but no longer? Has not R. Mari the son of R. Huna the son of R. Jeremiah b. Abba said in the name of R. Johanan: If a man erred and did not say the evening Tefillah, he says it twice in the morning. [If he erred] in the morning, he says it twice in the afternoon? — He may go on praying the whole day. But up to midday he is given the reward of saying the Tefillah in its proper time; thereafter he is given the reward of saying Tefillah, but not of saying Tefillah in its proper time.

The question was raised: If a man erred and did not say the afternoon Tefillah, should he say it twice in the evening? Should you argue from the fact that if he erred in the evening he prays twice in the morning, [I may reply that] this is because it is all one day, as it is written, And there was evening and there was morning, one day;[7] but in this case, prayer being in the place of sacrifice,[8] since the day has passed the sacrifice lapses. Or should we rather say that since prayer is supplication for mercy, a man may go on praying as long as he likes? — Come and hear: For R. Huna b. Judah said in the name of R. Isaac reporting R. Johanan: If a man erred and did not say the afternoon Tefillah, he says it twice in the evening, and we do not apply here the principle that if the day has passed the offering lapses. An objection was raised: That which is crooked cannot be made straight, and that which is wanting cannot be numbered.[9] 'That which is crooked cannot be made straight'; this applies to one who omitted the Shema' of the evening or the Shema' of the morning or the Tefillah of the evening or the Tefillah of the morning. 'And that which is wanting cannot be numbered': this applies to one whose comrades formed a group to perform a religious act and he was not included with them. — R. Isaac said in the name of
R. Johanan: With what case are we dealing here? With one who omitted deliberately.
R. Ashi said: The proof of this is that it says 'omitted', and it does not say, 'erred'. This proves it.

---

[1] This is explained in the Gemara.
[2] V. infra in the Gemara.
[3] Musaf, v. Glos.
[4] I.e., just after day-break.
[5] V. supra 9b.
[6] Gen. I, 5.
[7] V. infra 26b.
[8] Eccl. I, 25.
[9] In the teaching cited.

Berakoth 26b

Our Rabbis taught: If a man erred and did not say the afternoon prayer on the eve of Sabbath, he says the [Sabbath] Tefillah[1] twice on the night of the Sabbath. If he erred and did not say the afternoon Tefillah on Sabbath, he says the [weekday] Tefillah twice on the outgoing of the Sabbath; he says habdalah[2] in the first but not in the second;[3] and if he said habdalah in the second and not in the first, the second is counted to him, the first is not counted to him. This is equivalent, is it not, to saying that since he did not say habdalah in the first, it is as if he had not said the Tefillah and we make him say it again. To this was opposed the following: If one forgot and did not mention the miracle of rain[4] in the benediction for the resurrection of the dead[5] and prayed for rain in the benediction of the years,[6] he is turned back; if he forgot habdalah in 'who graciously grants knowledge',[7] he is not turned back, because he can say it over wine! — This is indeed a difficulty.

It has been stated: R. Jose son of R. Hanina said: The Tefillahs were instituted by the Patriarchs. R. Joshua b. Levi says: The Tefillahs were instituted[8] to replace the daily sacrifices. It has been taught in accordance with R. Jose b. Hanina, and it has been taught in accordance with R. Joshua b. Levi. It has been taught in accordance with R. Jose b. Hanina: Abraham instituted the morning Tefillah, as it says, And Abraham got up early in the morning to the place where he had stood,[9] and 'standing' means only prayer, as it says, Then stood up Phineas and prayed.[10] Isaac instituted the afternoon Tefillah, as it says, And Isaac went out to meditate in the field at eventide,[11] and 'meditation' means only prayer, as it says, A prayer of the afflicted when he fainteth and poureth out his meditation[12] before the Lord.[13] Jacob instituted the evening prayer, as it says, And he lighted [wa-yifga'] upon the place,[14] and 'pegi'ah' means only prayer, as it says, Therefore pray not thou for this people neither lift up prayer nor cry for them, neither make intercession to [tifga'] Me.[15] It has been taught also in accordance with R. Joshua b. Levi: Why did they say that the morning Tefillah could be said till midday? Because the regular morning sacrifice could be brought up to midday. R. Judah, however, says that it may be said up to the fourth hour because the regular morning sacrifice may be brought up to the fourth hour. And why did they say that the afternoon Tefillah can be said up to the evening? Because the regular afternoon offering can be brought up to the evening. R. Judah, however, says that it can be said only up to the middle[16] of the afternoon, because the evening offering could only be brought up to the middle of the afternoon. And why did they say that for the evening Tefillah there is

---

[1] V. Glosses. Vilna Gaon.
[2] V. P.B. p. 46.
[3] Because the one which is said in compensation is always said second.
[4] Lit., 'the (divine) power (manifested) in rain'.
[5] The second benediction.
[6] The ninth benediction.
[7] The fourth benediction.
[8] By the Men of the Great Synagogue.
[9] Gen. XIX, 27.
[10] Ps. CVI, 30.
[11] Gen. XXIV, 63.
[12] E.V. 'complaint'.
[13] Ps. CII, 1.
[14] Gen. XXVIII, 11.
[15] Jer. VII, 16.
[16] The precise time meant is discussed infra.

no limit? Because the limbs[1] and the fat[2] which were not consumed [on the altar] by the evening could be brought for the whole of the night. And why did they say that the additional Tefillahs[3] could be said during the whole of the day? Because the additional offering could be brought during the whole of the day. R. Judah, however, said that it can be said only up to the seventh hour, because the additional offering can be brought up to the seventh hour. Which is the 'greater afternoon'? From six hours and a half onwards.[4] And which is the 'small afternoon'? From nine hours and onwards.[5] The question was raised: Did R. Judah refer to the middle of the former afternoon-tide or the middle of the latter afternoon-tide?[6] Come and hear: for it has been taught: R. Judah said: They referred to the middle of the latter afternoon-tide, which is eleven hours less a quarter.[7] Shall we say that this is a refutation of R. Jose b. Hanina?[8] R. Jose b. Hanina can answer: I can still maintain that the Patriarchs instituted the Tefillahs, but the Rabbis found a basis for them in the offerings.

For if you do not assume this,[9] who according to R. Jose b. Hanina instituted the additional Tefillah? He must hold therefore that the Patriarchs instituted the Tefillahs and the Rabbis found a basis for them in the offerings.[10]

R. JUDAH SAYS: TILL THE FOURTH HOUR. It was asked: Is the point mentioned itself included in the UNTIL or is it not included?[11] — Come and hear: R. JUDAH SAYS, UNTIL THE MIDDLE OF THE AFTERNOON. If you say that the point mentioned is included in the UNTIL, then there is no difficulty; this is where the difference lies between

R. Judah and the Rabbis.[12] O But if you say that the point mentioned is not included,[13] then R. Judah says the same thing as the

---

[1] Of the burnt-offerings.
[2] Of the other offerings
[3] Said on Sabbaths, New Moons, and holy days.
[4] From 12.30 p.m. to 6 p.m. taking the day from 6 a.m. to 6 p.m.
[5] From 3.30 onwards.
[6] I.e., does he in his statement in the Mishnah mean midway between 12.30 and 6 or between 3.30 and 6?
[7] Viz., midway between 9 1/2 hours and 12.
[8] According to him it was the Patriarchs who instituted the prayers, and the time of the sacrifice should have no bearing on the time of the recital of the prayers.
[9] That R. Jose admits that the Rabbis based the Tefillah on the offerings.
[10] And accordingly added a musaf tefillah to those instituted by the Patriarchs, and for the same reason they made the time of the prayers to be determined by the time of the sacrifices.
[11] I.e., does he mean the beginning or the end of the fourth hour?
[12] Assuming that R. Judah meant the middle of the latter afternoontide, i.e., eleven hours less a quarter.
[13] So that 'until' means until the end of the point fixed by him.

Folio 27a

Rabbis? — You conclude then that the point mentioned is not included in the UNTIL? Look now at the next clause: THE TIME FOR THE ADDITIONAL PRAYERS IS THE WHOLE DAY; R. JUDAH SAYS, TILL SEVEN HOURS, and it has been taught: If a man had two Tefillahs to say, one for musaf[1] and one for minhah,[2] he says first the minhah prayer and afterwards the musaf one, because the former is daily and the latter is not daily.

R. Judah. however, says: He says the musaf one and afterwards the minhah one, because the [time for] the former [soon] lapses, while the [time for] the latter does not [so soon] lapse.[3] Now if you say that the point mentioned is included in the UNTIL there is no difficulty: on this supposition you can find a time which is appropriate to both of the Tefillahs.[4] But if you say that the point mentioned is not included in the UNTIL where can you find a time which is appropriate to both the Tefillahs?[5] As soon as the time for minhah has arrived, the time for musaf has passed! — What then? You say that the point mentioned is included in the UNTIL? Then there is the [afore-mentioned] difficulty of the first clause — what difference is there between R. Judah and the Rabbis? — Do you think that this MIDDLE OF THE AFTERNOON mentioned by R. Judah means the second half? It means the first half, and what he meant is this: When does the first half [of the second part of the afternoon] end and the second half begin? At the end of eleven hours less a quarter.

R. Nahman said: We also have learnt: R. Judah b. Baba testified five things — that they instruct a girl-minor to refuse,[6] that a woman may remarry on the evidence of one witness [that her husband is dead],[7] that a cock was stoned in Jerusalem because it killed a human being,[8] that wine forty days old was poured as a drink-offering on the altar,[9] and that the morning daily offering was brought at four hours.[10] This proves, does it not, that the point mentioned is included in the UNTIL? It does. R. Kahana said: The halachah follows R. Jose because we have learnt in the Select Tractate[11] as taught by him.

'And concerning the regular daily offering that it was brought at four hours'. Who is the authority for what we have learnt: And as the sun waxed hot it melted:[12] this was at four hours. You say at four hours; or is it not so, but at six hours? When it says 'in the heat of the day',[13] here we have the

---

[1] V. Glos.
[2] V. Glos.
[3] Musaf can be said up to seven hours and minhah up to eleven hours less a quarter.
[4] Viz., the second half of the seventh hour.
[5] Because when R. Judah says that the time for musaf is 'till the seventh hour', he must exclude the whole of the seventh hour itself.
[6] If a girl-minor who has lost her father is betrothed by her mother, when she becomes mature she can refuse to continue to be bound to her husband, and on some occasions the Beth din instruct her to refuse. V. Glos. s.v. mi'un; Yeb. 109a.
[7] V. Yeb. 122a.
[8] It pierced the skull of a child.
[9] Being no longer 'new wine', v. 'Ed. VI, 1.
[10] As R. Judah says; which shows that he included the 'four hours' in the 'until'.
[11] Behirta (selected). Eduyyoth is so called because all its statements are accepted as halachah; v. Introduction to 'Ed. (Sonc. ed.).
[12] Ex. XVI, 21.
[13] Gen. XVIII, 1. Here the word 'day' is used, implying that it was hot everywhere, and not only in the sun, v.

expression for six hours. What then am I to make of 'as the sun waxed hot it melted'? At four hours. Whose opinion does this represent? Apparently neither
R. Judah's nor the Rabbis'. For if we go by R. Judah, up to four hours also is still morning;[1] if we go by the Rabbis, up to six hours is also still morning! — If you like I can say it represents the opinion of R. Judah. and if you like of the Rabbis. 'If you like I can say it represents the opinion of the Rabbis': Scripture says, morning by morning,[2] thus dividing the morning into two.[3] 'If you like I can say R. Judah': this extra 'morning' indicates that they began [gathering] an hour beforehand.[4] At any rate all agree that 'as the sun waxed hot it melted' refers to four hours. How does the text imply this? R. Aha b. Jacob said: The text says, As the sun waxed hot it melted. Which is the hour when the sun is hot and the shade is cool? You must say, at four hours.

THE AFTERNOON TEFILLAH TILL EVENING. R. Hisda said to R. Isaac: In the other case [of the morning offering] R. Kahana said that the halachah follows R. Judah because we have learnt in the Select Tractate as [taught] by him. What is the decision in this case?
— He was silent, and gave him no answer at all. Said R. Hisda: Let us see for ourselves. Seeing that Rab says the Sabbath Tefillah on the eve of Sabbath while it is still day, we conclude that the halachah follows R. Judah![5] — On the contrary, from the fact that R. Huna and the Rabbis did not pray till night time, we conclude that the halachah does no follow R. Judah! Seeing then that it has not been stated definitely that the law follows either one or the other, if one follows the one he is right and if one follows the other he is right. Rab was once at the house of Genibah and he said the Sabbath Tefillah on the eve of Sabbath, and R. Jeremiah b. Abba was praying behind Rab and Rab finished but did not interrupt the prayer of R. Jeremiah.[6] Three things are to be learnt from this. One is that a man may say the Sabbath Tefillah on the eve of Sabbath. The second is that a disciple may pray behind his master. The third is that it is forbidden to pass in front of one praying. But is that so? Did not R. Ammi and R. Assi use to pass? — R. Ammi and R. Assi used to pass outside a four cubit limit. But how could R. Jeremiah act thus, seeing that Rab Judah has said in the name of Rab: A man should never pray

---

infra.

[1] It says that the Israelites gathered the manna every morning; why then had they stopped at this hour if it was still morning?
[2] Ex. loc. cit. Lit., 'in the morning, in the morning'.
[3] And the Israelites gathered in the first 'morning'.
[4] Thus finishing in the third hour of the day.
[5] That after the middle of the afternoon-tide, the afternoon Tefillah can no longer be said, and evening begins.
[6] By passing in front of him to resume his seat.

Berakoth 27b

either next to this master[1] or behind his master?[2] And it has been taught: R. Eleazar says: One who prays behind his master, and one who gives [the ordinary] greeting to his master[3] and one who returns a greeting to his master[4] and one who joins issue with [the teaching of] the Academy of his master and one who says something which he has not heard from his master causes the Divine Presence to depart from Israel? — R. Jeremiah b. Abba is different, because he was a disciple-colleague; and that is why R. Jeremiah b. Abba said to Rab: Have you laid aside,[5] and he replied: Yes, I have; and he did not say to him, Has the Master laid aside. But had he laid aside? Has not R. Abin related that once Rab said the Sabbath Tefillah on the eve of Sabbath and he went into the bath[6] and came out and taught us our section, while it was not yet dark? — Raba said: He went in merely to perspire, and it was before the prohibition had been issued.[7] But still, is this the rule?[8] Did not Abaye allow R. Dimi b. Levai to fumigate some baskets?[9] — In that case there was a mistake.[10] But can [such] a mistake be rectified? Has not Abidan said: Once [on Sabbath] the sky became overcast with clouds and the congregation thought that is was night-time and they went into the synagogue and said the prayers for the termination of Sabbath, and then the clouds scattered and the sun came out and they came and asked Rabbi, and he said to them, Since they prayed, they have prayed?[11] — A congregation is different, since we avoid troubling them [as far as possible].[12]

R. Hiyya b. Abin said: Rab used to say the Sabbath Tefillah on the eve of Sabbath;[13] R. Josiah said the Tefillah of the outgoing of Sabbath on Sabbath. When Rab said the Sabbath Tefillah on the eve of Sabbath, did he say sanctification over wine or not? — Come and hear: for R. Nahman said in the name of Samuel: A man may say the Tefillah of Sabbath on the eve of Sabbath, and say sanctification over wine; and the law is as stated by him. R. Josiah used to say the end-of-Sabbath Tefillah while it was yet Sabbath. Did he say habdalah over wine or did he not say habdalah over wine? — Come and hear: for Rab Judah said in the name of Samuel: A man may say the end-of-Sabbath Tefillah while it is yet Sabbath and say habdalah over wine. R. Zera said in the name of R. Assi reporting R. Eleazar who had it from R. Hanina in the name of Rab: At the side of this pillar R. Ishmael son of R. Jose said the Sabbath Tefillah on the eve of Sabbath. When 'Ulla came he reported that it was at the side of a palm tree and not at the side of a pillar, and that it was not R. Ishmael son of R. Jose but R. Eleazar son of R. Jose, and that it was not the Sabbath Tefillah on the eve of Sabbath but the end-of-Sabbath Tefillah on Sabbath.

---

[1] Because he seems to put himself on a level with him.
[2] This also is a sign of pride. Or perhaps, because he seems to be bowing down to him (Tosaf.).
[3] I.e., he says, 'Peace upon thee' simply instead of 'Pace upon thee, my master'.
[4] Omitted by Alfasi and Asheri.
[5] Have you laid aside all work, since you said the Sabbath Tefillah so early? Lit., 'have you made the distinction' (sc. between weekdays and Sabbath)?
[6] An act forbidden on the Sabbath.
[7] Against bathing and perspiring on Sabbath, v. Shab. 40a.
[8] That work may not be done after saying the Sabbath prayer early on Sabbath eve.
[9] After saying the Sabbath prayer.
[10] It was a dark afternoon, and he said the Sabbath prayer thinking that Sabbath had already commenced.
[11] And since the prayer need not be repeated, work in the case of Sabbath eve ought to be forbidden!
[12] To repeat the Tefillah.
[13] Before evening set in.

THE EVENING PRAYER HAS NO FIXED LIMIT. What is the meaning of HAS NO FIXED LIMIT? Shall I say it means that if a man wants he can say the Tefillah any time in the night? Then let it state, 'The time for the evening Tefillah is the 'whole night'! — But what in fact is the meaning of HAS NO FIXED LIMIT? It is equivalent to saying, The evening Tefillah is optional. For Rab Judah said in the name of Samuel: With regard to the evening Tefillah, Rabban Gamaliel says it is compulsory, whereas R. Joshua says it is optional. Abaye says: The halachah is as stated by the one who says it is compulsory; Raba says the halachah follows the one who says it is optional.

It is related that a certain disciple came before R. Joshua and asked him, Is the evening Tefillah compulsory or optional? He replied: It is optional. He then presented himself before Rabban Gamaliel and asked him: Is the evening Tefillah compulsory or optional? He replied: It is compulsory. But, he said, did not R. Joshua tell me that it is optional? He said: Wait till the champions[1] enter the Beth ha-Midrash. When the champions came in, someone rose and inquired, Is the evening Tefillah compulsory or optional? Rabban Gamaliel replied: It is compulsory. Said Rabban Gamaliel to the Sages: Is there anyone who disputes this? R. Joshua replied to him: No. He said to him: Did they not report you to me as saying that it is optional? He then went on: Joshua, stand up and let them testify against you! R. Joshua stood up and said: Were I alive and he [the witness] dead, the living could contradict the dead. But now that he is alive and I am alive, how can the living contradict the living?[2] Rabban Gamaliel remained sitting and expounding and R. Joshua remained standing, until all the people there began to shout and say to Huzpith the turgeman,[3] Stop! and he stopped. They then said: How long is he [Rabban Gamaliel] to go on insulting him [R. Joshua]? On New Year last year he insulted him;[4] he insulted him in the matter of the firstborn in the affair of R. Zadok;[5] now he insults him again! Come, let us depose him! Whom shall we appoint instead? We can hardly appoint R. Joshua, because he is one of the parties involved. We can hardly appoint R. Akiba because perhaps Rabban Gamaliel will bring a curse on him because he has no ancestral merit. Let us then appoint R. Eleazar b. Azariah, who is wise and rich and the tenth in descent from Ezra. He is wise, so that if anyone puts a question to him he will be able to answer it. He is rich, so that if occasion arises for paying court[6] to Caesar he will be able to do so. He is tenth in descent from Ezra, so that he has ancestral merit and he [Rabban Gamaliel] cannot bring a curse on him. They went and said to him: Will your honour consent to become head of the Academy? He replied: I will go and consult the members of my family. He went and consulted his wife. She said to him:

---

[1] Lit., 'masters of bucklers', 'shield-bearers', i.e., great scholars. The Rabbis often applied warlike terms to halachic discussion.
[2] I.e., how can I deny that I said this?
[3] Lit., 'interpreter', the man who expounded the ideas of the teacher to the public. The more usual later name is Amora.
[4] By telling him to appear before him on the Day of Atonement with his staff and wallet. V. R.H. 25a.
[5] V. Bek. 36a.
[6] Lit., 'serve'.

Folio 28a

Perhaps they will depose you later on. He replied to her: [There is a proverb:] Let a man use a cup of honour[1] for one day even if it be broken the next. She said to him: You have no white hair. He was eighteen years old that day, and a miracle was wrought for him and eighteen rows of hair [on his beard] turned white. That is why R. Eleazar b. Azariah said: Behold I am about seventy years old,[2] and he did not say [simply] seventy years old. A Tanna taught: On that day the doorkeeper was removed and permission was given to the disciples to enter. For Rabban Gamaliel had issued a proclamation [saying]. No disciple whose character does not correspond to his exterior[3] may enter the Beth ha-Midrash. On that day many stools[4] were added. R. Johanan said: There is a difference of opinion on this matter between Abba Joseph b. Dosethai and the Rabbis: one [authority] says that four hundred stools were added, and the other says seven hundred. Rabban Gamaliel became alarmed and said: Perhaps, God forbid, I withheld Torah from Israel![5] He was shown in his dream white casks full of ashes.[6] This, however, really meant nothing; he was only shown this to appease him.[7]

A Tanna taught: Eduyyoth[8] was formulated on that day — and wherever the expression 'on that day' is used, it refers to that day — and there was no halachah about which any doubt existed in the Beth ha-Midrash which was not fully elucidated. Rabban Gamaliel also did not absent himself from the Beth ha-Midrash a single hour, as we have learnt: On that day Judah, an Ammonite proselyte, came before them in the Beth ha-Midrash. He said to them: Am I permitted to enter the assembly?[9] R. Joshua said to him: You are permitted to enter the congregation. Said Rabban Gamaliel to him: Is it not already laid down, At Ammonite or a Moabite shall not enter into the assembly of the Lord?[10] R. Joshua replied to him: Do Ammon and Moab still reside in their original homes? Sennacherib king of Assyria long ago went up and mixed up all the nations, as it says, I have removed the bounds of the peoples and have robbed their treasures and have brought down as one mighty their inhabitants;[11] and whatever strays [from a group] is assumed to belong to the larger section of the group.[12] Said Rabban Gamaliel to him: But has it not been said: But afterward I will bring back the captivity of the children of Ammon, saith the Lord,[13] so that they have already returned? To which R. Joshua replied: And has it not been said, And I will turn the captivity of My people Israel,[14] and they have not yet returned? Forthwith they permitted him to enter the congregation. Rabban Gamaliel thereupon said: This being

---

[1] I.e., one used on state occasions. Aliter: 'a cup of filigree work'.
[2] V. supra p. 72 n. 7.
[3] Lit., 'whose inside is not as his outside'; a common Talmudic expression.
[4] Or 'benches'.
[5] By keeping out so many disciples.
[6] Signifying that those he kept out were in fact not genuine.
[7] I.e., they were in fact genuine.
[8] Lit., 'testimonies' not necessarily the Tractate Eduyyoth which we now have.
[9] I.e., marry a Jewess.
[10] Deut. XXIII, 4.
[11] Isa. X, 13.
[12] E.g., if there are nine shops in a street selling kasher meat and one selling trefa, and we find a piece of meat in the street, we presume that it came from one of the kasher shops, v. Keth. 15a. So here, we presume that this man came from one of the other nations.
[13] Jer. XLIX, 6.
[14] Amos IX, 24.

the case,[1] I will go and apologize to R. Joshua. When he reached his house he saw that the walls were black. He said to him: From the walls of your house it is apparent that you are a charcoal-burner.[2] He replied: Alas for the generation of which you are the leader, seeing that you know nothing of the troubles of the scholars, their struggles to support and sustain themselves! He said to him: I apologize.[3] forgive me. He paid no attention to him. Do it, he said, out of respect for my father. He then became reconciled to him. They said: Who will go and tell the Rabbis? A certain fuller said to them: I will go. R. Joshua sent a message to the Beth hamidrash saying: Let him who is accustomed to wear the robe wear it;[4] shall he who is not accustomed to wear the robe[5] say to him who is accustomed to wear it, Take off your robe and I will put it on? Said R. Akiba to the Rabbis: Lock the doors so that the servants of Rabban Gamaliel should not come and upset the Rabbis.[6] Said R. Joshua: I had better get up and go to them. He came and knocked at the door. He said to them: Let the sprinkler son of a sprinkler[7] sprinkle; shall he who is neither a sprinkler nor the son of a sprinkler say to a sprinkler son of a sprinkler, Your water is cave water[8] and your ashes are oven ashes?[9] Said R. Akiba to him: R. Joshua, you have received your apology, have we done anything except out of regard for your honour? Tomorrow morning you and I will wait on him.[10] They said: How shall we do? Shall we depose him [R. Eleazar b. Azariah]? We have a rule that we may raise an object to a higher grade of sanctity but must not degrade it to a lower.[11] If we let one Master preach on one Sabbath and one on the next, this will cause jealousy. Let therefore Rabban Gamaliel preach three Sabbaths and R. Eleazar b. Azariah one Sabbath. And it is in reference to this that a Master said: 'Whose Sabbath was it? It was the Sabbath of R. Eleazar b. Azariah'.[12] And that disciple[13] was R. Simeon b. Yohai.

THE TIME FOR THE ADDITIONAL PRAYER IS THE WHOLE DAY. R. Johanan said: And he is [nevertheless] called a transgressor.[14]

Our Rabbis taught: If a man had two Tefillahs to say, one for minhah and one for musaf, he says the one for minhah, and afterwards he says the one for musaf. because the one is daily[15] and the other is not daily. R. Judah says: He says the musaf one first and then he says the minhah one; the former is an obligation that will soon lapse[16] while the other is an obligation that will not lapse. R. Johanan said: The halachah is that he says the minhah Tefillah first and then the musaf one. When R. Zera was tired from studying, he used to go and sit by the door of the school of R. Nathan b. Tobi. He said

---

[1] Since he is held in such high respect.
[2] Aliter 'smith'.
[3] Lit., 'I am humbled to thee'.
[4] I.e., let Rabban Gamaliel be restored to the presidency.
[5] I.e., R. Eleazar b. Azariah.
[6] The Rabbis did not want Rabban Gamaliel to be restored, being afraid of his autocratic disposition.
[7] I.e., a priest, son of a priest, sprinkle the water of purification. The reference is again to Rabban Gamaliel who had an hereditary claim to the presidency.
[8] And not living water as required, v. Num. XIX, 27.
[9] And not from the Red Heifer.
[10] I.e., on R. Eleazar b. Azariah. Lit., 'we will rise early to his door'.
[11] V. e.g. Yoma 22b.
[12] Hag. 3a.
[13] Who asked the question about the evening Tefillah.
[14] If he delays too much.
[15] Lit., 'continual', 'regular'.
[16] Its time being limited, in the view of R. Judah, until the seventh hour.

to himself: When the Rabbis pass by, I will rise before them and earn a reward.[1] R. Nathan b. Tobi came out. He said to him: Who enunciated a halachah in the Beth ha-Midrash? He replied: Thus said R. Johanan: The halachah does not follow R. Judah who said that a man first says the musaf Tefillah and then the minhah one. He said to him: Did R. Johanan say it? — He replied, Yes.[2] He repeated it after him forty times. He said to him: Is this the one [and only] thing you have learnt [from him][3] or it is a new thing to you?[4] He replied: It is a new thing to me, because I was not certain [whether it was not the dictum] of R. Joshua b. Levi.

R. Joshua b. Levi said: If one says the musaf Tefillah after seven hours, then according to R. Judah the Scripture says of him, I will gather them that are destroyed [nuge][5] because of the appointed season, who are of thee.[6] How do you know that the word 'nuge' here implies destruction? It is as rendered by R. Joseph [in his Targum]:[7] Destruction comes upon the enemies of Israel[8] because they put off till late the times of the appointed seasons[9] in Jerusalem.

R. Eleazar said: If one says the morning Tefillah after four hours, then according to R. Judah the Scripture says of him, 'I will gather them that sorrow because of the appointed season, who are of thee'. How do we know that this word nuge implies sorrow? Because it is written, My soul melteth away for heaviness [tugah].[10] R. Nahman b. Isaac said: We learn it from here: Her virgins are afflicted [nugoth] and she herself is in bitterness.

---

[1] In the next world.
[2] Var. lec. (v. D.S.): 'Who enunciated a halachah etc.'? He replied, R. Johanan. He said to him, What was it. He replied, A man may say first etc.'.
[3] Sc. R. Johanan.
[4] That you set so much store by it.
[5] E.V. 'Them that sorrow for'.
[6] Zeph. III, 28.
1.37. To R. Joseph is ascribed the Targum on the prophets, v. Graetz, Geschichte, IV, 2.326.
[7] Euphemism.
[8] I.e., the festival prayers.
[9] Ps. CXIX, 28.
[10] Lam. I, 4.

Berakoth 28b

R. 'Awia was once ill and did not go to hear the lecture of R. Joseph.[1] On the next day when he came Abaye tried to appease R. Joseph. He said to him [R. 'Awia]: Why did your honour not come to the lecture yesterday? He replied: I felt weak and was not able. He said to him: Why did you not take some food and come? He replied: Does not your honour hold with the dictum of R. Huna? For R. Huna said: It is forbidden to a man to taste anything until he has said the musaf Tefillah. He said to him: Your honour ought to have said the musaf Tefillah privately and taken something and come. He replied: Does not your honour hold with what R. Johanan has laid down, that it is forbidden for a man to say his Tefillah before the congregation says it? He said to him: Has it not been said in regard to this: This refers to when he is with the congregation? And the law is neither as stated by R. Huna nor by R. Joshua b. Levi. 'It is not as stated by R. Huna', namely in what we have just said.[2] 'It is not as stated by R. Joshua b. Levi', namely, in what R. Joshua b. Levi said: When the time for the minhah Tefillah arrives it is forbidden to a man to taste anything until he has said the minhah Tefillah.

MISHNAH. R. NEHUNIA B. HA-KANEH USED TO SAY A PRAYER AS HE ENTERED THE BETH HA-MIDRASH AND AS HE LEFT IT — A SHORT PRAYER. THEY SAID TO HIM: WHAT SORT OF PRAYER IS THIS? HE REPLIED: WHEN I ENTER I PRAY THAT NO OFFENCE SHOULD OCCUR THROUGH ME,[3] AND WHEN I LEAVE I EXPRESS THANKS FOR MY LOT.

GEMARA. Our Rabbis taught: On entering what does a man[4] say? 'May it be Thy will, O Lord my God, that no offence may occur through me, and that I may not err in a matter of halachah and that my colleagues may rejoice in me[5] and that I may not call unclean clean or clean unclean, and that my colleagues may not err in a matter of halachah and that I may rejoice in them'. On his leaving what does he say? 'I give thanks to Thee, O Lord my God, that Thou hast set my portion with those who sit in the Beth ha-Midrash and Thou hast not set my portion with those who sit in [street] corners,[6] for I rise early and they rise early, but I rise early for words of Torah and they rise early for frivolous talk; I labour and they labour, but I labour and receive a reward and they labour and do not receive a reward; I run and they run, but I run to the life of the future world and they run to the pit of destruction.

Our Rabbis taught: When R. Eliezer fell ill, his disciples went in to visit him. They said to him: Master, teach us the paths of life so that we may through them win the life of the future world. He said to them: Be solicitous for the honour of your colleagues, and keep your children from

---

[1] R. Joseph was the head of the school at Pumbeditha and he used to lecture every Sabbath morning before the musaf prayer.
[2] That he must not eat anything before saying musaf.
[3] E.g., by giving a wrong decision.
[4] Lit., 'he say'; referring perhaps to R. Nehunia.
[5] Rashi translates: so that my colleagues may rejoice over me, i.e., over my discomfiture, and so bring sin upon themselves; and similarly in the next clause.
[6] Rashi explains this to mean shopkeepers or ignorant people. For an alternative rendering v. Sanh., Sonc. ed., p. 6, n. 4.

meditation,[1] and set them between the knees of scholars, and when you pray know before whom you are standing and in this way you will win the future world.

When Rabban Johanan ben Zakkai fell ill, his disciples went in to visit him. When he saw them he began to weep. His disciples said to him: Lamp of Israel, pillar of the right hand,[2] mighty hammer! Wherefore weepest thou? He replied: If I were being taken today before a human king who is here today and tomorrow in the grave, whose anger if he is angry with me does not last for ever, who if he imprisons me does not imprison me for ever and who if he puts me to death does not put me to everlasting death, and whom I can persuade with words and bribe with money, even so I would weep. Now that I am being taken before the supreme King of Kings, the Holy One, blessed be He, who lives and endures for ever and ever, whose anger, if He is angry with me, is an everlasting anger, who if He imprisons me imprisons me for ever, who if He puts me to death puts me to death for ever, and whom I cannot persuade with words or bribe with money — nay more, when there are two ways before me, one leading to Paradise and the other to Gehinnom, and I do not know by which I shall be taken, shall I not weep? They said to him: Master, bless us. He said to them: May it be [God's] will that the fear of heaven shall be upon you like the fear of flesh and blood. His disciples said to him: Is that all?[3] He said to them: If only [you can attain this]! You can see [how important this is], for when a man wants to commit a transgression, he says, I hope no man will see me.[4] At the moment of his departure he said to them: Remove the vessels so that they shall not become unclean, and prepare a throne for Hezekiah the king of Judah who is coming.[5]

MISHNAH. RABBAN GAMALIEL SAYS: EVERY DAY A MAN SHOULD SAY THE EIGHTEEN BENEDICTIONS. R. JOSHUA SAYS: AN ABBREVIATED EIGHTEEN.[6] R. AKIBA SAYS: IF HE KNOWS IT FLUENTLY HE SAYS THE ORIGINAL EIGHTEEN, AND IF NOT AN ABBREVIATED EIGHTEEN. R. ELIEZER SAYS: IF A MAN MAKES HIS PRAYERS A FIXED TASK, IT IS NOT A [GENUINE] SUPPLICATION. R. JOSHUA SAYS: IF ONE IS TRAVELLING IN A DANGEROUS PLACE, HE SAYS A SHORT PRAYER, SAYING, SAVE, O LORD, THY PEOPLE THE REMNANT OF ISRAEL; IN EVERY TIME OF CRISIS[7] MAY THEIR REQUIREMENTS NOT BE LOST SIGHT OF BY THEE. BLESSED ART THOU, O LORD, WHO HEARKENEST TO PRAYER. IF HE IS RIDING ON AN ASS HE DISMOUNTS AND PRAYS. IF HE IS UNABLE TO DISMOUNT HE SHOULD TURN HIS FACE [TOWARDS JERUSALEM]; AND IF HE CANNOT TURN HIS FACE HE SHOULD CONCENTRATE HIS THOUGHTS ON THE HOLY OF HOLIES. IF HE IS TRAVELLING IN A SHIP OR ON A RAFT,[8] HE SHOULD CONCENTRATE HIS THOUGHTS ON THE HOLY OF HOLIES.

GEMARA. To what do these eighteen benedictions correspond? R. Hillel the son of Samuel b. Nahmani said: To the eighteen times that David mentioned the Divine Name in the Psalm, Ascribe

---

[1] Rashi explains this to mean too much reading of Scripture, or alternatively, childish talk. Others explain it as philosophic speculation.
[2] The reference is to the two pillars in the Temple. V. I Kings VII, 21.
[3] Should not the fear of God be more than that?
[4] And therefore if the fear of God is no more than this, it will keep him from many sins.
[5] Sc. to accompany me into the next world. Perhaps because he, like Hezekiah, had acted mightily for the spread of Torah; v. Sanh. 94b.
[6] Lit., 'like the eighteen'. V. infra in the Gemara.
[7] Lit., 'section of the crossing', i.e., transition from one condition to another.
[8] Aliter: in prison.

unto the Lord, O ye sons of might.[1] R. Joseph said: To the eighteen times the Divine Name is mentioned in the Shema'. R. Tanhum said in the name of R. Joshua b. Levi: To the eighteen vertebrae in the spinal column.

R. Tanhum also said in the name of R. Joshua b. Levi: In saying the Tefillah one should bow down [at the appropriate places] until all the vertebrae in the spinal column are loosened. 'Ulla says: Until an issar[2] of flesh is visible opposite his heart.[3] R. Hanina said: If he simply bows his head, he need do no more. Said Raba: This is only if it hurts him [to stoop] and he shows that he would like to bow down.

These eighteen are really nineteen? — R. Levi said: The benediction relating to the Minim[4] was instituted in Jabneh.[5] To what was it meant to correspond? — R. Levi said: On the view of R. Hillel the son of R. Samuel b. Nahmani,[6] to The God of Glory thundereth;[7] on the view of R. Joseph, to the word 'One'[8] in the Shema'; on the view of R. Tanhum quoting R. Joshua b. Levi, to the little vertebrae in the spinal column.

Our Rabbis taught: Simeon ha-Pakuli[9] arranged the eighteen benedictions in order before Rabban Gamaliel in Jabneh. Said Rabban Gamaliel to the Sages:[10] Can any one among you frame a benediction relating to the Minim?[11] Samuel the Lesser arose and composed it. The next year[12] he forgot it

---

[1] Ps. XXIX.
[2] A coin, v. Glos.
[3] I.e., till the flesh bulges.
[4] V. Glos. The reading 'Sadducees' in our edd. is a censor's correction.
[5] After the rest.
[6] This is a marginal correction of the reading in the text, R. Levi son of R. Samuel b. Nahmani said: R. Hillel etc.
[7] Ps. XXIX, 3. The Hebrew for God here is El.
[8] Which is also considered a Divine Name.
[9] Possibly this word means 'cotton seller'. On this passage. cf. Meg. 17.
[10] On a subsequent occasion.
[11] V. n. 3.
[12] Apparently this benediction was at that time not recited daily as now, but on special annual occasions.

Folio 29a

and he tried for two or three hours to recall it, and they did not remove him.[1] Why did they not remove him seeing that Rab Judah has said in the name of Rab: If a reader made a mistake in any of the other benedictions, they do not remove him, but if in the benediction of the Minim, he is removed, because we suspect him of being a Min? — Samuel the Lesser is different, because he composed it. But is there not a fear that he may have recanted? — Abaye said: We have a tradition that a good man does not become bad. But does he not? It is not written, But when the righteous turneth away from his righteousness and committeth iniquity?[2] — Such a man was originally wicked, but one who was originally righteous does not do so. But is that so? Have we not learnt: Believe not in thyself until the day of thy death?[3] For lo, Johanan the High Priest officiated as High Priest for eighty years and in the end he became a Min? Abaye said: Johanan[4] is the same as Jannai.[5] Raba said: Johanan and Jannai are different; Jannai was originally wicked and Johanan was originally righteous. On Abaye's view there is no difficulty, but on Raba's view there is a difficulty? — Raba can reply: For one who was originally righteous it is also possible to become a renegade. If that is the case, why did they not remove him?

— Samuel the Lesser is different, because he had already commenced to say it [the benediction]. For Rab Judah said in the name of Rab — or as some say. R. Joshua b. Levi: This applies only if he has not commenced to say it, but if he has commenced, he is allowed to finish.

To what do the seven blessings said on Sabbath[6] correspond? — R. Halefta b. Saul said: To the seven voices mentioned by David [commencing with] 'on the waters'.[7] To what do the nine said on New Year [Musaf Tefillah] correspond?[8] Isaac from Kartignin[9] said: To the nine times that Hannah mentioned the Divine Name in her prayer.[10] For a Master has said: On New Year Sarah, Rachel and Hannah were visited.[11] To what do the twenty-four said on a last day correspond?[12] R. Helbo said: To the twenty-four times that Solomon used the expression 'prayer' etc. on the occasion when he brought the ark into the Holy of Holies.[13] If that is so, then let us say them every day? — When did Solomon say them? On a day of supplication;[14] We also say them on a day of supplication.

R. JOSHUA SAYS: AN ABBREVIATED EIGHTEEN. What is meant by 'AN ABBREVIATED EIGHTEEN'? Rab said: An abbreviated form of each blessing; Samuel said: Give us discernment, O Lord, to know Thy ways, and circumcise our heart to fear Thee, and forgive us so that we may be

---

[1] From his post as reader.
[2] Ezek. XVIII, 24.
[3] Ab. II, 4.
[4] The Hasmonean king, John Hyrcanus, is meant.
[5] Alexander Jannaeus who was always hostile to the Pharisees, and who massacred Pharisaic Sages. Cf. Kid., Sonc. ed., p. 332. n. 22.
[6] In the Tefillah, instead of the eighteen on week-days. V. P.B. 136-142.
[7] Ps. XXIX, 3.
[8] V. P.B p. 239-242.
[9] Carthage or Carthagena in Spain.
[10] I Sam. II, 1-10.
[11] V. R.H. 11a.
[12] Ta'an. II, 3, where six additional blessings to be said on fast days are mentioned.
[13] I Kings VIII, 23-53.
[14] Because the gates would not open. V. M.K. 9a.

redeemed, and keep us far from our sufferings, and fatten us in the pastures of Thy land, and gather our dispersions from the four corners of the earth, and let them who err from Thy prescriptions be punished,[1] and lift up Thy hand against the wicked, and let the righteous rejoice in the building of Thy city and the establishment of the temple and in the exalting of the horn of David Thy servant and the preparation of a light for the son of Jesse Thy Messiah; before we call mayest Thou answer; blessed art Thou, O Lord, who hearkenest to prayer.[2] Abaye cursed anyone who prayed 'Give us discernment'.[3] R. Nahman said in the name of Samuel: A man may say 'Give us discernment' any time of the year except on the outgoing of Sabbath and of festivals, because he has to say habdalah in 'that graciously giveth knowledge'. Rabbah b. Samuel demurred to this. Let him, [he said] make a fourth blessing[4] of it by itself. Have we not learnt: R. Akiba says: He says it as a fourth blessing by itself; R. Eleazar says: He says it in the thanksgiving?[5] — Do we follow R. Akiba all the year that we should follow him now? Why do we not follow R. Akiba the rest of the year? Because eighteen blessings were instituted, not nineteen. Here too, seven were instituted,[6] not eight. Mar Zutra demurred to this. Let him [he said] include it[7] in 'Give us discernment' [by saying]. O lord, our God, who distinguisheth between holy and profane. — This is indeed a difficulty.

R. Bibi b. Abaye said: A man may say 'Give us discernment' any time in the year except in the rainy season, because he requires to make a request in the benediction of the years.[8] Mar Zutra demurred to this. Let him include it [by saying], And fatten us in the pastures of Thy land and give dew and rain? — He might become confused. If so, by saying habdalah[9] in 'that grantest discernment' he might equally become confused? They replied: In that case, since it comes near the beginning of the Tefillah he will not become confused, here, as it comes in the middle of the Tefillah he will become confused. R. Ashi demurred to this. Let him say it in 'that hearkenest to prayer'?[10] For R. Tanhum said in the name of R. Assi: If a man made a mistake and did not mention the miracle of rain[11] in the benediction of he resurrection of the dead, we turn him back;[12] [if he forgot] the request for rain in the benediction of the years,[13] we do not turn him back, because he can say it in 'that hearkenest unto prayer', and [if he forgot] habdalah in 'that grantest knowledge' we do not turn him back, because he can say it later over wine?[14] — A mistake is different.[15]

The text above [said]: R. Tanhum said in the name of R. Assi: If one made a mistake and did not mention the miracle of rain in the benediction of the resurrection, he is turned back; [if he forgot] the request in the benediction of the years he is not turned back, because he can say it in 'that hearkenest

---

[1] Rashi, following Halakoth Gedoloth emends, Let those who err in judgment, judge according to Thy word.
1.16. Thus Samuel included the contents of the twelve middle benedictions in one. (V.
2.P.B. p. 55.) The first and last three must in every case be said in full.
[2] Instead of the eighteen benedictions in full.
[3] After the first three.
[4] Infra 33a.
[5] I.e., the first and last three and 'Give us discernment'.
[6] The reference to habdalah.
[7] The twelfth.
[8] In the Tefillah on the termination of the Sabbath.
[9] Which is at the conclusion of the prayer.
[10] Lit., 'the (divine) might (manifested) in the rain'.
[11] Because this, not being a prayer, cannot be said in 'that hearkenest unto prayer'.
[12] V. P.B. p. 47.
[13] V. ibid. p. 216.
[14] From something which can confuse the person praying.
[15] When he repeats the 'Amidah. V. Glos.

unto prayer'; [if he forgot] habdalah in 'that grantest knowledge' he is not turned back, because he can say it later over wine. An objection was raised: If one made a mistake and did not mention the miracle of rain in the benediction of the resurrection, he is turned back; [if he forgot] the request in the benediction of the years, he is turned back; [if he forgot] habdalah in 'that grantest knowledge' he is not turned back because he can say it later over wine! — There is no contradiction; the one case where he is turned back refers to where he is saying it by himself, the other, with the congregation. What is the reason why he is not turned back when he says it with the congregation? Because he hears it from the Reader, is it not? If so then instead of 'because he can say it in "who hearkenest unto prayer"', we should have 'because he hears it from the Reader'?

— In fact in both cases he is saying it by himself, and still there is no contradiction; the one case refers to where he remembers before he comes to 'that hearkenest unto prayer'

Berakoth 29b

, the other case where he only remembers after 'that hearkenest unto prayer'.

R. Tanhum said in the name of R. Assi quoting R. Joshua b. Levi: If one made a mistake and did not mention the New Moon in the 'Abodah[1] benediction, he goes back to the 'Abodah. If he remembered in the 'thanksgiving',[2] he goes back to the 'Abodah; if he remembers in 'grant peace',[3] he goes back to the 'Abodah. If he has finished, he goes back to the beginning. R. Papa son of R. Aha b. Ada said: In saying that if he has finished he goes back to the beginning, we mean only, if he has moved his feet; but if he has not yet moved his feet[4] he goes back to the 'Abodah. He said to him: From where have you that?
— He replied: I have heard it from Abba,[5] and Abba Meri had it from Rab. R. Nahman
b. Isaac said: When we say that if he has moved his feet he goes back to the beginning, we mean this to apply only to one who is not accustomed to say a supplication after his Tefillah,[6] but if he is accustomed to say a supplication after his Tefillah, he goes back to the 'Abodah. Some report: R. Nahman b. Isaac said: When we say that if he has not moved his feet he goes back to the 'Abodah, we mean this to apply only to one who is accustomed to say a supplication after his Tefillah, but if he is not accustomed to say a supplication after his Tefillah, he goes back to the beginning.

R. ELIEZER SAYS: HE WHO MAKES HIS PRAYER A FIXED TASK etc. What is meant by a FIXED TASK? — R. Jacob b. Idi said in the name of R. Oshaiah: Anyone whose prayer is like a heavy burden on him. The Rabbis say: Whoever does not say it in the manner of supplication.[7] Rabbah and R. Joseph both say: Whoever is not able to insert something fresh in it.[8] R. Zera said: I can insert something fresh, but I am afraid to do so for fear I should become confused.[9] Abaye b. Abin and R. Hanina b. Abin both said: Whoever does not pray at the first and last appearance of the sun.[10] For R. Hiyya b. Abba said in the name of R. Johanan: It is a religious duty to pray with the first and last appearance of the sun. R. Zera further said: What text confirms this? — They shall fear Thee with the sun, and before the moon throughout all generations.[11] In the West they curse anyone who prays [minhah] with the last appearance of the sun. Why so? — Perhaps he will miss the time.[12]

R. JOSHUA SAYS: HE WHO IS WALKING IN A DANGEROUS PLACE SAYS A SHORT PRAYER ... IN EVERY TIME OF CRISIS. What is 'TIME OF CRISIS' ['ibbur]?
R. Hisda said in the name of Mar 'Ukba: Even at the time when Thou art filled with wrath ['ebrah]

---

[1] Lit., 'Service': the name of the sixteenth benediction.
[2] The last benediction but one.
[3] The last benediction.
[4] On concluding the Tefillah, one steps back three paces.
[5] Or, my father, my teacher.
[6] E.g., My God, keep my tongue from guile etc. V. P.B. p. 54. Cf. also supra 16b, 17a.
[7] I.e., as if he were really asking for a favour.
[8] So as to vary it in case of need.
[9] And not know where I broke off
1.10. I.e., the morning Tefillah in the former case and the afternoon one in the latter. Lit.,
2.(a) 'the reddening of the sun', (b) 'the stillness of the sun' i.e., the time in the morning and evening when the sun appears to stand still, v. Jast.
[10] Ps, LXXII, 5. E.V.'They shall fear Thee while the sun endureth, and so long as the moon'.
[11] Through delaying so long.
[12] There is a play here on the words 'ibbur (passage transition), 'ebrah (wrath) and 'ubereth (pregnant) Which are all from the same root, though with different meanings.

against them like a pregnant woman, may all their need not be overlooked by Thee.[13] Some there are who say that R. Hisda said in the name of Mar 'Ukba: Even at the time when they transgress ['oberim] the words of the Torah may all their requirements not be overlooked by Thee.

Our Rabbis taught: One who passes through a place infested with beasts or bands of robbers says a short Tefillah. What is a short Tefillah? — R. Eliezer says: Do Thy will in heaven above,[2] and grant relief[3] to them that fear Thee below and do that which is good in Thine eyes.[4] Blessed art Thou, O Lord, who hearest prayer. R. Joshua says: Hear the supplication of Thy people Israel and speedily fulfil their request. Blessed art Thou, O Lord, who hearest prayer. R. Eleazar son of R. Zadok says: Hear the cry of thy people Israel and speedily fulfil their request. Blessed art Thou, O Lord, who hearkenest unto prayer. Others say: The needs of Thy people Israel are many and their wit is small.[5] May it be Thy will, O Lord our God, to give to each one his sustenance and to each body what it lacks. Blessed art Thou, O Lord, who hearkenest unto prayer. R. Huna said: The halachah follows the 'Others'.

Said Elijah to Rab Judah the brother of R. Sala the Pious: Fall not into a passion and thou wilt not sin, drink not to excess and thou wilt not sin; and when thou goest forth on a journey, seek counsel of thy Maker and go forth. What is meant by 'seek counsel of thy Maker and go forth'? — R. Jacob said in the name of R. Hisda: This refers to the prayer before setting forth on a journey. R. Jacob also said in the name of R. Hisda: Whoever sets forth on a journey should say the prayer for a journey. What is it? — 'May it be Thy will, O Lord my God, to lead me forth in peace, and direct my steps in peace and uphold me in peace, and deliver me from the hand of every enemy and ambush by the way, and send a blessing on the works of my hands, and cause me to find grace, kindness, and mercy in Thy eyes and in the eyes of all who see me. Blessed art Thou, O Lord, who hearkenest unto prayer'. Abaye said: A man should always

---

[13] Among the angels who never merit punishment.
[2] Lit., 'ease of spirit', i.e., a clear mind without fear of danger.
[3] Cf. Judg. X, 15.
[4] I.e., they do not know how to ask for their needs.
[5] V. P. B. p. 310.

Folio 30a

associate himself with the congregation. How should he say? 'May it be Thy will, O Lord our God, to lead us forth in peace etc'. When should he say this prayer? — R. Jacob said in the name of R. Hisda: At the moment he starts on his journey. How long [is it still permissible to say it]?[1] — R. Jacob said in the name of R. Hisda: Until [he has gone][2] a parasang. How is he to say it? R. Hisda said: Standing still; R. Shesheth said: [He may] also [say it] while proceeding. Once R. Hisda and R. Shesheth were going along together, and R. Hisda stood still and prayed. R. Shesheth asked his attendant, What is R. Hisda doing?[3] — He replied: He is standing and praying. He thereupon said to him: Place me in position also that I may pray; if thou canst be good, do not be called bad.[4]

What is the difference between 'Grant us discernment' and the SHORT PRAYER? — 'Grant us discernment' requires to be accompanied by the first and last three blessings [of the 'Amidah], and when he returns home he need not say the Tefillah again. The 'short prayer does not require to be accompanied either by the first or the last three blessings, and when one returns home he must say the Tefillah. The law is that 'Grant us discernment' must be said standing, a 'short prayer' may be said either standing or journeying.

IF ONE WAS RIDING ON AN ASS etc. Our Rabbis taught: If one was riding on an ass and the time arrived for saying Tefillah, if he has someone to hold his ass, he dismounts and prays, if not, he sits where he is and prays. Rabbi says: In either case he may sit where he is and pray, because [otherwise] he will be worrying.[5] Rab — or, as some say, R. Joshua b. Levi — said: The halachah follows Rabbi.

Our Rabbis taught: A blind man or one who cannot tell the cardinal points should direct his heart towards his Father in Heaven, as it says, And they pray unto the Lord.[6] If one is standing outside Palestine, he should turn mentally towards Eretz Israel, as it says, And pray unto Thee towards their land.[7] If he stands in Eretz Israel he should turn mentally towards Jerusalem, as it says, And they pray unto the Lord toward the city which Thou hast chosen.[8] If he is standing in Jerusalem he should turn mentally towards the Sanctuary, as it says, If they pray toward this house.[9] If he is standing in the Sanctuary, he should turn mentally towards the Holy of Holies, as it says, If they pray toward this place.[10] If he was standing in the Holy of Holies he should turn mentally towards the mercy-seat.[11] If he was standing behind the mercy-seat[12] he should imagine himself to be in front of the mercy-seat. Consequently, if he is in the east he should turn his face to the west; if in the west he should turn his face to the east; if in the south he should turn his face to the north; if in the north he should turn his face to the south. In this way all Israel will be turning their hearts towards one place. R. Abin — or as

---

[1] Another rendering is: How long must the journey be before this prayer is required to be said.
[2] Or, (v. previous note) up to the distance of a parasang.
[3] R. Shesheth was blind.
[4] I.e., although I may pray walking, to pray standing is still better.
[5] At the delay of his journey.
[6] I Kings VIII, 44.
[7] Ibid. 48.
[8] Ibid. 44.
[9] II Chron. VI, 26.
[10] I Kings VIII, 35'
[11] V. Ex. XXV, 17.
[12] In the western part of the Forecourt of the Temple.

some say R. Abina — said: What text confirms this? — Thy neck is like the tower of David builded with turrets [talpioth],[1] the elevation [tel][2] towards which all mouths (piyyoth) turn.[3]

When Samuel's father and Levi were about to set out on a journey, they said the Tefillah before [dawn],[4] and when the time came to recite the Shema', they said it. Whose authority did they follow? — That of the following Tanna, as it has been taught: If a man got up early to go on a journey, they bring him [before dawn] a shofar and he blows,[5] a lulab[6] and he shakes it,[7] a megillah[8] and he reads it,[9] and when the time arrives for reciting the Shema', he recites it. If he rose early in order to take his place in a coach or in a ship,[10] he says the Tefillah,[11] and when the time arrives for reciting he Shema', he recites it. R. Simeon b. Eleazar says: In either case he recites the Shema' and then says the Tefillah, in order that he may say the ge'ullah next to the Tefillah. What is the ground of the difference between the two authorities? — One held that it is more important to say the Tefillah standing,[12] the other that it is more important to say ge'ullah next to Tefillah. Meremar and Mar Zutra used to collect ten persons on the Sabbath before a festival[13] and say the Tefillah, and then they went out and delivered their lectures.[14]

R. Ashi used to say the Tefillah while still with the congregation sitting.[15] and when he returned home he used to say it again standing. The Rabbis said to him: Why does not the Master do as Meremar and Mar Zutra did? — He replied: That[16] is a troublesome business. Then let the Master do like the father of Samuel and Levi? — He replied: I have not seen any of the Rabbis who were my seniors doing thus.[17]

MISHNAH. R. ELEAZAR B. AZARIAH SAYS: THE MUSAF PRAYERS ARE TO BE SAID ONLY WITH THE LOCAL CONGREGATION;[18] THE RABBIS, HOWEVER, SAY: WHETHER WITH OR WITH OUT THE CONGREGATION. R. JUDAH SAID IN HIS NAME:[19] WHEREVER THERE IS A CONGREGATION, AN INDIVIDUAL IS EXEMPT FROM SAYING THE MUSAF PRAYER.

---

[1] Cant. IV, 4.
[2] Taken as an expression for the Temple.
[3] Var. lec. omit 'mouths' and read: towards which all turn (ponim).
[4] So Rashi. Tosaf., however, says, before sunrise.
[5] On New Year.
[6] V. Glos.
[7] On Tabernacles.
[8] V. Glos.
[9] On Purim.
[10] Where he cannot stand.
[11] Before leaving.
[12] Which is not possible when journeying, hence the Tefillah is said at home before setting out.
[13] When they preached in public, before daybreak.
[14] Apparently the public who had gathered in the schoolhouse from early dawn said the Shema' before he came, and after the lecture they would not wait to say the Tefillah together, each saying it by himself
[15] In the course of his lecture, when the turgeman (v. Glos.) was explaining his remarks to the public. He did not stand, as the congregation would have felt it their duty to rise with him.
[16] To collect ten persons.
[17] Saying Tefillah before dawn before the Shema'.
1.29. I.e., in a place where at least ten Jews are living. On the term , a town organization,
2.v. Meg. Sonc. ed., p. 164, n. 1.
[18] The name of R. Eleazar b. Azariah.
[19] If he says prayers alone.

GEMARA. R. Judah says the same thing as the first Tanna? — They differ on the case of an individual living in a place where there is no congregation; the first Tanna holds that he is exempt, while R. Judah holds that he is not exempt. R. Huna b. Hinena said in the name of R. Hiyya b. Rab: The halachah follows R. Judah, citing R. Eleazar b. Azariah. Said R. Hiyya b. Abin to him: You are quite right; for Samuel said: All my life I have never said the musaf prayer alone

Berakoth 30b

in Nehardea except on that day when the king's forces came to the town and they disturbed the Rabbis and they did not say the Tefillah, and I prayed by myself, being an individual where there was no congregation. R. Hanina the Bible teacher[1] sat before R. Jannai and said: The halachah is as stated by R. Judah in the name of R. Eleazar b. Azariah. He said to him: Go and give your bible-reading outside; the halachah is not as stated by R. Judah citing R. Eleazar b. Azariah. R. Johanan said: I have seen R. Jannai pray [privately]. and then pray again.[2] R. Jeremiah said to R. Zera: Perhaps the first time he was not attending to what he said, and the second time he did attend? — He said to him: See what a great man it is who testifies concerning him.[3]

Although there were thirteen synagogues in Tiberias, R. Ammi and R. Assi prayed only between the pillars, the place where they studied.[4]

It has been stated: R. Isaac b. Abdimi said in the name of our Master:[5] The halachah is as stated by R. Judah in the name of R. Eleazar b. Azariah. R. Hiyya b. Abba prayed once and then prayed again. Said R. Zera to him: Why does the Master act thus? Shall I say it is because the Master was not attending? Has not R. Eleazar said: A man should always take stock of himself: if he can concentrate his attention he should say the Tefillah, but if not he should not say it? Or is it that the Master did not remember that it is New Moon?[6] But has it not been taught: If a man forgot and did not mention the New Moon in the evening Tefillah, he is not made to repeat, because he can say it in the morning prayer; if he forgot in the morning prayer, he is not made to repeat, because he can say it in the musaf if he forgot in musaf, he is not made to repeat, because he can say it in minhah? — He said to him: Has not a gloss been added to this: R. Johanan says: This applies only to prayer said in a congregation?[7]

What interval should be left between one Tefillah and another?[8] — R. Huna and R. Hisda gave different answers: one said, long enough for him to fall into a suppliant frame of mind; the other said,

---

[1] Heb. kara, a professional reciter of the Hebrew Scriptures.
[2] I.e., apparently, first the morning prayer and then the musaf.
[3] Viz., R. Johanan, who was not likely to have made a mistake.
[4] I.e., they said even the musaf there, privately.
[5] Rab (Rashi); Hyman (Toledoth, p. 785): Rabbi.
[6] And omitted the appropriate reference to it in the first prayer.
[7] Because then he hears the Reader repeat it, and as R. Hiyya b. Abba was praying privately he rightly repeated the Tefillah.
[8] On any occasion when two are to be said.

long enough to fall into an interceding frame of mind.[1] The one who says a suppliant frame of mind quotes the text, And I supplicated [wa-ethhanan] the Lord;[2] the one who says an interceding frame of mind quotes the text, And Moses interceded [wa-yehal].[3]

R. 'Anan said in the name of Rab: If one forgot and made no mention of New Moon in the evening prayer, he is not made to repeat, because the Beth din sanctify the New Moon only by day. Amemar said: This rule of Rab seems right in a full month,[4] but in a defective month he is made to repeat. Said R. Ashi to Amemar: Let us see: Rab gave a reason, so what does it matter whether it is full or defective? In fact there is no difference.

CHAPTER V

MISHNAH. ONE SHOULD NOT STAND UP TO SAY TEFILLAH SAVE IN A REVERENT FRAME OF MIND.[5] THE PIOUS MEN OF OLD[6] USED TO WAIT AN HOUR BEFORE PRAYING IN ORDER THAT THEY MIGHT CONCENTRATE THEIR THOUGHTS UPON THEIR FATHER IN HEAVEN. EVEN IF A KING GREETS HIM [WHILE PRAYING] HE SHOULD NOT ANSWER HIM: EVEN IF A SNAKE IS WOUND ROUND HIS HEEL HE SHOULD NOT BREAK OFF.

GEMARA. What is the [Scriptural] source of this rule? — R. Eleazar said: Scripture says, And she was in bitterness of soul.[7] But how can you learn from this? Perhaps Hannah was different because she was exceptionally bitter at heart! Rather, said R. Jose son of R. Hanina: We learn it from here: But as for me, in the abundance of Thy lovingkindness will I come into Thy house, I will bow down toward Thy holy temple in the fear of Thee.[8] But how can we learn from this? perhaps David was different, because he was exceptionally self-tormenting in prayer! Rather, said R. Joshua b. Levi, it is from here: Worship the Lord in the beauty of holiness.[9] Read not hadrath [beauty] but herdath [trembling]. But how can you learn from here? perhaps I can after all say that the word 'hadrath' is to be taken literally, after the manner of Rab Judah, who used to dress himself up before he prayed! Rather, said R. Nahman b. Isaac: We learn it from here: Serve the Lord with fear and rejoice with trembling.[10] What is meant by 'rejoice with trembling'?

— R. Adda b. Mattena said in the name of Rab: In the place where there is rejoicing there should also be trembling. Abaye was sitting before Rabbah, who observed that he seemed very merry. He said: It is written, And rejoice with trembling? — He replied: I am putting on tefillin.[11] R. Jeremiah was sitting before R. Zera who saw that he seemed very merry. He said to him: It is written, In all sorrow there is profit?[12] — He replied: I am wearing tefillin. Mar the son of Rabina made a marriage feast for

---

[1] The difference between them is little more than verbal.
[2] Deut. III, 23.
[3] Ex. XXXII, 11.
[4] When the preceding month is thirty days, two new moon days are observed, viz., the concluding day of the old month and the next day which is the first of the next; in this case if he omitted the reference on one evening, he can rectify the error on the next.
[5] Lit., 'with heaviness of head'. Cf. Latin gravitas.
[6] Perhaps identical with the wathikin. V. supra p. 49 n. 4.
[7] I Sam. I, 10.
[8] Ps. V, 8.
[9] Ibid. XXIX, 2.
[10] Ibid. II, 11.
[11] And this is a guarantee that I am not going too far.
[12] Prov. XIV, 23. E.V. 'In all labour'.

his son. He saw that the Rabbis were growing very merry,

Folio 31a

so he brought a precious cup[1] worth four hundred zuz and broke it before them, and they became serious. R. Ashi made a marriage feast for his son. He saw that the Rabbis were growing very merry, so he brought a cup of white crystal and broke it before them and they became serious. The Rabbis said to R. Hamnuna Zuti at the wedding of Mar the son of Rabina: please sing us something. He said to them: Alas for us that we are to die! They said to him: What shall we respond after you? He said to them: Where is the Torah and where is the mizwah that will shield us![2]

R. Johanan said in the name of R. Simeon b. Yohai: It is forbidden to a man to fill his mouth with laughter in this world, because it says, Then will our mouth be filled with laughter and our tongue with singing.[3] When will that be? At the time when 'they shall say among the nations, The Lord hath done great things with these'.[4] It was related of Resh Lakish that he never again filled his mouth with laughter in this world after he heard this saying from R. Johanan his teacher.

Our Rabbis taught: A man should not stand up to say Tefillah either immediately after trying a case or immediately after a [discussion on a point of] halachah;[5] but he may do so after a halachic decision which admits of no discussion.[6] What is an example of a halachic decision which admits of no discussion? — Abaye said: Such a one as the following of R. Zera; for R. Zera said:[7] The daughters of Israel have undertaken to be so strict with themselves that if they see a drop of blood no bigger than a mustard seed they wait seven [clean] days after it.[8] Raba said: A man may resort to a device with his produce and bring it into the house while still in its chaff[9] so that his animal may eat of it without its being liable to tithe.[10] Or, if you like, I can say, such as the following of R. Huna. For R. Huna said in the name of R. Zeiri:[11] If a man lets blood in a consecrated animal, no benefit may he derived from it [the blood] and such benefit constitutes a trespass. The Rabbis followed the rule laid down in the Mishnah,[12] R. Ashi that of the Baraitha.[13]

Our Rabbis taught: One should not stand up to say Tefillah while immersed in sorrow, or idleness, or laughter, or chatter, or frivolity, or idle talk, but only while still rejoicing in the performance of some

---

[1] Aliter: crystal cup.
[2] From the punishment that is to come.
[3] Ps. CXXVI, 2.
[4] Ibid. 3.
[5] Because through thinking of it he may be unable to concentrate on his prayer.
[6] Lit., 'a decided halachah'.
[7] Nid. 66a.
[8] Though Scripture requires this only if they saw three issues.
[9] I.e., before it is winnowed.
[10] Whereas if it had been winnowed before being brought into the house, it would have been liable to tithe, v. Pes., Sonc. ed. p. 39, n. 5.
[11] Me'il. 12b.
[12] That one should rise to pray only in a reverent frame of mind.
[13] That one should pray only after dealing with an undisputed halachah.

religious act.¹ Similarly a man before taking leave of his fellow should not finish off with ordinary conversation, or joking, or frivolity, or idle talk, but with some matter of halachah. For so we find with the early prophets that they concluded their harangues with words of praise and comfort; and so Mari the grandson of R. Huna the son of R. Jeremiah b. Abba learnt: Before taking leave of his fellow a man should always finish with a matter of halachah, so that he should remember him thereby. So we find that R. Kahana escorted R. Shimi b. Ashi from Pun, to Be-Zinyatha² of Babylon, and when he arrived there he said to him, Sir, do people really say that these palm trees of Babylon are from the time of Adam? — He replied: You have reminded me of the saying of R. Jose son of R. Hanina. For R. Jose son of R. Hanina said: What is meant by the verse, Through a land that no man passed through and where no man dwelt?³ If no one passed, how could anyone dwell? It is to teach you that any land which Adam decreed should be inhabited is inhabited, and any land which Adam decreed should not be inhabited is not inhabited.⁴ R. Mordecai escorted R. Shimi b. Abba from Hagronia to Be Kafi, or, as some report, to Be Dura.⁵

Our Rabbis taught: When a man prays, he should direct his heart to heaven. Abba Saul says: A reminder of this is the text, Thou wilt direct their heart, Thou wilt cause Thine ear to attend.⁶ It has been taught: Such was the custom of R. Akiba; when he prayed with the congregation, he used to cut it short and finish⁷ in order not to inconvenience the congregation,⁸ but when he prayed by himself, a man would leave him in one corner and find him later in another, on account of his many genuflexions and prostrations.

R. Hiyya b. Abba said: A man should always pray in a house with windows, as it says, Now his windows were open.⁹

I might say that a man should pray the whole day? It has already been expressly stated by the hand of Daniel, And three times. etc.¹⁰ But perhaps [this practice] began only when he went into captivity? It is already said, As he did aforetime.¹¹ I might say that a man may pray turning in any direction he wishes? Therefore the text states, Toward Jerusalem.¹² I might say that he may combine all three Tefillahs in one? It has already been clearly stated by David, as is written, Evening and morning and at noonday.¹³ I might say that he should let his voice be heard in praying? It has already been clearly stated by Hannah, as is said, But her voice could not be heard.¹⁴ I might say that a man should first ask for his own requirements¹⁵ and then say the Tefillah?¹⁶ It has been clearly stated by Solomon, as

---

¹ I.e., he should first say something like Ps. CXLIV.
² Lit., 'among the palms'. The district of the old city of Babylon which was rich in palms.
³ Jer. II, 6.
⁴ And Adam decreed that this should be inhabited, and so there have always been palm trees here. On the identification of all the places mentioned in this message v. Sotah, Sonc. ed., p. 243 notes.
⁵ The text here seems to be defective, as we are not told what either of the Rabbis said.
⁶ I.e., if the heart is directed to heaven, then God will attend. Ps. X, 17.
⁷ Lit., 'ascend', 'depart'.
⁸ By detaining them; the congregation would not resume the service until R. Akiba had finished his Tefillah.
⁹ Dan. VI, 11.
¹⁰ Ibid.
¹¹ Ibid.
¹² Ibid.
¹³ Ps. LV, 18.
¹⁴ I Sam. I, 13.
¹⁵ In the middle benedictions of the 'Amidah.
¹⁶ The first three benedictions.

is said, To hearken unto the cry and to the prayer:[1] 'cry' here means Tefillah. 'prayer' means [private] request. A [private] request is not made after 'True and firm',[2] but after the Tefillah, even the order of confession of the Day of Atonement[3] may be said. It has also been stated: R. Hiyya b. Ashi said in the name of Rab: Although it was laid down that a man asks for his requirements in 'that hearkenest unto prayer', if he wants to say something after his prayer, even something like the order of confession on the Day of Atonement, he may do so.

R. Hamnuna said: How many most important laws can be learnt from these verses relating to Hannah![4] Now Hannah, she spoke in her heart: from this we learn that one who prays must direct his heart. Only her lips moved: from this we learn that he who prays must frame the words distinctly with his lips. But her voice could not be heard: from this, it is forbidden to raise one's voice in the Tefillah. Therefore Eli thought she had been drunken: from this, that a drunken person is forbidden to say the Tefillah. And Eli said unto her, How long wilt thou be drunken, etc.[5] R. Eleazar said: From this we learn that one who sees in his neighbour

---

[1] I Kings VIII, 28.
[2] And before the first three benedictions.
[3] V. P.B. p. 258.
[4] I Sam. I, 10ff.
[5] Ibid. 14.

Berakoth 31b

something unseemly must reprove him. And Hannah answered and said, No, my lord.[1] 'Ulla, or as some say R. Jose b. Hanina, said: She said to him: Thou art no lord in this matter, nor does the holy spirit rest on thee, that thou suspectest me of this thing. Some say, She said to him: Thou art no lord, [meaning] the Shechinah and the holy spirit is not with you in that you take the harsher and not the more lenient view of my conduct.[2] Dost thou not know that I am a woman of sorrowful spirit: I have drunk neither wine nor strong drink.

R. Eleazar said: From this we learn that one who is suspected wrongfully must clear himself. Count not thy handmaid for a daughter of Belial;[3] a man who says the Tefillah when drunk is like one who serves idols. It is written here, Count not thy handmaid for a daughter of Belial, and it is written elsewhere, Certain sons of Belial have gone forth from the midst of thee.[4] Just as there the term is used in connection with idolatry, so here. Then Eli answered and said, Go in Peace.[5] R. Eleazar said: From this we learn that one who suspects his neighbour of a fault which he has not committed must beg his pardon;[6] nay more, he must bless him, as it says, And the God of Israel grant thy petition.[7]

And she vowed a vow and said, O Lord of Zebaoth [Hosts].[8] R. Eleazar said: From the day that God created His world there was no man called the Holy One, blessed be He, Zeboath [hosts] until Hannah came and called Him Zebaoth. Said Hannah before the Holy One, blessed be He: Sovereign of the Universe, of all the hosts and hosts that Thou hast created in Thy world, is it so hard in Thy eyes to give me one son? A parable: To what is this matter like? To a king who made a feast for his servants, and a poor man came and stood by the door and said to them, Give me a bite,[9] and no one took any notice of him, so he forced his way into the presence of the king and said to him, Your Majesty, out of all the feast which thou hast made, is it so hard in thine eyes to give me one bite?

If Thou wilt indeed look.[10] R. Eleazar said: Hannah said before the Holy One, blessed be He: Sovereign of the Universe, if Thou wilt look, it is well, and if Thou wilt not look, I will go and shut myself up with someone else in the knowledge of my husband Elkanah,[11] and as I shall have been alone[12] they will make me drink the water of the suspected wife, and Thou canst not falsify Thy law, which says, She shall be cleared and shall conceive seed.[13] Now this would be effective on the view of him who says that if the woman was barren she is visited. But on the view of him who says that if

---

[1] Ibid. 15.

[2] Lit., 'You have judged me in the scale of guilt and not of merit'.

[3] So lit. E.V. 'wicked woman'. V. Kid. 16.

[4] Deut. XIII, 14. E.V. 'certain base fellows'.

[5] I Sam. I, 17.

[6] Lit., 'appease him'.

[7] I Sam. I, 17.

[8] Ibid. 11.

[9] Lit., 'morsel' (sc. of bread).

[10] Ibid.

[11] So that he will become jealous and test me.

[12] Lit., 'as I will have been hidden'.

[13] Num. V, 28.

she bore with pain she bears with ease, if she bore females she now bears males, if she bore swarthy children she now bears fair ones, if she bore short ones she now bears tall ones, what can be said? As it has been taught: 'She shall be cleared ad shall conceive seed': this teaches that if she was barren she is visited. So R. Ishmael. Said K. Akiba to him, If that is so, all barren women will go and shut themselves in with someone and she who has not misconducted herself will be visited! No, it teaches that if she formerly bore with pain she now bears with ease, if she bore short children she now bears tall ones, if she bore swarthy ones she now bears fair ones, if she was destined to bear one she will now bear two. What then is the force of 'If Thou wilt indeed look'? — The Torah used an ordinary form of expression.

If Thou wilt indeed look on the affliction of Thy handmaid … and not forget Thy handmaid, but wilt give unto Thy handmaid etc. R. Jose son of R. Hanina said: Why these three 'handmaids'? Hannah said before the Holy One, blessed be He: Sovereign of the Universe, Thou hast created in woman three criteria [bidke] of death[1] (some say, three armour-joints [dibke] of death),[2] namely, niddah, hallah and the kindling of the light [on Sabbath].[3] Have I transgressed in any of them?

But wilt give unto Thy handmaid a man-child. What is meant by 'a man-child'? Rab said: A man among men;[4] Samuel said: Seed that will anoint two men, namely, Saul and David; R. Johanan said: Seed that will be equal to two men, namely, Moses and Aaron, as it says, Moses and Aaron among His priests and Samuel among them that call upon His name;[5] the Rabbis say: Seed that will be merged among men.[6] When R. Dimi came [from Palestine] he explained this to mean: Neither too tall nor too short, neither too thin nor too corpulent,[7] neither too pale nor too red, neither overclever[8] nor stupid.

I am the woman that stood by thee here.[9] R. Joshua b. Levi said: From this we learn that it is forbidden to sit within four cubits of one saying Tefillah.[10]

For this child I prayed.[11] R. Eleazar said: Samuel was guilty of giving a decision in the presence of his teacher; for it says, And when the bullock was slain, the child was brought to Eli.[12] Because the bullock was slain, did they bring the child to Eli? What it means is this. Eli said to them: Call a priest and let him come and kill [the animal]. When Samuel saw them looking for a priest to kill it, he said to them, Why do you go looking for a priest to kill it? The shechitah may be performed by a layman! They brought him to Eli, who asked him, How do you know this? He replied: Is it written, 'The priest shall kill'? It is written, The priests shall present [the blood]:[13] the office of the priest begins with the

---

[1] Three things by which she is tested to see whether she deserves death.
[2] I.e., three vulnerable points. Hannah plays on the resemblance of the word amateka (thy handmaid) to mithah (death).
[3] V. Shab. 32a: For three transgressions woman die in childbirth; because they are not careful with niddah, with hallah and with the kindling of the light.
[4] I.e., conspicuous among men.
[5] Ps. XCIX, 6.
[6] I.e., average, not conspicuous.
[7] So Rashi.
[8] So as not to be talked about and so become exposed to the evil eye.
[9] I Sam. I, 26.
[10] Because the words imply that Eli also was standing.
[11] I Sam. I, 27.
[12] Ibid. 25.
[13] Lev. I, 5

receiving of the blood, which shows that shechitah may be performed by a layman.[1] He said to him: You have spoken very well, but all the same you are guilty of giving a decision in the presence of your teacher, and whoever gives a decision in the presence of his teacher is liable to the death penalty. Thereupon Hannah came and cried before him: 'I am the woman that stood by thee here etc.'. He said to her: Let me punish him and I will pray to God and He will give thee a better one than this. She then said to him: 'For this child I prayed'.

Now Hannah, she spoke in[2] her heart.[3] R. Eleazar said in the name of R. Jose b. Zimra: She spoke concerning her heart. She said before Him: Sovereign of the Universe, among all the things that Thou hast created in a woman, Thou hast not created one without a purpose, eyes to see, ears to hear, a nose to smell, a mouth to speak, hands to do work, legs to walk with, breasts to give suck. These breasts that Thou hast put on my heart, are they not to give suck? Give me a son, so that I may suckle with them.

R. Eleazar also said in the name of R. Jose b. Zimra: If one keeps a fast on Sabbath,[4] a decree of seventy years standing against him is annulled;[5] yet all the same he is punished for neglecting to make the Sabbath a delight. What is his remedy? R. Nahman b. Isaac said: Let him keep another fast to atone for this one.

R. Eleazar also said: Hannah spoke insolently[6] toward heaven, as it says, And Hannah prayed unto[7] the Lord.[8] This teaches that she spoke insolently toward heaven.

R. Eleazar also said: Elijah spoke insolently toward heaven, as it says, For Thou didst turn their heart backwards.[9] R. Samuel b. Isaac said: Whence do we know that the Holy One, blessed be He, gave Elijah right?

---

[1] V. Zeb. 32a.
[2] Lit., 'upon'.
[3] I Sam. I, 13.
[4] E.g., to avert the omen of a dream.
[5] I.e., even though it is high time that it was carried out (Rashi).
[6] Lit., 'she hurled words'.
[7] The Hebrew word is 'al, lit., 'upon', 'against'.
[8] I Sam. I, 10.
[9] I Kings XVIII, 37. As much as to say, it was God's fault that they worshipped idols.

Folio 32a

Because it says, And whom I have wronged.[1]

R. Hama said in the name of R. Hanina: But for these three texts,[2] the feet of Israel's enemies[3] would have slipped. One is Whom I have wronged; a second, Behold as the clay in the potter's hand, so are ye in My hand, O house of Israel;[4] the third, And I will take away the stony heart out of your flesh, and I will give you a heart of flesh.[5] R. papa said: We learn it from here: And I will put My spirit within you and cause you to walk in My statutes.[6]

R. Eleazar also said: Moses spoke insolently towards heaven, as it says, And Moses prayed unto the Lord.[7] Read not el [unto] the Lord, but 'al [upon] the Lord, for so in the school of R. Eliezer alefs were pronounced like 'ayins and 'ayins like alefs. The school of R. Jannai learnt it from here: And Di-Zahab.[8] What is 'And Di-Zahab'? They said in the school of
R. Jannai: Thus spoke Moses before the Holy One, blessed be He: Sovereign of the Universe, the silver and gold [zahab] which Thou didst shower on Israel until they said, Enough [dai], that it was which led to their making the Calf. They said in the school of R. Jannai: A lion does not roar over a basket of straw but over a basket of flesh. R. Oshaia said: It is like the case of a man who had a lean but large-limbed cow. He gave it lupines to eat and it commenced to kick him. He said to it: What led you to kick me except the lupines that I fed you with? R. Hiyya b. Abba said: It is like the case of a man who had a son; he bathed him and anointed him and gave him plenty to eat and drink and hung a purse round his neck and set him down at the door of a bawdy house. How could the boy help sinning?
R. Aha the son of R. Huna said in the name of R. Shesheth: This bears out the popular saying: A full stomach is a bad sort, as It says, When they were fed they became full, they were filled and their heart was exalted; therefore they have forgotten Me.[9] R. Nahman learnt it from here: Then thy heart be lifted up and thou forget the Lord.[10] The Rabbis from here: And they shall have eaten their fill and waxen fat, and turned unto other gods.[11] Or, if you prefer, I can say from here. But Jeshurun waxed fat and kicked.[12]
R. Samuel b. Nahmani said in the name of R. Jonathan. Whence do we know that the Holy One, blessed be He, in the end gave Moses right? Because it says, And multiplied unto her silver and gold, which they used for Baal.[13]

---

[1] Micah IV, 6. This is taken to mean that God admits having wronged sinners by creating in them the evil impulse. E.V. 'afflicted'.
[2] Which show that God is responsible for the evil impulse.
[3] Euphemism.
[4] Jer. XVIII, 6.
[5] Ezek. XXXVI, 26.
[6] Ibid. 27.
[7] Num. XI, 2.
[8] Deut. I, I.
[9] Hos. XIII, 6.
[10] Deut. VIII, 24.
[11] Ibid. XXXI, 20.
[12] Ibid. XXXII, 15.
[13] Hos. II, 10.

And the Lord spoke unto Moses, Go, get thee down.[1] What is meant by 'Go, get thee down'? R. Eleazar said: The Holy One, blessed be He, said to Moses: Moses, descend from thy greatness. Have I at all given to thee greatness save for the sake of Israel? And now Israel have sinned; then why do I want thee? Straightway Moses became powerless and he had no strength to speak. When, however, [God] said, Let Me alone that I may destroy them,[2] Moses said to himself: This depends upon me, and straightway he stood up and prayed vigorously and begged for mercy. It was like the case of a king who became angry with his son and began beating him severely. His friend was sitting before him but was afraid to say a word until the king said, Were it not for my friend here who is sitting before me I would kill you. He said to himself, This depends on me, and immediately he stood up and rescued him.

Now therefore let Me alone that My wrath may wax hot against them, and that I may consume them, and I will make of thee a great nation.[3] R. Abbahu said: Were it not explicitly written, it would be impossible to say such a thing: this teaches that Moses took
hold of the Holy One, blessed be He, like a man who seizes his fellow by his garment and said before Him: Sovereign of the Universe, I will not let Thee go until Thou forgivest and pardonest them.

And I will make of thee a great nation etc. R. Eleazar said: Moses said before the Holy One, blessed be He: Sovereign of the Universe, seeing that a stool with three legs[4] cannot stand before Thee in the hour of Thy wrath, how much less a stool with one leg! And moreover, I am ashamed before my ancestors, who will now say: See what a leader he has set over them! He sought greatness for himself, but he did not seek mercy for them!

And Moses besought [wa-yehal] the Lord his God.[5] R. Eleazar said: This teaches that Moses stood in prayer before the Holy One, blessed be He, Until he [so to speak] wearied Him [hehelahu]. Raba said: Until he remitted His vow for Him. It is written here wa-yehal, and it is written there [in connection with vows], he shall not break [yahel] his word;[6] and a Master has said: He [himself] cannot break, but others may break for him.[7] Samuel says: It teaches that he risked his life for them,[8] as it says, And if not, blot me, I pray Thee, out of Thy book which Thou hast written.[9] Raba said in the name of R. Isaac: It teaches that he caused the Attribute of Mercy to rest [hehelah] on them. The Rabbis say: It teaches that Moses said before the Holy One, blessed be He: Sovereign of the Universe, it is a profanation [hullin] for Thee to do this thing.
And Moses besought the Lord. It has been taught: R. Eliezer the Great says: This teaches that Moses stood praying before the Holy One, blessed be He, until an ahilu seized him. What is ahilu? R. Eleazar says: A fire in the bones. What is a fire in the bones? Abaye said: A kind of fever.

Remember Abraham, Isaac and Israel Thy servants, to whom Thou didst swear by Thyself.[10] What is the force of 'by Thyself'? R. Eleazar said: Moses said before the Holy One, blessed be He: Sovereign

---

[1] Ex. XXXII, 7.
[2] Deut. IX, 14.
[3] Ex XXXII, 10.
[4] The three Patriarchs.
[5] Ex. XXXII, 11.
[6] Num. XXX, 3.
[7] I.e., find a ground of absolution.
[8] Connecting wayehal with halal, slain.
[9] Ex. XXXII, 32.
[10] Ibid. 13.

of the Universe, hadst Thou sworn to them by the heaven and the earth, I would have said, Just as the heaven and earth can pass away, so can Thy oath pass away. Now, however, Thou hast sworn to them by Thy great name: just as Thy great name endures for ever and ever, so Thy oath is established for ever and ever.

And saidst unto them, I will multiply your seed as the stars of heaven and all this land that I have spoken of etc.[1] 'That I have spoken of? It should be, 'That Thou hast spoken of'![2] — R. Eleazar said: Up to this point the text records the words of the disciple,[3] from this point the words of the master.[4] R. Samuel b. Nahmani, however, said: Both are the words of the disciple, only Moses spoke thus before the Holy One, blessed be He: Sovereign of the Universe, the things which Thou didst tell me to go and tell Israel in Thy name I did go and tell them in Thy name; now what am I to say to them?

Because the Lord was not able [yekoleth].[5] It should be yakol![6] R. Eleazar said: Moses said before the Holy One, blessed be He: Sovereign of the Universe, now the nations of the world will say, He has grown feeble like a female and He is not able to deliver. Said the Holy One, blessed be He, to Moses: Have they not already seen the wonders and miracles I performed for them by the Red Sea? He replied: Sovereign of the Universe, they can still say, He could stand up against one king, He cannot stand up against thirty. R. Johanan said: How do we know that in the end the Holy One, blessed be He, gave Moses right? Because it says, And the Lord said, I have pardoned according to thy word.[7] It was taught in the school of R. Ishmael: According to thy word: the nations of the world will one day say, Happy is the disciple to whom the master gives right!

But in very deed, as I live.[8] Raba said in the name of R. Isaac: This teaches that the Holy One, blessed be He, said to Moses: Moses, you have revived Me[9] with your words.

R. Simlai expounded: A man should always first recount the praise of the Holy One, blessed be He, and then pray. Whence do we know this? From Moses; for it is written, And I besought the Lord at that time,[10] and it goes on, O Lord God, Thou hast begun to show Thy servant Thy greatness and Thy strong hand; for what god is there in heaven and earth who can do according to Thy works and according to Thy mighty acts, and afterwards is written, Let me go over, I pray Thee, and see the good land etc.

(Mnemonic: Deeds, charity, offering, priest, fast, lock, iron.)[11]

---

[1] Ex. XXXII, 13.
[2] If Moses were reporting God's promises to the Patriarchs, the words, 'that I have spoken of' are out of place.
[3] Moses.
[4] God.
[5] Num. XIV, 16.
[6] The ordinary form, which is masculine, while yekoleth, the word used, is feminine.
[7] Ibid. 20.
[8] Ibid. 21.
[9] I.e., preserved My estimation among the nations (Rashi).
[10] Deut. III, 23ff.
[11] This is a mnemonic for the seven dicta of R. Eleazar which follow.

Berakoth 32b

R. Eleazar said: prayer is more efficacious even than good deeds, for there was no-one greater in good deeds than Moses our Master, and yet he was answered only after prayer, as it says, Speak no more unto Me,[1] and immediately afterwards, Get thee up into the top of Pisgah.[2]

R. Eleazar also said: Fasting is more efficacious than charity. What is the reason? One is performed with a man's money, the other with his body.

R. Eleazar also said: Prayer is more efficacious than offerings, as it says, To what purpose is the multitude of your sacrifices unto Me,[3] and this is followed by, And when ye spread forth your hands.[4] R. Johanan said: A priest who has committed manslaughter should not lift up his hands [to say the priestly benediction], since it says [in this context], 'Your hands are full of blood'.

R. Eleazar also said: From the day on which the Temple was destroyed the gates of prayer have been closed, as it says, Yea, when I cry and call for help He shutteth out my prayer.[5] But though the gates of prayer are closed, the gates of weeping are not closed, as it says, Hear my prayer, O Lord, and give ear unto my cry; keep not silence at my tears.[6] Raba did not order a fast on a cloudy day because it says, Thou hast covered Thyself with a cloud so that no prayer can pass through.[7]

R. Eleazar also said: Since the day that the Temple was destroyed, a wall of iron has intervened between Israel and their Father in Heaven, as it says, And take thou unto thee an iron griddle, and set it for a wall of iron between thee and the city.[8]

R. Hanin said in the name of R. Hanina: If one prays long his prayer does not pass unheeded. Whence do we know this? From Moses our Master; for it says, And I prayed unto the Lord,[9] and it is written afterwards, And the Lord hearkened unto me that time also.[10] But is that so? Has not R. Hiyya b. Abba said in the name of R. Johanan: If one prays long and looks for the fulfilment of his prayer, in the end he will have vexation of heart, as it says, Hope deferred maketh the heart sick?[11] What is his remedy? Let him study the Torah, as it says, But desire fulfilled is a tree of life;[12] and the tree of life is nought but the Torah, as it says, She is a tree of life to them that lay hold on her![13] — There is no contradiction: one statement speaks of a man who prays long and looks for the fulfilment of his

---

[1] Ibid. 26. The meaning is apparently that his good deeds did not avail to procure him permission to enter the land, but his prayer procured for him the vision of Pisgah.
[2] Ibid. 27.
[3] Isa. I, 11.
[4] Ibid. 15. Since spreading of hands is mentioned after sacrifice, it must be regarded as more efficacious.
[5] Lam. III, 8.
[6] Ps. XXXIX, 13. This shows that the tears are at any rate observed.
[7] Lam. III, 44.
[8] Ezek. IV, 3. This wall was symbolical of the wall separating Israel from God.
[9] Deut. IX, 26. This seems to be quoted in error for, And I fell down before the Lord forty days and forty nights, in v. 18; v. MS.M.
[10] Ibid. 19.
[11] Prov. XIII, 12.
[12] Ibid.
[13] Ibid. III, 18.

prayer, the other of one who prays long without looking for the fulfilment of his prayer.[1] R. Hama son of R. Hanina said: If a man sees that he prays and is not answered, he should pray again, as it says, Wait for the Lord, be strong and let thy heart take courage; yea, wait thou for the Lord.[2]

Our Rabbis taught: Four things require to be done with energy,[3] namely, [study of] the Torah, good deeds, praying, and one's worldly occupation. Whence do we know this of Torah and good deeds? Because it says, Only be strong and very courageous to observe to do according to all the law:[4] 'be strong' in Torah, and 'be courageous in good deeds. Whence of prayer? Because it says, 'Wait for the Lord, be strong and let thy heart take courage, yea, wait thou for the Lord'. Whence of worldly occupation? Because it says, Be of good courage and let us prove strong for our people.[5]

But Zion said, The Lord hath forsaken me, and the Lord hath forgotten me.[6] Is not 'forsaken' the same as 'forgotten'? Resh Lakish said: The community of Israel said before the Holy One, blessed be He: Sovereign of the Universe, when a man takes a second wife after his first, he still remembers the deeds of the first. Thou hast both forsaken me and forgotten me! The Holy One, blessed be He, answered her: My daughter, twelve constellations have I created in the firmament, and for each constellation I have created thirty hosts, and for each host I have created thirty legions, and for each legion I have created thirty cohorts, and for each cohort I have created thirty maniples, and for each maniple I have created thirty camps, and to each camp[7] I have attached three hundred and sixty-five thousands of myriads of stars, corresponding to the days of the solar year, and all of them I have created only for thy sake, and thou sayest, Thou hast forgotten me and forsaken me! Can a woman forsake her sucking child ['ullah]?[8] Said the Holy One, blessed be He: Can I possibly forget the burn-offerings ['olah] of rams and the firstborn of animals[9] that thou didst offer to Me in the wilderness? She thereupon said: Sovereign of the Universe, since there is no forgetfulness before the Throne of Thy glory, perhaps Thou wilt not forget the sin of the Calf? He replied: 'Yea, "these "[10] will be forgotten'. She said before Him: Sovereign of the Universe, seeing that there is forgetfulness before the Throne of Thy glory, perhaps Thou wilt forget my conduct at Sinai? He replied to her: 'Yet "the I"[11] will not forget thee'. This agrees with what R. Eleazar said in the name of R. Oshaia: What is referred to by the text, 'yea, "these" will be forgotten'? This refers to the sin of the Calf. 'And yet "the I" will not forget thee': this refers to their conduct at Sinai.

THE PIOUS MEN OF OLD USED TO WAIT AN HOUR. On what is this based? — R. Joshua b. Levi said: On the text, Happy are they that dwell in Thy house.[12] R. Joshua b. Levi also said: One who says the Tefillah should also wait an hour after his prayer, as it says, Surely the righteous shall

---

[1] V. B.B. (Sonc. ed.) p. 717, n. 8.
[2] Ps. XXVII, 14.
[3] Lit., 'require vigour'.
[4] Joshua I, 7.
[5] II Sam. X, 12.
[6] Isa. XLIX, 14.
[7] These terms are obviously taken from Roman military language. There is, however, some difficulty about identifying rahaton (cohorts) and karton (maniples) in the text.
[8] Ibid. 25.
[9] Lit., 'opening of the womb'.
[10] Referring to the golden calf incident when Israel exclaimed 'These are thy gods', Ex. XXXII, 4'
[11] Referring to the revelation at Sinai when God declared, 'I am the Lord Thy God'. This incident will not be forgotten. R.V. 'Yet will I not forget thee'.
[12] Ps. LXXXIV, 5.

give thanks unto Thy name, the upright shall sit in Thy presence.[1] It has been taught similarly: One who says the Tefillah should wait an hour before his prayer and an hour after his prayer. Whence do we know [that he should wait] before his prayer? Because it says: 'Happy are they that dwell in Thy house'. Whence after his prayer? Because it says, 'Surely the righteous shall give thanks unto Thy name, the upright shall dwell in Thy presence'. Our Rabbis taught: The pious men of old used to wait for an hour and pray for an hour and then wait again for an hour. But seeing that they spend nine hours a day over prayer, how is their knowledge of Torah preserved and how is their work done? [The answer is] that because they are pious, their Torah is preserved[2] and their work is blessed.[3]

EVEN IF A KING GREETS HIM HE SHOULD NOT ANSWER HIM. R. Joseph said: This was meant to apply only to Jewish kings, but for a king of another people he may interrupt. An objection was raised: If one was saying Tefillah and he saw a robber[4] coming towards him or a carriage coming towards him, he should not break off but curtail it and clear off! — There Is no contradiction: where it is possible for him to curtail [he should curtail, otherwise he should break off].[5]

Our Rabbis taught: It is related that once when a certain pious man was praying by the roadside, an officer came by and greeted him and he did not return his greeting. So he waited for him till he had finished his prayer. When he had finished his prayer he said to him: Fool![6] is it not written in your Law, Only take heed to thyself and keep thy soul diligently,[7] and it is also written, Take ye therefore good heed unto your souls?[8] When I greeted you why did you not return my greeting? If I had cut off your head with my sword, who would have demanded satisfaction for your blood from me? He replied to him: Be patient and I will explain to you. If, [he went on], you had been standing before an earthly king and your friend had come and given you greeting, would you

---

[1] Ibid. CXL, 14.

[2] I.e., they do not forget it.

[3] I.e., a little goes a long way.

[4] The Heb. annes usually means 'a man of violence'. Some suppose that it is here equivalent to hamor, ass, which is actually found in J.T.

[5] Alfasi reads: In the one case it is possible for him to curtail, in the other it is not possible; where he can curtail he should, otherwise he may break off.

[6] Raka; v. supra p. 133, n. 3.

[7] Deut. IV, 9.

[8] Ibid. 15. 'Soul' in these texts is taken to mean 'life'.

Folio 33a

have returned it? No, he replied. And if you had returned his greeting, what would they have done to you? They would have cut off my head with the sword, he replied. He then said to him: Have we not here then an a fortiori argument: If [you would have behaved] in this way when standing before an earthly king who is here today and tomorrow in the grave, how much more so I when standing before the supreme King of kings, the Holy One, blessed be He, who endures for all eternity? Forthwith the officer accepted his explanation, and the pious man returned to his home in peace.

EVEN IF A SNAKE IS WOUND ROUND HIS FOOT HE SHOULD NOT BREAK OFF.
R. Shesheth said: This applies only in the case of a serpent, but if it is a scorpion, he breaks off.[1] An objection was raised: If a man fell into a den of lions [and was not seen again] one cannot testify concerning him that he is dead; but if he fell into a trench full of serpents or scorpions, one can testify concerning him that he is dead! — The case there is different, because on account of his crushing them [in falling] they turn and bite him. R. Isaac said: If he sees oxen [coming towards him] he may break off; for R. Oshaia taught: One should remove from a tam[2] ox fifty cubits, and from a mu'ad[3] ox out of sight. It was taught in the name of R. Meir: If an ox's head is in a [fodder] basket,[4] go up to a roof and kick the ladder away.[5] Samuel said: This applies only to a black ox and in the month of Nisan, because then Satan is dancing between his horns.[6]

Our Rabbis taught: In a certain place there was once a lizard[7] which used to injure people. They came and told R. Hanina b. Dosa. He said to them: Show me its hole. They showed him its hole, and he put his heel over the hole, and the lizard came out and bit him, and it died. He put it on his shoulder and brought it to the Beth ha-Midrash and said to them: See, my sons, it is not the lizard that kills, it is sin that kills! On that occasion they said: Woe to the man whom a lizard meets, but woe to the lizard which R. Hanina b. Dosa meets![8]

MISHNAH. THE MIRACLE OF THE RAINFALL[9] IS MENTIONED IN THE BENEDICTION OF THE RESURRECTION, AND THE PETITION[10] FOR RAIN IN THE BENEDICTION OF THE YEARS, AND HABDALAH[11] IN 'THAT GRACIOUSLY GRANTEST KNOWLEDGE'.[12] R. AKIBA SAYS: HE SAYS IT AS A FOURTH BLESSING[13] BY ITSELF; R. ELIEZER SAYS: IT IS

---

[1] A scorpion is more certain to sting.
[2] One which has 'lot gored before.
[3] One which has gored three times. For these terms, v. Glos.
[4] I.e., even if it is busy eating.
[5] This is a humorous exaggeration.
[6] I.e., it is high spirited and full of mischief in the spring.
[7] Heb. yarod, apparently a cross-breed of a snake and a lizard.
[8] According to J.T. a spring of water had miraculously opened at the feet of R. Hanina, and that sealed the fate of the lizard, for (it is asserted) when a lizard bites a man, if the man reaches water first, the lizard dies, but if the lizard reaches water first the man dies.
[9] The formula 'that causest the wind to blow' etc., P.B. P. 44.
[10] The words 'and grant dew and rain for a blessing', ibid. p. 47.
[11] V. Glos.
[12] Ibid. p. 46.
[13] After the first three.

SAID IN THE THANKSGIVING BENEDICTION![1]

GEMARA. THE MIRACLE OF THE RAINFALL etc. What is the reason? — R. Joseph said: Because it is put on a level with the resurrection of the dead, therefore it was inserted in the benediction of the resurrection.

THE PETITION FOR RAIN IN THE BENEDICTION OF THE YEARS. What is the reason? — R. Joseph said: Because [the petition] refers to sustenance, therefore it was inserted in the benediction of sustenance.

HABDALAH IN THAT GRACIOUSLY GRANTEST KNOWLEDGE'. What is the reason? — R. Joseph said: Because it is a kind of wisdom,[2] it was inserted in the benediction of wisdom. The Rabbis, however, say: Because the reference is to a weekday, therefore it was inserted in the weekday blessing. R. Ammi said: Great is knowledge, since it was placed at the beginning of the weekday blessings. R. Ammi also said: Great is knowledge since it was placed between two names,[3] as it says, For a God of knowledge is the Lord.[4] And if one has not knowledge, it is forbidden to have mercy on him, as it says, For it is a people of no understanding, therefore He that made them will have no compassion upon them.[5] R. Eleazar said: Great is the Sanctuary, since it has been placed between two names, as it says, Thou hast made, O Lord, the sanctuary, O Lord.[6]
R. Eleazar also said: Whenever there is in a man knowledge, it is as if the Sanctuary had been built in his days; for knowledge is set between two names, and the Sanctuary is set between two names. R. Aha Karhina'ah demurred to this. According to this, he said, great is vengeance since it has been set between two names, as it says, God of vengeance, O Lord;[7] He replied: That is so; that is to say, it is great in its proper sphere; and this accords with what 'Ulla said: Why two vengeances here?[8] One for good and one for ill. For good, as it is written, He shined forth from Mount Paran;[9] for ill, as it is written, God of vengeance, O Lord, God of vengeance, shine forth.[10]

R. AKIBA SAYS: HE SAYS IT AS A FOURTH BLESSING, etc. R. Shaman b. Abba said to R. Johanan: Let us see: It was the Men of the Great Synagogue[11] who instituted for Israel blessings and prayers, sanctifications and habdalahs.[12] Let us see where they inserted them! — He replied: At first they inserted it [the habdalah] in the Tefillah: when they [Israel] became richer, they instituted that it should be said over the cup [of wine]; when they became poor again they again inserted it in the Tefillah; and they said that one who has said habdalah in the Tefillah must say it [again] over the cup [of wine]. It has also been stated: R. Hiyya b. Abba said in the name of R. Johanan: The Men of the Great Synagogue instituted for Israel blessings and prayers, sanctifications and habdalahs. At first

---

[1] Ibid. p. 51.
[2] Viz., discerning between holy and profane and between clean and unclean etc.
[3] I.e., two mentions of the Deity. Lit., 'letters'; var. lec. 'words'.
[4] I Sam. II, 3.
[5] Isa. XXVII, 11.
[6] Ex. XV, 17. (lit. trans.).
[7] Ps. XCIV, 1.
[8] The word 'vengeance' is written twice in the verse cited from Psalms.
[9] Deut. XXXIII, 2. It is difficult to see what this has to do with vengeance. It seems that in fact the text does not explain the statement of 'Ulla, and instead shows how there are two kinds of 'shining forth'. V. Sanh. 92a.
[10] Ps. XCIV, 1.
[11] V. Aboth I, 1.
[12] The various divisions mentioned in the habdalah benediction.

they inserted the habdalah in the Tefillah. When they [Israel] became richer, they instituted that it should be said over the cup [of wine]. When they became poor again, they inserted it in the Tefillah; and they said that one who says habdalah in the Tefillah must [also] say it over the cup [of wine]. It has also been stated: Rabbah and R. Joseph both say: One who has said habdalah in the Tefillah must [also] say it over the cup [of wine]. Said Raba: We can bring an objection against this ruling [from the following]: If a man forgot and did not mention the miracle of the rain in the resurrection blessing, or petition for rain in the blessing of the years, he is made to repeat the Tefillah. If, however, he forgot habdalah in 'that graciously grantest knowledge', he is not made to repeat, because he can say it over the cup [of wine]![1] Do not read, because he can say it over the cup [of wine], but read, because he says it over the cup [of wine].

It has also been stated: R. Benjamin b. Jephet said: R. Jose asked R. Johanan in Sidon — some report, R. Simeon b. Jacob from Tyre asked R. Johanan: But I have heard that one who has said habdalah in the Tefillah says it over the cup [of wine]; or is it not so? He replied to him: He must say it over the cup [of wine].

The question was raised: If one has said habdalah over the cup [of wine], need he say it [again] in the Tefillah? — R. Nahman b. Isaac replied: We learn the answer a fortiori from the case of Tefillah. The essential place of the habdalah is in the Tefillah, and yet it was laid down that one who has said it in the Tefillah must say it also over the cup [of wine]. Does it not then stand to reason that if he has said it over the cup [of wine], which is not its essential place, he must say it [again] in the Tefillah? R. Aha Arika[2] recited in the presence of R. Hinena: He who says habdalah in the Tefillah is more praiseworthy than he who says it over the cup [of wine], and if he says it in both, may blessings rest on his head! This statement contains a contradiction. It says that he who says habdalah in the Tefillah is more praiseworthy than he who says it over the cup [of wine], which would show that to say it in Tefillah alone is sufficient, and again it teaches, 'and if he says it in both, may blessings rest on his head', but since he has said it in one he is quit, the second is a blessing which is not necessary, and Raba, or as some say Resh Lakish, or again as some say, both Resh Lakish and R. Johanan, have said: Whoever says a blessing which is not necessary transgresses the command of 'thou shalt not take [God's name in vain]'![3] Rather read thus: If he has said habdalah in one and not in the other, blessings shall rest upon his head.

R. Hisda inquired of R. Shesheth: If he forgot in both,[4] what is he to do? — He replied: If one forgot in both, he says the whole again.[5]

---

[1] V. infra 26b. Which seems to show that it is optional.
[2] The Tall.
[3] Ex. XX, 7.
[4] In the case of habdalah over the cup, he failed to say the last benediction which contains the enumeration of the various divisions. V. D.S. a.l.
[5] He recites anew the Tefillah and the benediction over the cup of wine.

Berakoth 33b

Rabina said to Raba: What is the law?[1] He replied to him: The same as in the case of sanctification. Just as the sanctification, although it has been said in the Tefillah, is also said over the cup [of wine], so habdalah, although it has been said in the Tefillah, is also to be said over the cup [of wine].

R. ELIEZER SAYS: IN THE THANKSGIVING BENEDICTION. R. Zera was once riding on an ass, with R. Hiyya b. Abin following on foot.[2] He said to him: Did you really say in the name of R. Johanan that the halachah is as stated by R. Eliezer on a festival that falls after Sabbath?[3] He replied: Yes, that is the halachah. Am I to assume [he replied] that they [the Rabbis] differ from him?[4] — And do they not differ? Surely the Rabbis differ!
— I would say that the Rabbis differ in regard to the other days of the year, but do they differ in regard to a festival which falls after a Sabbath? — But surely R. Akiba differs?[5]
— Do we follow R. Akiba the rest of the year that we should now[6] commence to follow him? Why do we not follow R. Akiba all the rest of the year? Because eighteen blessings were instituted, not nineteen. Here too [on the festival] seven were instituted, not eight![7]

[R. Zera then] said to him: It was not stated that such is the halachah,[8] but that we incline to this view.[9] It has been stated: R. Isaac b. Abdimi said in the name of our teacher [Rab]: Such is the halachah, but some say, we [merely] incline to this view. R. Johanan said: [The Rabbis] agree [with R. Eliezer].[10] R. Hiyya b. Abba said: This appears correct.[11] R. Zera said: Choose the statement of R. Hiyya b Abba, for he is very accurate in repeating the statements of his teacher, like Rahaba of Pumbeditha. For Rahaba said in the name of Rabbi Judah: The Temple Mount was a double stoa — a stoa within a stoa.[12] R. Joseph said: I know neither one nor the other,[13] but I only know that Rab and Samuel instituted for us a precious pearl in Babylon:[14] 'And Thou didst make known unto us, O Lord our God, Thy righteous judgments and didst teach us to do the statutes that Thou hast willed, and hast made us inherit seasons of gladness and festivals of freewill-offering, and didst transmit to us the holiness of Sabbath and the glory of the appointed season and the celebration of the festival. Thou hast divided between the holiness of Sabbath and the holiness of the festival, and hast sanctified the seventh day above the six working days: Thou hast separated and sanctified Thy people Israel with

---

[1] About saying habdalah over wine, after having mentioned it in the Tefillah.
[2] Lit., 'betaking himself and going'.
[3] I.e., on Saturday night, when the fourth benediction 'that graciously grantestknowledge' is not said.
[4] Because otherwise there would be no need to say that the halachah follows him.
[5] R. Akiba provides for habdalah a benediction by itself. Consequently is was necessary to declare the halachah follows R. Eliezer on at festival which follows Sabbath, to exclude the view of R. Akiba.
[6] On a festival following Sabbath.
[7] Why then is it necessary to say that the halachah is as R. Eliezer, not as stated by R. Akiba?
[8] And is to be taught as such in public.
[9] And we advise individuals to act thus if they inquire.
[10] When a festival falls on Saturday night.
[11] We do not recommend this, but if one does so, we do not interfere.
[12] Though the word used in the Mishnah of Pes. (13a) is not stoa (colonnade) but the more familiar iztaba which has the same meaning. V. Pes. (Sonc. ed.) P. 59. nn. 10-11 and Bez. (Sonc. ed.) p. 54 n. 9.
[13] That we incline towards the view of R. Eliezer or that we regard it as probable.
[14] To be inserted in the fourth benediction of the festival 'Amidah.

Thy holiness. And Thou hast given us' etc.[1]

MISHNAH. IF ONE [IN PRAYING] SAYS 'MAY THY MERCIES EXTEND TO A BIRD'S NEST',[2] 'BE THY NAME MENTIONED FOR WELL-DOING', OR 'WE GIVE THANKS, WE GIVE THANKS', HE IS SILENCED.[3]

GEMARA. We understand why he is silenced if he says 'WE GIVE THANKS, WE GIVE THANKS', because he seems to be acknowledging two powers;[4] also if he says, 'BE THY NAME MENTIONED FOR WELL-DOING', because this implies, for the good only and not for the bad, and we have learnt, A man must bless God for the evil as he blesses Him for the good.[5] But what is the reason for silencing him if he says 'THY MERCIES EXTEND TO THE BIRD'S NEST? — Two Amoraim in the West, R. Jose b. Abin and R. Jose b. Zebida, give different answers; one says it is because he creates jealousy among God's creatures,[6] the other, because he presents the measures taken by the Holy One, blessed be He, as springing from compassion, whereas they are but decrees.[7] A certain [reader] went down [before the Ark] in the presence of Rabbah and said, 'Thou hast shown mercy to the bird's nest, show Thou pity and mercy to us'. Said Rabbah: How well this student knows how to placate his Master! Said Abaye to him: But we have learnt, HE IS SILENCED? — Rabbah too acted thus only to test[8] Abaye.

A certain [reader] went down in the presence of R. Hanina and said, O God, the great, mighty, terrible, majestic, powerful, awful, strong, fearless, sure and honoured. He waited till he had finished, and when he had finished he said to him, Have you concluded all the praise of your Master? Why do we want all this? Even with these three that we do say,[9] had not Moses our Master mentioned them in the Law[10] and had not the Men of the Great Synagogue come and inserted them in the Tefillah, we should not have been able to mention them, and you say all these and still go on! It is as if an earthly king had a million denarii of gold, and someone praised him as possessing silver ones. Would it not be an insult to him?

R. Hanina further said: Everything is in the hand of heaven except the fear of heaven,[11] as it says, And now, Israel, what doth the Lord thy God require of thee but to fear.[12] Is the fear of heaven such a little thing? Has not R. Hanina said in the name R. Simeon b. Yohai: The Holy One, blessed be He, has in His treasury nought except a store of the fear of heaven, as it says, The fear of the Lord is His treasure?[13] — Yes; for Moses it was a small thing; as R. Hanina said: To illustrate by a parable, if a man is asked for a big article and he has it, it seems like a small article to him; if he is asked for a small article and he does not possess it, it seems like a big article to him.

---

[1] This form of habdalah prayer is used with slight variants on a festival that follows Sabbath, v. P.B. p. 227.
[2] V. Deut. XXII, 6.
[3] For the reasons, v. the Gemara. This Mishnah is found in Meg. 26a with a somewhat different reading.
[4] The dualism of the Persian — the God of darkness and the God of light.
[5] Infra 54a.
[6] By implying that this one is favoured above others.
[7] V. Meg. (Sonc. ed.) p. 149 notes.
[8] Lit., 'sharpen'. He wanted to see if he knew the law.
[9] Great, mighty, and terrible, in the first benediction.
[10] Deut. X, 17.
[11] I.e., all a man's qualities are fixed by nature, but his moral character depends on his own choice.
[12] Deut. X, 12.
[13] Isa. XXXIII, 6.

WE GIVE THANKS, WE GIVE THANKS, HE IS SILENCED. R. Zera said: To say 'Hear, hear', [in the Shema'] is like saying 'We give thanks, we give thanks'. An objection was raised: He who recites the Shema' and repeats it is reprehensible. He is reprehensible, but we do not silence him? — There is no contradiction; in the one case he repeats each word as he says it,[1] in the other each sentence.[2] Said R. papa to Abaye: But perhaps [he does this because] at first he was not attending to what he said and the second time he does attend? — He replied:

Folio 34a

Can one behave familiarly with Heaven? If he did not recite with attention at first, we hit him with a smith's hammer until he does attend.

MISHNAH. [IF ONE SAYS, LET THE GOOD BLESS THEE, THIS IS A PATH OF HERESY].[3] IF ONE WAS PASSING BEFORE THE ARK AND MADE A MISTAKE, ANOTHER SHOULD PASS IN HIS PLACE, AND AT SUCH A MOMENT ONE MAY NOT REFUSE. WHERE SHOULD HE COMMENCE? AT THE BEGINNING OF THE BENEDICTION IN WHICH THE OTHER WENT WRONG. THE READER[4] SHOULD NOT RESPOND AMEN AFTER [THE BENEDICTIONS OF] THE PRIESTS[5] BECAUSE THIS MIGHT CONFUSE HIM. IF THERE IS NO PRIEST THERE EXCEPT HIMSELF, HE SHOULD NOT RAISE HIS HANDS [IN PRIESTLY BENEDICTION], BUT IF HE IS CONFIDENT THAT HE CAN. RAISE HIS HANDS AND GO BACK TO HIS PLACE IN HIS PRAYER,[6] HE IS PERMITTED TO DO SO.

GEMARA. Our Rabbis taught: If one is asked to pass before the Ark, he ought to refuse,[7] and if he does not refuse he resembles a dish without salt; but if he persists too much in refusing he resembles a dish which is over-salted. How should he act? The first time he should refuse; the second time he should hesitate; the third time he should stretch out his legs and go down.
Our Rabbis taught: There are three things of which one may easily have too much[8] while a little is good, namely, yeast, salt, and refusal.

R. Huna said: If one made a mistake in the first three [of the Tefillah] blessings, he goes back to the beginning; if in the middle blessings, he goes back to 'Thou graciously grantest knowledge;'[9] if in the last blessings, he goes back to the 'Abodah.[10] R. Assi, however, says that in the middle ones the order

---

[1] This is merely reprehensible.
[2] In this case he is silenced since this is as if he were addressing two Powers.
[3] Minuth, (v. Glos. s.v. Min) implying that only the good are invited to bless God. This passage is wanting in the separate editions of the Mishnah, but occurs in Meg. 25a.
[4] Lit., 'he who passes before the Ark'.
[5] V. P.B. 283a (15th ed.).
[6] Without making a mistake in the prayers.
[7] As feeling himself unworthy for the sacred duty.
[8] Lit., 'a large quantity is hard'.
[9] The fourth benediction in the Tefillah, v. P.B. p. 46.
[10] Lit., 'service'. The seventeenth blessing, v. P.B. p. 50.

need not be observed.[1] R. Shesheth cited in objection: 'Where should he commence? At the beginning of the benediction in which the other went wrong'.[2] This is a refutation of R. Huna, is it not?[3] — R. Huna can reply: The middle blessings are all one.[4]

Rab Judah said: A man should never petition for his requirements either in the first three benedictions or in the last three, but in the middle ones. For R. Hanina said: In the first ones he resembles a servant who is addressing a eulogy to his master; in the middle ones he resembles a servant who is requesting a largess from his master, in the last ones he resembles a servant who has received a largess from his master and takes his leave.

Our Rabbis taught: Once a certain disciple went down[5] before the Ark in the presence of R. Eliezer, and he span out the prayer to a great length. His disciples said to him: Master, how longwinded this fellow is! He replied to them: Is he drawing it out any more than our Master Moses, of whom it is written: The forty days and the forty nights [that I fell down]?[6] Another time it happened that a certain disciple went down before the Ark in the presence of R. Eliezer, and he cut the prayer very short. His disciples said to him: How concise this fellow is! He replied to them: Is he any more concise than our Master Moses, who prayed, as it is written: Heal her now, O God, I beseech Thee?[7] R. Jacob said in the name of R. Hisda: If one prays on behalf of his fellow, he need not mention his name, since it says: Heal her now, O God, I beseech Thee', and he did not mention the name of Miriam.

Our Rabbis taught: These are the benedictions in saying which one bows [in the Tefillah]: The benediction of the patriarchs,[8] beginning and end, and the thanksgiving, beginning and end.[9] If one wants to bow down at the end of each benediction and at the beginning of each benediction, he is instructed not to do so. R. Simeon b. Pazzi said in the name of R. Joshua b. Levi, reporting Bar Kappara: An ordinary person bows as we have mentioned;

---

[1] And if one was accidentally omitted it can be inserted anywhere. So Rashi. Tosaf., however, say that he goes back to that blessing and continues from there.
[2] So M.S. M. cur. edd. read: 'To where does he go back'.
[3] Because it shows that he need not go back to 'Thou graciously grantest'.
[4] And if one errs in any of them he has to go back to 'Thou graciously grantest'.
[5] The reading desk was at a lower level than the floor of the Synagogue. (v. supra 10); hence the expression 'went down'.
[6] Deut. IX, 25.
[7] Num. XII, 13.
[8] The first benediction.
[9] V. P.B. 51 and 53.

Berakoth 34b

a high priest at the end of each benediction; a king at the beginning of each benediction and at the end of each benediction.[1] R. Isaac b. Nahmani said: It was explained to me by R. Joshua b. Levi that an ordinary person does as we have mentioned; a high priest bows at the beginning of each blessing; and a king, once he has knelt down, does not rise again [until the end of the Tefillah], as it says: And it was so that when Solomon had made an end of praying, ... he arose from before the Altar of the Lord, from kneeling on his knees.[2]

Kidah [bowing] is upon the face, as it says: Then Bath-Sheba bowed with her face to the ground.[3] Keri'ah [kneeling] is upon the knees, as it says: From kneeling on his knees, prostration is spreading out of hands and feet, as it says: Shall I and thy mother and thy brethren come to prostrate ourselves before thee on the ground.[4]

R. Hiyya the son of R. Huna said: I have observed Abaye and Raba bending to one side.[5] One [Baraitha] taught: To kneel in the thanksgiving benediction is praiseworthy, while another taught: It is reprehensible? — There is no contradiction: one speaks of the beginning,[6] the other of the end. Raba knelt in the thanksgiving at the beginning and at the end. The Rabbis said to him: Why does your honour act thus? He replied to them: I have seen R. Nahman kneeling, and I have seen R. Shesheth doing thus. But it has been taught: To kneel in the thanksgiving is reprehensible — That refers to the thanksgiving in Hallel.[7] But it has been taught: To kneel in the thanksgiving and in the thanksgiving of Hallel is reprehensible? — The former statement refers to the thanksgiving in the Grace after Meals.[8]

MISHNAH. IF ONE MAKES A MISTAKE IN HIS TEFILLAH IT IS A BAD SIGN FOR HIM, AND IF HE IS A READER OF THE CONGREGATION[9] IT IS A BAD SIGN FOR THOSE WHO HAVE COMMISSIONED HIM, BECAUSE A MAN'S AGENT IS EQUIVALENT TO HIMSELF. IT WAS RELATED OF R. HANINA BEN DOSA THAT HE USED TO PRAY FOR THE SICK AND SAY, THIS ONE WILL DIE, THIS ONE WILL LIVE. THEY SAID TO HIM: HOW DO YOU KNOW? HE REPLIED: IF MY PRAYER COMES OUT FLUENTLY,[10] I KNOW THAT HE IS ACCEPTED, BUT IF NOT, THEN I KNOW THAT HE IS REJECTED.[11]

GEMARA. In which blessing [is a mistake a bad sign]? — R. Hiyya said in the name of R. Safra who had it from a member of the School of Rabbi: In the blessing of the Patriarchs.[12] Some attach this statement to the following: 'When one says the Tefillah he must say all the blessings attentively, and

---

[1] I.e., the greater the individual, the more he humbles himself.
[2] I Kings VIII, 54.
[3] Ibid. I, 31.
[4] Gen. XXXVII, 10.
[5] And not completely prostrating themselves.
[6] This is praiseworthy.
[7] The verse, Give thanks unto the Lord, for he is good, etc., v. P.B. p. 222.
[8] P.B. p. 281.
[9] Lit., 'An agent of the congregation'.
[10] Lit., 'is fluent in my mouth'.
[11] Lit., 'he is torn'. The word, however, may refer to the Prayer, meaning that it is rejected.
[12] The first blessing in the Tefillah.

if he cannot say all attentively he should say one attentively'. R. Hiyya said in the name of R. Safra who had it from a member of the School of Rabbi: This one should be the blessing of the Patriarchs.

IT WAS RELATED OF RABBI HANINA etc. What is the [Scriptural] basis for this? — R. Joshua b. Levi said: Because Scripture says: Peace to him that is far off and to him that is near, saith the Lord that createth the fruit of the lips, and I will heal him.[1]

R. Hiyya b. Abba said in the name of R. Johanan: All the prophets prophesied only on behalf of[2] one who gives his daughter in marriage to a scholar and who conducts business on behalf of a scholar and who allows a scholar the use of his possessions. But as for the scholars themselves, Eye hath not seen, oh God, beside Thee what He will do for him that waiteth for Him.[3]
R. Hiyya b. Abba also said in the name of R. Johanan: All the prophets prophesied only for the days of the Messiah, but as for the world to come, 'Eye hath not seen, oh God, beside Thee'. These Rabbis differ from Samuel; for Samuel said: There is no difference between this world and the days of the Messiah except [that in the latter there will be no] bondage of foreign powers, as it says: For the poor shall never cease out of the land.[4]

R. Hiyya b. Abba also said in the name of R. Johanan: All the prophets prophesied only on behalf of penitents; but as for the wholly righteous, 'Eye hath not seen, oh God, beside Thee'. He differs in this from R. Abbahu. For R. Abbahu said: In the place where penitents stand even the wholly righteous cannot stand, as it says: Peace, peace to him that was far and to him that is near[5] — to him that was far first, and then to him that is near. R. Johanan, however, said: What is meant by 'far'? One who from the beginning was far from transgression. And what is meant by 'near'? That he was once near to transgression and now has gone far from it.[6] What is the meaning of 'Eye hath not seen'? R. Joshua b. Levi said: This is the wine which has been preserved in its grapes from the six days of Creation.[7] R. Samuel b. Nahmani said: This is Eden,[8] which has never been seen by the eye of any creature, perhaps you will say, Where then was Adam? He was in the garden. Perhaps you will say, the garden and Eden are the same? Not so! For the text says: And a river went out of Eden to water the garden[9] — the garden is one thing and Eden is another.

Our Rabbis taught: Once the son of R. Gamaliel fell ill. He sent two scholars to R. Hanina
b. Dosa to ask him to pray for him. When he saw them he went up to an upper chamber and prayed for him. When he came down he said to them: Go, the fever has left him; They said to him: Are you a prophet? He replied: I am neither a prophet nor the son of a prophet, but I learnt this from experience. If my prayer is fluent in my mouth, I know that he is accepted: but if not, I know that he is rejected.[10] They sat down and made a note of the exact moment. When they came to R. Gamaliel, he said to them: By the temple service! You have not been a moment too soon or too late, but so it happened: at

---

[1] Isa. LVII, 19. Bore translated 'created' has also the meaning 'strong', hence the verse is rendered to mean: if the fruit of the lips (prayer) is strong (fluent) then I will heal him.
[2] I.e., their promises and consolations had reference to.
[3] Isa. LXIV, 3.
[4] Deut. XV, 11. 'Never' i.e., not even in the Messianic era.
[5] Isa. LVII, 19.
[6] I.e., the Penitent.
[7] To feast the righteous in the future world.
[8] Paradise.
[9] Gen. II, 10.
[10] V. supra, p. 214 n. 4.

that very moment the fever left him and he asked for water to drink.

On another occasion it happened that R. Hanina b. Dosa went to study Torah with R. Johanan ben Zakkai. The son of R. Johanan ben Zakkai fell ill. He said to him: Hanina my son, pray for him that he may live. He put his head between his knees and prayed for him and he lived. Said R. Johanan ben Zakkai: If Ben Zakkai had stuck his head between his knees for the whole day, no notice would have been taken of him. Said his wife to him: Is Hanina greater than you are? He replied to her: No; but he is like a servant before the king,[2] and I am like a nobleman before a king.[3]

R. Hiyya b. Abba said in the name of R. Johanan: A man should not pray save in a room which has windows,[4] since it says, Now his windows were open in his upper chamber towards Jerusalem.[5]

R. Kahana said: I consider a man impertinent who prays in a valley.[6] R. Kahana also said: I consider a man impertinent who openly[7] recounts his sins, since it is said, Happy is he whose transgression is forgiven, whose sin is covered.[8]

---

[2] Who has permission to go in to him at anytime.
[3] Who appears before him only at fixed times.
[4] So that he should have a view of the heavens.
[5] Dan. VI, 11.
[6] A level stretch of ground where people constantly pass; one should pray in an enclosed and secluded spot.
[7] As though unashamed.
[8] Lit., trans. E.V. 'whose sin is Pardoned' Ps. XXXII, 1.

Folio 35a

CHAPTER VI

MISHNAH. WHAT BLESSINGS ARE SAID OVER FRUIT? OVER FRUIT OF THE TREE ONE SAYS, WHO CREATEST THE FRUIT OF THE TREE, EXCEPT FOR WINE, OVER WHICH ONE SAYS, WHO CREATEST THE FRUIT OF THE VINE. OVER THAT WHICH GROWS FROM THE GROUND ONE SAYS: WHO CREATEST THE FRUIT OF THE GROUND, EXCEPT OVER BREAD, FOR WHICH ONE SAYS, WHO BRINGEST FORTH BREAD FROM THE EARTH. OVER VEGETABLES ONE SAYS, WHO CREATEST THE FRUIT OF THE GROUND; R. JUDAH, HOWEVER, SAYS: WHO CREATEST DIVERS KINDS OF HERBS.

GEMARA. Whence is this derived?[1] — As our Rabbis have taught: The fruit thereof shall be holy, for giving praise unto the Lord.[2] This[3] teaches that they require a blessing both before and after partaking of them. On the strength of this R. Akiba said: A man is forbidden to taste anything before saying a blessing over it.

But is this the lesson to be learnt from these words 'Holy for giving praise'? Surely they are required for these two lessons: first, to teach that the All-Merciful has declared: Redeem it[4] and then eat it, and secondly, that a thing which requires a song of praise requires redemption,[5] but one that does not require a song of praise does not require redemption,[6] as has been taught by R. Samuel b. Nahmani in the name of R. Jonathan. For R. Samuel b. Nahmani said in the name of R. Jonathan: Whence do we know that a song of praise is sung only over wine?[7] Because it says, And the vine said unto them: Should I leave my wine which cheereth God and man?[8] If it cheers man, how does it cheer God? From this we learn that a song of praise is sung only over wine.

Now this reasoning[9] is valid for him who teaches 'The planting of the fourth year'.[10] But for him who teaches 'The vineyard of the fourth year', what can be said? For it has been stated: R. Hiyya and R. Simeon the son of Rabbi [taught differently]. One taught, 'Vineyard of the fourth year', the other taught, 'Planting of the fourth year'. — For him who teaches 'Vineyard of the fourth year' also there is no difficulty if he avails himself of a gezerah shawah.[11] For it has been taught: Rabbi says: It says there, that it may yield unto you more richly the increase thereof,[12] and it says in another place, the

---

[1] That a benediction is necessary before partaking of any food.
[2] Lev. XIX, 24, with reference to the fruit of the fourth year.
[3] The fact that the word hillulim (praise) is in the plural, indicating that there must be two praises.
[4] The fruit of the fourth year, if it is to be eaten outside Jerusalem.
[5] This is learnt from a play on the word hillulim, which is read also as hillulim(profaned, i.e., redeemed).
[6] Thus limiting the law relating to the fruit of the fourth year only to the vine, as infra.
[7] By the Levites at the offering of the sacrifices.
[8] Judg. IX, 13.
[9] That we learn the requirement of saying a blessing from the word hillulim.
[10] I.e., that the verse quoted from Leviticus refers to all fruit of the fourth year and not to the vine only. In this case the word hillulim can not be used to prove that only the vine requires redemption. and is available for teaching that a blessing must be said over fruit.
[11] v. Glos.
[12] Lev. XIX, 25.

increase of the vineyard.¹ Just as in the latter passage 'increase' refers to the vineyard, so here it refers to the vineyard. Thus one hillul is left over to indicate that a blessing is required. But if he does not avail himself of a gezerah shawah, how can he derive this lesson? And even if he does avail himself of a gezerah shawah, while we are satisfied that a blessing is required after it,² whence do we learn that it is required [before partaking]? — This is no difficulty. We derive it by argument a fortiori: If he says a blessing when he is full, how much more so ought he to do so when he is hungry?³

We have found a proof for the case of [the produce of the vineyard]: whence do we find [that a benediction is required] for other species?⁴ It can be learnt from the vineyard. Just as the vineyard being something that is enjoyed requires a blessing, so everything that is enjoyed requires a blessing. But this may be refuted: How can we learn from a vineyard, seeing that it is subject to the obligation of the gleanings?⁵ — We may cite the instance of corn.⁶ How can you cite the instance of corn, seeing that it is subject to the obligation of hallah?⁷ — We may then cite the instance of the vineyard, and the argument goes round in a circle: The distinguishing feature of the first instance is not like that of the second, and vice versa. The feature common to both is that being things which are enjoyed they require a blessing; similarly everything which is enjoyed requires a blessing. But this [argument from a] common feature [is not conclusive], because there is with them⁸ the common feature that they are offered on the altar!⁹ We may then adduce also the olive from the fact that it is offered on the altar. But is [the blessing over] the olive derived from the fact that it is offered on the altar? It is explicitly designated kerem,¹⁰ as it is written, And he burnt up the shocks and the standing corn and also the olive yards [kerem]?¹¹ —

R. Papa replied: It is called an olive kerem but not kerem simply. Still the difficulty remains: How can you learn [other products] from the argument of a common factor, seeing that [wine and corn] have the common feature of being offered on the altar? — Rather it is learnt from the seven species.¹² Just as the seven species are something which being enjoyed requires a blessing,¹³ so everything which is enjoyed requires a blessing. How can you argue from the seven species. seeing that they are subject to the obligation of first-fruits? And besides, granted that we learn from them that a blessing is to be said after partaking, how do we know it is to be said before? — This is no difficulty, being learnt a fortiori: If he says a blessing when he is full, how much more should he do so when he is hungry? Now as for the one who reads 'planting of the fourth year', we may grant he has proved his point with regard to anything planted. But whence does he derive it in regard to things that are not planted, such as meat, eggs and fish? — The fact is that it is a reasonable supposition that it is forbidden to a man to enjoy anything of this world without saying a blessing.¹⁴

---

¹ Deut. XXII, 9.

² On the analogy of grace after meals as prescribed in Deut. VIII, 10.

³ And is about to satisfy his hunger.

⁴ On the view that Lev. XIX, 24 refers only to a vineyard.

⁵ Cf. Lev. XIX, 10. And this may be the reason why it requires a blessing.

⁶ Which is not subject to the obligation of gleanings, and yet requires a blessing, as laid down in Deut VIII, 10.

⁷ The heave-offering of the dough.

⁸ I.e., wine and corn.

⁹ In the form of drink-offering and meal-offering.

¹⁰ Lit. 'vineyard', and therefore it is on the same footing as wine.

¹¹ Judg. XV. 5.

¹² Mentioned in Deut. VIII, 8.

¹³ As distinctly prescribed in Deut. VIII, 8.

¹⁴ Whether we take the law of the fourth year to apply to the vine or to all fruit trees, we cannot derive from it the law for saying a blessing over all things — in the former case because of the difficulty about the altar, in the latter because of the difficulty about things other than plants. Nor can we derive the law from the 'seven kinds',

Our Rabbis have taught: It is forbidden to a man to enjoy anything of this world without a benediction, and if anyone enjoys anything of this world without a benediction, he commits sacrilege.[1] What is his remedy? He should consult a wise man. What will the wise man do for him? He has already committed the offence! — Said Raba: What it means is that he should consult a wise man beforehand, so that he should teach him blessings and he should not commit sacrilege. Rab Judah said in the name of Samuel: To enjoy anything of this world without a benediction is like making personal use of things consecrated to heaven, since it says. The earth is the Lord's and the fulness there of.[2] R. Levi contrasted two texts. It is written, 'The earth is the Lord's and the fulness thereof', and it is also written, The heavens are the heavens of the Lord, but the earth hath He given to the children of men![3] There is no contradiction: in the one case it is before a blessing has been said

Berakoth 35b

in the other case after. R. Hanina b. Papa said: To enjoy this world without a benediction is like robbing the Holy One, blessed be He, and the community of Israel, as it says. Whoso robbeth his father or his mother and saith, It is no transgression, the same is the companion of a destroyer;[4] and 'father' is none other but the Holy One, blessed be He, as it says. Is not He thy father that hath gotten thee;[5] and 'mother' is none other than the community of Israel, as it says, Hear, my son, the instruction of thy father, and forsake not the teaching of thy mother.[6] What is the meaning of 'he is the companion of a destroyer'? — R. Hanina
b. Papa answered: He is the companion of Jeroboam son of Nebat who destroyed Israel's [faith in] their Father in heaven.[7]
R. Hanina b. Papa pointed out a contradiction. It is written, Therefore will I take back My corn in the time thereof, etc.,[8] and it is elsewhere written, And thou shalt gather in thy corn, etc.![9] There is no difficulty: the one text speaks of where Israel do the will of the Omnipresent, the other of where they do not perform the will of the Omnipresent.[10]

Our Rabbis taught: And thou shalt gather in thy corn.[11] What is to be learnt from these words? Since it says, This book of the law shall not depart out of thy mouth,[12] I might think that this injunction is to be taken literally. Therefore it says, 'And thou shalt gather in thy corn', which implies that you are to

---

because of the difficulty about first-fruits. Hence we are driven back upon 'reasonable supposition'.
[1] Heb. ma'al, the technical term for the personal use of consecrated things by a layman.
[2] Ps. XXIV. 1.
[3] Ibid. CXV, 16.
[4] Prov. XXVIII, 24. To rob God can only mean to enjoy something without saying a blessing, in recognition that it comes from Him.
[5] Deut. XXXII, 6.
[6] Prov. I, 8.
[7] Likewise he who enjoys things without a blessing sets a bad example to others.
[8] Hos. II, 11.
[9] Deut. XI, 14.
[10] Who accordingly takes back the corn and shows that it is His.
[11] Deut. XI, 14.
[12] Joshua I, 8.

combine the study of them¹ with a worldly occupation. This is the view of R. Ishmael. R. Simeon b. Yohai says: Is that possible? If a man ploughs in the ploughing season, and sows in the sowing season, and reaps in the reaping season, and threshes in the threshing season, and winnows in the season of wind, what is to become of the Torah? No; but when Israel perform the will of the Omnipresent, their work is performed by others, as it says. And strangers shall stand and feed your flocks. etc.,² and when Israel do not perform the will of the Omnipresent their work is carried out by themselves, as it says, And thou shalt gather in thy corn.³ Nor is this all, but the work of others also is done by them, as it says. And thou shalt serve thine enemy etc.⁴ Said Abaye: Many have followed the advice of Ishmael, and it has worked well; others have followed R. Simeon b. Yohai and it has not been successful. Raba said to the Rabbis: I would ask you not to appear before me during Nisan and Tishri⁵ so that you may not be anxious about your food supply during the rest of the year.

Rabbah b. Bar Hanah said in the name of R. Johanan, reporting R. Judah b. Ila'i: See what a difference there is between the earlier and the later generations. The earlier generations made the study of the Torah their main concern and their ordinary work subsidiary to it, and both prospered in their hands. The later generations made their ordinary work their main concern and their study of the Torah subsidiary, and neither prospered in their hands.

Rabbah b. Bar Hanah further said in the name of R. Johanan reporting R. Judah b. Ila'i: Observe the difference between the earlier and the later generations. The earlier generations used to bring in their produce by way of the kitchen-garden⁶ purposely in order to make it liable to tithe, whereas the later generations bring in their produce by way of roofs or courtyards or enclosures in order to make it exempt from tithe. For R. Jannai has said: Untithed produce is not subject to tithing⁷ until it has come within sight of the house, since it says. I have put away the hallowed things out of my house.⁸ R. Johanan, however, says that even [sight of] a courtyard imposes the obligation, as it says, That they may eat within thy gates and be satisfied.⁹

EXCEPT OVER WINE. Why is a difference made for wine? Shall I say that because [the raw material of] it is improved¹⁰ therefore the blessing is different? But in the case of oil also [the raw material of] it is improved, yet the blessing is not different, as Rab Judah has laid down in the name of Samuel, and so R. Isaac stated in the name of R. Johanan, that the blessing said over olive oil is 'that createst the fruit of the tree'?¹¹ — The answer given is that in the case of oil it is not possible to change the blessing. For what shall we say? Shall we say, 'That createst the fruit of the olive'? The fruit itself is called olive!¹² But we can say over it, 'That createst the fruit of the olive tree'? — Rather [the real reason is], said Mar Zutra, that wine has food value but oil has no food value. But has oil no food value? Have we not learnt: One who takes a vow to abstain from food is allowed to partake of water and salt,¹³ and we argued from this as follows: 'Water and salt alone are not called food, but all

---

¹ Sc. the words of the Torah.
² Isa. LXI, 5.
³ Tosaf. point out that this homily conflicts with that given above on the same verse by R. Hanina b. Papa.
⁴ Deut. XXVIII, 48.
⁵ Nisan being the time of the ripening of the corn and Tishri of the vintage and olive pressing.
⁶ I.e., direct to the house, by the front way. V. infra.
⁷ I.e., according to the Torah. The Rabbis, however, forbade a fixed meal to be made of any untithed produce.
⁸ Deut. XXVI, 13.
⁹ Ibid. 12; v. Git. 81a.
¹⁰ Lit., 'it has been changed for the better'.
¹¹ As over the olive itself.
¹² There is no special name in Hebrew for the olive tree as there is for the vine.
¹³ 'Er. 26b.

other stuffs are called food? May we not say that this is a refutation of Rab and Samuel, who say that the blessing "who createst various kinds of food" is said only over the five species [of cereals]?¹ and R. Huna solved the problem by saying that [the Mishnah] refers to one who says, 'I vow to abstain from anything that feeds'; which shows that oil has food value?² — Rather [say the reason is that] wine sustains³ and oil does not sustain. But does wine sustain? Did not Raba use to drink wine on the eve of the Passover in order that he might get an appetite and eat much unleavened bread? — A large quantity gives an appetite, a small quantity sustains. But does it in fact give any sustenance? Is it not written, And wine that maketh glad the heart of man … and bread that stayeth man's heart,⁴ which shows that it is bread which sustains, not wine? — The fact is that wine does both, it sustains and makes glad, whereas bread sustains but does not cheer. If that is the case, let us say three blessings after it?⁵ — People do not make it the basis of the meal. R. Nahman b. Isaac asked Raba: Suppose a man makes it the basis of his meal. what then? — He replied: When Elijah comes he will tell us whether it can really serve as a basis; at present, at any rate, no man thinks of such a thing.⁶

The text [above] stated: 'Rab Judah said in the name of Samuel, and so too said R. Isaac in the name of R. Johanan, that the blessing said over olive oil is "that createst the fruit of the tree"'. How are we to understand this? Are we to say that it is drunk? If so, it is injurious, as it has been taught: If one drinks oil of terumah,⁷ he repays the bare value, but does not add a fifth.⁸ If one anoints himself with oil of terumah, he repays the value and also a fifth in addition. Do we suppose then that he consumes it with bread? In that case, the bread would be the main ingredient and the oil subsidiary, and we have learnt: This is the general rule: If with one article of food another is taken as accessory, a blessing is said over the main article, and this suffices also for the accessory!⁹ Do we suppose then that he drinks it with elaiogaron? (Rabbah b. Samuel has stated: Elaiogaron is juice of beetroots; oxygaron is juice of

---

¹ wheat, barley, oats, spelt, and rye.
² Even according to Rab and Samuel.
³ And has more than merely food value.
⁴ Ps. CIV, 15.
⁵ As after bread, v. infra 37a.
⁶ Aliter 'His opinion is rejected by all men'.
⁷ V. Glos.
⁸ Because the fifth is added only for what can be called food, since it says, And if a man eat of the holy thing through error (Lev. XXII, 14).
⁹ V. infra 41a.

Folio 36a

all other boiled vegetables.) In that case the elaiogaron would be the main thing and the oil subsidiary, and we have learnt: This is the general rule: If with one article of food another is taken as accessory, a blessing is said over the main article, and this suffices for the accessory! — What case have we here in mind?[1] The case of a man with a sore throat, since it has been taught: If one has a sore throat, he should not ease it directly with oil on Sabbath,[2] but he should put plenty of oil into elaiogaron and swallow it.[3] This is obvious![4] — You might think that since he intends it as a medicine he should not say any blessing over it. Therefore we are told that since he has some enjoyment from it he has to say a blessing.

Over wheaten flour[5] Rab Judah says that the blessing is 'who createst the fruit of the ground' [6] while R. Nahman says it is, 'By whose word all things exist'. Said Raba to R. Nahman: Do not join issue with Rab Judah, since R. Johanan and Samuel would concur with him. For Rab Judah said in the name of Samuel, and likewise R. Isaac said in the name of R. Johanan: Over olive oil the blessing said is 'that createst the fruit of the tree', which shows that although it has been transformed it is fundamentally the same. Here too, although it has been transformed, it is fundamentally the same. But are the two cases alike? In that case [of olive oil] the article does not admit of further improvement, in this case it does admit of further improvement, by being made into bread; and when it is still capable of further improvement we do not say over it the blessing 'that createst the fruit of the ground', but 'by whose word all things exist'! — But has not R. Zera said in the name of R. Mattena reporting Samuel: Over raw cabbage and barley-flour we say the blessing 'by whose word all things exist', and may we not infer from this that over wheat-flour we say 'who createst the fruit of the ground'? — No; over wheat-flour also we say 'by whose word all things exist'. Then let him state the rule for wheat-flour, and it will apply to barley-flour as a matter of course?[7] — If he had stated the rule as applying to wheat-flour, I might have said: That is the rule for wheat-flour, but over barley-flour we need say no blessing at all. Therefore we are told that this is not so. But is barley-flour of less account than salt or brine, of which we have learnt:[8] Over salt and brine one says 'by whose word all things exist'? — It was necessary [to lay down the rule for barley-flour]. You might argue that a man often puts a dash of salt or brine into his mouth [without harm], but barley-flour is harmful in creating tapeworms, and therefore we need say no blessing over it. We are therefore told that since one has some enjoyment from it he must say a blessing over it.

Over the palm-heart,[9] Rab Judah says that the blessing is 'that createst the fruit of the ground', while Samuel says that it is 'by whose word all things exist'. Rab Judah says it is 'that createst the fruit of the ground', regarding it as fruit, whereas Samuel says that it is 'by whose word all things exist', since

---

[1] When it is stated that oil requires a benediction.
[2] Medicine being forbidden on Sabbath, for fear one might come to pound drugs.
[3] For in this case it is not obvious that he is taking it as a medicine.
[4] That in this case one should make a blessing over the oil, because the oil is here the principal item.
[5] When eaten raw.
[6] Which is the blessing over crushed wheat, v. infra 37a.
[7] Since it is inferior to wheat-flour.
[8] More correctly, 'as it has been taught', v. infra 40b.
[9] An edible part of the young palm, which afterwards hardens and becomes part of the tree.

subsequently it grows hard. Said Samuel to Rab Judah:

Shinnena![1] Your opinion is the more probable, since radish eventually hardens and over it we say 'who createst the fruit of the ground'. This, however, is no proof; radishes are planted for the sake of the tuber,[2] but palms are not planted for the sake of the heart. But [is it the case that] wherever one thing is not planted for the sake of another [which it later becomes], we do not say the blessing [for that other]?[3] What of the caper-bush which is planted for the sake of the caper-blossom, and we have learnt: In regard to the various edible products of the caper-bush, over the leaves and the young shoots, 'that createst the fruit of the ground' is said, and over the berries and buds,[4] 'that createst the fruit of the tree'! — R. Nahman b. Isaac replied: Caper-bushes are planted for the sake of the shoots, but palms are not planted for the sake of the heart. And although Samuel commended Rab Judah, the halachah is as laid down by Samuel.

Rab Judah said in the name of Rab: In the case of an 'uncircumcised'[5] caper-bush outside of Palestine,[6] one throws away the berries and may eat the buds. This is to say that the berries are fruit but the buds are not fruit — A contradiction was pointed out [between this and the following]: In regard to the various edible articles produced by the caper-bush, over the leaves and the young shoots 'that createst the fruit of the ground' is said; over the buds and the berries 'that createst the fruit of the tree' is said! — [Rab Judah] followed R. Akiba, as we have learnt: R. Eliezer says: From the caper-bush tithe is given from the berries and buds. R. Akiba, however, says that the berries alone are tithed, because they are fruit.[7] Let him then say that the halachah is as laid down by R. Akiba? — Had he said that the halachah is as laid down by R. Akiba, I should have thought that this was so even in the Holy Land. He therefore informs us that if there is an authority who is more lenient in regard to [uncircumcised products in] the Holy Land, the halachah follows him in respect of [such products] outside of the Holy Land, but not in the Land itself. But let him then say that the halachah is as laid down by R. Akiba for outside the Holy Land, because if an authority is more lenient with regard to the Land, the halachah follows him in the case of outside the Land? — Had he said so, I should have argued that this applies to tithe of fruit which in the Holy Land itself was ordained only by the Rabbis,[8] but that in the case of 'orlah, the law for which is stated in the Torah, we should extend it to outside the Land. Therefore he tells us that we do not do so.

Rabina once found Mar b. R. Ashi throwing away [uncircumcised] caper-berries and eating the buds. He said to him: What is your view? Do you agree with R. Akiba who is more lenient?[9] Then follow Beth Shammai, who are more lenient still, as we have learnt: With regard to the caper-bush, Beth Shammai say that it constitutes kil'ayim[10] in the vineyard, whereas Beth Hillel hold that it does not constitute kil'ayim in the vineyard, while both agree that it is subject to the law of 'orlah. Now this statement itself contains a contradiction. You first say that Beth Shammai hold that a caper-bush

---

[1] An affectionate designation given by Samuel to his disciple Rab Judah. Apparently it means 'sharp-witted'. V. B.K. (Sonc. ed.) p. 60, n. 2.
[2] To be eaten before it becomes hard and woody.
[3] But 'by whose word all things exist'.
[4] Aliter: 'caper-flowers', or 'husks'.
[5] I.e., in its first three years. V. Lev. XIX, 23 (A.V.).
[6] To which the Rabbis extended the obligation of 'orlah, (v. Glos.).
[7] But the buds are not fruit.
[8] Since according to the written Torah, tithe was to be given only on corn, oil and wine.
[9] In not exacting tithe for the buds.
[10] Diverse seeds, v. Glos.

constitutes kil'ayim in a vineyard, which shows that it is a kind of vegetable,[1] and then you say that both agree that it is subject to the law of 'orlah, which shows that it is a kind of tree![2] — This is no difficulty; Beth Shammai were in doubt [whether it was a fruit or a vegetable], and accepted the stringencies of both. In any case,[3] Beth Shammai regard it [the caper-bush] as a doubtful case of 'orlah, and we have learnt: Where there is a doubt if a thing is subject to 'orlah, in the Land of Israel, it is prohibited, but in Syria it is allowed; and outside of Palestine one may go down

Berakoth 36b

and buy it, provided he does not see the man plucking it![4] — When R. Akiba conflicts with R. Eliezer, we follow him, and the opinion of Beth Shammai when it conflicts with that of Beth Hillel is no Mishnah.[5] But then let us be guided by the fact that it [the bud] is a protection for the fruit, and the All-Merciful said, Ye shall observe its uncircumcision along with its fruit;[6] 'with' refers to that which is attached to its fruit, namely, that which protects its fruit?[7] — Raba replied: When do we say a thing is a protection for the fruit? When it does so both when [the fruit is] still attached [to the tree] and after it is plucked. In this case it protects while [the fruit is] attached, but not after it is plucked.

Abaye raised an objection: The top-piece of the pomegranate is counted in with it,[8] but its blossom is not counted in.[9] Now since it says that its blossom is not counted in with it, this implies that it is not food: and it was taught in connection with 'orlah: The skin of a pomegranate and its blossom, the shells of nuts and their kernels are subject to the law of 'orlah![10] — We must say, then, said Raba, that we regard something as a protection to the fruit only where it is so at the time when the fruit becomes fully ripe; but this caper-bud falls off when the fruit ripens. But is that so? Has not R. Nahman said in the name of Rabbah b. Abbuha: The calyces surrounding dates in the state of 'orlah are forbidden, since they are the protection to the fruit. Now when do they protect the fruit? In the early stages of its growth [only]. Yet he calls them a protection to the fruit'? — R. Nahman took the same view as R. Jose, as we have learnt: R. Jose says, The grape-bud is forbidden because it is fruit; but the Rabbis differ from him.[11] R. Shimi from Nehardea demurred: Do the Rabbis differ from him in respect of other trees?[12] Have we not learnt: At what stage must we refrain from cutting trees in the seventh

---

[1] Otherwise it would not constitute kil'ayim in a vineyard.
[2] Vegetables are not subject to the law of 'orlah.
[3] Rabina resumes here his argument against Mar b. R. Ashi.
[4] Consequently Mar b. R. Ashi should have eaten also the berries.
[5] Consequently the caper-bud is certainly subject to the law of 'orlah.
[6] Lit. trans. E.V, 'Then ye shall count the fruit thereof as forbidden'. Lev. XIX. 23.
[7] How then did he eat the buds?
[8] To bring it to the size of an egg and so render it susceptible to uncleanness.
[9] The blossom bears the same relationship to the pomegranate that the caper-bud bears to the berry.
[10] Although the blossom of the pomegranate does not protect it after it is plucked. The same should apply to the caper-bud.
[11] And the halachah follows the Rabbis, who are the majority. And similarly the caper-bud is not subject to 'orlah.
[12] And can we say therefore that the halachah does not follow R. Nahman following R. Jose?

year?¹ Beth Shammai say: In the case of all trees, from the time they produce fruit; Beth Hillel say: In the case of carob-trees, from the time when they form chains [of carobs]; in the case of vines, from the time when they form globules; in the case of olive-trees, from the time when they blossom; in the case of all other trees, from the time when they produce fruit; and R. Assi said: Boser and garua'² and the white bean are all one. ('White bean', do you say?³ — Read instead: the size [of them] is that of the white bean.) Now which authority did you hear declaring that the boser is fruit but the grape-bud is not? It is the Rabbis;⁴ and it is they who state that we must refrain from cutting down all other trees from the time when they produce fruit!⁵ — No, said Raba. Where do you say that something is the protection to the fruit? Where if you take it away the fruit dies, Here⁶ you can take it away and the fruit does not die. In an actual case, they once took away the blossom from a pomegranate and it withered; they took away the flower from a caper and it survived.⁷ (The law is as [indicated by] Mar b.

R. Ashi when he threw away the caper-berries and ate the buds. And since for purposes of 'orlah they [the buds] are not fruit, for the purposes of benedictions also they are not fruit, and we do not say over them, 'who createst the fruit of the tree', but, 'who createst the fruit of the ground'.)⁸

With regard to pepper, R. Shesheth says that the blessing is 'by whose word all things exist'; Raba says: It requires no blessing at all.⁹ Raba in this is consistent; for Raba said: If a man chews peppercorns on the Day of Atonement he is not liable [to kareth];¹⁰ if he chews ginger on the Day of Atonement he is not liable. An objection was raised: R. Meir says: Since the text says. Ye shall count the fruit thereof as forbidden,¹¹ do I not know that it is speaking of a tree for food? Why then does it say [in the same context], ['and shall have planted all manner of] trees for food'? To include a tree of which the wood has the same taste as the fruit. And which is this? The pepper tree, This teaches you that pepper is subject to the law of 'orlah, and it also teaches you that the land of Israel lacks nothing, as it says, A land wherein thou shalt eat bread without scarceness, thou shalt not lack anything in it!¹² — There is no contradiction; one statement refers to moist pepper,¹³ the other to dried. The Rabbis¹⁴ said to Meremar: One who chews ginger on the Day of Atonement is not liable [to kareth]. But has not Raba said: The preserved ginger which comes from India is permitted,¹⁵ and we say over it the benediction 'Who createst the fruit of the ground'?¹⁶ — There is no contradiction: one statement refers to moist ginger, the other to dried.

---

¹ Cf. Ex, XXIII, 21; Lev. XXV, 4.
² Boser is the sour grape; garua' the grape when the stone is formed inside.
³ Lit., can you imagine'.
⁴ Who differ from R. Jose.
⁵ Which shows that in other cases the halachah is according to R. Jose.
⁶ In the case of the caper-bud.
⁷ And therefore you cannot argue from one to the other.
⁸ The passage in brackets reads like a marginal gloss.
⁹ Not being regarded as food.
¹⁰ V. Glos.
¹¹ Lev. XIX, 23.
¹² Deut. VIII, 9. This contradicts Raba.
¹³ I.e., preserved only in this condition does it become an article of food.
¹⁴ MS.M. Rabina.
¹⁵ In spite of the fact that it has been prepared by heathens.
¹⁶ Which shows that it is food. How then does the chewing thereof on the Day of Atonement not carry with it the guilt of kareth.

With regard to habiz[17] boiled in a pot, and also pounded grain, Rab Judah says the blessing is 'by whose word all things exist', while R. Kahana says that it is 'who createst various kinds of foods'. In the case of simple pounded grain all agree that the correct blessing is 'who createst various kinds of foods'. Where they differ is in respect of pounded grain made like boiled habiz.[18] Rab Judah says that the blessing for this is 'by whose word etc.', considering that the honey is the main ingredient; R. Kahana holds that the blessing is 'who createst all kinds of food', considering the flour the main ingredient. R. Joseph said: The view of R. Kahana is the more probable, because Rab and Samuel have both laid down that over anything containing an ingredient from the five species [of cereals] the blessing is 'who createst all kinds of foods'.

The [above] text [states]: 'Rab and Samuel both lay down that over anything containing an ingredient from the five species [of cereals] the blessing is 'who createst all kinds of foods'. It has also been stated: Rab and Samuel both lay down that over anything made of the five species the blessing is 'who createst all kinds of foods'. Now both statements are necessary. For if I had only the statement 'anything made of etc.', I might say, this is because the cereal is still distinguishable, but if it is mixed with something else, this is not [the blessing].

---

[17] This is described later as a kind of pull made of flour, honey, and oil.
[18] I.e., to which honey has been added.

Folio 37a

We are told therefore, 'anything containing an ingredient etc.'. If again I had only the statement, anything containing an ingredient etc.', I might think that this applies to the five species [of cereals], but not to rice and millet when they are mixed with other things; but when they are distinguishable the blessing even over rice and millet is 'who createst various kinds of foods'. So we are told that over anything which is made of the five species we say 'who createst various kinds of foods', excluding rice and millet, over which we do not say 'who createst various kinds of foods' even when they are distinguishable.

And over rice and millet do we not say, 'who createst various kinds of foods'? Has it not been taught: If one is served with rice bread or millet bread, he says blessings before and after it as for a cooked dish [of the five species]; and with regard to cooked dishes, it has been taught: He says before partaking, 'Who createst various kinds of foods', and after it, he says one blessing which includes three?[1] — It is on a par with cooked dishes in one way and not in another. It resembles cooked dishes in requiring a benediction before and after, and it differs from cooked dishes, because the blessing before these is 'who createst various kinds of foods' and the blessing after is the one which includes three, whereas in this case the blessing before is 'by whose word all things exist', and the blessing after. 'Who createst many living beings with their wants, for all which He has created etc.[2]

But is not rice a 'cooked dish'?[3] Has it not been taught: The following count as cooked dishes: spelt groats, wheat groats, fine flour, split grain, barley groats, and rice? Whose opinion is this?[4] That of R. Johanan b. Nuri; for it has been taught: R. Johanan b. Nuri says: Rice is a kind of corn, and when leavened it can entail the penalty of kareth,[5] and it can be used to fulfil the obligation of [eating unleavened bread on] Passover.[6] The Rabbis, however, do not admit this.[7] But do not the Rabbis admit this? Has it not been taught: If one chews wheat, he says over it the benediction, 'who createst the fruit of the ground'. If he grinds and bakes it and then soaks it [in liquid], so long as the pieces are still whole[8] he says before [partaking the blessing], 'who bringest forth bread from the earth' 'and after, the grace of three blessings;[9] if the pieces are no longer whole, he says before partaking 'that createst various kinds of foods', and after it one blessing that includes three.[10] If one chews rice, he says before partaking 'who createst the fruit of the ground'. If he grinds and bakes it and then soaks it, even if the pieces are still whole, he says before partaking who createst various kinds of foods', and after it the one blessing which includes three? Now whose opinion is this? Shall I say it is R. Johanan b. Nuri's? But he said that rice is a kind of corn, and therefore [according to him] the blessing should be 'who bringest forth food from the earth' and the grace the one of three blessings! It must therefore be the Rabbis'; and this is a refutation of Rab and Samuel, is it not? — It is a refutation.

---

[1] Ibid. p. 290.
[2] For the purpose of a blessing.
[3] That rice counts as a cooked dish.
[4] If eaten on Passover. V. Glos.
[5] V. Ex. XII, 19.
[6] I.e., have not been softened into a pulp.
[7] If eaten on Passover. V. Glos.
[8] The grace after meals which originally consisted of three blessings. V. infra 46a.
[9] Who requires (infra 40a) a separate blessing for each kind of fruit or vegetable.
[10] Who requires (infra 40a) a separate blessing for each kind of fruit or vegetable.

The Master said [above]: 'If one chews wheat 'he says over it the blessing, "who createst the fruit of the ground"'. But it has been taught: 'Who createst various kinds of seeds'? There is no contradiction: one statement represents the view of R. Judah,[1] the other that of the Rabbis, as we have learnt: Over vegetables one says, 'who createst the fruit of the ground';
R. Judah. however, says: 'Who createst various kinds of herbs'.

The Master said [above]: 'If one chews rice he says over it "Who createst the fruit of the ground". If he grinds and bakes it and then soaks it, even if the pieces are still whole, he says before it, "Who createst the various kinds of foods", and after it one blessing which includes three'. But it has been taught: After it he need not say any blessing at all?[2] —
R. Shesheth replied: There is no contradiction: the one statement expresses the view of R. Gamaliel, the other that of the Rabbis, as it has been taught: This is the general rule: after partaking of anything that belongs to the seven species,[3] R. Gamaliel says that three blessings should be said, while the Rabbis say, one that includes three. Once R. Gamaliel and the elders were reclining in an upper chamber in Jericho, and dates[4] were brought in and they ate, and R. Gamaliel gave permission to R. Akiba to say grace. and R. Akiba said quickly the one blessing which includes three. Said R. Gamaliel to him: Akiba, how long will you poke your head into quarrels?[5] He replied: Master, although you say this way and your colleagues say the other way, you have taught us, master, that where an individual joins issue with the majority, the halachah is determined by the majority. R. Judah said in his [R. Gamaliel's] name: [After partaking of] any food from the seven species

---

[1] The benediction, 'for the nourishment and the sustenance etc.', V. infra 44a; v. P.B. p. 287ff.
[2] Enumerated in Deut. VIII, 8.
[3] One of the 'seven species', being included in the term 'honey' in Deut. VIII, 8.
[4] I.e., go against me.
[5] So Rashi. We should rather, however, expect it to be R. Akiba's, as R. Gamaliel is mentioned in the statement, and R. Judah can hardly have been a disciple of R. Gamaliel.

Berakoth 37b

, not being a kind of corn or which belongs to one of the kinds of corn but has not been made into bread, R. Gamaliel says that three blessings are to be said, while the Sages say, only one blessing [which includes three]. [After] anything which belongs neither to the seven species nor to any kind of corn, for instance bread of rice or millet, R. Gamaliel says that one blessing which includes three is to be said, while the Sages say, no grace at all. To which authority do you then assign this statement?[1] To R. Gamaliel. Look now at the latter half of the first statement[2] viz., 'if the pieces are no longer whole, he says before partaking "who createst various kinds of foods", and after partaking one blessing which includes three'. Whose view does this express? Shall I say that of R. Gamaliel? Seeing that
R. Gamaliel requires a grace of three blessings after dates and pounded grain,[3] is there any question that he should require it if the pieces are no longer whole?[4] Hence, obviously, it must be the view of the Rabbis.[5] If that is the case, there is a contradiction between two statements of the Rabbis?[6] — No; I still say, it is the view of the Rabbis; and in connection with rice you should read, 'after partaking he does not say any blessing'.

Raba said: Over the rihata[7] f the field workers, in which there is a large quantity of flour, the blessing said is 'who createst various kinds of foods'. What is the reason? The flour is the main ingredient. Over the rihata of the townspeople in which there is not so much flour, the blessing said is 'by whose word all things exist'. What is the reason? The main ingredient is the honey. Raba, however, corrected himself and said: Over both the blessing is 'who createst various kinds of foods'. For Rab and Samuel both laid down that over anything containing one of the five species as an ingredient, the blessing to be said is 'who createst various kinds of foods'.

R. Joseph said: If in a habiz there are pieces of bread[8] as big as an olive, the blessing said before it is 'who bringest forth bread from the earth', and after it a grace of three blessings is said. If there are no pieces as big as an olive in it, the blessing said before it is 'who createst various kinds of foods', and after it one blessing which includes three. Said R. Joseph: Whence do I derive this? Because it has been taught: If one[9] is in the act of offering meal-offerings in Jerusalem, he says, 'Blessed be He that hath kept us alive and preserved us and brought us to this season'. When he[10] takes them up in order to eat them, he says the blessing, 'Who bringest forth bread from the earth', and it was taught in this connection. They are all[11] broken into fragments of the size of an

---

[1] That after rice one has to say the one blessing including three.
[2] In the above-cited Baraitha, 'if one chews wheat etc.', supra p. 232.
[3] Which is the same as 'corn which has not been made into bread', mentioned in the Baraitha quoted above.
[4] Since they were originally bread.
[5] Who hold that after pounded grain (v. n. 2) only the one blessing which includes three is said, and where the pieces are no longer whole the cooked wheat is treated like pounded grain.
[6] There the Rabbis declare that after bread made of rice no benediction is necessary, while in the previously cited Baraitha they are said to require one benediction which includes three.
[7] A dish resembling the habiz, and containing the same ingredients.
[8] I.e., if bread is broken up into it.
[9] According to Rashi, this is the layman who gives it to the priest to offer; according to Tosaf., the priest himself.
[10] The priest.
[11] I.e., all the various kinds of meal-offerings mentioned in Lev. II.

olive.¹² Said Abaye to him: If that is so, then similarly according to the Tanna of the school of R. Ishmael who says that he crushes them until he reduces them to flour, he should not require to say who bringest forth bread from the earth'? And should you reply that that is indeed the case, has it not been taught: If he scraped together as much as an olive from all of them¹³ and ate [all of] it, if it is leaven he is punished with kareth,¹⁴ and if it is unleaven a man may perform his obligation with it on Passover?¹⁵ — With what case are we dealing here?¹⁶ If he re-kneaded the crumbs.¹⁷ If so, look at the next clause: This is only if he ate them within the time which it takes to eat half [a roll].¹⁸ Now if they are re-kneaded, instead of saying 'to eat them', it should say, 'to eat it'? [Rather] with what case are we here dealing? When it comes from a large loaf.¹⁹ Now what do we decide upon this matter? R. Shesheth said: If the crumbs of bread in a habiz are even less than an olive, the benediction 'who bringest forth bread from the earth' is said over it. Raba added: This is only if they still have the appearance of bread.

Troknin⁹ is subject to the law of hallah. When Rabin came, he said in the name of R. Johanan: Troknin is not subject to the law of hallah. What is Troknin? — Abaye said: [Dough baked] in a cavity made in the ground.

Abaye also said: Tarita is exempt from the obligation of hallah. What is tarita? — Some say, dough just lightly baked;¹⁰ others say, bread baked on a spit;¹¹ others again, bread used for kuttah.¹² R. Hiyya said: Bread used for kuttah is not liable to hallah. But it has been taught that it is liable for hallah? — There the reason is stated: Rab Judah says that the way it is made shows what it is; if it is made

---

¹² V. Lev. II, 6. This proves that crumbs must be at least the size of an olive for the benediction 'Who bringest forth bread' to be said.
¹³ The various kinds of meal-offerings. Tosaf., however, refers it to ordinary crumbs of different species of cereals, since the continuation, 'if it is leaven etc.', could not apply to meal-offerings which had to be unleavened.
¹⁴ If he eats it on Passover.
¹⁵ And of course the prescribed blessing 'who bringest forth etc.', must be said over it also.
¹⁶ In the teaching last cited.
¹⁷ Making them into a compact mass.
¹⁸ A piece of bread the size of four eggs. If he does not eat the size of an olive within this time, it does not count for any purpose.
¹⁹ Some of which still remains unbroken, even though he did not reknead the bread crumbs.
⁹ Bread baked in a hole in the ground.
¹⁰ By being poured on the hot hearth and formed into fritters.
¹¹ And covered with oil, or eggs and oil. Aliter: 'Indian bread.'
¹² A dish made of bread mixed with sour milk and baked in the sun.

Folio 38a

like cakes, it is liable for hallah, if like boards,[1] it is not liable.

Abaye said to R. Joseph: What blessing is said over dough baked in a cavity in the ground? — He replied: Do you think it is bread? It is merely a thick mass, and the blessing said over it is 'who createst various kinds of foods'. Mar Zutra made it the basis of his meal and said over it the blessing, 'who bringest forth bread from the earth' and three blessings after it. Mar son of R. Ashi said: The obligation of Passover can be fulfilled with it. What is the reason? We apply to it the term, 'bread of affliction.

Mar son of R. Ashi also said: Over honey of the date-palm we say, 'by whose word all things exist'.[2] What is the reason? — Because it is merely moisture [of the tree]. With whose teaching does this accord? — With that of the following Tanna, as we have learnt: With regard to the honey of the date-palm and cider and vinegar from stunted grapes[3] and other fruit juices of terumah. R. Eliezer requires [in case of sacrilege] payment of the value and an additional fifth,[4] but R. Joshua exempts [from the additional fifth].[5]

One of the Rabbis asked Raba: What is the law with regard to trimma?[6] Raba did not quite grasp what he said. Rabina was sitting before Raba and said to the man: Do you mean of sesame[7] or of saffron[8] or of grape-kernels?[9] Raba thereupon bethought himself[10] and said: You certainly mean hashilta;[11] and you have reminded me of something which R. Assi said: It is permissible to make trimma[12] of dates of terumah, but forbidden to make mead of them.[13] The law is that over dates which have been used to make into trimma we say the blessing 'who createst the fruit of the tree'. What is the reason? They are still in their natural state.

With regard to shatitha,[14] Rab said that the blessing is 'by whose word all things were made', while Samuel said that it is 'who createst various kinds of foods'. Said R. Hisda: They do not really differ: the latter is said over the thick variety, the former over the thin. The thick is made for eating, the thin for a medicine. R. Joseph raised an objection to this: Both alike[15] say that we may stir up a shatitha on Sabbath and drink Egyptian beer. Now if you think that he intends it as a remedy, is a medicine permitted on Sabbath? — Abaye replied: And do you hold that it is not? Have we not learnt: All

---

[1] I.e., in flat thick pieces not resembling bread.
[2] Not 'who createst the fruit of the tree'.
[3] I.e., which never come to maturity. So Rashi; v.l. 'winter grapes'.
[4] V. Lev. V, 15ff.
[5] Because he does not regard these things as fruit.
[6] , something pounded but not out of recognition; here, a brew made of pounded fruit.
[7] Pounded sesame over which wine is poured.
[8] Saffron pounded to extract its oil.
[9] Over which water is poured to make mead.
[10] Rabina's question suggested to Raba the meaning of the question put to him.
[11] A brew made with rounded date-stones.
[12] I.e., a mere brew, not so strong as mead.
[13] Because then they completely lose their identity.
[14] Flour of dried barleycorns mixed with honey.
[15] R. Judah and R. Jose b. Judah; v. Shab. 156a.

foods may be eaten on Sabbath for medical purposes and all drinks may be drunk?[1] But what you must say is: in these cases the man intends it for food;[2] here too, the man intends it for food. (Another version of this is: But what you can say is that the man intends it for food and the healing effect comes of itself. So here too. the man intends it for food, and the healing effect comes of itself.) And it was necessary to have this statement of Rab and Samuel.[3] For if I had only the other statement[4] I might think that [he says a blessing because] he intends it for food and the healing effect comes of itself; but in this case, since his first intention is to use it for healing. I might think that he should not say any blessing at all over it. We are therefore told that since he derives some enjoyment from it, he has to say a blessing.

FOR OVER BREAD IS SAID, WHO BRINGEST FORTH etc. Our Rabbis taught: What does he say? 'Who bringest forth [ha-mozi] bread from the earth'. R. Nehemiah says: 'Bringing [mozi][5] forth bread from the earth'. Both agree that the word mozi means 'who has brought forth',[6] since it is written, God who brought them forth [moziam] from Egypt.[7] Where they disagree is as to the meaning of ha-mozi. The Rabbis held that ha-mozi means 'who has brought forth', as it is written, Who brought thee forth [ha-mozi] water out of the rock of flint,[8] whereas R. Nehemiah held that ha-mozi means 'who is bringing forth', as it says, Who bringeth you out [ha-mozi] from under the burden of the Egyptians.[9] The Rabbis, however, say that those words spoken by the Holy One, blessed be He, to Israel were meant as follows: When I shall bring you out, I will do for you something which will show you that it is I who brought you forth from Egypt, as it is written, And ye shall know that I am the Lord your God who brought you out.[10]

The Rabbis used to speak highly to R. Zera of the son of R. Zebid[11] the brother of R. Simeon son of R. Zebid as being a great man and well versed in the benedictions. He said to them: When you get hold of him bring him to me. Once he came to his house and they brought him a loaf, over which he pronounced the blessing mozi. Said R. Zebid: Is this the man of whom they say that he is a great man and well versed in benedictions? Had he said ha-mozi,

---

[1] Shab. 109b.
[2] And the healing effect is produced incidentally.
[3] That shatitha though used for medicinal purpose is treated as food and requires a benediction, in addition to the teaching that it is regarded as food and may be partaken of on Sabbath.
[4] That all foods may be consumed on Sabbath for medical purposes.
[5] Mozi is the present participle; ha-mozi is the same with the definite article.
[6] Which is the meaning required.
[7] Num. XXIII, 22.
[8] Deut. VIII, 15.
[9] Ex. VI, 7.
[10] Ex. VI, 7.
[11] So the text. There seems to be some corruption. and Goldschmidt reads: The Rabbis praised the father of R. Simeon b. Zebid to R. Zera b. Rab; cf. D.S.

Berakoth 38b

he would have taught us the meaning of a text and he would have taught us that the halachah is as stated by the Rabbis. But when he says mozi, what does he teach us?[1] In fact he acted thus so as to keep clear of controversy. And the law is that we say, ha-mozi bread from the earth', since we hold with the Rabbis who say that it means 'who has brought forth'.

OVER VEGETABLES ONE SAYS etc. Vegetables are placed [by the Mishnah] on a par with bread: just as over bread which has been transformed by fire [the same blessing is said], so [the same blessing is said over] vegetables when they have been changed by fire. Rabinnai said in the name of Abaye: This means to say that over boiled vegetables we say 'who createst the fruit of the ground'. [How? — Because the Mishnah puts vegetables on a par with bread].[2]
R. Hisda expounded in the name of our Teacher, and who is this? Rab: Over boiled vegetables the blessing to be said is 'who createst the fruit of the ground'. But teachers who came down from the land of Israel, and who are these? 'Ulla in the name of R. Johanan, said: Over boiled vegetables the blessing to be said is 'by whose word all things exist'. I say, however,[3] that wherever we say over a thing in its raw state 'who createst the fruit of the ground', if it is boiled we say 'by whose word all things exist'; and wherever we say over it in the raw state 'by whose word all things exist', if it is boiled we say 'who createst the fruit of the ground'. We quite understand that where the blessing over a thing in its raw state is 'by whose word all things were created', if it is boiled we say, 'who createst the fruit of the ground';[4] you have examples in cabbage, beet, and pumpkin. But where can you find that a thing which in its raw state requires 'who createst the fruit of the ground' should, when boiled, require 'by whose word all things exist'?[5] — R. Nahman b. Isaac replied: You have an instance in garlic and leek.

R. Nahman expounded in the name of our teacher, and who is this? Samuel: Over boiled vegetables the blessing to be said is 'who createst the fruit of the ground'; but our colleagues who came down from the Land of Israel, and who are these? 'Ulla in the name of R. Johanan, say: Over boiled vegetables the blessing to be said is 'by whose word all things exist'. I personally say that authorities[6] differ on the matter, as it has been taught: One may satisfy the requirement [of eating unleavened bread on Passover] with a wafer which has been soaked, or which has been boiled, provided it has not been dissolved. So R. Meir.
R. Jose, however, says: One fulfils the requirements with a wafer which has been soaked, but not with one which has been boiled, even though it has not been dissolved. But this is not the case.[7] All [in fact] would agree that over boiled vegetables the blessing is 'who createst the fruit of the ground'; and R. Jose was more particular in the case of the wafer only because we require the taste of unleavened bread and it is not there. In this case, however, even R. Jose would admit [that boiling does not alter its character].

---

[1] Seeing that all are agreed as to its meaning.
[2] These words seem to be a needless repetition, and are bracketed in the text.
[3] In order to reconcile the two opinions.
[4] Because usually it is improved by boiling.
[5] I.e., should deteriorate through being boiled.
[6] I.e., Tannaim.
[7] That the authorities differ with regard to vegetables and that R. Jose supports R. Johanan.

R. Hiyya b. Abba said in the name of R. Johanan: Over boiled vegetables the blessing to be said is 'who createst the fruit of the ground'. R. Benjamin b. Jefet, however, said in the name of R. Johanan: Over boiled vegetables the blessing to be said is 'by whose word all things exist'. R. Nahman b. Isaac said: 'Ulla[3] became confirmed in his error by accepting the word of R. Benjamin b. Jefet. R. Zera expressed his astonishment.[4] How [he said], can you mention R. Benjamin b. Jefet along with R. Hiyya b. Abba? R. Hiyya b. Abba was very particular to get the exact teaching of R. Johanan his master, whereas R. Benjamin b. Jefet was not particular. Further, R. Hiyya b. Abba used to go over what he had learnt every thirty days with his teacher R. Johanan, while R. Benjamin b. Jefet did not do so. Besides, apart from these two reasons[5] there is the case of the lupines which were cooked seven times in the pot, and eaten as dessert,[6] and when they came and asked R. Johanan about them, he told them that the blessing to be said was 'who createst the fruit of the ground'. Moreover R. Hiyya b. Abba said: I have seen R. Johanan eat salted olives and say a blessing both before and after. Now if you hold that boiled vegetables are still regarded as the same, we can understand this: before eating he said 'who createst the fruit of the tree', and after it a grace of one blessing which includes three.[7] But if you hold that vegetables after being boiled are not regarded as the same, no doubt he could say before eating 'by whose word all things are created', but what could he say after? — Perhaps he said, 'who createst many living things and their requirements for all that he has created'.

R. Isaac b. Samuel raised an objection: With regard to the herbs with which one may fulfil the requirement [of eating bitter herbs on] Passover,[8] both they and their stalks may serve this purpose, but not if they are pickled or cooked or boiled.[9] Now if you maintain that after boiling they are still regarded as the same, why may they not be used boiled? — The case is different there. because we require the taste of bitter herbs, and this we do not find.

R. Jeremiah asked R. Zera: How could R. Johanan make a blessing over a salted olive? Since the stone had been removed,

---
[3] Who reported supra in the name of R. Johanan that the blessing is 'by whose word etc.'.
[4] That this difference of opinion should have been recorded.
[5] Showing that R. Johanan did not make the statement attributed to him by R.Benjamin b. Jefet.
[6] And therefore required a separate blessing.
[7] Because in spite of the salting, it was still regarded as an olive.
[8] V. Ex. XII, 8.
[9] I.e., reduced to a pulp. V. Pes. 39a.

Folio 39a

it was less than the minimum size! — He replied: Do you think the size we require is that of a large olive? We require only that of a medium sized olive, and that was there, for the one they set before R. Johanan was a large one, so that even when its stone had been removed it was still of the requisite size. For so we have learnt: The 'olive' spoken of[1] means neither a small nor a large one, but a medium one. This is the kind which is called aguri. R. Abbahu, however, said: Its name is not aguri but abruti, or, according to others, samrusi. And why is it called aguri? Because its oil is collected [agur] within it.[2]

May we say that this controversy [about the blessing to be said over boiled vegetables] is found between Tannaim? For once two disciples were sitting before Bar Kappara, and cabbage, Damascene plums and poultry were set before him. Bar Kappara gave permission to one of them to say a blessing, and he at once said the blessing over the poultry.[3] The other laughed at him, and Bar Kappara was angry, He said: I am not angry with the one who said the blessing, but with the one who laughed. If your companion acts like one who has never tasted meat in his life, is that any reason for you to laugh? Then he corrected himself and said: I am not angry with the one who laughed, but with the one who said the blessing. If there is no wisdom here, is there not old age here?[4] A Tanna taught: Neither of them saw the year out.[5] Now did not their difference lie in this, that the one who said the blessing held that the benediction over both boiled vegetables and poultry is 'by whose word all things exist', and therefore the dish he liked best had the preference,[6] while the one who laughed held that the blessing over boiled vegetables is 'who createst the fruit of the ground', and that over poultry is 'by whose word all things were created', and therefore the vegetables should have had the preference?[7] — Not so. All agree that for both boiled vegetables and poultry the blessing is 'by whose word all things exist', and their difference lies in this, that one held that what is best liked should have the preference, and the other held that the cabbage should have the preference, because it is nourishing.[8]

R. Zera said: When we were with R. Huna, he told us that with regard to the tops of turnips, if they are cut into large pieces, the blessing is 'who createst the fruit of the ground', but if they are cut into small pieces, 'by whose word all things exist'.[9] But when we came to Rab Judah, he told us that for both the blessing is 'who createst the fruit of the ground', since the reason for their being cut into small pieces is to make them taste sweeter.

R. Ashi said: When we were with R. Kahana, he told us that over a broth of beet, in which not much flour is put, the blessing is 'who createst the fruit of the ground', but for a broth of turnip, in which much flour is put, the blessing is 'who createst all kinds of foods'. Subsequently, however, he said that

---

[1] As a standard of quantity.
[2] I.e., can be squeezed out immediately. Probably all these names refer to the place of origin of different kinds of olive.
[3] As being the principal dish.
[4] And why did you not consult me?
[5] As a punishment for the disrespect shown to Bar Kappara.
[6] I.e., he said the blessing over that one first and commenced to eat it.
[7] Even though he liked the poultry better, because the blessing over vegetables is more dignified.
[8] I.e., more than poultry. v. infra 44b.
[9] Because they have been more or less spoilt.

the blessing for both is 'who createst the fruit of the ground', since the reason why much flour is put in it is only to make it cohere better.

R. Hisda said: A broth of beet is beneficial for the heart and good for the eyes, and needless to say for the bowels. Said Abaye: This is only if it is left on the stove till it goes tuk, tuk.[2]

R. Papa said: It is quite clear to me that beet-water is on the same footing as beet,[3] and turnip-water on the same footing as turnips. and the water of all vegetables on the same footing as the vegetables themselves. R. Papa, however, inquired: What about aniseed water? Is its main purpose to sweeten the taste[4] [to the dish] or to remove the evil smell?[5] — Come and hear: Once the aniseed has given a taste to the dish, the law of terumah no longer applies to it,[6] and it is not liable to the uncleanness of foods.[7] This proves that its main purpose is to sweeten the dish, does it not? — It does.

R. Hiyya b. Ashi said: Over a dry crust which has been put in a pot [to soak], the blessing is 'who bringeth forth bread etc.'. This view conflicts with that of R. Hiyya; for R. Hiyya said: The bread should be broken with the conclusion of the blessing.[8] Raba demurred to this. What [he said], is the reason [why hamozi should not be said] in the case of dry crust? Because, you say, when the blessing is concluded, it is concluded over a broken piece. But when it is said over a loaf, it finishes over a broken piece!

---

[2] I.e., has been brought to the boil. .
[3] And the blessing to be said over it is 'who createst the fruit of the earth'.
[4] And is the blessing to be said over it 'who createst the fruit of the ground'.
[5] And the blessing will be 'by whose word etc.'.
[6] It is regarded as merely wood, not liable to terumah.
[7] 'Uk. III, 4.
[8] But this has already been broken off, and therefore the blessing is 'by whose word'

Berakoth 39b

The fact is, said Raba, that the benediction is said first and then the loaf is broken.[1] The Nehardeans acted as prescribed by R. Hiyya, while the Rabbis acted as prescribed by Raba. Rabina said: Mother told me: Your father acted as prescribed by R. Hiyya; for R. Hiyya said: The bread should be broken with the conclusion of the blessing, whereas the Rabbis acted as prescribed by Raba. The law is as laid down by Raba, that one says the blessing first and afterwards breaks the loaf.

It has been stated: If pieces and whole loaves are set before one, R. Huna says that the benediction can be said over the pieces,[2] and this serves also for the whole loaves, whereas R. Johanan says that the religious duty is better performed if the blessing is said over the whole one. If, however, a broken piece of wheat bread and a whole loaf of barley bread are set before one, all agree that the benediction is said over the piece of wheaten bread, and this serves also for the whole loaf of barley bread. R. Jeremiah b. Abba said: There is the same difference of opinion between Tannaim:[3] Terumah is given from a small whole onion, but not from the half of a large onion. R. Judah says: Not so, but also from the half of a large onion.[4] Are we to say that the point in which they differ is this: one authority holds that the fact of being worth more is more important, while the other holds that the fact of being whole is more important? — Where a priest is on the spot,[5] all agree that the fact of being worth more is more important. Where they differ is when there is no priest on the spot, since we have learnt: Wherever a priest is on the spot, terumah is given from the best of the produce; where the priest is not on the spot,[6] terumah is set aside from that which will keep best. R. Judah said: Terumah is in all cases given from the best.[7] R. Nahman b. Isaac said: A Godfearing man will seek to satisfy both.[8] Who is such a one? Mar the son of Rabina. For Mar the son of Rabina used to put the broken piece under[9] the whole loaf and then break the bread.[10] A Tanna recited in the presence of R. Nahman b. Isaac: One should place the broken piece under the whole loaf and then break and say the benediction. He said to him: What is your name? Shalman, he replied. He said to him: Thou art peace [shalom] and thy Mishnah is faultless [shelemah], for thou hast made peace between the scholars.

R. Papa said: All admit that on Passover one puts the broken cake under the whole one and breaks [them together]. What is the reason? Scripture speaks of 'Bread of poverty'.[11] R. Abba said: On Sabbath one should break bread from two loaves. What is the reason? Scripture speaks of 'double bread'.[12] R. Ashi said: I have observed R. Kahana take two and break one. R. Zera used to break off [a piece of bread] sufficient for the whole meal [on Sabbath]. Said Rabina to R. Ashi: Does not this look like greediness? He replied: Since every other day he does not act thus and today he acts thus, it does

---

[1] So that when the blessing is concluded the bread is still whole.
[2] Especially if they are larger than the whole loaf, in which case preference must be given to the broken one (Rashi).
[3] In the case where the broken one is of wheat and the whole one of barley.
[4] Ter. II, 5.
[5] And the terumah can be given to him immediately.
[6] And the produce has to be kept till he turns up.
[7] Ibid. 4.
[8] I.e., both points of view, sc. of R. Huna and R. Johanan.
[9] V. Rashi.
[10] From both, v. Rashi.
[11] Deut. XVI, 3. (E.V. 'affliction'). A poor man has usually only a piece.
[12] Ex. XVI. 22, of the manna on Friday. (E.V. 'twice as much bread').

not look like greediness. When R. Ammi and R. Assi happened to get hold of a loaf which had been used for an 'erub,[1] they used to say over it the blessing, 'who bringest forth bread from the earth', saying, Since one religious duty has been performed with it, let us perform with it still another.

---

[1] For allowing transport through the courts on Sabbath. V. Glos.

Folio 40a

Rab said: [If the host says to his guests,][1] Take, the benediction has been said,[2] take, the benediction has been said, he [the host] need not say the benediction [again].[3] If he said [between the benediction and the eating], Bring salt, bring relish, he must say the benediction [again]. R. Johanan, however, said that even if he said, Bring salt, bring relish, the benediction need not be repeated. If he said, Mix fodder for the oxen, mix fodder for the oxen, he must repeat the blessing; R. Shesheth. however, said that even if he said, Mix fodder for the oxen, he need not repeat; for Rab Judah said in the name of Rab: A man is forbidden to eat before he gives food to his beast, since it says. And I will give grass in thy fields for thy cattle, and then, thou shalt eat and be satisfied.[4]

Raba b. Samuel said in the name of R. Hiyya: The one who is about to break the bread is not permitted to do so before salt or relish is placed before each one at table. Raba b. Samuel was once at the house of the Exilarch, and they brought him bread and he broke it at once. They said to him: Has the Master retraced his own teaching? — He replied: This requires no condiment.[5]

Raba b. Samuel also said in the name of R. Hiyya: Urine is never completely discharged except when sitting.[6] R. Kahana said: If over loose earth, even when standing. If there is no loose earth, one should stand on a raised spot and discharge down a declivity.

Raba b. Samuel also said in the name of R. Hiyya: After every food eat salt, and after every beverage drink water, and you will come to no harm. It has been taught similarly: After every food eat salt, and after every beverage drink water, and you will come to no harm. It has been taught elsewhere: If one ate any kind of food without taking salt after it, or drank any kind of liquor without taking water after it, by day he is liable to be troubled with an evil-smelling mouth, and by night with croup. The Rabbis taught: One who swills down his food with plenty of water will not suffer with his bowels. How much should he drink? R. Hisda says: A cupful to a loaf.

R. Mari said in the name of R. Johanan: If one takes lentils regularly once in thirty days, he will keep croup away from his house.[7] He should not, however, take them every day. Why so? Because they cause a bad smell in the mouth. R. Mari also said in the name of R. Johanan: If one takes mustard regularly once in thirty days, he keeps sickness away from his house. He should not, however, take it every day. Why so? Because it is weakening for the heart. R. Hiyya b. Ashi said in the name of Rab: One who eats regularly small fish will not suffer with his bowels. Moreover, small fish stimulate propagation and strengthen a man's whole body. R. Hama b. Hanina said: One who takes regularly black cumin will not suffer from heartburn.[8] The following was cited in objection to this: R. Simeon

---

[1] After saying the blessing on behalf of all.

[2] Lit., '(the bread) has been blessed'.

[3] In spite of the fact that there has been an interruption between the saying and the eating, because the words spoken have reference to the benediction.

[4] Deut. XI, 15.

[5] So Jast. Rashi translates: no delay (in waiting for the salt).

[6] Because one who discharges standing is afraid of the drops falling on his clothes (Rashi).

[7] Rashi explains that they keep away indigestion which is the cause of croup.

[8] Lit., 'pain of the heart'.

b. Gamaliel says: Black cumin is one of the sixty poisons. and if one sleeps on the east side of the place where it is stored, his blood will be on his own head?[1] — There is no contradiction: The latter statement speaks of its smell, the former of its taste. The mother of
R. Jeremiah used to bake bread for him and stick [black cumin] on it[2] and then scrape it off.[3]

R. JUDAH SAYS, WHO CREATEST DIVERS KINDS OF HERBS. R. Zera, or as some say R. Hinnena b. Papa, said: The halachah is not as stated by R. Judah. R. Zera, or as some say, R. Hinnena b. Papa, further said: What is R. Judah's reason? Scripture says, Blessed be the Lord day by day.[4] Are we then to bless Him by day and not bless Him by night?
What it means to tell us is that every day we should give Him the blessing appropriate to the day.[5] So here, for every species we should give Him the appropriate blessing.

R. Zera, or as some say, R. Hinnena b. Papa, further said: Observe how the character of the Holy One, blessed be He, differs from that of flesh and blood. A mortal can put something into an empty vessel[6] but not into a full one. But the Holy One, blessed be He, is not so; He puts more into a full vessel[7] but not into an empty one; for it says, If hearkening thou wilt hearken,[8] implying, if thou hearkenest [once] thou wilt go on hearkening, and if not, thou wilt not hearken. Another explanation is: If thou hearkenest to the old,[9] thou wilt hearken to the new, but if thy heart turns away, thou wilt not hear any more.

MISHNAH. IF ONE SAYS OVER FRUIT OF THE TREE THE BENEDICTION, 'WHO CREATEST THE FRUIT OF THE GROUND, HE HAS PERFORMED HIS OBLIGATION. BUT IF HE SAID OVER PRODUCE OF THE GROUND, 'WHO CREATEST THE FRUIT OF THE TREE', HE HAS NOT PERFORMED HIS OBLIGATION. IF HE SAYS 'BY WHOSE WORD ALL THINGS EXIST OVER ANY OF THEM, HE HAS PERFORMED HIS OBLIGATION.

GEMARA. What authority maintains that the essence of the tree is the ground? — R. Nahman b. Isaac replied: It is R. Judah, as we have learnt: If the spring has dried up or the tree has been cut down,[10] he brings the first-fruits but does not make the declaration.[11] R. Judah, however, says that he both brings them and makes the declaration.[12]

OVER FRUIT OF THE GROUND etc. This is obvious, is it not? — R. Nahman b. Isaac said: It required to be stated in view of the opinion of R. Judah, who maintains that wheat is a kind of tree. For it has been taught: R. Meir holds that the tree of which Adam ate was the vine, since the thing

---

[1] Because the west wind will carry the odour to him and poison him.
[2] So that it should absorb the taste.
[3] To remove the smell.
[4] Ps. LXVIII, 20.
[5] E.g., on Sabbath the Sabbath blessing, on festivals the festival blessing. etc.
[6] Lit., 'in the case of a mortal man, an empty vessel can be made to hold, etc.'.
[7] I.e., He gives more wisdom to the wise.
[8] Ex. XV, 26, lit. trans. E.V. 'If thou wilt diligently hearken'.
[9] I.e., constantly revise what you have learnt.
[10] If one has gathered first-fruits, and before he takes them to Jerusalem the spring which fed the tree dries up, or the tree is cut down.
[11] V. Deut. XXVI, 5-10, because it contains the words 'of the land which Thou, O Lord, hast given me', and the land is valueless without the tree or the spring.
[12] Because the land is the essence, not the tree; v. Bik. I, 6.

that most causes wailing to a man is wine, as it says, And he drank of the wine and was drunken.[1] R. Nehemiah says it was the fig tree, so that they repaired their misdeed with the instrument of it, as it says, And they sewed fig leaves together.[2]

R. Judah says it was wheat, since a child does not know how to call 'father' and 'mother' until it has had a taste of corn.[3] Now you might think that because R. Judah says that wheat is a kind of tree, therefore we should say over it the benediction 'who createst the fruit of the tree'. Therefore we are told that we say 'who createst the fruit of the tree' only in those cases where if you take away the fruit the stem still remains to produce fruit again

---

[1] Gen. IX, 21. The reference is to Noah.
[2] Ibid. III, 7.
[3] Hence the Tree of Knowledge must have been some kind of corn.

Berakoth 40b

, but in cases where if you take the fruit the stem does not remain to produce again, the benediction is not 'who createst the fruit of the tree' but 'who createst the fruit of the ground'.

IF HE SAYS, BY 'WHOSE WORD ALL THINGS EXIST' etc. It has been stated: R. Huna said: Except over bread and wine.[1] R. Johanan, however, said: Even over bread and wine. May we say that the same difference of opinion is found between Tannaim? [For it was taught:] 'If a man sees a loaf of bread and says, What a fine loaf this is! Blessed be the Omnipresent that has created it! he has performed his obligation. If he sees a fig and says, What a fine fig this is! Blessed be the Omnipresent that has created it! he has performed his obligation. So R. Meir. R. Jose says: If one alters the formula laid down by the Sages in benedictions, he has not performed his obligation'. May we say that R. Huna concurs with
R. Jose and R. Johanan with R. Meir? — R. Huna can reply to you: I can claim even R. Meir as a supporter of my view. For R. Meir went as far as he did in that case only because the bread is actually mentioned, but where the bread is not actually mentioned even R. Meir would admit [that the obligation is not fulfilled]. And R. Johanan can reply to you: I may claim R. Jose also as a supporter of my view. For R. Jose only went as far as he did in that case because he made a benediction which was not instituted by the Sages, but if he says, 'by whose word all things exist', which has been instituted by the Sages, even R. Jose would admit [that he has performed his obligation].

Benjamin the shepherd made a sandwich[2] and said, Blessed be the Master of this bread,[3] and Rab said that he had performed his obligation. But Rab has laid down that any benediction in which God's name is not mentioned is no benediction? — We must suppose he said, Blessed be the All-Merciful, the Master of this bread. But we require three blessings?[4] — What did Rab mean by saying that he had performed his obligation? He had performed the obligation of the first blessing. What does this tell us [that we did not already know]? That [he has performed his obligation] even if he says it in a secular language. But we have already learnt this: 'The following may be said in any language: the section of the Unfaithful wife,[5] the confession over tithe,[6] the recital of the Shema', and the Tefillah and grace after food?[7] — It required to be stated. For you might have thought that this is the case only if one says the grace in a secular language in the same form as was instituted by the Rabbis in the holy tongue, but if one does not say it in the secular language in the same form as was instituted by the Rabbis in the holy tongue, he has not performed his obligation. We are therefore told [that this is not so].

It was stated above: Rab said that any benediction in which the Divine Name is not mentioned is no benediction. R. Johanan, however, said: Any benediction in which [God's] Kingship is not mentioned is no benediction. Abaye said: The opinion of Rab is the more probable. For it has been taught: I have

---

[1] Bread because it is the mainstay of the meal, wine because many special benedictions are said over it.
[2] Lit., 'doubled (wrapped) a loaf', which seems to mean that he made a sandwich of bread and some relish.
[3] He said it in Aramaic.
[4] It was assumed that he said this formula after eating.
[5] Num. V, 21ff.
[6] Deut. XXVI, 13-15.
[7] V. Sot. 32a.

not transgressed any of Thy commandments, neither have I forgotten.¹ This means: 'I have not transgressed' so as not to bless Thee,² 'neither have I forgotten' to mention Thy name therein. Of sovereignty, however, there is no mention here. R. Johanan, however, reads: 'Neither have I forgotten' to mention Thy name and Thy sovereignty therein.

MISHNAH. OVER ANYTHING WHICH DOES NOT GROW FROM THE EARTH ONE SAYS: 'BY WHOSE WORD ALL THINGS EXIST'. OVER VINEGAR, NOBELOTH³ AND LOCUSTS ONE SAYS, 'BY WHOSE WORD ALL THINGS EXIST'. R. JUDAH SAYS: OVER ANYTHING TO WHICH A KIND OF CURSE ATTACHES NO BENEDICTION IS SAID.⁴ IF ONE HAS SEVERAL VARIETIES BEFORE HIM, R. JUDAH SAYS THAT IF THERE IS AMONG THEM SOMETHING OF THE SEVEN KINDS,⁵ HE MAKES THE BLESSING OVER THAT, BUT THE SAGES SAY THAT HE MAY MAKE THE BLESSING OVER ANY KIND THAT HE PLEASES.

GEMARA. Our Rabbis taught: Over anything which does not grow from the ground, such as the flesh of cattle, beasts and birds and fishes, one says 'by whose word all things were created'. Over milk, eggs and cheese one says, 'by whose word, etc.'. Over bread which has become mouldy and over wine on which a film has formed and cooked food which has become spoilt one says, 'by whose word'. Over salt and brine and morils and truffles one says, 'by whose word'. This would imply that morils and truffles do not grow from the ground. But has it not been taught: If one vows to abstain from fruit of the ground, he is forbidden to eat of fruit of the ground but is allowed to eat morils and truffles? If he said, I vow abstention from all that grows from the ground, he is forbidden to eat morils and truffles also?⁶ — Abaye said: They do indeed spring up from the earth, but their sustenance is not derived⁷ from the earth. But it says, 'over anything which grows from the earth'? — Read: Over anything which draws sustenance from the earth.

OVER NOBELOTH. What are NOBELOTH? — R. Zera and R. El'a [gave different answers]. One said: fruit parched by the sun;⁸ the other said: dates blown down by the wind. We have learnt: R. JUDAH SAYS: OVER ANYTHING TO WHICH A KIND OF CURSE ATTACHES NO BLESSING IS SAID. This accords with the view of the one who says that nobeloth are fruit parched by the sun, which can rightly be called something to which a curse attaches. But if we say they are dates blown down by the wind, what has 'a kind of curse' to do with them? — This expression relates to the other things [mentioned].⁹

Some report as follows: On the view of him who says that they are fruit parched by the sun, it is quite right that we should say 'by whose word, etc.'; but according to the one who says that they are dates blown down by the wind, we should say, 'who createst the fruit of the tree'?¹⁰ — The fact is that all are agreed that nobeloth in general are fruit parched by the sun. The difference arises over nobeloth

---

¹ Deut. XXVI, 13 in reference to the tithe.
² The benediction, 'Blessed be He … who commanded us to set aside terumah and tithe'.
³ Lit., 'withering products'. This is explained in the Gemara.
⁴ And the things just mentioned come under this heading.
⁵ Enumerated in Deut. VIII, 8.
⁶ V. Ned. 55b.
⁷ Lit., 'they do not suck'.
⁸ While still on the tree.
⁹ Viz., vinegar and locusts.
¹⁰ Since they are still dates.

of the date-palm, since we have learnt:[1] Things in regard to which the law of demai is not so strict[2] are shittin, rimin, 'uzradin, benoth shuah, benoth shikmah, gofnin, nizpah and the nobeloth of the date-palm. Shittin, according to Rabbah b. Bar Hanah reporting R. Johanan, are a kind of figs. Rimin are lote. 'Uzradin are crabapples. Benoth shuah, according to Rabbah b. Bar Hanah reporting R. Johanan, are white figs. Benoth shikmah, according to Rabbah b. Bar Hanah reporting R. Johanan, are sycamore figs. Gofnin are winter grapes. Nizpah is the caper-fruit. Nobeloth of the date-palm are explained differently by R. Zera and R. El'a. One says that they are fruit parched by the sun, the other that they are dates blown down by the wind. Now the view of him who says that they are fruit parched by the sun accords well with what it teaches [concerning them], 'things about which the law of demai is not so strict', and if there is a doubt about them, they are free from the obligation of tithe, which shows that if there is no doubt[3] they are subject to it. But on the view of him who says that they are dates blown down by the wind, must, in case of certainty, tithe be given from them? They are hefker![4] — With what case are we dealing here? Where one made a store of them. For R. Isaac said in the name of R. Johanan reporting R. Eliezer b. Jacob: If [a poor man] has made a store of gleanings, forgotten sheaves and produce of the corner,[5] they are liable for tithe.

Some report as follows:

---

[1] Demai I, 1.

[2] I.e., which a haber (v. Glos.) need not tithe if he buys them from an 'am ha-arez (v. Glos.). These things being of little value, the presumption is that they have been tithed.

[3] That they have not been tithed.

[4] I.e., ownerless (v. Glos.) and not subject to tithe.

[5] Which he had gathered and which are ordinarily not titheable.

Folio 41a

The view of him who says that [they[1] are] dates blown down by the wind accords well with the fact that in one place[2] nobeloth simply[3] are spoken of and in the other[4] nobeloth of the date-palm. But on the view of him who says they[5] are fruit parched by the sun, in both places we should have nobeloth of the date-palm,[6] or in both places nobeloth simply, should we not?[7] — This is indeed a difficulty.

IF ONE HAD SEVERAL VARIETIES BEFORE HIM etc. 'Ulla said: Opinions differ only in the case where the blessings [over the several varieties] are the same; in such a case R. Judah holds that belonging to the seven kinds is of more importance, while the Rabbis held that being better liked is of more importance. But where they have not all the same benediction, all agree that a blessing is to be said first on one variety[8] and then on another. An objection was raised: If radishes and olives are set before a person, he says a benediction over the radish, and this serves for the olive also! — With what case are we dealing here? When the radish is the main item.[9] If so, look at the next clause: R. Judah says that the benediction is said over the olive, because the olive is one of the seven species.[10] Now would not R. Judah accept the teaching which we have learnt: Whenever with one article of food another is taken as subsidiary to it, a blessing is said over the main article and this serves for the subsidiary one also?[11] And should you be disposed to maintain that in fact he does not accept it, has it not been taught: R. Judah said, If the olive is taken on account of the radish, a blessing is said for the radish and this serves for the olive? — In fact we are dealing with a case where the radish is the main item,[12] and the difference of opinion between R. Judah and the Rabbis is really over a different matter, and there is a lacuna in the text and it should read as follows: If radish and olives are set before a person, he says a benediction over the radish and this serves for the olive also. When is this the case? When the radish is the main item; but if the radish is not the main item, all agree that he says a blessing over one and then a blessing over the other. If there are two varieties of food[13] which have the same blessing, he says it over whichever he prefers.
R. Judah, however, says that he says the blessing over the olive, since it is of the seven species.

R. Ammi and R. Isaac Nappaha understood this differently. One said that the difference between R. Judah and the Rabbis arises when the blessings over the two kinds of food are the same, R. Judah holding that the fact of belonging to the seven kinds is more important, while the Rabbis held that the fact of being better liked was more important; but where the blessings are not the same, both agreed that a blessing is first said over one kind and then over the other. The other said that R. Judah and the Rabbis differ even when the blessings are not the same. Now accepting the view of him who says that

---

[1] The nobeloth mentioned in Demai.
[2] In our Mishnah.
[3] Denoting fruit parched by the sun.
[4] In the passage from Demai.
[5] The nobeloth mentioned in Demai.
[6] Because it is necessary to distinguish the two kinds of nobeloth.
[7] Because both passages are speaking about the same thing.
[8] Which he likes best.
[9] And the olive was only eaten to counteract the sharp taste.
[10] This shows that we are not dealing with the case where one of the two articles is more important.
[11] V. supra 35b.
[12] And we cannot say that in all cases a blessing is said first over one variety and then over the other.
[13] One of which is of the seven species, e.g., olives.

the difference arises when the blessings are the same, we find no difficulty. But accepting the view that they differ also when the blessings are not the same, [we have to ask] on what ground do they differ?[1] — R. Jeremiah replied: They differ on the question of precedence. For R. Joseph. or as some say. R. Isaac, said: Whatever comes earlier in this verse has precedence in the matter of benediction, viz., A land of wheat and barley, and vine and fig-trees and pomegranates, a land of olive trees and honey.[2]

[In the exposition of this verse, R. Isaac] differs from R. Hanan. For R. Hanan said: The whole purpose of the verse was to mention things which serve as standards of measurements. 'Wheat', as we have learnt: If one enters a house stricken with leprosy with his garments on his shoulder and his sandals and his rings in his hands, both he and they become unclean immediately. If he is wearing his garments and his sandals and has his rings on his fingers, he is immediately unclean but they remain clean until he stays in the house long enough to eat a piece of wheat bread,[3] but not of barley bread, reclining and taking with it a relish.[4] 'Barley', as we have learnt: A bone as large as a barleycorn renders unclean by touch and carrying, but it does not render a tent unclean.[5] 'Vine', the measurement for a Nazirite[6] is a fourth [of a log] of wine.[7] 'Figtree', a dried fig is the measurement of what may be taken out of the house on Sabbath. 'Pomegranates', as we have learnt: For utensils of a private person[8]

---

[1] Surely in this case the benediction for the one does not serve the other!
[2] Deut. VIII, 8. R. Judah agrees with R. Isaac, and therefore a fortiori holds that any of these species should have precedence over other species, whereas the Rabbis agree with the view of R. Hanan which follows.
[3] Which is eaten more quickly than barley bread.
[4] Neg. XIII, 9.
[5] Oh. II, 3.
[6] The quantity of grapes which he may eat without spoiling his Naziriteship.
[7] Which is somewhat larger than a log (v. Glos.) of water.
[8] As opposed to an artificer who makes them.

Berakoth 41b

the measurement[1] is a pomegranate.[2] 'A land of olive trees', R. Jose son of R. Hanina said: A land in which the olive is the standard for all measurements. All measurements, do you say? What of those we have just mentioned? — Say rather, in which the olive is the standard for most measurements. 'Honey',[3] as much as a large date [is the quantity which renders one liable for eating] on the Day of Atonement. What says the other to this? — Are these standards laid down explicitly? They were instituted by the Rabbis, and the text is only an asmekta.[4]

R. Hisda and R. Hamnuna were seated at a meal, and dates and pomegranates were set before them. R. Hamnuna took some dates and said a blessing over them. Said R. Hisda to him: Does not the Master agree with what R. Joseph, or as some say R. Isaac, said: Whatever is mentioned earlier in this verse has precedence in the matter of benediction? — He replied: This [the date] comes second after the word 'land', and this [the pomegranate] comes fifth.[5] He replied: Would that we had feet of iron so that we could always [run and] listen to you!

It has been stated: If figs and grapes were set before them in the course of the meal, R. Huna says that they require a benediction before but they do not require a blessing after;[6] and so said R. Nahman: They require a blessing before but they do not require a blessing after. R. Shesheth, however, said: They require a blessing both before and after, since there is nothing requiring a blessing before which does not also require a blessing after, save bread taken with the sweets.[7] This is at variance with R. Hiyya; for R. Hiyya said: [A blessing said over] bread suffices for all kinds of food [taken in the meal], and a blessing said over wine for all kinds of drink. R. Papa said: The law is that things which form an integral part of the meal when taken in the course of the meal require no blessing either before or after; things which do not form an integral part of the meal when taken in the course of the meal require a blessing before but not after, and when taken after the meal require a blessing both before and after.

Ben Zoma was asked: Why was it laid down that things which form an integral part of the meal when taken in the course of a meal require no blessing either before or after? — He replied: Because the [blessing over] bread suffices for them. If so, [they said] let the blessing over bread suffice for wine also? — Wine is different, he replied

---

[1] The size of a breakage which renders the utensil incapable of becoming unclean.
[2] V. Kel. XVI, 1.
[3] According to the Rabbis, the honey of dates is meant.
[4] Lit., 'support'; here, a kind of mnemonic. For further notes on this passage v. Suk. (Sonc. ed.) pp. 19ff.
[5] The verse referred to is Deut. VIII, 8, where two lists are given of the products of the Land of Israel, each introduced with the word 'land', and in the first pomegranates are mentioned fifth, while in the second honey (i.e., date honey) is mentioned second.
[6] The grace after meals serves for them too.
[7] More exactly, 'nibblings' — things like nuts or dates brought in to nibble after the grace after meals.

Folio 42a

because it is itself a motive for benediction.[1]

R. Huna ate thirteen rolls[2] of three to a kab without saying a blessing after them. Said R. Nahman to him: This is what [you call] hunger.[3] [R. Nahman is consistent with his own view, for R. Nahman said:][4] Anything which others make the mainstay of a meal requires a grace to be said after it.

Rab Judah gave a wedding feast for his son in the house of R. Judah b. Habiba.[5] They set before the guests bread such as is taken with dessert. He came in and heard them saying the benediction ha-Mozi.[6] He said to them: What is this zizi that I hear? Are you perhaps saying the blessing 'who bringest forth bread from the earth'? — They replied: We are, since it has been taught: R. Muna said in the name of R. Judah: Over bread which is taken with dessert the benediction 'who bringest forth bread' is said; and Samuel said that the halachah is as stated by R. Muna. He said to them: It has been stated that the halachah is not as stated by R. Muna. They said to him: Is it not the Master himself who has said in the name of Samuel that bread wafers may be used for an erub,[7] and the blessing said over them is 'who bringest forth bread'? — [He replied]: There [we speak] of a different case, namely, where they are made the basis of the meal; but if they are not the basis of the meal, this does not apply.

R. Papa was once at the house of R. Huna the son of R. Nathan. After they had finished the meal, eatables were set before them and R. Papa took some and commenced to eat. They said to him: Does not the Master hold that after the meal is finished it is forbidden to eat?[8] He replied: 'Removed'[9] is the proper term.[10]

Raba and R. Zera once visited the Exilarch. After they had removed the tray from before them, a gift [of fruit] was sent them from the Exilarch. Raba partook, but R. Zera did not partake. Said the latter to him: Does not the Master hold that if the food has been removed it is forbidden to eat? He replied: We can rely on the tray of the Exilarch.[11]

Rab said: If one is accustomed to [rub his hands with] oil [after a meal], he can wait for the oil.[12] R. Ashi said: When we were with R. Kahana he said to us: I, for instance, who am accustomed to use oil, can wait for the oil. But the law is not as stated in all those dicta reported above, but as thus

---

[1] When used for such purposes as sanctification, and not merely as a beverage.
[2] With the 'nibblings'.
[3] I.e., such is enough to satisfy any hunger, and therefore should necessitate grace after it. The original is obscure and the meaning doubtful.
[4] Inserted with MS.M. and deleting 'but' of cur. edd.
[5] Var. lec., R. Habiba.
[6] The ordinary blessing over bread.
[7] I.e., they are reckoned as substantial food.
[8] Until grace after meals had first been said, after which a fresh benediction has to be said.
[9] I.e., it is permissible (if grace has not yet been said) to eat as long as the table has not actually been cleared away.
[10] Lit., 'it has been stated'.
[11] I.e., we can be sure that more food will come.
[12] I.e., he can go on eating till the oil is brought, even if the table has been cleared. Lit., 'the oil impedes him'.

stated by R. Hiyya b. Ashi in the name of Rab: Three things should follow immediately one on the other. The killing [of the sacrifice] should follow immediately on the laying on of hands. Tefillah should follow immediately on ge'ullah.[13] Grace should follow immediately on the washing of hands.[14] Abaye said: We will add another case. A blessing follows immediately on [the entertaining of] scholars, since it says, The Lord hath blessed me for thy sake.[15] If you prefer, I can learn it from here: The Lord blessed the Egyptian's house for Joseph's sake.[16]

MISHNAH. A BLESSING SAID OVER THE WINE TAKEN BEFORE THE MEAL[6] SERVES ALSO FOR THE WINE TAKEN AFTER THE MEAL.[7] A BLESSING OVER THE HORS D'OEUVRES[8] TAKEN BEFORE THE MEAL SERVES FOR THE SWEETS[9] TAKEN AFTER THE MEAL. A BLESSING OVER BREAD SERVES FOR THE SWEETS BUT A BLESSING OVER THE HORS D'OEUVRES DOES NOT SERVE FOR THE BREAD. BETH SHAMMAI SAY: NEITHER [DOES IT SERVE] FOR A COOKED DISH. IF [THOSE AT THE TABLE] ARE SITTING UPRIGHT,[10] EACH ONE SAYS GRACE FOR HIMSELF; IF THEY HAVE RECLINED, ONE SAYS GRACE FOR ALL.

---

[13] v. supra. 4b, 9b.
[14] The second washing, at the end of the meal, the 'latter water' (v. infra 53b). and this washing is the signal that the meal is finished, whether or not the table has been cleared.
[15] Gen. XXX, 27.
[16] Ibid. XXXIX, 5.
[6] As an appetizer.
[7] Before grace is said.
[8] Lit., 'dainty'.
[9] Lit., 'dainty'.
[10] I.e., do not form a party.

Berakoth 42b

IF WINE IS BROUGHT TO THEM IN THE COURSE OF THE MEAL, EACH ONE SAYS A BENEDICTION FOR HIMSELF; IF AFTER THE MEAL, ONE SAYS IT FOR ALL. THE SAME ONE SAYS [THE BENEDICTION] OVER THE PERFUME,[1] ALTHOUGH THE PERFUME IS NOT BROUGHT IN TILL AFTER THE MEAL.[2]

GEMARA. Rabbah b. Bar Hanah said in the name of R. Johanan: This[3] was meant to apply only to Sabbaths and festivals, because then a man makes wine an essential part of his meal.[4] On others days of the year, however, a blessing is said over each cup,[5] it has also been reported: Rabbah b. Mari said in the name of R. Joshua b. Levi: This was meant to apply only to Sabbaths and festivals, and to meals taken when a man leaves the bath or after bloodletting, because on such occasions a man makes wine an essential part of the meal. On other days of the year, however, a blessing is said over each cup. Rabbah b. Mari was once at the house of Raba on a weekday. He saw him say a blessing [over the wine taken] before the meal and again after the meal. He said to him: 'Well done; and so said R. Joshua b. Levi!'

R. Isaac b. Joseph visited Abaye on a festival, and saw him say a blessing over each cup. He said to him: Does your honour not hold with the rule laid down by R. Joshua b. Levi?
— He replied: I have just changed my mind.[6]

A question was asked: If wine was brought round in the course of the meal [but not before], can a blessing over it serve for the wine taken after the meal as well? Should you cite the ruling that A BLESSING SAID OVER THE WINE TAKEN BEFORE THE MEAL SERVES FOR WINE TAKEN AFTER THE MEAL, this may be because both are [drunk] for the sake of drinking. Here, however, where one cup is for steeping [the food in] and the other for drinking. shall I say that this is not the rule, or perhaps it makes no difference? — Rab replied that it does serve; R. Kahana that it does not; R. Nahman held that it does serve; R. Shesheth that it does not serve. R. Huna and Rab Judah and all the disciples of Rab held that it does not serve. Raba raised an objection to R. Nahman: IF WINE IS BROUGHT TO THEM IN THE COURSE OF THE MEAL, EACH ONE SAYS A BLESSING FOR HIMSELF; IF AFTER THE MEAL, ONE SAYS IT FOR ALL.[7] — He replied: The meaning is this: If no wine was brought in during the course of the meal but only after the meal, one says the blessing on behalf of all.

A BLESSING OVER BREAD SERVES FOR THE SWEETS, BUT A BLESSING OVER THE HORS D'OEUVRES DOES NOT SERVE FOR THE BREAD. BETH SHAMMAI SAY: NEITHER [DOES IT SERVE] FOR A COOKED DISH. The question was asked: Do Beth Shammai differ with

---

[1] I.e., spices put on coals and brought in after grace is said.
[2] And grace has intervened between it and the vine.
[3] That a blessing said over wine before the meal serves for wine after the meal. The reason is that from the beginning there is an intention to drink later.
[4] Rashi: he intends to linger at the table after the meal and drink wine.
[5] Because each cup requires a separate intention.
[6] To drink an additional cup, as I did not intend at first to take more wine after the meal.
[7] Assuming that the grace after the meal refers to a second serving of wine, this seems to show that wine taken in the course of the meal does not serve for wine taken after.

regard to the first part of the statement or the second part? [Do we understand] that the First Tanna said that A BLESSING OVER BREAD SERVES FOR THE SWEETS and a fortiori for cooked dishes, and Beth Shammai on the contrary maintained that not merely does the blessing over bread not suffice for the sweets but it does not serve even for the cooked dishes; or are we perhaps to understand that they differ as to the second half of the statement, that A BLESSING OVER THE HORS D'OEUVRES DOES NOT SERVE FOR THE BREAD, which implies that it does not indeed serve for bread but it does serve for cooked dishes, and Beth Shammai on the contrary maintain that it does not serve even for cooked dishes? — This is left undecided.

IF [THEY] ARE SITTING UPRIGHT, EACH ONE etc. If they are reclining he may, if not he may not. With this was contrasted the following: If ten persons were travelling on the road, even though all eat of one loaf, each one says grace for himself; but if they sat down to eat, even though each one eats of his own loaf, one may say grace on behalf of all. It says here, 'sat', which implies, although they did not recline? — R. Nahman b. Isaac replied: This is the case if for instance, they say: Let us go and eat bread in such and such a place.[1]

When Rab died, his disciples followed his bier. When they returned[2] they said, Let us go and eat a meal by the river Danak.[3] After they had eaten, they sat and discussed the question: When we learnt 'reclining', is it to be taken strictly, as excluding sitting, or perhaps, when they say, Let us go and eat bread in such and such a place, it is as good as reclining? They could not find the answer. R. Adda b. Ahabah rose

---

[1] Which is equivalent to making a party.
[2] Rab was buried in another town from that in which his Academy was situated.
[3] Perhaps a mistake for Anak, a river near Sura; v. MS.M.

Folio 43a

and turned the rent in his garment[1] from front to back and made another rent, saying, Rab is dead, and we have not learnt the rules about grace after meals! At length an old man came and pointed out the contradiction between the Mishnah and the Baraitha, and solved it by saying, Once they have said, Let us go and eat bread in such and such a place, it is as if they were reclining.

IF THEY HAVE RECLINED, ONE SAYS GRACE: Rab said: The rule is that only bread requires reclining, but wine does not require reclining.[2] R. Johanan, however, says that wine also requires reclining. Some report thus: Rab said, This applies only to bread, for which reclining is of effect,[3] but for wine reclining is not of effect. R. Johanan, however, says that for wine also reclining is of effect.

The following was cited in objection [to Rab]: 'What is the procedure for reclining? The guests[4] enter and sit on stools and chairs till they are all assembled. When water is brought, each one washes one hand.[5] When wine is brought, each one says a blessing for himself. When they go up [on to the couches] and recline, and water is brought to them, although each one of them has already washed one hand, he now again washes both hands. When wine is brought to them, although each one has said a blessing for himself, one now says a blessing on behalf of all.[6] Now according to the version which makes Rab say that 'this applies only to bread which requires reclining, but wine does not require reclining'. there is a contradiction between his view and the first part of this statement?[7] — Guests are different, since they intend to shift their place.[8] According to the version which makes Rab say that this applies only to bread for which reclining is of effect, but for wine reclining is of no effect, there is a contradiction with the second part?[9] — The case is different there because, since reclining is of effect for bread, it is also of effect for wine.[10]

Ben Zoma was asked: Why was it laid down that if wine is brought in the course of the meal, each one says a blessing for himself, but if after the meal, one may say a blessing for all? He replied: Because [during meals] the gullet is not empty.[11]

THE SAME ONE SAYS [THE BENEDICTION] OVER THE PERFUME. Since it says, THE SAME ONE SAYS [THE BENEDICTION] OVER THE PERFUME, we may infer that there is present someone superior to him. Why then does he say it? — Because he washed his hands first [after the meal]. This supports Rab; for R. Hiyya b. Ashi said in the name of Rab: The one who first washes his

---

[1] Which he had made on hearing of the death of Rab.
[2] To constitute a party, and even without it one may say the blessing on behalf of all.
[3] For the purpose of constituting a party.
[4] Probably a party of Haberim (v. Glos.) is referred to.
[5] To take the wine which is to be offered before the meal.
[6] Since they now form a party.
[7] Which says that, till they have reclined, each one says a blessing for himself over wine.
[8] I.e., to go up from the stools on to the couches.
[9] Which says that having reclined one says a blessing on behalf of all also for wine.
[10] Since the guests on this occasion have been invited to partake of bread, the reclining is of effect also for the wine.
[11] The guests might be eating at the moment when the blessing was pronounced and would not be able to answer Amen (Tosaf).

hands [after the meal] can claim the right[1] to say grace. Rab and R. Hiyya were once sitting before Rabbi at dinner. Rabbi said to Rab: Get up and wash your hands. He [R. Hiyya] saw him trembling.[2] Said R. Hiyya to him: Son of Princes![3] He is telling you to think over the grace after meals.[4]

R. Zera said in the name of Raba b. Jeremiah: When do they say the blessing over the perfume? As soon as the smoke column ascends. Said R. Zera to Raba b. Jeremiah: But he has not yet smelt it! He replied: According to your reasoning, when one says 'Who brings forth bread from the earth', he has not yet eaten! But [he says it because] it is his intention to eat. So here, it is his intention to smell.

R. Hiyya the son of Abba b. Nahmani said in the name of R. Hisda reporting Rab — according to others, R. Hisda said in the name of Ze'iri: Over all incense-perfumes the blessing is 'who createst fragrant woods', except over musk, which comes from a living creature and the blessing is, 'who createst various kinds of spices'. An objection was raised: The benediction 'who createst fragrant woods' is said only over the balsam-trees of the household of Rabbi and the balsam-trees of Caesar's household and over myrtle everywhere![5] — This is a refutation.

R. Hisda said to R. Isaac: What blessing is said over this balsam-oil? — He replied: Thus said Rab Judah: 'Who createst the oil of our land',[6] He then said to him: Leaving out Rab Judah, who dotes on the Land of Israel, what do ordinary people say? — He replied: Thus said R. Johanan: 'Who createst pleasant oil'. R. Adda b. Ahabah said: Over costum the blessing is, 'Who createst fragrant woods', but not over oil in which it is steeped. R. Kahana, however, says: Even over oil in which it is steeped, but not over oil in which it has been ground. The Nehardeans say: Even over oil in which it has been ground.

---

[1] Lit., 'he is prepared'.
[2] He thought Rab had told him to do this because his hands were dirty or something of the sort.
[3] V. supra p. 79' n. 6.
[4] So as to be able to say it fluently.
[5] I.e., over plants of which the wood itself is fragrant.
[6] Balsam-trees grew near Jericho.

Berakoth 43b

.R. Giddal said in the name of Rab: Over jasmine[1] the blessing is 'who createst fragrant woods'. R. Hananel said in the name of Rab: Over sea-rush[2] the blessing is 'who createst fragrant woods'. Said Mar Zutra: What Scriptural verse confirms this? She had brought them up to the roof and hid then, with the stalks of fax.[3] R. Mesharsheya said: Over garden narcissus the blessing is 'who createst fragrant woods'; over wild narcissus, 'who createst fragrant herbs'. R. Shesheth said: Over violets the blessing is, 'who createst fragrant herbs'. Mar Zutra said: He who smells a citron or a quince should say. 'Blessed be He who has given a sweet odour to fruits'. Rab Judah says: If one goes abroad in the days of Nisan [spring time] and sees the trees sprouting, he should say, 'Blessed be He who hath not left His world lacking in anything and has created in it goodly creatures and goodly trees for the enjoyment of mankind'. R. Zutra b. Tobiah said in the name of Rab: Whence do we learn that a blessing should be said over sweet odours? Because it says, Let every soul[4] praise the Lord.[5] What is that which gives enjoyment to the soul and not to the body? — You must say that this is fragrant smell.

Mar Zutra b. Tobiah further said in the name of Rab: The young men of Israel[6] are destined to emit a sweet fragrance like Lebanon,[7] as it says His branches shall spread, and his beauty shall be as the olive tree, and his fragrance as Lebanon.[8]

R. Zutra b. Tobiah further said in the name of Rab: What is the meaning of the verse. He hath made everything beautiful in its time?[9] It teaches that the Holy One, blessed be He, made every man's trade seem fine in his own eyes. R. Papa said: This agrees with the popular saying:[10] Hang the heart of a palm tree on a pig, and it will do the usual thing with it.[11]

R. Zutra b. Tobiah further said in the name of Rab: A torch is as good as two [persons][12] and moonlight as good as three. The question was asked: Is the torch as good as two counting the carrier, or as good as two besides the carrier? — Come and hear: 'Moonlight is as good as three'. If now you say, 'including the carrier there is no difficulty. But if you say, 'besides the carrier', why do I want four, seeing that a Master has said: To one [person] an evil spirit may show itself and harm him; to two it may show itself, but without harming them; to three it will not even show itself? We must therefore say that a torch is equivalent to two including the carrier; and this may be taken as proved.

R. Zutra b. Tobiah further said in the name of Rab — according to others. R. Hanah b. Bizna said it

---

[1] According to Krauss, it should be 'elder-tree'.
[2] Which has stalks like flax.
[3] Lit., 'flax of the tree'. Josh. II, 6.
[4] Heb. neshamah, lit., 'breath'.
[5] Ps. CL, 6.
[6] MS.M. adds here: 'who have not tasted sin', and this seems to be the proper reading.
[7] From its trees and blossoms.
[8] Hos. XIV, 7.
[9] Eccl. III, 11.
[10] Lit., 'this is what people say'.
[11] Sc. takes it to the dungheap.
[12] In respect of the injunction that a man should not go abroad at night unaccompanied, for fear of evil spirits.

in the name of R. Simeon the Pious, and according to others again. R. Johanan said it in the name of R. Simeon b Yohai: It is better for a man that he should cast himself into a fiery furnace rather than that he should put his fellow to shame in public.[1] Whence do we know this? From Tamar, of whom it says, When she was brought forth etc.[2]

Our Rabbis taught: If oil and myrtle are brought before one,[3] Beth Shammai say that he first says a benediction over the oil and then over the myrtle, while Beth Hillel say that he first says a benediction over the myrtle and then over the oil. Said Rabban Gamaliel: I will turn the scale.[4] Of oil we have the benefit both for smelling and for anointing; of myrtle we have the benefit for smelling but not for anointing. R. Johanan said: The halachah follows the one who turned the scale. R. Papa was once visiting R. Huna the son of R. Ika. Oil and myrtle were brought before him and he took up the myrtle and said the blessing over it first, and then he said the blessing over the oil. Said the other to him: Does not your honour hold that the halachah follows the one who turned the scale? He replied: Thus said Raba: The halachah follows Beth Hillel. This was not correct,[5] however; he said so only to excuse himself.

Our Rabbis taught: If oil and wine are brought before one,[6] Beth Shammai say that he first takes the oil in his right hand and the wine in his left hand and says a blessing over the oil[7] and then a blessing over the wine. Beth Hillel, however, say that he takes the wine in his right hand and the oil in his left, and says the blessing over the wine and then over the oil. [Before going out] he smears it on the head of the attendant; and if the attendant is a man of learning, he smears it on the wall, since it is unbecoming for a scholar to go abroad scented.

Our Rabbis taught: Six things are unbecoming for a scholar. He should not go abroad scented; he should not go out by night alone; he should not go abroad in patched sandals; he should not converse with a woman in the street; he should not take a set meal[8] in the company of ignorant persons; and he should not be the last to enter the Beth ha-Midrash. Some add that he should not take long strides nor carry himself stiffly.[9]

'He should not go abroad scented'. R. Abba the son of R. Hiyya b. Abba said in the name of
R. Johanan: This applies only to a place where people are suspected of pederasty. R. Shesheth said: This applies only to [the scenting of] one's clothes; but [perfuming] the body removes the perspiration. R. Papa said: The hair is on the same footing as clothes; others, however, say: as the body.

'He should not go out at night alone', so as not to arouse suspicion.[10] This is the case only if he has no appointment [with his teacher]; but if he has an appointment, people know that he is going to his appointment.

---

[1] Lit., 'cause his face to blanch'.
[2] Gen. XXXVIII, 25. Even to save herself from the stake, Tamar did not mention Judah's name.
[3] After a meal, oil for removing dirt from the hands, myrtle for scent.
[4] In favour of Beth Shammai.
[5] That Raba ever said so.
[6] After a meal on a weekday. the perfumed oil being for scent.
[7] 'Blessed is He that created pleasant oil'.
[8] Lit., 'recline'.
[9] Lit., 'with erect stature'.
[10] Of immoral practices.

'He should not go abroad in patched sandals'. This supports R. Hiyya b. Abba; for R. Hiyya b. Abba said: It is unseemly for a scholar to go abroad in patched sandals. Is that so? Did not R. Hiyya b. Abba go out in such? — Mar Zutra the son of R. Nahman said: He was speaking of one patch on top of another. And this applies only to the upper, but if it is on the sole, there is no objection. On the upper too this applies only to the public way; but in the house there is no objection. Further, this is the case only in summer; but in the rainy season there is no objection.[4]

'He should not converse with a woman in the street'. R. Hisda said: Even with his wife. It has been taught similarly: Even with his wife, even with his daughter, even with his sister, because not everyone knows who are his female relatives.

'He should not take a set meal with ignorant persons'. What is the reason? — Perhaps he will be drawn into their ways.

'He should not be last to enter the Beth ha-Midrash', because he will be called a transgressor.[5]

'Some add that he should not take long strides'; because a Master has said: Long strides diminish a man's eyesight by a five-hundredth part. What is the remedy? He can restore it with [drinking] the sanctification wine of Sabbath eve.[6]

'Nor should he carry himself stiffly'; since a Master has said: If one walks with a stiff bearing even for four cubits, it is as if he pushed against the heels of the Divine Presence,[7] since it is written, The whole earth is full of His glory.[8]

---

[4] Because the mud will hide it.
[5] Var. lec.: 'idler', which in any case is the meaning.
[6] V. Shab. 113b.
[7] I.e., acted haughtily against God.
[8] Isa. VI, 3.

Folio 44a

MISHNAH. IF SALTED FOOD IS SET BEFORE HIM AND BREAD WITH IT, HE SAYS A BLESSING OVER THE SALTED FOOD AND THIS SERVES FOR THE BREAD, SINCE THE BREAD IS ONLY SUBSIDIARY TO IT. THIS IS THE GENERAL PRINCIPLE: WHENEVER WITH ONE KIND OF FOOD ANOTHER IS TAKEN AS SUBSIDIARY, A BENEDICTION IS SAID OVER THE PRINCIPAL KIND AND THIS SERVES FOR THE SUBSIDIARY.

GEMARA. But is it ever possible for salted food to be the principal item and bread subsidiary to it? — R. Aha the son of R. 'Awira replied, citing R. Ashi: This rule applies to [one who eats] the fruit of Genessareth.[1] Rabbah b. Bar Hannah said: When we went after R. Johanan to eat the fruit of Genessareth, when there were a hundred of us we used each to take him ten, and when we were ten we used each to take him a hundred, and a hundred could not be got into a basket holding three se'ahs, and he used to eat them all and swear that he had not tasted food. Not tasted food, do you say? — Say rather: that he had not had a meal. R. Abbahu used to eat of them [so freely] that a fly slipped off his forehead.[2] R. Ammi and R. Assi used to eat of them till their hair fell out. R. Simeon b. Lakish ate until his mind began to wander, and R. Johanan told the household of the Nasi, and R. Judah the Prince send a band of men[3] for him and they brought him to his house.

When R. Dimi came [from Palestine], he stated that King Jannaeus[4] had a city in the King's Mountain[5] where they used to take out sixty myriads of dishes of salted fish for the men cutting down fig-trees from one week-end to the next.[6] When Rabin came, he stated that King Jannaeus used to have a tree on the King's Mountain from which they used to take down forty se'ahs of young pigeons from three broods every month. When R. Isaac came, he said: There was a town in the Land of Israel named Gofnith[7] in which there were eighty pairs of brothers, all priests, who were married to eighty pairs of sisters, also all of priestly family. The Rabbis searched from Sura to Nehardea and could not find [a similar case] save the daughters of R. Hisda who were married to Rami b. Hama and to Mar 'Ukba
b. Hama; and while they were priestesses, their husbands were not priests.

Rab said: A meal without salt is no meal. R. Hiyya b. Abba said in the name of R. Johanan: A meal without gravy[8] is no meal.

MISHNAH. IF ONE HAS EATEN GRAPES, FIGS OR POMEGRANATES HE SAYS A GRACE OF THREE BLESSINGS AFTER THEM. SO R. GAMALIEL. THE SAGES, HOWEVER, SAY: ONE BLESSING WHICH INCLUDES THREE. R. AKIBA SAYS: IF ONE ATE ONLY BOILED VEGETABLES, AND THAT IS HIS MEAL, HE SAYS AFTER IT THE GRACE OF THREE BLESSINGS. IF ONE DRINKS WATER TO QUENCH HIS THIRST, HE SAYS THE

---

[1] Which is highly prized. Tosaf. explains that the rule applies to salted food taken after the fruit of Genessareth to correct the excessive sweetness.
[2] They made his skin so smooth that it could not obtain a footing.
[3] Lit., 'searchers', 'officials'.
[4] Of the Hasmonean House.
[5] Probably some district in Judea was known by this name.
[6] So many workers were required for the task.
[7] Supposed to be the Biblical Ophni, modern Jifna.
[8] So Rashi. Aliter: 'vegetable juices'; aliter: 'something sharp'. In all cases the idea is to aid digestion.

BENEDICTION 'BY WHOSE WORD ALL THINGS EXIST. R. TARFON SAYS: 'WHO CREATEST MANY LIVING THINGS AND THEIR REQUIREMENTS.

GEMARA. What is the reason of R. Gamaliel? — Because it is written, A land of wheat and barley. etc.,[1] and it is also written, A land wherein thou shalt eat bread without scarceness,[2] and it is written, And thou shalt eat and be satisfied and bless the Lord thy God.[3] The Rabbis, however, hold that the word 'land'[4] makes a break in the context.

R. Gamaliel also must admit that 'land' makes a break in the context? — He requires that for excluding one who chews wheat [from the necessity of saying grace].[5]

R. Jacob b. Idi said in the name of R. Hanina: Over anything belonging to the five species [of cereals],[6] before partaking the blessing 'who createst all kinds of food' is said, and after partaking one blessing which includes three. Rabbah b. Mari said in the name of R. Joshua b. Levi: Over anything belonging to the seven kinds,[7] before partaking the blessing 'who createst the fruit of the tree' is said, and after it the grace of one blessing which includes three.

Abaye asked R. Dimi: What is the one blessing which includes three? — He replied: Over fruit of the tree he says: 'For the tree and for the fruit of the tree and for the produce of the field and for a desirable, goodly, and extensive land which Thou didst give our ancestors to inherit to eat of its fruit and to be satisfied with its goodness. Have mercy, O Lord our God, on Israel Thy people and on Jerusalem Thy city and on Thy Sanctuary and on Thy altar, and build Jerusalem Thy holy city speedily in our days and bring us up into the midst thereof and rejoice us therein,[8] for Thou art good and doest good to all'.[9] Over the five species [of cereals] one says: 'For the provision and the sustenance and the produce of the field etc.', and he concludes, 'For the land and for the sustenance'.

How does one conclude [in the case of fruits]? When R. Dimi came, he said in the name of Rab: On New Moon one concludes, Blessed is He who sanctifies Israel and New Moons.[10]

What do we say in this case [over fruit]? — R. Hisda said: 'For the land and for its fruits';
R. Johanan said: 'For the land and for the fruits'. R. Amram said: They are not at variance: the one blessing[11] is for us [in Babylon], and the other for them [in Palestine].[12] R. Nahman b. Isaac demurred to this: Shall they eat and we bless?[13] You must therefore reverse the names, thus: R. Hisda said: For the land and for the fruits; R. Johanan said, For the land and for its fruits.

---

[1] Deut. VIII, 8.
[2] Ibid. 9.
[3] Ibid. 10. The first two verses show that grapes etc. are on the same footing as bread, while the third verse contains a hint of three blessings, as explained infra 48b.
[4] In the second half of v. 9 so that 'and thou shalt bless' in v. 10 refers only to 'bread' mentioned in v. 9.
[5] The break is necessary to indicate that 'wheat' mentioned must first be made into 'bread' before the three benedictions are necessary.
[6] Viz., wheat, barley, oats, rye and spelt.
[7] Mentioned in v. 8, other than corn.
[8] Var. lec. (Similarly P.B.): Rejoice us in its rebuilding. MS.M. add (similarly P.B.): May we eat of the fruits of the land and be satisfied with its goodness and bless Thee for it in holiness and purity.
[9] Cf. P.B. p. 287.
[10] This paragraph seems to be out of place here and is deleted by Wilna Gaon. MS.M.: On New Moon one concludes etc. What do we say in this case?
[11] R. Hisda's.
[12] R. Hisda was from Babylon and R. Johanan from Palestine.
[13] They eat the fruit of Palestine, and we say its fruits!

Berakoth 44b

R. Isaac b. Abdimi said in the name of our Master:[1] Over eggs and over all kinds of meat the blessing said before partaking is 'by whose word etc.', and after partaking 'who createst many living creatures etc.', vegetables, however, require no blessing [after]. R. Isaac, however, says that even vegetables also require a blessing [after], but not water. R. Papa says: Water also. Mar Zutra acted as prescribed by R. Isaac b. Abdimi and R. Shimi b. Ashi as prescribed by R. Isaac. (To remember which is which think of one[2] acting as two and two as one.)[3] R. Ashi said: When I think of it, I do as prescribed by all of them.[4]

We have learnt: Whatever requires a blessing to be said after it requires a blessing before it, but some things require a blessing before but not after.[5] Now this is right on the view of R. Isaac b. Abdimi, since it is to exclude vegetables, and on the view of R. Isaac to exclude water; but on the view of R. Papa, what does it exclude? — It is to exclude the performance of religious duties.[6] And according to the Palestinians[7] who after removing their tefillin say 'Blessed be Thou ... who hast sanctified us with Thy commandments and commanded us to observe Thy statutes' — what does it exclude? — It excludes scents.

R. Jannai said in the name of Rabbi: An egg is superior [in food value] to the same quantity of any other kind of food. When Rabin came [from Palestine] he said: A lightly roasted egg is superior to six kaysi[8] of fine flour. When R. Dimi came, he said: A lightly roasted egg is better than six [kaysi]; a hard baked egg than four;[9] and a [boiled] egg is better than the same quantity of any other kind of boiled food except meat.

R. AKIBA SAYS: EVEN IF ONE ATE BOILED VEGETABLES etc. Is there any kind of boiled vegetable of which one can make a meal? — R. Ashi replied: The rule applies to the stalk of cabbage.

Our Rabbis taught: Milt is good for the teeth but bad for the bowels; horse-beans are bad for the teeth but good for the bowels. All raw vegetables make the complexion pale and all things not fully grown retard growth. Living beings[10] restore vitality[11] and that which is near the vital organs[12] restores vitality. Cabbage for sustenance and beet for healing. Woe to the house[13] through which vegetables are always passing!

---

[1] V. supra p. 185. n. 4.
[2] Lit., 'and thy sign is'.
[3] I.e., the authority who was mentioned alone without his father (Mar Zutra). acted as prescribed by the authority who is mentioned with his father (R. Isaac b. Abdimi) and vice versa.
[4] Saying even after water.
[5] Nid. 51b.
[6] Which require a blessing before the performance of them but not after, such as taking off the tefillin, laying aside of the lulab, etc.
[7] Lit., 'the sons of the West'.
[8] A measure equal to a log.
[9] Var. lec.: a lightly baked egg is better than four hard-baked and a hard-baked than four boiled.
[10] Taken whole, like small fish.
[11] Lit., 'soul'.
[12] Of a slaughtered animal.
[13] I.e., stomach.

The Master has said, 'Milt is good for the teeth and bad for the bowels.' What is the remedy? — To chew it well and then spit it out. 'Horse-beans are bad for the teeth but good for the bowels'. What is the remedy? — To boil them well and swallow them. 'All raw vegetables make the complexion pale'. R. Isaac said: That is, in the first meal taken after blood-letting. R. Isaac also said: If one eats vegetables before the fourth hour [of the day],[1] it is forbidden to talk with him. What is the reason? Because his breath smells. R. Isaac also said: It is forbidden to a man to eat raw vegetables before the fourth hour. Amemar and Mar Zutra and R. Ashi were once sitting together when raw vegetables were set before them before the fourth hour. Amemar and R. Ashi ate, but Mar Zutra would not eat. They said to him: What is your reason? Because R. Isaac said that if one eats vegetables before the fourth hour it is forbidden to converse with him because his breath smells? See, we have been eating, and you have been conversing with us? He replied: I hold with that other saying of R. Isaac, where he said that it is forbidden to a man to eat raw vegetables before the fourth hour.[2] 'Things not fully grown retard growth'. R. Hisda said: Even a kid worth a zuz.[3] This, however, is the case only with that which has not attained a fourth of its full size; but if it has attained a fourth, there is no objection. 'Living being restore vitality'. R. Papa said: Even tiny fishes from the pools. 'That which is near the vital organs restores vitality'. R. Aha b. Jacob said: Such as the neck.[4] Raba said to his attendant: When you buy a piece of meat for me, see that you get it from a place near where the benediction is said.[5] 'Cabbage for sustenance and beet for healing'. Is cabbage then good only for sustenance and not for healing? Has it not been taught: Six things heal a sick person of his disease with a permanent cure, namely, cabbage, beet, a decoction of dry[6] poley, the maw, the womb, and the large lobe of the liver'? — What you must say is that the cabbage is good for sustenance also. 'Woe to the house through which vegetables are always passing'. Is that so? Did not Raba say to his attendant: If you see vegetables in the market, do not stop to ask me, What will you put round your bread.[7] — Abaye said: [It means, when they are cooked] without meat;[8] Raba said: [It means, when they are taken] without wine. It has been stated: Rab says, without meat, Samuel says, without wood,[9] and R. Johanan says, without wine. Said Raba to R. Papa the brewer:[10] We neutralize[11] it with meat and wine; you who have not much wine, how you neutralize it?

— He replied: With chips [of wood]. R. Papa's wife when she cooked vegetables neutralized their evil effects by using eighty Persian twigs.[12]

Our Rabbis taught: A small salted fish is sometimes deadly, namely on the seventh, the seventeenth and the twenty-seventh day of its salting. Some say, on the twenty-third. This is the case only if it is imperfectly roasted; but if it is well roasted, there is no harm in it. And even if it is not well roasted there is no harm in it unless one neglects to drink beer after it; but if one drinks beer after it, there is no harm.

---

[1] When the first meal was taken.
[2] But it is not forbidden to converse with him.
[3] I.e., a good fat one.
[4] Which is near the heart.
[5] I.e., the neck, on cutting which a benediction is said.
[6] Reading ihach for acs in the text, as infra.
[7] To eat with it as a kind of sandwich.
[8] The juices of which neutralize the evil effects of the vegetables.
[9] I.e., a good fire to cook it.
[10] Aliter: (a) the landowner (v. Obermeyer p. 309); (b) 'Man of Mystery!', i.e., acquainted with the divine mysteries (v. 'Aruch).
[11] Lit., 'break (the evil effects)'.
[12] Twigs from Persian trees.

IF ONE QUENCHES HIS THIRST WITH WATER etc. What does this exclude? — R. Idi b. Abin said: It excludes one

Folio 45a

who is choked by a piece of meat.[1]

R. TARFON SAYS: WHO CREATEST MANY LIVING THINGS AND THEIR REQUIREMENTS. Raba son of R. Hanan said to Abaye, according to others to R. Joseph: What is the law? He replied: Go forth and see how the public are accustomed to act.[2]

CHAPTER VII

MISHNAH. IF THREE PERSONS HAVE EATEN TOGETHER, IT IS THEIR DUTY TO INVITE [ONE ANOTHER TO SAY GRACE].[3] ONE WHO HAS EATEN DEMAI,[4] OR FIRST TITHE[5] FROM WHICH TERUMAH HAS BEEN REMOVED,[6] OR SECOND TITHE OR FOOD BELONGING TO THE SANCTUARY THAT HAS BEEN REDEEMED,[7] OR AN ATTENDANT WHO HAS EATEN AS MUCH AS AN OLIVE OR A CUTHEAN MAY BE INCLUDED [IN THE THREE]. ONE WHO HAS EATEN TEBEL[8] OR FIRST TITHE FROM WHICH THE TERUMAH HAS NOT BEEN REMOVED, OR SECOND TITHE OR SANCTIFIED FOOD WHICH HAS NOT BEEN REDEEMED,[9] OR AN ATTENDANT WHO HAS EATEN LESS THAN THE QUANTITY OF AN OLIVE OR A GENTILE MAY NOT BE COUNTED. WOMEN, CHILDREN AND SLAVES MAY NOT BE COUNTED IN THE THREE. HOW MUCH [MUST ONE HAVE EATEN] TO COUNT? AS MUCH AS AN OLIVE; R. JUDAH SAYS, AS MUCH AS AN EGG.

GEMARA. Whence is this derived?[10] — R. Assi says: Because Scripture says, O magnify ye the Lord with me, and let us exalt His name together.[11] R. Abbahu derives it from here: When I [one] proclaim the name of the Lord, ascribe ye [two] greatness unto our God.[12]

R. Hanan b. Abba said: Whence do we learn that he who answers Amen should not raise his voice above the one who says the blessing? Because it says, O magnify ye the Lord with me and let us exalt His name together.[13] R. Simeon b. Pazzi said: Whence do we learn that the one who translates[14] is not permitted to raise his voice above that of the reader? Because it says, Moses spoke and God answered him by a voice.[15] The words 'by a voice' need not have been inserted. What then does 'by a voice'

---

[1] And drinks simply to wash it down.
[2] And the general practice is to say 'by whose word' before and 'that createst many living beings' after.
[3] By means of the responses given in P.B. p. 279. This invitation is technically known as zimmun (inviting).
[4] Produce from which it is doubtful whether the tithe has been given.
[5] Due to the Levite, v. Num. XVIII, 21.
[6] The terumah (v. Glos) mentioned here is apparently the tithe, v. ibid. 26.
[7] And so has been made available for being eaten out of Jerusalem (cf. Deut. XIV, 22ff) or by a layman. All these are kinds of food which may be legitimately partaken of.
[8] Food from which it is known that tithe has not been separated.
[9] These are foods of which it is not legitimate to partake.
[10] That three who eat together should invite one another to say grace.
[11] Ps. XXXIV, 4. 'Ye' implies two, besides the speaker.
[12] Deut. XXXII, 3. E.V. 'For I will proclaim etc..
[13] I.e., one not louder than the other.
[14] The public reading of the Pentateuch in Hebrew was followed by a translation in Aramaic.
[15] Ex. XIX, 19. Moses is here compared to a reader and God to a translator, v.however Tosaf. s.v. .

mean? [It means], by the voice of Moses.[1] It has been taught similarly: The translator is not permitted to raise his voice above that of the reader. If the translator is unable to speak as loud as the reader, the reader should moderate his voice and read.

It has been stated: If two have eaten together, Rab and R. Johanan differ [as to the rule to be followed]. One says that if they wish to invite one another [to say grace] they may do so, the other says that even if they desire to invite one another they may not do so. We have learnt: IF THREE PERSONS HAVE EATEN TOGETHER IT IS THEIR DUTY TO INVITE ONE ANOTHER. That means to say, three but not two? — No; there [in the case of three] it is a duty, here [in the case of two] it is optional.

Come and hear: If three persons have eaten together, it is their duty to invite one another [to say grace], and they are not permitted to separate. This means to say, three but not two, does it not?[2] — No; there is a special reason there [why they may not separate], because from the outset of the meal they laid upon themselves the duty to invite one another.[3]
Come and hear: If an attendant is waiting on two persons he may eat with them even without their giving him permission;[4] if he was waiting on three, he may not eat with them unless they give him permission! — There is a special reason there

---

[1] I.e., a voice not raised above that of Moses.
[2] Because if two are sufficient, why may not one of the three separate?
[3] And though two may invite one another, yet to perform an obligation is more meritorious.
[4] And we assume that they approve of it so that they may be able to invite oneanother, and this is not presumptuous on his part.

Berakoth 45b

, because [we assume that] it is with their approval[1] since he [thereby] makes [the zimmun] obligatory on them.[2]

Come and hear: Women by themselves invite one another, and slaves by themselves invite one another, but women, slaves and children together even if they desire to invite one another may not do so. Now[3] a hundred women are no better then two men,[4] and yet it says, Women by themselves invite one another and slaves by themselves invite one another? — There is a special reason there, because each has a mind of her own.[5] If that is so, look at the next clause: Women and slaves together, even though they desire to invite one another may not do so. Why not? Each has a mind! — There is a special reason in that case, because it might lead to immorality.

We may conclude that it was Rab who said, 'Even though they [two] desire to invite one another they may not do so', because R. Dimi b. Joseph said in the name of Rab: If three persons ate together and one of them went out, the others call to him and count him for zimmun.[6] The reason is, is it not, that they call him, but if they did not call him they could not [invite one another]? — There is a special reason there, that the obligation to invite one another devolved upon them from the outset. Rather you may conclude that it is

R. Johanan who said that even though they desire to invite one another they may not do so. For Rabbah b. Bar Hanah said in the name of R. Johanan: If two persons eat together, one of them is exempted by the benediction of his fellow; and we were perplexed to know what it was that he tells us; for we have learnt: If he heard without responding [Amen], he has performed his obligation, and R. Zera explained that he tells us that they do not invite one another to say grace.[7] We may therefore draw this conclusion.

Raba b. R. Huna said to R. Huna: But the Rabbis who came from the West[8] say that if they desire to invite one another they may do so; and must they not have heard this from R. Johanan?[9] — No; they heard it from Rab before he went down to Babylon.[10]

The [above] text [stated]: 'R. Dimi b. Joseph said in the name of Rab: If three persons ate together and one of them went out into the street, they can call to him and count him for zimmun'. Abaye says: This is only when they call to him and he responds.[11] Mar Zutra said: This applies only to three; but if it is for [the purpose of completing] ten,[12] they must wait till he comes. R. Ashi demurred to this. We should rather [he said], suppose the contrary; for nine look like ten, but two do not look like three.

---

[1] That the attendant joins them.
[2] Cur. edd. add in brackets 'from the outset', which is best omitted.
[3] Cur. edd. read here in brackets, 'and surely as for women even a hundred' which is best omitted.
[4] In respect of the obligation of zimmun. This proves that two by themselves are not sufficient to form a zimmun.
[5] Lit., 'there are minds' and therefore thanksgiving from three women is morevaluable than from two men.
[6] Even while he remains outside, provided he joins in the response v. infra.
[7] But one may be exempted by the other.
[8] Palestine.
[9] Who lived in Palestine.
[10] From Palestine to settle there, v. Git. (Sonc. ed.) p. 17. n. 3.
[11] I.e., he joins in the responses.
[12] V. infra 49b.

The law, however, is as laid down by Mar Zutra. What is the reason? — Since they [ten] have to mention God's name,[1] it is not proper that there should be less than ten.

Abaye said: We have a tradition that if two persons have eaten together, it is their duty to separate.[2] It has been taught similarly: If two persons have eaten together, it is their duty to separate. When is this case? When they are both educated men. But if one is educated and the other illiterate, the educated one says the benedictions and this exempts the illiterate one.

Raba said: The following statement was made by me independently and a similar statement has been made in the name of R. Zera: If three persons have been eating together, one breaks off to oblige two,[3] but two do not break off to oblige one. But do they not? Did not R. Papa break off for Abba Mar his son, he and another with him? — R. Papa was different because he went out of his way[4] to do so.[5] Judah b. Meremar and Mar son of R. Ashi and R. Aha from Difti took a meal with one another. No one of them was superior to the other[6] that he should have the privilege of saying grace.[7] They said: Where the Mishnah learnt[8] that IF THREE PERSONS HAVE EATEN TOGETHER IT IS THEIR DUTY TO INVITE [ONE ANOTHER TO SAY GRACE], this is only where one of them is superior [to the others], but where they are all on a level, perhaps it is better that the blessings should be separate. They thus said [the grace] each one for himself. Thereupon they came before Meremar and he said to them: You have performed the obligation of grace, but you have not performed the obligation of zimmun. Should you say, Let us start again with zimmun, zimmun cannot be said out of its place.[9]

If one came and found three persons saying grace,[10] what does he say after them? — R. Zebid says: Blessed and to be blessed [be His Name]. R. Papa said: He answers, Amen. They are not really at variance; the one speaks of the case where he found them saying 'Let us say grace', and the other where he found them saying 'Blessed'. If he found them saying 'Let us say grace', he answers 'Blessed and to be blessed'; if he found them saying 'Blessed', he answers 'Amen'.

One [Baraitha] taught: One who answers 'Amen' after his own blessings is to be commended, while another taught that this is reprehensible! — There is no contradiction: the one speaks of the benediction 'who buildest Jerusalem',[11] the other of the other benedictions. Abaye used to give the response[12] in a loud voice so that the workmen should hear and rise,[13] since the benediction 'Who is

---

[1] In the response, 'Blessed is our God of whose food we have eaten'. V. P.B. p. 279.
[2] For the purpose of saying grace.
[3] If one has not yet finished, he interrupts his meal to join with the two who have finished for the purpose of zimmun.
[4] Lit., 'acted within the limits of strict justice'.
[5] To show respect to his son.
[6] In years or learning.
[7] So MS.M. Cur. edd. add: 'for them'.
[8] Emended reading. v. Marginal Gloss. The text has, They sat and discussed the question. When the Mishnah says. etc.
[9] Lit., 'retrospectively'. I.e., it must come before the actual grace.
[10] Sc. the zimmun responses.
[11] The last of the three Scriptural benedictions in the Grace, v. P.B. p. 282.
[12] To this third benediction.
[13] To go to their work.

good and does good"[1] is not prescribed by the Torah.[2] R. Ashi gave the response in a low voice, so that they should not come to think lightly of the benediction 'Who is good and does good'.

---

[1] Which follows 'Who buildest Jerusalem'; v. P.B. p. 283.
[2] Which prescribes only the first three.

Folio 46a

R. Zera once was ill. R. Abbahu went to visit him, and made a vow, saying, If the little one with scorched legs[1] recovers, I will make a feast for the Rabbis. He did recover, and he made a feast for all the Rabbis. When the time came to begin the meal,[2] he said to R. Zera: Will your honour please commence for us.[3] He said to him: Does not your honour accept the dictum of R. Johanan that the host should break bread? So he [R. Abbahu] broke the bread for them. When the time came for saying grace he said to him [R. Zera], Will your honour please say grace for us, He replied: Does your honour not accept the ruling of
R. Huna from Babylon,[4] who said that the one who breaks bread says grace? Whose view then did R. Abbahu accept? — That expressed by R. Johanan in the name of R. Simeon b. Yohai: The host breaks bread and the guest says grace. The host breaks bread so that he should do so generously,[5] and the guest says grace so that he should bless the host. How does he bless him? 'May it be God's will that our host should never be ashamed in this world nor disgraced in the next world'. Rabbi added some further items: 'May he be very prosperous with all his estates, and may his possessions and ours be prosperous and near a town,[6] and may the Accuser have no influence either over the works of his hands or of ours, and may neither our host nor we be confronted with[7] any evil thought or sin or transgression or iniquity from now and for all time'.

To what point does the benediction of zimmun extend?[8] — R. Nahman says: Up to [the conclusion of] 'Let us bless';[9] R. Shesheth says: Up to [the conclusion of] 'Who sustains',[10] May we say that there is the same difference between Tannaim? For one [authority] taught: The grace after meals is either two or three benedictions,[11] while another has taught: Either three or four. Now we assume that all agree that 'Who is good and does good' is not Scriptural. Is not then the difference [between the two authorities cited] this, that the one who says two or three holds that [the benediction of zimmun] extends up to 'Who sustaineth',[12] while the one who says three or four holds that it extends up to 'Let

---

[1] A nickname of R. Zera, explained in B.M. 85a.
[2] By breaking bread.
[3] I.e., break the bread.
[4] R. Huna's place of origin is mentioned here because the meal was taking place in Palestine.
[5] Lit., 'with a pleasant eye'.
[6] So that he can visit them without difficulty.
[7] Lit., 'may there not leap before him or us'.
[8] The point of this query is not clear. Rashi takes it to mean, How much is said by three which is not said by two or one; but in this case the answer of R. Shesheth is unintelligible, since all agree that one says the blessing 'Who sustaineth'. Tosaf. therefore explain that it refers to the statement above that one person may interrupt his meal to join two others in zimmun, and the question is now asked, How long must he wait before resuming.
[9] The zimmun responses proper.
[10] The first benediction.
[11] Emended reading, the numeral being in the feminine, v, Marginal Gloss. In the text the numeral is in the masculine, and we must translate (with Tosaf.), 'with either two or three men'. Tosaf. ad loc. accept this reading and explain it to mean that the recital of the blessings can be shared out between a number of people if no-one knows the whole of it, by assigning to each one benedictions which he happens to know.
[12] So that if zimmun is said there are three blessings, the zimmun formula together with the first blessing constituting on this view one benediction, otherwise two.

us bless'?[1] — No; R. Nahman explains according to his view and R. Shesheth explains according to his view. R. Nahman explains according to his view: All agree that it extends to 'Let us bless'. On the view of him who says, 'three or four', this creates no difficulty.[2] The one who says 'two or three' can say that here we are dealing with a grace said by work-people, regarding which a Master has said, He commences with 'Who sustaineth' and includes 'Who builds Jerusalem' in the benediction of the land.[3] R. Shesheth can also explain according to his view: All agree that the blessing of zimmun extends up to 'Who sustaineth'. On the view of him who says 'two or three', this creates no difficulty; while the one who says 'three or four' holds that the benediction 'Who is good and does good' is Scriptural.

R. Joseph said: You may know that the benediction 'who is good and does good' is not Scriptural from the fact that workpeople omit it. R. Isaac b. Samuel b. Martha said in the name of Rab: You may know that the benediction 'who is good and does good' is not Scriptural from the fact that it commences with 'Blessed' but does not conclude with 'Blessed', for so it has been taught: All benedictions commence with 'Blessed' and close with 'Blessed', except the blessing over fruits, the blessings said over the performance of precepts, one blessing which joins on to another, and the last blessing after the recital of the Shema'.[4] Some of these commence with 'Blessed' but do not close with 'Blessed'[5]

---

[1] So that without zimmun there are three and with the zimmun there is an extra one.
[2] If grace is said with zimmun, there are four blessings, if without, three.
[3] They combine the second and third benedictions into one, and thus when two labourers eat together there are two benedictions, when three, they form zimmun and say three.
[4] Which is separated by the Shema' from the two blessings before it, though it is really a continuation of these.
[5] E.g., the benediction to be said before the putting on of tefillin.

Berakoth 46b

, while some close with 'Blessed' but do not open with 'Blessed';[1] and 'who is good and does good' opens with 'Blessed' but does not close with 'Blessed'. This shows that it is a separate blessing. R. Nahman b. Isaac said: You may know that 'who is good and does good' is not Scriptural from the fact that it is omitted in the house of a mourner,[2] as it has been taught: What blessing is said in the house of a mourner? 'Blessed is He that is good and does good'. R. Akiba says: 'Blessed be the true Judge'. And does one [according to the first authority] say. 'Blessed be He that is good and does good', and not 'Blessed be the true Judge'? — Read: He says also,'Blessed be He that is good and does good'. Mar Zutra visited
R. Ashi when the latter had suffered a bereavement, and in the grace after meals he began and uttered the benediction: 'Who is good and does good, God of truth, true Judge, who judges in righteousness and takes away in righteousness, who is Sovereign in His universe to do as pleaseth Him in it, for all His ways are judgment; for all is His, and we are His people and His servants, — and for everything it is incumbent upon us to give thanks to Him and to bless Him. He who closes up the breaches of Israel will close up this breach in Israel, granting life'.

Where does he[3] commence again? — R. Zebid says in the name of Abaye: At the beginning; the Rabbis say, at the place where he left off.[4] The law is, at the place where he left off.

Said the Exilarch to R. Shesheth: Although you are venerable Rabbis, yet the Persians are better versed than you in the etiquette[5] of a meal. When there are two couches [in the set],[6] the senior guest takes his place first and then the junior one above him.[7] When there are three couches, the senior occupies the middle one, the next to him in rank takes the place above him, and the third one below him.[8] R. Shesheth said to him: So when he wants to talk to him,[9] he has to stretch himself and sit upright to do so![10] He replied: This does not matter to the Persians, because they speak with gesticulation. [R. Shesheth asked the Exilarch:] With whom do they commence the washing of the hands before the meal? — He replied: With the senior one. Is then the senior one to sit still [he

---

[1] E.g., the benedictions in the Tefillah.
[2] According to R. Akiba.
[3] Rashi explains this to mean the one who has interrupted his meal to join with two others in zimmun, (cf. supra 45b) and the question is, on the view of R. Shesheth, (cf. supra) where should he resume his grace.
[4] Viz., (on the view of R. Shesheth) at the second blessing. Tosaf. remark on this that it is very difficult to suppose that he is excused saying the first blessing after having eaten again. They accordingly refer it to the man who leads in the grace, and the question is, after the others have responded 'Blessed be He of whose bounty we have partaken and through whose goodness we live', where does he go on, and the reply is, on Abaye's view, that he repeats his own formula with the addition 'Blessed be He of whose bounty etc.', whereas according to the Rabbis he merely says 'Blessed be He of whose bounty etc.', v. P.B. p. 280.
[5] Lit., 'requirements'.
[6] It was usual for guests at a set meal to recline on couches arranged in sets of two or three (the latter being the Roman triclinium).
[7] I.e., head to head.
[8] I.e., with his head to the other's feet.
[9] When the senior wishes to speak to the one who is above him.
[10] If he wants to face him.

exclaimed] and watch his hands[1] until they have all washed? — He replied: They bring a table before him immediately.[2] With whom do they begin the washing after the meal [he asked him]? — He replied: With the junior one present. And is the senior one to sit with greasy hands until all have washed? — He replied: They do not remove the table from before him till water is brought to him.[3] R. Shesheth then said: I only know a Baraitha, in which it is taught: 'What is the order of reclining? When there are two couches in a set, the senior one reclines first, and then the junior takes his place below him. When there are three couches, the senior takes his place first, the second next above him, and then the third one below him. Washing before the meal commences with the senior one, washing after the meal, if there are five, commences with the senior, and if there are a hundred[4] it commences with the junior until five are left, and then they start[5] from the senior one. The saying of grace is assigned to the one to whom the washing thus reverts'.[6] This supports Rab; for R. Hiyya b. Ashi said in the name of Rab: Whoever washes his hands first at the end of the meal has the right to say grace. Rab and R. Hiyya were once dining with Rabbi. Rabbi said to Rab: Get up and wash your hands. R. Hiyya saw him trembling and said to him: Son of princes, he is telling you to think over the grace.[7] Our Rabbis taught: We do not give precedence [to others][8] either on the road or on a bridge

---

[1] I.e., do nothing. Aliter: 'guard them against impurity'.
[2] It was usual to place a small table before each guest.
[3] And meanwhile he can go on eating.
[4] Sc., any number more than five.
[5] I.e., removing the table (Rashi).
[6] I.e., either the senior one, or the one to whom he delegates the honour.
[7] V. supra p. 262, nn. 9 and 10.
[8] Lit., 'honour', i.e., ask another to go first, out of politeness.

Folio 47a

or in the washing of the greasy hands [at the end of a meal]. Once Rabin and Abaye were on the road and the ass of Rabin got in front of Abaye, and he [Rabin] did not say to him, Will your honour proceed. Said Abaye: Since this student has come up from the West,[1] he has grown proud. When he arrived at the door of the synagogue, he said, Will your honour please enter. He said to him: Was I not 'Your honour', up to now? — He replied: Thus said R. Johanan: One gives precedence only in a doorway in which there is a mezuzah.[2] [You say] only where there is a mezuzah, but not where there is no mezuzah. If that is so, then in the case of a synagogue and Beth hamidrash also where there is no mezuzah we do not give precedence? What you must say is, in a doorway which is suitable for a mezuzah.[3]

R. Judah the son of R. Samuel b. Shilath said in the name of Rab: The guests may not eat anything until the one who breaks bread has tasted. R. Safra sat and stated: The statement was, 'May not taste'.[4] What difference does it make [in practice]? — [It teaches that] one must repeat the exact words of his teacher.

Our Rabbis taught: Two wait for one another[5] before commencing on the dish,[6] but three need not wait.[7] The one who has broken bread stretches out his hand first, but if he wishes to show respect to his teacher or to anyone senior to himself, he may do so. Rabbah
b. Bar Hanah made a marriage feast for his son in the house of R. Samuel son of R. Kattina, and he first sat down and taught his son: The one who acts as host[8] may not break the bread until the guests have finished responding, Amen. R. Hisda said: The bulk of the guests. Rama b. Hama said to him: Why should this be the case only with the majority? Presumably it is because the benediction had not yet been completed.[9] The same should apply also to a minority, for the benediction has not yet been completed? — He replied: What I say is that whoever [draws out] the response of Amen longer than necessary is in error.[10]

Our Rabbis taught: The Amen uttered in response should be neither hurried[11] nor curtailed[12] nor orphaned,[13] nor should one hurl the blessing, as it were, out of his mouth.[14] Ben 'Azzai says: If a man says an 'orphaned' Amen in response, his sons will be orphans; if a hurried Amen, his days will be snatched away; if a curtailed Amen, his days will be curtailed. But if one draws out the Amen, his

---

[1] Palestine.
[2] V. Glos.
[3] Excluding open roads and bridges.
[4] And not 'may not eat'.
[5] When one interrupts his eating, the other must wait till he resumes. This was according to the old custom when all diners ate from the same dish.
[6] After breaking bread, it was the custom for each of the guests to take something out of the dish.
[7] If one interrupts his eating.
[8] Who in this case would be the bridegroom. Lit., 'he who breaks (the bread)'.
[9] As long as the Amen response had not been finished.
[10] And the minority who unduly prolong the Amen response need not be taken into consideration.
[11] I.e., the A should not be slurred over.
[12] The N should be clearly pronounced.
[13] Said by one who has not heard the blessing itself but only the others responding Amen.
[14] He should not gabble it.

days and years will be prolonged. Once Rab and Samuel were sitting at a meal and R. Shimi b. Hiyya joined them and ate very hurriedly.[1] Said Rab to him: What do you want? To join us? We have already finished. Said Samuel to him: If they were to bring me mushrooms, and pigeon to Abba,[2] would we not go on eating?[3] The disciples of Rab were once dining together when R. Aha entered. They said: A great man has come who can say grace for us. He said to them: Do you think that the greatest present says the grace? One who was there from the beginning must say grace! The law, however, is that the greatest says grace even though he comes in at the end.

ONE WHO HAD EATEN DEMAI etc. But this is not a proper food for him?[4] — If he likes he can declare his possessions hefker[5] in which case he becomes a poor man, and it is suitable for him. For we have learnt: Demai may be given to the poor to ear and also to billeted soldiers.[6] And R. Huna said: A Tanna taught: Beth Shammai say that demai is not given to the poor and to billeted soldiers to eat.[7]

OR FIRST TITHE FROM WHICH TERUMAH HAS BEEN REMOVED. This is obvious!
— This had to be stated, for the case in which the Levite came beforehand [and thus obtained the first tithe] in the ear and he separated the terumah of the tithe,[8] but not the great terumah.[9] And the rule stated follows R. Abbahu; for R. Abbahu said in the name of Resh Lakish: First tithe for which [the Levite] has come beforehand [and obtained] in the ear is not liable to great terumah, since it says, ye shall offer up an heave offering of it for the Lord, even a tenth part of the tithe.[10] I bid you offer a tithe from the tithe, not the great terumah plus the terumah of the tithe from the tithe. Said R. Papa to Abaye: If that is so, the same should be the case even if he anticipates it at the heap?[11] — He replied: It was in anticipation of your question that the text says,

---

[1] So as to be able to join them in the grace.
[2] A name of endearment given by Samuel to Rab.
[3] As dessert, these being our favourite dishes. Therefore it is as though we had not finished and he may join us.
[4] Sc. and it is as though he ate stolen property, over which it is forbidden to make a blessing.
[5] V. Glos.
[6] Dem. III, 1.
[7] I.e., it is only Beth Shammai who provided demai to the poor but Beth Hillel, with whom the law agrees, differ from them.
[8] The tithe given by the Levite to the priest.
[9] The ordinary terumah, (v. Glos. s.v. terumah).
[10] Num. XVIII, 26.
[11] The grain after winnowing, but before being ground.

Berakoth 47b

Out of all your tithes ye shall offer.[1] But still what reason have you [for including corn in the ear and not grain]? — One has been turned into corn the other has not.[2]

SECOND TITHE OR FOOD BELONGING TO THE SANCTUARY THAT HAS BEEN REDEEMED. This is obvious! — We are dealing here with a case where, for instance, he has given the principal but not the additional fifth;[3] and he teaches us here that the fact that the fifth has not been given is no obstacle.[4]

OR IF AN ATTENDANT WHO HAS EATEN AS MUCH AS AN OLIVE etc. This is obvious! — You might object that the attendant does not sit through the meal.[5] This teaches, therefore, [that this is no objection].

A CUTHEAN MAY BE INCLUDED [IN THE THREE]. Why so? Wherein is he better than an 'am ha-arez, and it has been taught: An 'am ha-arez is not reckoned in for zimmun?
— Abaye replied: It refers to a Cuthean who is a haber. Raba said: You may even take it to refer to a Cuthean who is an 'am ha-arez, the passage cited referring to an 'am ha-arez as defined by the Rabbis who join issue in this matter with R. Meir. For it has been taught: Who is an 'am ha-arez[6] Anyone who does not eat non-sacred food in ritual cleanness. So
R. Meir. The Rabbis, however, say: Anyone who does not tithe his produce in the proper way. Now these cutheans do tithe their produce in the proper way, since they are very scrupulous about any injunction written in the Torah; for a Master has said: Whenever the Cutheans have adopted a mizwah, they are much more particular with it than the Jews.[7]

Our Rabbis taught: Who is an 'am ha-arez[8] Anyone who does not recite the Shema' evening and morning. This is the view of R. Eliezer. R. Joshua says: Anyone who does not put on tefillin. Ben 'Azzai says: Anyone who has not a fringe on his garment. R. Nathan says: Anyone who has not a mezuzah on his door. R. Nathan b. Joseph says: Anyone who has sons and does not bring them up to the study of the Torah. Others say: Even if one has learnt Scripture and Mishnah, if he has not ministered to the disciples of the wise,[9] he is an 'am ha-arez. R. Huna said: The halachah is as laid down by 'Others'.

Rami b. Hama refused to count to zimmun R. Menashiah b. Tahalifa who could repeat Sifra,[10] Sifre,[11] and halachah. When Rami b. Hama died, Raba said: Rami b. Hama died only because he would not count R. Menashiah b. Tahalifa for zimmun. But it has been taught: Others say that even if one has

---

[1] Num, XVIII, 29. The actual word in the text is 'gifts'.
[2] And it is only from what can be called 'corn' that terumah has to be given.
[3] Required for the redemption of second tithe or anything belonging to the Sanctuary.
[4] To render the redemption valid.
[5] He has always to be getting up to wait on the guests.
[6] Hence a Cuthean may be reckoned in.
[7] Hence a Cuthean may be reckoned in.
[8] Hence a Cuthean may be reckoned in.
[9] Rashi explains this to mean that he has not learnt Gemara, which explains the Mishnah.
[10] The Midrash on Leviticus.
[11] The Midrash on Deuteronomy.

learnt Scripture and Mishnah but has not ministered to the disciples of the wise, he is an 'am ha-arez? — R. Menashiah b. Tahalifa was different because he used to minister to the Rabbis, and it was Rami b. Hama who did not make proper inquiries about him. According to another version, he used to hear discussions from the mouth of the Rabbis and commit them to memory. and he was therefore like a Rabbinical scholar.

ONE WHO HAS EATEN TEBEL AND FIRST TITHE etc. In the case of tebel this is obvious! — It required to be stated for the case of that which is tebel only by the ordinance of the Rabbis. What for instance? Food grown in a pot without a hole in the bottom.[1]

FIRST TITHE etc. This is obvious! — It required to be stated for the case where [the Levite] anticipated [the priest] at the heap. You might think that the law is as indicated by
R. Papa's question to Abaye;[2] this teaches that it is as indicated by the latter's answer.
SECOND TITHE etc. This is obvious! — It is required for the case in which the tithe etc., has been redeemed, but not properly redeemed. Second tithe, for instance, if it has been redeemed for
bar silver,[3] since the All-Merciful said; Thou shalt bind up [we-zarta] the silver in thy hands,[4] implying, silver on which a form [zurah] is stamped. As to FOOD BELONGING TO THE SANCTUARY, if for instance it has been rendered profane for its equivalent in land but has not been redeemed for money, whereas the All Merciful laid down, He shall give the money and it shall be assured unto him.[5]

OR THE ATTENDANT WHO HAS EATEN LESS THAN AN OLIVE. This is obvious!
— Since the first clause states the rule for the quantity of an olive, the second clause states it for less than an olive.

A GENTILE MAY NOT BE COUNTED. This is obvious! — We are dealing here with the case of a proselyte who has been circumcised but has not yet made ablution. For R. Zera said in the name of R. Johanan: One does not become a proselyte until he has been circumcised and has performed ablution; and so long as he has not performed ablution he is a gentile.

WOMEN SLAVES AND CHILDREN ARE NOT COUNTED [IN THE THREE]. R. Jose said: An infant in the cradle may be counted for zimmun. But we have learnt: WOMEN SLAVES AND CHILDREN MAY NOT BE COUNTED? — He adopts the view of R. Joshua b. Levi. For R. Joshua b. Levi said: Although it was laid down that an infant in a cradle cannot be counted for zimmun, yet he can be counted to make up ten. R. Joshua b. Levi also said: Nine and a slave may be joined [to make up ten].[6]

The following was cited in objection: Once R. Eliezer entered a synagogue and not finding there ten he liberated his slave and used him to complete the ten. This was because he liberated him, otherwise he could not have done so? — He really required two, and he liberated one and one he used to make up the ten. But how could he act so seeing that Rab Judah has said: If one liberates his slave he

---

[1] So that the earth in it is not in contact with the soil.
[2] V. supra 46b ad fin.
[3] I.e., silver not turned into current coin.
[4] Deut. XIV, 25.
[5] Lev. XXVII, 19. The exact words of the text are: he shall add the fifth part of the money of thy valuation unto it, and it shall be assured to him; v. B.M. (Sonc. ed.) p. 321, n. 1.
[6] For a congregational service which requires a minimum quorum of ten males over the age of thirteen.

transgresses a positive precept, since it says, they shall be your bondmen for ever?[1] — If it is for a religious purpose. It is different. But this is a religious act which is carried out by means of a transgression? — A religious act which affects a whole company[2] is different.

R. Joshua b. Levi also said: A man should always rise early to go to synagogue so that he may have the merit of being counted in the first ten; since if even a hundred come after him he receives the reward of all of them. 'The reward of all of them', say you? — Say rather: He is given a reward equal to that of all of them.

R. Huna said: Nine and the Ark join together [to be counted as ten]. Said R. Nahman to him: Is the Ark a man? I mean, said R. Huna, that when nine look like ten, they may be joined together. Some say [this means] when they are all close together,[3] others say when they are scattered. R. Ammi said: Two and the Sabbath may be joined together. Said
R. Nahman to him: Is the Sabbath a man? What R. Ammi really said was that two scholars who sharpen one another in the knowledge of the halachah may count as three [for zimmun].[4] R. Hisda gave an example: For instance, I and R. Shesheth. R. Shesheth gave an example: For instance, I and R. Hisda.[5]
R. Johanan said: A boy [who has reached puberty] before his years[6] may be counted for zimmun. It has been taught similarly: A boy who has grown two hairs may be counted for zimmun, but if he has not grown two hairs he may not be counted; and we are not particular about a boy. Now this seems to contain a contradiction. You first say that if he has grown two hairs he may count and if not he may not, and then you say, We are not particular with a boy. What case does this include? Is it not

---

[1] Lev. XXV, 46. V. Git. 38b.
[2] As in the case of R. Eliezer.
[3] In which case the absence of one is not so noticeable. The Ark is probably mentioned as being a focal point which enables us to determine whether the worshippers are close together or scattered.
[4] is accordingly explained as an abbreviation for (two) who study the Law; v. Goldschmidt.
[5] R. Shesheth and R. Hisda represented each a different type of scholar, the former's forte being an extensive knowledge of traditions, the latter's keen dialectical powers; v. 'Er. 67a.
[6] I.e., before reaching the age of thirteen years and one day.

Folio 48a

to include a boy who shows signs of puberty before his years? The law, however, is not as laid down in all these statements, but as in this statement of R. Nahman: A boy who knows to whom the benediction is addressed may be counted for zimmun. Abaye and Raba [when boys] were once sitting in the presence of Rabbah. Said Rabbah to them: To whom do we address the benedictions? They replied: To the All-Merciful. And where does the All-Merciful abide? Raba pointed to the roof; Abaye went outside and pointed to the sky. Said Rabbah to them: Both of you will become Rabbis. This accords with the popular saying: Every pumpkin can be told from its stalk.[1]

Rab Judah the son of R. Samuel b. Shilath said in the name of Rab: If nine persons have eaten corn and one vegetables, they may combine.[2] R. Zera said: I asked Rab Judah, What of eight, what of seven,[3] and he replied: It makes no difference. Certainly if six [were eating corn][4] I did not need to ask. Said R. Jeremiah to him: You were quite right not to ask. What was the reason there [in the first case]? Because there is a majority [eating corn]; here too there is a majority. He, however, thought that perhaps an easily recognizable majority is required.[5]

King Jannai and his queen were taking a meal together. Now after he had put the Rabbis to death,[6] there was no-one to say grace for them. He said to his spouse: I wish we had someone to say grace for us. She said to him: Swear to me that if I bring you one you will not harm him. He swore to her, and she brought Simeon b. Shetah, her brother.[7] She placed him between her husband and herself, saying. See what honour I pay you. He replied: It is not you who honour me but it is the Torah which honours me, as it is written, Exalt her and she shall promote thee,[8] [she shall bring thee to honour when thou dost embrace her].[9] He [Jannai] said to her: You see that he[10] does not acknowledge any authority![11] They gave him a cup of wine to say grace over.[12] He said: How shall I say the grace? [Shall I say] Blessed is He of whose sustenance Jannai and his companions have eaten? So he drank that cup, and they gave him another and he said grace over it. R. Abba the son of R. Hiyya b. Abba said: Simeon b. Shetah in acting thus[13] followed his own view. For thus said R. Hiyya b. Abba in the name of Johanan: A man cannot say grace on behalf of others until he has eaten at least the size of an olive of

---

[1] Var. lec. from its sap; i.e., as soon as it begins to emerge from the stalk.
[2] To say the zimmun formula for ten, v. next Mishnah.
[3] Who ate corn while two or three ate vegetables.
[4] Aliter: If six were eating corn and four vegetables (omitting 'certainly'). Rashi's reading (which is found also in Ber. Rab. XCI) is: I am sorry I did not ask what is the rule if six eat (corn). This accords better with what follows.
[5] And even if he were to permit in the first case, he would not permit in the case of six.
[6] V. Kid. (Sonc. ed.) pp. 332ff. notes.
[7] Who was a Pharisaic leader and had been in hiding
[8] Prov. IV, 8.
[9] Cf. Ecclus. XI, 1.
[10] Simeon b. Shetah.
[11] So according to some edd. Cur. edd.: He said to him, See how they (i.e., the Pharisees) do not accept my authority! His reply to the king was regarded by Jannai as an affront and evidence of the Pharisees' hostility to the throne.
[12] Though he had not joined in the meal.
[13] In saying grace without having eaten anything.

corn food with them. Even as it was taught:[1] R. Simeon b. Gamaliel says: If one went up [on the couch] and reclined with them, even though he only dipped [a little bit] with them in brine and ate only one fig with them, he can be combined with them [for zimmun]. Now he can be combined with them, but he cannot say grace on behalf of others until he eats the quantity of an olive of corn food. It has also been stated: R. Hanah b. Judah said in the name of Raba:

---

[1] So BaH. Cur. edd.: An objection was raised.

Berakoth 48b

Even though he only dipped [a little bit] with them in brine or ate with them only one fig, he can be combined with them; but for saying grace on behalf of others he is not qualified until he eats the quantity of an olive of corn food with them. R. Hanah b. Judah said in the name of Raba: The law is that if he ate with them a vegetable-leaf and drank a cup of wine, he can be combined; but he cannot say grace on behalf of others until he eats with them the quantity of an olive of corn food.

R. Nahman said: Moses instituted for Israel the benediction 'Who feeds'[1] at the time when manna descended for them. Joshua instituted for them the benediction of the land[2] when they entered the land. David and Solomon instituted the benediction which closes 'Who buildest Jerusalem'.[3] David instituted the words. 'For Israel Thy people and for Jerusalem Thy city',[4] and Solomon instituted the words 'For the great and holy House'.[5] The benediction 'Who is good and bestows good'[6] was instituted in Jabneh with reference to those who were slain in Bethar. For R. Mattena said: On the day on which permission was given to bury those slain in Bethar,[7] they ordained in Jabneh that 'Who is good and bestows good' should be said: 'Who is good', because they did not putrefy, and 'Who bestows good', because they were allowed to be buried.

Our Rabbis taught: The order of grace after meals is as follows. The first benediction is that of 'Who feeds'. The second is the benediction of the land. The third is 'Who buildest Jerusalem'. The fourth is 'Who is good and bestows good'. On Sabbath [the third blessing] commences with consolation and closes with consolation.[8] and the holiness of the day is mentioned in the middle [of this blessing]. R. Eliezer says: If he likes he can mention it in the consolation, or he can mention it in the blessing of the land,[9] or he can mention it in the benediction which the Rabbis instituted in Jabneh.[10] The Sages, however, say that it must be said in the consolation blessing. The Sages say the same thing as the First Tanna?
— They differ in the case where he actually did say it [in some other place].[11]

Our Rabbis taught: Where is the saying of grace intimated in the Torah? In the verse, And thou shalt eat and be satisfied and bless:[12] this signifies the benediction of 'Who feeds'.[13] 'The Lord Thy God': this signifies the benediction of zimmun.[14] 'For the land': this signifies the blessing for the land. 'The

---

[1] The first benediction of the grace.
[2] The second benediction.
[3] The third benediction.
[4] In the third benediction.
[5] In the third benediction.
[6] The fourth benediction.
[7] The scene of the last stand of the Bar Kocheba Wars, in 135 C.E.
[8] I.e., no change is made. The third blessing commences with 'Have mercy', and ends with a prayer for the rebuilding of Jerusalem, which is also a prayer for 'consolation'.
[9] I.e., the second.
[10] The fourth.
[11] In which case the First Tanna insists that it must be said again in the proper place.
[12] Deut. VIII. 10.
[13] This appears to be a mistake for 'zimmun'. V. Wilna Gaon Glosses.
[14] This appears to be a mistake for 'Who feeds'. V. Wilna Gaon Glosses.

good': this signifies 'Who buildest Jerusalem'; and similarly it says This good mountain and Lebanon.[1] 'Which he has given thee': this signifies the blessing of 'Who is good and bestows good'. This accounts for the grace after [meals]; how can we prove that there should be a blessing before [food]? — You have an argument a fortiori; if when one is full he says a grace, how much more so should he do so, when he is hungry! Rabbi says: This argument is not necessary. 'And thou shalt eat and be satisfied and bless' signifies the benediction of 'Who feeds'. The responses of zimmun are derived from O magnify the Lord with me.[2] 'For the land': this signifies the blessing of the land. 'The good': this signifies, 'Who buildest Jerusalem'; and so it says, 'This goodly mountain and Lebanon'. 'Who is good and bestows good' was instituted in Jabneh. This accounts for the grace after [meals]; whence do I learn that a blessing must be said before [food]? — Because it says, 'Which He has given thee', implying, as soon as He has given thee.[3] R. Isaac says: This is not necessary. For see, it says, And He shall bless thy bread and thy water.[4] Read not u-berak [and he shall bless] but u-barek [and say a blessing]. And when is it called 'bread'? Before it is eaten. R. Nathan says: This is not necessary. For see, it says, As soon as ye be come into the city ye shall straightway find him, before he go up to the high place to eat; for the people will not eat until he come, because he doth bless the sacrifice, and afterwards they eat that be bidden.[5] Why did they[6] make such a long story of it? Because[7] women are fond of talking. Samuel, however, says that it was so that they might feast their eyes on Saul's good looks, since it is written, From his shoulders and upward he was higher than any of the people;[8] while R. Johanan says it was because one kingdom cannot overlap another by a hair's breadth.[9]

We have found warrant for blessing over food; whence do we derive it for the blessing over the Torah? R. Ishmael says: It is learnt a fortiori: If a blessing is said for temporal life, how much more should it be said for eternal life! R. Hiyya b. Nahmani, the disciple of R. Ishmael, said in the name of R. Ishmael: This is not necessary. For see, it says, 'For the good land which He has given thee', and in another place it says, And I will give thee the tables of stone and a law and commandments, etc.[10] (R. Meir says: Whence do we learn that just as one says a blessing for good hap, so he should say one for evil hap? — Because it says, Which the Lord thy God hath given thee, [as much as to say,] which He hath judged thee[11] — for every judgment which He has passed on thee, whether it is a doom of happiness or a doom of suffering.) R. Judah b. Bathyrah says: This is not necessary. For see, it says 'the good' where it need only have said 'good'. 'Good' signifies the Torah; and so it says, For I give you a good doctrine.[12] 'The good' signifies the building of Jerusalem; and so it says, This good mount and Lebanon.[13]

It has been taught: If one does not say the words 'a desirable, good and extensive land' in the blessing

---

[1] Deut. III, 25.
[2] Ps. XXXIV, 4.
[3] Even before partaking thereof.
[4] Ex. XXIII, 25.
[5] I Sam. IX, 13.
[6] The women who were talking to Saul.
[7] MS.M. inserts, Rab said: Hence (is proved) that women etc.
[8] Ibid. 2.
[9] Samuel's regime was destined to cease as soon as Saul's commenced.
[10] Ex. XXIV, 12; the derivation here is based on the principle of Gezerah Shawah.
[11] So BaH. Cur. edd.: 'Thy Judge', explaining the term 'thy God Elohim', which in Rabbinic thought represents God as Judge.
[12] Prov. IV, 2.
[13] The text is in disorder, v. D.S. a.l.

of the land and does not mention the kingdom of the house of David in the blessing 'Who buildest Jerusalem', he has not performed his obligation. Nahum the Elder says: He must mention in it [the second blessing] the covenant. R. Jose says: He must mention in it the Torah. Pelimo says: He must mention the covenant before the Torah, since the latter was given with only three covenants[1]

---

[1] At Mount Sinai (or the Tent of Meeting). at Mount Gerizim and in the plains of Moab.

Folio 49a

but the former with thirteen.[1] R. Abba[2] says: He must express thanksgiving at the beginning and end of it, or at the very least once; and one who omits to do so at least once is blameworthy. And whoever concludes the blessing of the land with 'Who givest lands in inheritance' and 'Who buildest Jerusalem' with the words 'Saviour of Israel' is a boor.[3] And whoever does not mention the covenant and the Torah in the blessing of the land and the kingdom of the house of David in 'Who buildest Jerusalem' has not performed his obligation. This supports R. Ela; for R. Ela said in the name of R. Jacob b. Aha in the name of our Teacher:[4] 'Whoever omits to mention covenant and Torah in the blessing of the land and the kingdom of the house of David in 'Who buildest Jerusalem' has not performed his obligation. There is a difference of opinion between Abba Jose b. Dosethai and the Rabbis. One authority says that [God's] kingship must be mentioned in the blessing 'Who is good and bestows good', the other says it need not be mentioned. The one who says it must be mentioned holds that this blessing has only Rabbinic sanction,[5] the one who says it need not be mentioned holds that it has Scriptural sanction.

Our Rabbis taught: How does one conclude the blessing of the building of Jerusalem? — R. Jose son of R. Judah says: Saviour of Israel. 'Saviour of Israel' and not 'Builder of Jerusalem'? Say rather, 'Saviour of Israel' also. Rabbah b. Bar Hanah was once at the house of the Exilarch. He mentioned one[6] at the beginning of [the third blessing] and both at the end.[7] R. Hisda said: Is it a superior way to conclude with two? And has it not been taught: Rabbi says that we do not conclude with two?

The [above] text [stated]: Rabbi says that we do not conclude with two. In objection to this Levi pointed out to Rabbi that we say 'for the land and for the food'?[8] It means, [he replied] a land that produces food. [But we say,] 'for the land and for the fruits'?[9] — [It means,] a land that produces fruits. [But we say], 'Who sanctifiest Israel and the appointed seasons'?[10] [It means,] Israel who sanctify the seasons. [But we say,] Who sanctifiest Israel and New Moons? — [It means,] Israel who sanctify New Moons. [But we say,] Who sanctifies the Sabbath, Israel and the seasons?[11] — This is

---

[1] The word of 'covenant' occurring thirteen times in the section of the circumcision of Abraham, Gen. XVII, 1-14.
[2] Rab is here intended, v. Marginal Gloss.
[3] Probably because he leaves out the reference to Palestine and Jerusalem; v. infra.
[4] This must refer to Rabbi, Rab, who is usually so designated, being excluded here, since Rab has already stated his view. (V. p. 294, n. 7.)
[5] Hence it is not a continuation of the preceding blessings, which are Scriptural; and therefore kingship must be mentioned afresh in it.
[6] Either Israel or Jerusalem. The third blessing begins 'Have mercy ... upon Israel Thy people and upon Jerusalem Thy city'.
[7] Of the third blessing.
[8] In concluding the second blessing.
[9] V. P.B. p. 289.
[10] Ibid. p. 229.
[11] V. P.B. p. 229.

the exception.¹ Why then should it be different? — In this case it² is one act, in the other two, each distinct and separate.³ And what is the reason for not concluding with two? — Because we do not make religious ceremonies into bundles.⁴ How do we decide the matter? — R. Shesheth says: If one opens with 'Have mercy on Thy people Israel' he concludes with 'Saviour of Israel'; If one opens with 'Have mercy on Jerusalem', he concludes with 'Who buildest Jerusalem'. R. Nahman, however, said: Even if one opens with 'Have mercy on Israel', he concludes with 'Who buildest Jerusalem', because it says. The Lord doth build up Jerusalem. He gathereth together the dispersed of Israel,⁵ as if to say: When does God build Jerusalem? — When He gathereth the dispersed of Israel.

R. Zera said to R. Hisda: Let the Master come and teach us [grace]. He replied: The grace after meals I do not know myself, and shall I teach it to others? — He said to him: What do you mean? — Once, he replied. I was at the house of the Exilarch, and I said grace after the meal, and R. Shesheth stretched out his neck at me like a serpent,⁶ and why? — Because I had made no mention either of covenant or of Torah⁷ or of kingship.⁸ And why did you not mention them [asked R. Zera]? Because, he replied. I followed R. Hananel citing Rab; for R. Hananel said in the name of Rab: If one has omitted to mention covenant, Torah and kingship he has still performed his obligation: covenant, because it does not apply to women; 'Torah and kingship' because they apply neither to women nor to slaves. And you [he exclaimed] abandoned all those other Tannaim and Amoraim and followed Rab!

Rabbah b. Bar Hanah said in the name of R. Johanan: The blessing 'Who is good and bestows good' must contain mention of [God's] kingship. What does he tell us? That any benediction which does not contain mention of [God's] kingship is no proper blessing? R. Johanan has already said this once!⁹ R. Zera said: He tells us that it requires kingship to be mentioned twice,¹⁰ once for itself and once for the benediction 'Who buildest Jerusalem'.¹¹ If that is so, we should require three times, once for itself, once for 'Who buildest Jerusalem', and once for the blessing of the land?¹² Hence what you must say is: Why do we not require one for the blessing of the land? — Because it is a benediction closely connected with the one which precedes it. Then 'Who buildest Jerusalem' should also not require it, being a benediction closely connected with the one which precedes it?

— The fact is that, strictly speaking, the blessing 'Who buildest Jerusalem' also does not require it, but since the kingdom of the house of David is mentioned,¹³ it is not seemly that the kingship of heaven also should not be mentioned.¹⁴ R. Papa said: What he [R. Johanan] meant is this: It requires two mentions of the kingship [of heaven] besides its own.¹⁵

R. Zera was once sitting behind R. Giddal, and R. Giddal was sitting facing R. Huna, and as he [R.

---

¹ Israel do not sanctify the Sabbath by means of a formal proclamation, hence we cannot here apply the same explanation as in the case of festivals and New Moons.
² God's sanctifying of the Sabbath and Israel.
³ Saving Israel and building Jerusalem.
⁴ Cf. Pes. 102b.
⁵ Ps. CXLVII. 2.
⁶ In astonishment.
⁷ In the second benediction.
⁸ The kingship of the house of David in the third benediction.
⁹ V. supra 40b.
¹⁰ As in fact we find in the benediction of 'Who is good etc.', which begins with the formula, 'Blessed art Thou … King of the Universe …' and goes on, 'Our father, our King …'.
¹¹ Which does not conclude with the formula, 'Blessed art Thou … King of the universe,
¹² Which also concludes without the kingship formula.
¹³ In the third blessing.
¹⁴ And therefore we repair the omission in the next benediction.
¹⁵ And in fact the benediction proceeds, 'Our father our King … the king who is good etc.'.

Giddal] sat, he said: If one forgot and did not mention in the grace Sabbath, he says, 'Blessed be He who gave Sabbaths for rest to His people Israel in love for a sign and a covenant, blessed is He who sanctifies the Sabbath!' He [R. Huna] said to him: Who made this statement? — He replied, Rab. He then continued: If one forgot and did not mention the festival, he says, 'Blessed is He who gave holy days to His people Israel for joy and for remembrance, blessed is He who sanctifies Israel and the festivals'. He again asked him who made the statement, and he answered, Rab. He then continued: If one forgot and did not mention the New Moon, he says, 'Blessed is He who gave New Moons to His people Israel for a remembrance'. But, said R. Zera: I do not know whether he also said that he must add 'for joy', or not, whether he concluded with a benediction or not, or whether he said it on his own authority or was repeating the words of his teacher.[1]

Once when R. Giddal b. Manyumi was in the presence of R. Nahman, R. Nahman made a mistake [in the grace],[2]

---

[1] Rab.
[2] I.e., forgot to mention Sabbath or New Moon.

Berakoth 49b

and he went back to the beginning. He said to him: What is the reason why your honour does this? — He replied: Because R. Shila said in the name of Rab: If one makes a mistake, he goes back to the beginning. But R. Huna has said in the name of Rab: If he goes wrong, he says, 'Blessed be He who gave [etc.]'? — He replied: Has it not been stated in reference to this that R. Menashia b. Tahalifa said in the name of Rab: This is the case only where he has not commenced, 'Who is good and bestows good'; but if he has commenced 'Who is good and bestows good', he goes back to the beginning.

R. Idi b. Abin said in the name of R. Amram quoting R. Nahman who had it from Samuel: If one by mistake omitted to mention New Moon in the Tefillah, he is made to begin again; if in the grace after meals, he is not made to begin again. Said R. Idi b. Abin to R. Amram: Why this difference between Tefillah and grace? — He replied: I also had the same difficulty, and I asked R. Nahman, and he said to me: From Mar Samuel personally I have not heard anything on the subject, but let us see for ourselves. [I should say that] in the case of Tefillah, which is obligatory, he is made to begin again, but in the case of a meal, which he can eat or not eat as he pleases, he is not made to begin again. But if that is so [said the other], in the case of Sabbaths and festivals, on which it is not possible for him to abstain from eating, I should also say that if he makes a mistake he must go back to the beginning? — He replied: That is so; for R. Shila said in the name of Rab: If one goes wrong, he goes back to the beginning. But has not R. Huna said in the name of Rab that if one goes wrong he says 'Blessed is He who gave [etc.]'? — Has it not been stated in reference to this that this is the case only if he has not commenced 'Who is good and bestows good', but if he has commenced, 'Who is good and bestows good', he goes back to the beginning?

HOW MUCH [MUST ONE HAVE EATEN] TO COUNT etc. This would seem to show that R. Meir's standard is an olive and R. Judah's an egg. But we understand the opposite, since we have learnt: Similarly, if one has left Jerusalem and remembers that he has in his possession holy flesh, if he has gone beyond Zofim[1] he burns it on the spot, and if not he goes back and burns it in front of the Temple with some of the wood piled on the altar. For what minimum quantity do they turn back? R. Meir says: In either case,[2] the size of an egg; R. Judah says: In either case the size of an olive.[3] R. Johanan said: The names must be reversed. Abaye said: There is no need to reverse. In this case [of zimmun] they differ in the interpretation of a Scriptural text. R. Meir holds that 'thou shalt eat' refers to eating and 'thou shalt be satisfied' to drinking, and the standard of eating is an olive. R. Judah holds that 'And thou shalt eat and be satisfied' signifies an eating which gives satisfaction, and this must be as much as an egg. In the other case, they differ in their reasoning. R. Meir considers that the return for a thing should be analogous to its defilement; just as its defilement is conditioned by the quantity of an egg, so is the return for it conditioned by the quantity of an egg.[4] R. Judah held that the return for it should be analogous to its prohibition. Just as the prohibition thereof comes into force for the quantity of an olive, so is the return for it conditioned by the quantity of an olive.

---

[1] Mt. Scopus, the furthest point from which the Temple was still visible.
[2] The case of holy flesh just mentioned, and the case of leaven which one who is bringing the Paschal lamb remembers that he has not cleared out of his house.
[3] V. Pes. (Sonc. ed.) p. 23 notes.
[4] Less than the quantity of an egg does not communicate defilement in case of food.

MISHNAH. WHAT IS THE FORMULA FOR ZIMMUN? IF THERE ARE THREE, HE [THE ONE SAYING GRACE] SAYS, 'LET US BLESS [HIM OF WHOSE BOUNTY WE HAVE EATEN]'. IF THERE ARE THREE BESIDE HIMSELF HE SAYS, 'BLESS'. IF THERE ARE TEN, HE SAYS, LET US BLESS OUR GOD'; IF THERE ARE TEN BESIDE HIMSELF HE SAYS,'BLESS'. IT IS THE SAME WHETHER THERE ARE TEN OR TEN MYRIADS.[1] IF THERE ARE A HUNDRED HE SAYS, 'LET US BLESS THE LORD OUR GOD'; IF THERE ARE A HUNDRED BESIDE HIMSELF HE SAYS, 'BLESS'. IF THERE ARE A THOUSAND HE SAYS 'LET US BLESS THE LORD OUR GOD, THE GOD OF ISRAEL'; IF THERE ARE A THOUSAND BESIDE HIMSELF HE SAYS 'BLESS'. IF THERE ARE TEN THOUSAND HE SAYS, 'LET US BLESS THE LORD OUR GOD, THE GOD OF ISRAEL, THE GOD OF HOSTS, WHO DWELLS AMONG THE CHERUBIM, FOR THE FOOD WHICH WE HAVE EATEN'. IF THERE ARE TEN THOUSAND BESIDE HIMSELF HE SAYS, 'BLESS'. CORRESPONDING TO HIS INVOCATION THE OTHERS RESPOND, 'BLESSED BE THE LORD OUR GOD THE GOD OF ISRAEL, THE GOD OF HOSTS, WHO DWELLS AMONG THE CHERUBIM, FOR THE FOOD WHICH WE HAVE EATEN'. R. JOSE THE GALILEAN SAYS: THE FORMULA OF INVOCATION CORRESPONDS TO THE NUMBER ASSEMBLED, AS IT SAYS: BLESS YE GOD IN FULL ASSEMBLIES, EVEN THE LORD, YE THAT ARE FROM THE FOUNTAIN OF ISRAEL.[2] SAID R. AKIBA: WHAT DO WE FIND IN THE SYNAGOGUE? WHETHER THERE ARE MANY OR FEW[3] THE READER SAYS, 'BLESS YE THE LORD.[4] R. ISHMAEL SAYS: BLESS YE THE LORD WHO IS BLESSED.

GEMARA. Samuel said: A man should never exclude himself from the general body.[5] We have learnt: IF THERE ARE THREE BESIDE HIMSELF HE SAYS 'BLESS'? —

---

[1] This is the opinion of R. Akiba, as appears infra.
[2] Ps. LXVIII, 27.
[3] Provided there are ten.
[4] V. P.B. p. 37 and p. 68.
[5] He should always say 'Let us bless'.
[6] Thus excluding himself from their company.

Folio 50a

Read: he may also say 'Bless'; but all the same to say 'Let us bless' is preferable. For R. Adda b. Ahabah said: The school of Rab say: We have learnt that [a company consisting of from] six to ten may divide.[1] Now if you say that 'Let us bless' is preferable, we can see a reason why they should divide. But if you say that 'Bless' is preferable, why should they divide?[2] You must therefore conclude that 'Let us bless' is preferable; and so we do conclude.

It has been taught to the same effect: Whether he says 'Bless' or 'Let us bless', no fault is to be found with him for this. But those who are punctilious do find fault with him for this.[3] And from the way a man says the benedictions it may be recognized whether he is a scholar or not. For example, Rabbi says: If he says 'and by his goodness', he is a scholar; if he says 'and from his goodness', he shows himself an ignoramus.[4] Said Abaye to R. Dimi: But it is written, And from thy blessing let the house of thy servant be blessed for ever.?[5] — In a petition it is different.[6] But of a petition also it is written, Open thy mouth wide and I will fill it?[7] — That was written with reference to words of Torah. It has been taught: Rabbi says: If one says, 'And by his goodness we live', he shows himself a scholar; if he says 'they live', he shows himself an ignoramus.[8] The scholars of Neharbel[9] state the opposite,[10] but the law is not as stated by the scholars of Neharbel. R. Johanan says: If one says 'let us bless Him of whose bounty we have partaken' he shows himself a scholar; if he says 'Let us bless the one of whose bounty we have partaken', he shows himself an ignoramus.[11] Said R. Aha the son of Raba to R. Ashi: But do we not say 'We will bless the one who wrought for our ancestors and for us all these miracles'?[12] — He replied: There the meaning is obvious, for who performs miracles? The Holy One, blessed be He.

R. Johanan said: If one says 'Blessed is He of whose bounty we have eaten', he shows himself a scholar. If he says, 'For the food which we have eaten',[13] he shows himself an ignoramus. R. Huna the son of R. Joshua said: This is the case only where there are three, since the name of heaven is not mentioned [in the zimmun],[14] but if there are ten, since the name of heaven is mentioned, it is clear what is meant, as we have learnt: CORRESPONDING TO HIS INVOCATION THE OTHERS RESPOND,'BLESSED BE THE LORD OUR GOD, THE GOD OF ISRAEL, THE GOD OF HOSTS, WHO DWELLS AMONG THE CHERUBIM, FOR THE FOOD WHICH WE HAVE EATEN.'

IT IS THE SAME WHETHER THERE ARE TEN OR TEN MYRIADS. There seems here to be a

---

[1] I.e., form groups of three or four. But ten may not divide, since they will not then be able to say 'Our God'.
[2] Rashi reads: 'Why should six divide?' If they form two groups of three, neither can say 'bless'.
[3] For excluding himself from the group.
[4] Because he belittles the goodness of the Almighty.
[5] II Sam. VII, 29.
[6] The Petitioner likes to be modest in his request.
[7] Ps. LXXXI, 11.
[8] Because he excludes himself from their company.
[9] Neharbel, east of Bagdad.
[10] Taking 'they live' to refer to the whole of mankind.
[11] Because this form may be taken to refer to the host.
[12] In the Haggadah on Passover eve.
[13] Without assigning its ownership to God.
[14] In the responses 'Let us bless our God'.

contradiction. You say, IT IS THE SAME WHETHER THERE ARE TEN OR TEN MYRIADS, which would show that they are all alike. Then it states: IF THERE ARE A HUNDRED HE SAYS so and so, IF THERE ARE A THOUSAND HE SAYS, IF THERE ARE TEN THOUSAND HE SAYS? — R. Joseph said: There is no contradiction; the one statement expresses the view of R. Akiba, the other of R. Jose the Galilean, since we have learnt: R. JOSE THE GALILEAN SAYS: THE FORMULA OF INVOCATION CORRESPONDS TO THE NUMBER ASSEMBLED, AS IT SAYS: BLESS YE GOD IN ALL ASSEMBLIES, EVEN THE LORD, YE THAT ARE FROM THE FOUNTAIN OF ISRAEL.

SAID R. AKIBA: WHAT DO WE FIND IN THE SYNAGOGUE etc. And what does R. Akiba make of the verse cited by R. Jose the Galilean? — He wants it for the following lesson, as it has been taught: R. Meir used to say: Whence do we learn that even children [yet unborn] in their mothers' womb chanted a song by the Red Sea? — Because it says, Bless ye the Lord in full assemblies, even the Lord, ye that are from the fountain of Israel.[1] What says the other [R. Jose] to this? — He derives the lesson from the word 'fountain'.

Raba said: The halachah is as laid down by R. Akiba. Rabina and R. Hama b. Buzi once dined at the house of the Exilarch, and R. Hama got up and commenced to look about for a hundred. Said Rabina to him: There is no need for this. For thus said Raba: The halachah is as stated by R. Akiba.

Raba said: When we take a meal at the house of the Exilarch, we say grace in groups of three.[2] Why not in groups of ten?[3] — Because the Exilarch might hear them and be angry.[4] But could not the grace of the Exilarch suffice for them? — Since everybody would respond loudly, they would not hear the one who says grace.

Raba Tosfa'ah said: If three persons had a meal together and one said grace for himself before the others, his zimmun is effective for them but theirs is not effective for him,[5] since zimmun cannot be said out of its place.[6]

R. ISHMAEL SAYS. Rafram b. Papa once attended the synagogue of Abi Gobar.[7] He was called up to read in the Scroll and he said, 'Bless ye the Lord' and stopped, without adding 'who is to be blessed'. The whole congregation cried out, 'Bless ye the Lord who is to be blessed'. Raba said to him: You black pot![8] Why do you want to enter into controversy?[9] And besides, the general custom is to use the formula of R. Ishmael.

MISHNAH. IF THREE PERSONS HAVE EATEN TOGETHER THEY MAY NOT SEPARATE [FOR GRACE].[10] SIMILARLY WITH FOUR AND SIMILARLY WITH FIVE.[11] SIX MAY

---

[1] The lesson being derived from the word 'assemblies'.
[2] Before the Exilarch finishes and says grace.
[3] So as to add the word 'Our God'.
[4] At their not waiting for him.
[5] I.e., he does not perform the mizwah of zimmun.
[6] V. supra. p. 278. n. 6.
[7] Be Gobar, in the vicinity of Mahuzah.
[8] Probably he was of swarthy complexion.
[9] I.e., follow a minority view.
[10] But must say zimmun together.
[11] One or two may not say grace for themselves.

DIVIDE,[1] [AND HIGHER NUMBERS] UP TO TEN; BETWEEN TEN AND TWENTY THEY MAY NOT DIVIDE. IF TWO GROUPS EAT IN THE SAME ROOM, AS LONG AS SOME OF THE ONE CAN SEE SOME OF THE OTHER THEY COMBINE [FOR ZIMMUN], BUT OTHERWISE EACH GROUP MAKES ZIMMUN FOR ITSELF. A BLESSING IS NOT SAID OVER THE WINE UNTIL WATER IS PUT IN IT.[2](27) SO R. ELIEZER. THE SAGES, HOWEVER, SAY THAT THE BLESSING MAY BE SAID.

GEMARA. What does this tell us? We have already learnt it once: Three persons who have eaten together must say zimmun?[3] — This teaches us the same thing as was stated by
R. Abba in the name of Samuel: If three persons have sat down to eat, even though they have not yet commenced, they are not at liberty to separate. Another version: R. Abba said in the name of Samuel: What is meant is this: if three persons sit down to eat together, even though each eats of his own loaf, they are not at liberty to separate. Or [it may teach us] the same as R. Huna; for R. Huna said: If three persons from these groups come together,[4] they are not at liberty to separate.[5] R. Hisda said: This is only if they come from three groups of three men each.[6] Raba said:

---

[1] Into two groups of three.
[2] To dilute it, otherwise it is too strong to be drunk.
[3] V. supra 45b.
[4] Each having left his group for one reason or another.
[5] But they must say grace together even though they have not eaten together.
[6] So that each of them was under the obligation of zimmun.

Berakoth 50b

This applies only if the groups had not already counted them for zimmun; but if they had reckoned upon them where they were,[1] the obligation of zimmun has departed from them. Said Raba: Whence do I derive this rule? Because we have learnt: If the half of a bed has been stolen or lost, or if a bed has been divided by brothers or partners, it cannot receive uncleanness. If it is restored [to its original state] it can receive uncleanness thenceforward. Thenceforward it can, but not retrospectively.[2] This shows that from the time it was divided, uncleanness no longer attached to it.[3] So here, once they had used them for zimmun, the obligation of zimmun no longer attached to them.[4]

TWO GROUPS etc. A Tanna taught: If there is an attendant waiting on both, the attendant combines them.[5]

A BLESSING IS NOT SAID OVER WINE. Our Rabbis taught: If wine has not yet been mixed with water, we do not say over it the blessing 'Who createst the fruit of the vine',[6] but 'Who createst the fruit of the tree', and it can be used for washing the hands.[7] Once water has been mixed with it, we say over it the blessing 'Who createst the fruit of the vine', and it may not be used for washing the hands. So R. Eliezer. The Sages, however, say: In either case we say over it the blessing 'Who createst the fruit of the vine', and we do not use it for washing the hands. Whose view is followed in this statement of Samuel: A man may use bread for any purpose he likes?[8] — Whose view? That of R. Eliezer. R. Jose son of
R. Hanina said: The Sages agree with R. Eliezer in the matter of the cup of wine used for grace, that a blessing should not be said over it until water has been added. What is the reason? — R. Oshaiah said: For a religious ceremony we require the best. And according to the Rabbis — for what kind of drink is undiluted wine suitable? — It is suitable for [mixing with] karyotis.[9]

Our Rabbis taught: Four things have been said with reference to bread. Raw meat should not be placed on bread; a full cup should not be passed along over bread;[10] bread should not be thrown; and a dish should not be propped up on bread. Amemar and Mar Zutra and
R. Ashi were once taking a meal together. Dates and pomegranates were served to them, and Mar Zutra took some and threw them in front of R. Ashi as his portion. He said to him: Does not your honour agree with what has been taught, that eatables should not be thrown?
— [He replied]: That was laid down with reference to bread. But it has been taught that just as bread is not to be thrown, so eatables should not be thrown? But, he replied. it has also been taught that although bread is not to be thrown, eatables may be thrown? But in fact there is no contradiction; one

---

[1] I.e., if the party to which they belonged consisted of four persons each and they had left only after their respective parties has said the zimmun formula introducing the grace.
[2] Kelim XVIII, 9.
[3] An incomplete article does not contract defilement.
[4] Lit., 'flew away from them'.
[5] Even though they do not see one another.
[6] Because as yet it shows no improvement over its original condition. This, of course, refers to the very strong wine of the ancients.
[7] Like fruit juice.
[8] I.e., wiping his hands after a meal, in spite of the general rule that food must not be wasted.
[9] A kind of date with the shape of a nut, used for medicinal purpose.
[10] For fear some should spill on the bread.

statement refers to things which are spoilt by throwing,[1] the other to things which are not spoilt.

Our Rabbis taught: Wine can be run through pipes[2] before the bridegroom and the bride, and roasted ears of corn and nuts may be thrown in front of them in the summer season but not in the rainy season;[3] while cakes may not be thrown in front of them either in the summer or the rainy season.[4]

Rab Judah said: If one forgot and put food into his mouth without saying a blessing, he shifts it to the side of his mouth and says the blessing. One [Baraitha] taught that he swallows it, and another taught that he spits it out, and yet another taught that he shifts it to one side. There is no contradiction. Where it says that he swallows it, the reference is to liquids; where it says that he spits it out, the reference is to something which is not spoilt thereby; and when it says that he shifts it, the reference is to something which would be spoilt [by being spat out].

---

[1] I.e., ripe, juicy figs.
[2] This was done either as a symbol of prosperity, or for the purpose of diffusing a pleasant odour; it could be caught up in cups and so not wasted.
[3] Because they may be spoilt by the muddy roads.
[4] Because in either case they may be spoilt.

Folio 51a

But why should he not also shift to one side anything which would not be spoilt and say the blessing? — R. Isaac Kaskasa'ah[1] gave the reason in the presence of R. Jose son of R. Abin, quoting R. Johanan: Because it says, My mouth shall be filled with Thy praise.[2]

R. Hisda was asked: If one has eaten and drunk without saying a blessing, should he say the blessing afterwards? — He replied: If one has eaten garlic so that his breath smells, should he eat more garlic so that his breath should go on smelling?[3] Rabina said: Therefore[4] even if he has finished his meal he should say the blessing retrospectively, since it has been taught: If a man has taken a ritual immersion and come out of the water, he should say on his emerging, 'Blessed be He who has sanctified us with His commandments and commanded us concerning immersion'. This, however, is not correct. In that case [of immersion] the man at the outset was not in a fit state to say a blessing;[5] in this case the man at the outset was in a fit state, and once it has been omitted it must remain omitted.

Our Rabbis taught: Asparagus brew[6] is good for the heart and good for the eyes, and, needless to say, for the bowels. If one uses it regularly it is good for the whole body, but if one gets drunk on it it is bad for the whole body. Since it is stated that it is good for the heart, we infer that we are dealing with a brew of wine. Yet it states that it is, needless to say, good for the bowels; but surely it has been taught: For La'AT[7] it is good. for Ramat[8] it is bad? — Our statement[9] was made with reference to a brew of old wine,[10] as we have learnt: If one takes a vow to abstain from wine because it is bad for the bowels and they say to him, Is not the old wine good for the bowels, and he says nothing, he is forbidden to drink new wine but permitted to drink old wine.[11] This proves [that we are dealing with old wine].

Our Rabbis taught: Six things were said with reference to asparagus. It is only taken when the wine is undiluted and from a [full] cup; it is received in the right hand and held in the left hand when drunk; one should not talk after drinking it, nor stop in the middle of drinking it, and it should be returned only to the person who served it; one should spit after drinking it, and he should take immediately after it[12] only something of the same kind. But it has been taught: He should take immediately after it only bread? — There is no contradiction: the one statement applies to a brew of wine, the other to a brew of beer.[13]

---

[1] The reading is not certain.
[2] Ps. LXXI, 8. There should be no room for anything besides the benediction.
[3] I.e., having made one mistake, should he make another by not saying a blessing over the part he has still to eat (Maharsha).
[4] Since he stops in the middle to say the blessing which he did not say at thebeginning.
[5] Having been unclean.
[6] A beverage made by soaking certain roots in wine or beer.
[7] L = leb (heart); 'A = 'ayin (eyes); T = tehol (milt).
[8] R = rosh (head); M = me'ayim (bowels); T = tahtonioth (piles).
[9] Lit., 'that'.
[10] At least three years old (Rashi).
[11] Ned. 66a.
[12] Lit., 'he must only support it with'.
[13] According to Rashi, bread should be taken after wine; according to the Aruch, after beer.

One [authority] teaches: It is good for La'AT and bad for Ramat, while another teaches that it is good for Ramat and bad for La'AT! There is no contradiction: one statement speaks of a brew of wine, the other of a brew of beer. One [authority] teaches that if he spits after it he will suffer, another that if he does not spit after it he will suffer! There is no contradiction: the one statement speaks of a brew of wine, the other of a brew of beer. R. Ashi said: Now that you say that if he does not spit after it he will suffer, he should eject the liquid even in the presence of a king.

R. Ishmael b. Elisha said: Three things were told me by Suriel the Officer of the [Divine] Presence.[1] Do not take your shirt from the hand of your attendant when dressing in the morning,[2] and do not let water be poured over your hands by one who has not already washed his own hands, and do not return a cup of asparagus brew to anyone save the one who has handed it to you, because a company of demons (according to others, a band of destroying angels) lie in wait for a man and say, When will the man do one of these things so that we can catch him.

R. Joshua b. Levi says: Three things were told me by the Angel of Death. Do not take your shirt from your attendant when dressing in the morning, and do not let water be poured on your hands by one who has not washed his own hands,[3] and do not stand in front of women when they are returning from the presence of a dead person, because I go leaping in front of them with my sword in my hand, and I have permission to harm. If one should happen to meet them what is his remedy? — Let him turn aside four cubits; if there is a river, let him cross it, and if there is another road let him take it, and if there is a wall, let him stand behind it;[4] and if he cannot do any of these things, let him turn his face away and say, And the Lord said unto Satan, The Lord rebuke thee, O Satan etc.,[5] until they have passed by.

R. Zera said in the name of R. Abbahu — according to others, it was taught in a Baraitha: Ten things have been said in connection with the cup used for grace after meals. It requires to be rinsed and washed, it must be undiluted and full, it requires crowning and wrapping,[6] it must be taken up with both hands and placed in the right hand, it must be raised a handbreadth from the ground, and he who says the blessing must fix his eyes on it. Some add that he must send it round to the members of his household. R. Johanan said: We only know of four: rinsing, washing, undiluted and full. A Tanna taught: Rinsing refers to the inside, washing to the outside. R. Johanan said: Whoever says the blessing over a full cup is given an inheritance without bounds, as it says, And full with the blessing of the Lord; possess thou the sea and the south.[7] R. Jose son of R. Hanina says: He is privileged to inherit two worlds, this world and the next. 'Crowning': Rab Judah crowned it with disciples;[8] R. Hisda surrounded it with cups. 'And undiluted': R. Sheshet said: Up to the blessing of the land.[9] 'Wrapping': R. Papa used to wrap himself in his robe and sit down [to say grace over a cup]; R. Assi spread a kerchief over his head. 'It is taken in both hands': R. Hinena b. Papa said: What is the

---

[1] I.e., an angel of high rank.
[2] But get it yourself.
[3] MS.M. inserts: and do not return the cup of asparagus brew to anyone save the one who has handed it to you. Do not enter alone a synagogue in which children are not being taught, because I hide there my weapons; and when there is a pestilence raging in the city do not walk in the middle of the road but on the side, and when there is peace in the city, do not walk on the side but in the middle of the road.
[4] MS.M. inserts: and turn his face to the wall.
[5] Zech. III, 2.
[6] This is explained infra.
[7] Deut. XXXIII, 23.
[8] I.e., made them sit around him.
[9] I.e., up to this point he leaves it undiluted, then he adds water. This is the reading of Alfasi; the reading of our text which has the words 'R. Hanan said' before 'and undiluted' is not intelligible.

Scriptural warrant for this? — Lift up your hands in holiness and bless ye the Lord.[1] 'And placed in the right hand'. R. Hiyya b. Abba said in the name of R. Johanan: The earlier [students] asked: Should the left hand support the right? — R. Ashi said: Since the earlier [students] inquired and the question was not decided

---
[1] Ps. CXXXIV, 2.

Berakoth 51b

we will follow the more stringent view.[1] 'He raises it a handbreadth from the ground': R. Aha b. Hanina said: What Scriptural text have we for this? — I will lift up the cup of salvation and call upon the name of the Lord.[2] 'He fixes his eyes on it': so that his attention should not wander from it. 'He sends it round to the members of his household': so that his wife may be blessed.

'Ulla was once at the house of R. Nahman. They had a meal and he said grace, and he handed the cup of benediction to R. Nahman. R. Nahman said to him: Please send the cup of benediction to Yaltha.[3] He said to him: Thus said R. Johanan: The fruit of a woman's body is blessed only from the fruit of a man's body, since it says, He will also bless the fruit of thy body.[4] It does not say the fruit of her body, but the fruit of thy body. It has been taught similarly: Whence do we know that the fruit of a woman's body is only blessed from the fruit of a man's body? Because it says: He will also bless the fruit of thy body. It does not say the fruit of her body, but the fruit of thy body. Meanwhile Yaltha heard,[5] and she got up in a passion and went to the wine store and broke four hundred jars of wine. R. Nahman said to him: Let the Master send her another cup. He sent it to her with a message: All that wine[6] can be counted as a benediction. She returned answer: Gossip comes from pedlars and vermin from rags.[7]

R. Assi said: One should not speak over the cup of benediction.[8] R. Assi also said: One should not speak over the cup of punishment. What is the cup of punishment? — R. Nahman b. Isaac said: a second cup.[9] It has been taught similarly: He who drinks an even number[10] should not say grace,[11] because it says, Prepare to meet thy God, O Israel,[12] and this one is not fitly prepared.

R. Abbahu said (according to others, it was taught in a Baraitha): One who eats as he walks says grace standing; if he eats standing up he says grace sitting; if he eats reclining he sits up to say grace. The law is that in all cases he says grace sitting.

---

[1] And do not support with the left.
[2] Ibid. CXVI, 13.
[3] R. Nahman's wife.
[4] Deut. VII, 13.
[5] That 'Ulla had refused to send her the cup.
[6] I.e., all the wine of the flask from which the cup of benediction was poured.
[7] As much as to say, what could he expected from a man like 'Ulla.
[8] Once it is taken up for grace, it is not permitted to speak.
[9] Even numbers were supposed to he unlucky.
[10] Lit., 'Doubles'.
[11] Probably it means, lead in the grace.
[12] Amos IV, 12.

CHAPTER VIII

MISHNAH. THESE ARE THE POINTS [OF DIFFERENCE] BETWEEN BETH SHAMMAI AND BETH HILLEL IN RELATION TO A MEAL. BETH SHAMMAI SAY THAT THE BENEDICTION IS FIRST SAID OVER THE DAY[1] AND THEN OVER THE WINE, WHILE BETH HILLEL SAY THAT THE BENEDICTION IS FIRST SAID OVER THE WINE AND THEN OVER THE DAY. BETH SHAMMAI SAY THAT WASHING THE HANDS PRECEDES THE FILLING OF THE CUP,[2] WHILE BETH HILLEL SAY THAT THE FILLING OF THE CUP PRECEDES THE WASHING OF THE HANDS. BETH SHAMMAI SAY THAT AFTER WIPING HIS HANDS WITH A NAPKIN THE DINER PLACES IT ON THE TABLE, WHILE BETH HILLEL SAY THAT HE PLACES IT ON THE CUSHION.[3] BETH SHAMMAI SAY THAT [AFTER THE MEAL] THE FLOOR IS SWEPT BEFORE THE WASHING OF THE HANDS,[4](16) WHILE BETH HILLEL SAY THAT [THE DINERS] WASH THEIR HANDS AND THEN THE FLOOR IS SWEPT. BETH SHAMMAI SAY THAT [THE PROPER ORDER[5] IS] LIGHT, GRACE, SPICES, AND HABDALAH, WHILE BETH HILLEL SAY: LIGHT, SPICES, GRACE, AND HABDALAH.[6] BETH SHAMMAI SAY [THAT THE BLESSING OVER LIGHT CONCLUDES WITH THE WORDS], WHO CREATED THE LIGHT OF THE FIRE, WHILE BETH HILLEL SAY [THAT THE WORDS ARE], WHO IS CREATING THE LIGHTS OF THE FIRE.

A BENEDICTION MAY NOT BE SAID OVER THE LIGHTS OR THE SPICES OF IDOLATERS OR OVER THE LIGHTS OR THE SPICES OF DEAD,[7] OR OVER THE LIGHTS OR THE SPICES OF IDOLATRY, AND A BLESSING IS NOT SAID OVER THE LIGHT UNTIL IT HAS BEEN UTILIZED.

IF ONE HAS EATEN AND FORGOTTEN TO SAY GRACE, BETH SHAMMAI SAY THAT HE MUST RETURN TO THE PLACE WHERE HE ATE AND SAY THE GRACE, WHILE BETH HILLEL SAY THAT HE SHOULD SAY IT IN THE PLACE WHERE HE REMEMBERED. UNTIL WHEN CAN HE SAY THE GRACE? UNTIL SUFFICIENT TIME HAS PASSED FOR THE FOOD IN HIS STOMACH TO BE DIGESTED. IF WINE IS SERVED TO THEM AFTER THE FOOD, AND THAT IS THE ONLY CUP THERE, BETH SHAMMAI SAY THAT A BLESSING IS FIRST SAID OVER THE WINE AND THEN [THE GRACE] OVER THE FOOD, WHILE BETH HILLEL SAY THAT A BLESSING IS FIRST SAID OVER THE FOOD AND THEN OVER THE WINE. ONE SAYS AMEN AFTER A BLESSING SAID BY AN ISRAELITE BUT NOT AFTER A BLESSING SAID BY A CUTHEAN, UNLESS THE WHOLE OF IT HAS BEEN HEARD[8].

GEMARA. Our Rabbis taught: The points of difference between Beth Shammai and Beth Hillel in relation to a meal are as follows: Beth Shammai say that the blessing is first said over the [sanctity of] the day and then over the wine, because it is on account of the day that the wine is used, and

---

[1] E.g., Sabbath or festival.
[2] The cup of benediction drunk before meals, v. supra 43a.
[3] The reason is given in the Gemara.
[4] The 'latter water' before grace.
[5] After a meal on the conclusion of the Sabbath or festival when habdalah (v. Glos.) has to be said.
[6] I.e., the principal benediction in the habdalah, v. Glos.
[7] Used at a funeral, cf. Roman turibula and faces.
[8] For fear he may have made all allusion to Mount Gerizim.

[moreover] the day has already become holy[1] before the wine has been brought. Beth Hillel say that a blessing is said over the wine first and then over the day, because the wine provides the occasion for saying a benediction.[2] Another explanation is that the blessing over wine is said regularly[3] while the blessing of the day is said only at infrequent intervals, and that which comes regularly always has precedence over that which comes infrequently. The halachah is as laid down by Beth Hillel. What is the point of the 'other explanation'? — Should you say that there [in explanation of Beth Shammai's view] two reasons are given and here [in explanation of Beth Hillel's] only one, we reply, there are two here also, [the second one being that] the blessing over wine is regular and the blessing of the day infrequent, and that which is regular has precedence over that which is infrequent, 'And the halachah is as stated by Beth Hillel'. This is self-evident, for the Bath Kol[4] went forth [and proclaimed so]![5] If you like I can reply that this statement was made before the Bath Kol [had issued forth], and if you like I can say that it was made after the Bath Kol

---

[1] At sunset or before by the formal acceptance of the sanctity of the day in prayers or otherwise.
[2] If there is no wine or its equivalent, no benediction is said.
[3] I.e., practically every day.
[4] Lit., 'daughter of a voice', 'A heavenly voice'.
[5] V. 'Er. 13b.

Folio 52a

and that it represents the view of R. Joshua, who said that we pay no attention to a Bath Kol.[1]

But do Beth Shammai hold that the blessing over the day is more important, seeing that it has been taught: 'When one goes into his house on the outgoing of Sabbath, he says blessings over wine and light and spices and then he says the habdalah [benediction].[2] If he has only one cup, he keeps it for after the meal and then says the other blessings in order after it? — But how do you know that this represents the view of Beth Shammai? Perhaps it represents the view of Beth Hillel? — Do not imagine such a thing. For it mentions first light and then spices; and who is it that we understand to hold this view? Beth Shammai, as it has been taught: R. Judah says: Beth Shammai and Beth Hillel concurred in holding that the grace after food comes first and the habdalah [benediction] last. In regard to what did they differ? In regard to the light and the spices, Beth Shammai holding that light should come first and then spices, and Beth Hillel that spices should come first and then light. And how do you know that this represents the view of Beth Shammai as reported by R. Judah? Perhaps it represents the view of Beth Hillel as reported by R. Meir![3] — Do not imagine such a thing. For it states here, BETH SHAMMAI SAY, LIGHT, GRACE AND SPICES, AND HABDALAH; WHILE BETH HILLEL SAY LIGHT, SPICES, GRACE, AND HABDALAH, and there in the Baraitha it says, 'If he has only one cup he keeps it for grace and says the others in order after it'. This shows that it represents the view of Beth Shammai as reported by R. Judah. In any case there is a difficulty?[4] — Beth Shammai hold that the entrance of a [holy] day is different from its outgoing. At its entrance, the earlier we can make it the better, but at its exit, the longer we can defer it the better, so that it should not seem to be a burden on us.

But do Beth Shammai hold that grace requires a cup [of wine] seeing that we have learnt: IF WINE IS SERVED TO THEM AFTER THE FOOD,[5] AND THAT IS THE ONLY CUP THERE, BETH SHAMMAI SAY THAT A BLESSING IS FIRST SAID OVER THE WINE AND THEN [THE GRACE] OVER THE FOOD. Does not this mean that he says a blessing over it and drinks it?[6] No; he says a blessing over it and puts it aside.[7] But a Master has said: [After saying the blessing] one must taste it? — He does taste it. But a Master has said: If he tastes it he spoils it?[8] — He tastes it with his finger. But a Master has said: The cup of benediction must have a certain quantity, and he diminishes it? — We must suppose that he has more than the prescribed quantity. But it says, 'If there is only that cup'? — There is not enough for two but more than enough for one. But R. Hiyya taught: Beth Shammai say that he says a blessing over wine and drinks it and then says grace? — Two Tannaim report Beth Shammai differently.[9]

BETH SHAMMAI SAY etc. Our Rabbis taught: Beth Shammai say that washing of the hands

---

[1] 'Er. 7a.
[2] Which is the blessing of the day.
[3] Infra.
[4] That Beth Shammai seem to give precedence to the blessing over wine over that of the day.
[5] But before grace has been said.
[6] That is if he wishes, he can drink the wine before the grace.
[7] To serve as the cup of benediction.
[8] For other ceremonial purposes.
[9] R. Hiyya reporting them as saying that the grace after meals does not require a cup of benediction.

precedes the filling of the cup. For should you say that the filling of the cup comes first, there is a danger lest liquid on the back of the cup will be rendered unclean through one's hands and it in turn will render the cup unclean. But would not the hands make the cup itself unclean? — Hands receive uncleanness in second degree,[1] and that which has received uncleanness in the second degree cannot pass on the uncleanness to a third degree in the case of non-sacred things, save through liquids.[2] Beth Hillel, however, say that the cup is first filled and then the hands are washed. For if you say that the hands are washed first, there is a danger lest the liquid on the hands should become unclean through the cup[3] and should then in turn make the hands unclean. But would not the cup make the hands themselves unclean? — A vessel does not make a man unclean. But would not [the cup] render unclean the liquid inside it? — We are here dealing with a vessel the outside of which has been rendered unclean by liquid, in which case its inside is clean and its outside unclean, as we have learnt: If the outside of a vessel has been rendered unclean by liquids, its outside is unclean

---

[1] They are rendered unclean by something which has become unclean through touching something by its nature unclean.
[2] This is a Rabbinic rule enunciated in Toh. II, 3.
[3] Supposing that this happens to be unclean.

Berakoth 52b

while its inside, its rim, its handle and its haft are clean. If its inside has been rendered unclean, it is all unclean. What is the point at issue between them? — Beth Shammai hold that it is forbidden to use a vessel the outside of which has been rendered unclean by liquids for fear of drippings,[1] and consequently there is no need to fear that the liquid on the hands will be rendered unclean by the cup.[2] Beth Hillel on the other hand hold that it is permitted to use a vessel the outside of which has been rendered unclean by liquids, considering that drippings are unusual, and consequently there is a danger lest the liquid on the [undried] hands should be rendered unclean through the cup.[3] Another explanation is, so that the meal should follow immediately the washing of the hands. What is the point of this 'other explanation'? — Beth Hillel argued thus with Beth Shammai: Even from your standpoint, that it is forbidden to use a vessel the outside of which has been rendered unclean by liquids, for fear of drippings, even so our ruling is superior, because the washing of the hands is immediately followed by the meal.

BETH SHAMMAI SAY THAT AFTER WIPING HIS HAND WITH THE NAPKIN etc. Our Rabbis taught: Beth Shammai say that [the diner] after wiping his hands with the napkin places it on the table. For if you say that he places it on the cushion, there is a danger lest liquid on the napkin may be rendered unclean through the cushion and then in turn render the hands unclean. But will not the cushion make the napkin itself unclean? — One vessel does not render another unclean. But will not the cushion make the man himself unclean? — A vessel does not render a man unclean. Beth Hillel, however, say that he puts it on the cushion. For if you say that he puts it on the table there is a fear lest the liquid on the napkin should be rendered unclean through the table and should in turn render the food unclean. But will not the table render the food on it unclean? — We are dealing here with a table which is unclean in the second degree, and that which is unclean in the second degree does not pass on uncleanness to a third degree in the case of non-sacred things, save through the medium of liquids. What is the point at issue between them? — Beth Shammai hold that it is forbidden to use a table which is unclean in the second degree for fear lest it may be used by persons eating terumah,[4] while Beth Hillel hold that it is permissible to use a table which is unclean in the second degree since persons who eat terumah are careful [to avoid such]. Another explanation is that washing of hands for non-sacred food is not prescribed by the Torah. What is the point of the 'other explanation'? — Beth Hillel argued thus with Beth Shammai: Should you ask what reason is there for being particular in the case of food[5] and not being particular in the case of hands, even granting this, our rule is better, since washing of hands for non-sacred food is not prescribed by the Torah. It is better that hands, the rule for which has no basis in the Torah, should become unclean, rather than food, the rule for which has a basis in the Torah.

BETH SHAMMAI SAY THAT THE FLOOR IS SWEPT etc. Our Rabbis taught: Beth Shammai say: The floor is swept and then they wash their hands. For should you say that the hands are washed first,

---

[1] Drops from the inside may spill on to the outside, and in virtue of the uncleanness of the cup the drops would render the hands unclean.
[2] Since ex hypothesi the cup may not be used. Hence it is quite safe to wash the hands before filling the cup.
[3] Hence it is safer to wash the hands after the cup has been filled.
[4] And terumah would be rendered unclean by a table unclean in the second degree.
[5] To protect it from uncleanness.

the result might be to spoil the food. (Beth Shammai do not hold that the washing of the hands comes first.)[1] What is the reason? — On account of the crumbs [of bread]. Beth Hillel, however, say that if he the attendant is a scholar, he removes the crumbs which are as large as an olive and leaves those which are smaller than an olive. This supports the dictum of R. Johanan; for R. Johanan said: It is permissible to destroy wilfully crumbs [of bread] smaller than an olive.[2] What is the ground of their difference? — Beth Hillel hold that it is not permissible to employ an attendant who is an 'am ha-arez,[3] while Beth Shammai hold that is is permissible to employ an attendant who is an 'am ha-arez. R. Jose b. Hanina said in the name of R. Huna: In all this chapter the halachah is as stated by Beth Hillel, save in this point where it is as stated by Beth Shammai. R. Oshaia, however, reverses the teaching[4] and in this point also the halachah follows Beth Hillel.

BETH SHAMMAI SAY, LIGHT, GRACE, etc. R. Huna b. Judah was once at the house of Raba, and he saw Raba say the blessing over spices first.[5] He said to him: Let us see. Beth Shammai and Beth Hillel do not differ with respect to the light [that it should come first], as we learnt: BETH SHAMMAI SAY, [THE ORDER IS] LIGHT, GRACE, SPICES, AND HABDALAH, WHILE BETH HILLEL SAY THAT IT IS LIGHT, SPICES, GRACE AND HABDALAH! — Raba answered after[6] him: These are the words of R. Meir, but
R. Judah said: Beth Shammai and Beth Hillel agreed that grace comes first and habdalah last. Where they differed was in respect of light and spices, Beth Shammai maintaining that light comes first and then spices, while Beth Hillel held that spices comes first and then light; and R. Johanan has stated: The public have adopted the custom of following Beth Hillel as reported by R. Judah.

BETH SHAMMAI SAY, WHO CREATED etc. Raba said: All are agreed that the word bara[7] refers to the past. Where they differ is with respect to the word bore.[8] Beth Shammai maintain that bore means 'who will create in the future', while Beth Hillel hold that bore can also refer to the past. R. Joseph cited in objection [to Beth Shammai] the verses, I form the light and create [bore] darkness,[9] He formeth the mountains and createth [bore] the wind,[10] He that created [bore] the heavens and stretched them forth.[11] Rather, said R. Joseph: Both sides are agreed that both bara and bore can refer to the past. Where they differ is as to whether ma'or [light] or me'- ore [lights] should be said. Beth Shammai are of the opinion that there is only one light in the fire, while Beth Hillel are of the opinion that there are several.[12] It has been taught to the same effect: Said Beth Hillel to Beth Shammai: There are several illuminations in the light.

A BLESSING IS NOT SAID etc. There is a good reason in the case of the light [of idolaters],

---

[1] This sentence seems to be an interpolation.
[2] In spite of the prohibition against wasting food.
[3] Who would not know the difference between crumbs of the size of an olive and those of smaller size. Probably a meal of haberim (v. Glos.) is referred to.
[4] I.e., ascribes to Beth Hillel the teaching that an 'am ha-arez may be employed, and consequently the floor is swept first.
[5] I.e., before the light.
[6] I.e., supplemented the reading in our Mishnah as follows.
[7] Past tense, 'he created'.
[8] Participle, 'creating', or 'who creates'.
[9] Isa. XLV, 7.
[10] Amos. IV, 13.
[11] Isa. XLII, 5.
[12] I.e., several colours in the light-red, white, green etc.

because it has not 'rested'.[1] But what reason is there in the case of the spices? — Rab Judah said in the name of Rab: We are dealing here with [spices used at] a banquet of idolaters[2] because ordinarily a banquet of idolaters is held in honour of idolatry. But since it is stated further on, OR OVER THE LIGHT OR THE SPICES OF IDOLATRY, we may infer that the earlier statement does not refer to idolaters? — R. Hanina of Sura replied: The latter statement is explanatory. What is the reason why a blessing is not said over the light and the spices of idolaters? Because ordinarily a banquet of idolaters is in honour of idolatry.

Our Rabbis taught: A blessing may be said over a light which has 'rested', but not over one which has not 'rested'. What is meant by 'which has not rested'?

---

[1] I.e., forbidden work has been done by its light.
[2] Lit., 'Cutheans' which throughout this passage is probably a censor's correction for 'Gentiles'.

Folio 53a

Shall we say that it has not rested on account of work [done by it], even permissible work?[1] But it has been taught: A blessing may be said over a light used for a woman in confinement or for the sake of a sick person? — R. Nahman b. Isaac replied: What is meant by 'rested'? That it rested from work which is a transgression on Sabbath. It has been taught to the same effect: A blessing may be said over a lamp which has been burning throughout the day[2] to the conclusion of Sabbath.[3]

Our Rabbis taught: We may say the blessing over a light kindled by a Gentile[4] from an Israelite or by an Israelite from a Gentile, but not by a Gentile from a Gentile. What is the reason for barring a light kindled by a Gentile from a Gentile? Because it may not have rested.[5] But a light kindled by an Israelite from a Gentile also may not have rested? Perhaps you will say that the prohibited [flame] has vanished and the light is now a different one and is reborn in the hand of the Israelite.[6] What then of this which has been taught: If one carries out a flame to the public way [on Sabbath],[7] he is liable to a penalty.[8] Why is he liable? That which he took up he did not set down and that which he set down he did not take up?[9] — We must say therefore that [in our present case] the prohibited flame is still present, only the blessing which he says is said over the additional permitted part. If that is the case [a blessing over] a light kindled by a Gentile from a Gentile should also be permitted? — That is so; but [the prohibition is] a precaution on account of the first Gentile[10](10) and the first flame.[11]

Our Rabbis taught: If one was walking [at the termination of Sabbath] outside the town and saw a light, if the majority [of the inhabitants] are Gentiles he should not say a benediction, but if the majority are Israelites he may say the benediction. This statement is self-contradictory. You first say, 'if the majority are Gentiles, he may not say the blessing', which implies that if they are half and half he may say it, and then it states, 'if the majority are Israelites, he may say it', which implies that if they are half and half he may not say it!
— Strictly speaking, even if they are half and half he may say it, but since in the first clause it says 'the majority are Gentiles', in the second clause it says 'the majority are Israelites'.

Our Rabbis taught: If a man was walking outside the town and saw a child with a torch in its hands,

---

[1] E.g., a light lit for the sake of a sick person.
[2] I.e., which was lit before Sabbath came in.
[3] Because no Sabbath transgression had been performed with it.
[4] On the termination of Sabbath.
[5] I.e., some forbidden work has been done by its light.
[6] The llght being regarded as not having a continuous existence but as consisting of a series of flashes.
[7] E.g., if burning wick is placed in oil in a potsherd so small that the prohibition of carrying on Sabbath does not apply to it.
[8] For transferring from one domain to another on Sabbath, v. Bezah 39a.
[9] Such transference renders liable only when the same object is taken up from its place in one domain and set down in its place in the other. Here the flame which is taken from its place in the house is not the same as is set down outside. The reason therefore why he is liable must be because the flame is in fact considered throughout to be one and the same.
[10] I.e., against the light kindled by a Gentile on Sabbath.
[11] Lit., 'pillar'. The first flame of the light kindled on Saath, by the Gentile.

he makes inquiries about it; if it is an Israelite child, he may say the benediction, but if it is a Gentile he may not. Why does it speak of a child? The same applies even to a grown-up! — Rab Judah said in the name of Rab: We suppose this to happen immediately after sunset. In the case of a grown-up it is obvious that he must be a Gentile.[1] In the case of a child, I can suppose that it is an Israelite child who happened to take hold [of the light].

Our Rabbis taught: If one was walking outside the town at the termination of Sabbath and saw a light, if it is thick like the opening of a furnace he may say the benediction over it,[2] otherwise not. One [authority] states: A benediction may be said over the light of a furnace, while another says that it may not! — There is no contradiction: one speaks of the beginning of the fire, the other of the end.[3] One [authority] teaches: A benediction may be said over the light of an oven or a stove, while another says that it may not, and there is no contradiction: one speaks of the beginning of the fire, the other of the end.[4] One [authority] teaches: The benediction may be said over the light of the synagogue or the Beth ha-Midrash, while another says it may not, and there is no contradiction: one speaks of a case where an eminent man is present,[5] the other of a case where no eminent man is present. Or if you like, I can say that both speak of where an eminent man is present, and there is no contradiction: one speaks of where there is a beadle,[6] and the other of where there is no beadle. Or if you like, I can say that both speak of where there is a beadle, and there is no contradiction; one speaks of where there is moonlight,[7] the other of where there is no moonlight.

Out Rabbis taught: If people were sitting in the Beth ha-Midrash and light was brought in [at the termination of the Sabbath], Beth Shammai say that each one says a blessing over it for himself, while Beth Hillel say that one says a blessing on behalf of all, because it says, In the multitude of people is the King's glory.[8] Beth Hillel at any rate explain their reason; but what is the reason of Beth Shammai? — It is probably to avoid an interruption of study.[9] It has been taught similarly: The members of the household of Rabban Gamaliel did not use to say 'Good health'[10] in the Beth ha-Midrash so as not to interrupt their study.

A BENEDICTION MAY NOT BE SAID OVER THE LIGHTS OR THE SPICES OF THE DEAD. What is the reason? — The light is kindled only in honour of the dead, the spices are to remove the bad smell. Rab Judah said in the name of Rab: Wherever [the person buried is of such consequence that] a light would be carried before him either by day or by night, we do not say a blessing over the light [if he is buried on the termination of Sabbath];[11] but if he is one before whom a light would be carried only at night, we may say the blessing.[12]

---

[1] Since a grown-up Israelite would not use a light immediately on the termination of the Sabbath, before saying habdalah.
[2] Because this is a genuine light.
[3] A furnace (of lime burners) is first lit to burn the lime, but afterwards it is kept alight for the purpose of lighting.
[4] The fire is lit for cooking, but afterwards chips are thrown in to give light.
[5] In whose honour the light has been kindled.
[6] Who has his meals in the synagogue.
[7] Which suffices for the beadle, and the light must have been kindled out of respect for an eminent man.
[8] Prov. XIV, 28.
[9] One may be in the middle of a difficult part just at the moment for saying Amen.
[10] To someone who sneezed.
[11] Because the light is carried for his honour.
[12] Because the light is really to give light.

R. Huna said: A blessing is not said over spices used in a privy[1] or oil used for removing grease [from the hands].[2] This implies that wherever [spice] is not used for scent no blessing is said over it. An objection was raised [to this]: If one enters a spice-dealer's shop and smells the fragrance, even though he sits there the whole day he makes only one blessing, but if he is constantly going in and out he makes a blessing each time he enters. Now here is a case where it is not used for smell,[3](26) and yet one makes a blessing?
— In fact it is used for smell, the object being that people should smell and come and make purchases thereof.

Our Rabbis taught: If one was walking outside the town and smelt an odour [of spices], if the majority of the inhabitants are idolaters he does not say a blessing, but if the majority are Israelites he does say a blessing. R. Jose says: Even if the majority are Israelites he does not say a blessing, because the daughters of Israel use incense for witchcraft. Do all of them use incense for witchcraft? — The fact is that a small part is used for witchcraft and a small part for scenting garments, with the result that the greater part of it is not used for smell, and wherever the greater part is not used for smell a blessing is not said over it. R. Hiyya b. Abba said in the name of R. Johanan: If one was walking on the eve of Sabbath in Tiberias, or at the conclusion of Sabbath in Sepphoris, and smelt an odour [of spices], he does not say a blessing, because the probability is that they are being used only to perfume garments. Our Rabbis taught: If one was walking in a street of idolaters and smelt the spices willingly, he is a sinner.

---

[1] To counteract the bad smell.
[2] This oil contained spices, and the blessing said over it was that for oil and not for spices.
[3] But for sale.

Berakoth 53b

. A BLESSING IS NOT SAID OVER THE LIGHT TILL IT HAS BEEN UTILIZED. Rab Judah said in the name of Rab: This does not mean literally till it has been utilized, but it means a light which can be serviceable if one stands near enough to it, and then even those at a distance [may say the blessing]. So too said R. Ashi: We have learnt that it serves for those at a distance.

An objection was raised: If one had a light hidden in the folds of his dress or in a lamp, or if he could see a flame but could not use its light, or if he could do something by the light but saw no flame, he should not say the blessing; he must both see a flame and be able to use the light. We understand the statement 'he can use its light but sees no flame'; this can happen when the light is in a corner. But how can it happen that he sees the flame and cannot make use of the light? Is it not when he is at a distance? — No; it is when, for instance, the flame keeps on flickering.

Our Rabbis taught: We may say the blessing over glowing coals but not over dying coals. How do you define 'glowing'? — R. Hisda replied: This means coals from which a chip, if inserted between them, will catch of itself. The question was asked: Is the proper form omemoth or 'omemoth?[1] — Come and hear: for R. Hisda b. Abdimi quoted the verse, The cedars in the garden of God could not darken ['amamuhu] it.[2]

Rab, however,[3] said that [the Mishnah means literally] 'utilize it'. How near must one be?
— 'Ulla said: Near enough to distinguish between an as and a dupondium.[4] Hezekiah said: Near enough to distinguish between a meluzma[5] of Tiberias and one of Sepphoris. Rab Judah used to say the blessing over the light in the house of Adda the waiter.[6] Raba said the blessing over the light in the house of Guria b. Hama.[7] Abaye said it over the light in the house of Bar Abbuha. Rab Judah said in the name of Rab: We do not go looking for a light[8] in the same way as we do in the case of other commandments. R. Zera said: At first I used to go looking for a light. But since hearing this statement of Rab Judah reporting Rab, I also do not look for one, but if one comes my way I say the blessing over it.

IF ONE HAS EATEN etc. R. Zebid, or as some say R. Dimi b. Abba, said: Opinions differ only in the case where one forgot, but if he omitted wilfully he must return to his place and say grace. This is obvious! The Mishnah says 'HAS FORGOTTEN'? — You might think that the rule is the same even if he did it purposely, and the reason why it says 'HAS FORGOTTEN' is to show you how far Beth Shammai are prepared to go. Therefore we are told [that this is not so]. It has been taught: Beth Hillel said to Beth Shammai: according to you, if one ate at the top of the Temple Mount and forgot and descended without having said grace, he should return to the top of the Temple Mount and say grace?

---

[1] I.e., does the word translated 'dying' commence with an alef or an 'ayin.
[2] Ezek. XXXI, 8.
[3] This goes back to the statement of Rab Judah in the name of Rab above.
[4] A dupondium was twice the size of an as.
[5] According to Rashi, a weight; according to Jastrow, a stamp of a coin.
[6] Which was some distance away.
[7] Which was quite near.
[8] To say the blessing.

Beth Shammai replied to Beth Hillel: According to you, if one forgot a purse at the top of the Temple Mount, is he not to go up and get it? And if he will ascend for his own sake, surely he should do so all the more for the honour of Heaven!

There were once two disciples who omitted to say grace. One who did it accidentally followed the rule of Beth Shammai[1] and found a purse of gold, while the other who did it purposely[2] followed the rule of Beth Hillel,[3] and he was eaten by a lion. Rabbah b. Bar Hanah was once travelling with a caravan, and he took a meal and forgot to say grace. He said to himself: What shall I do? If I say to the others, I have forgotten to say grace, they will say to me, Say it [here]: wherever you say the benediction you are saying it to the All-Merciful. I had better tell them that I have forgotten a golden dove. So he said to them: Wait for me, because I have forgotten a golden dove. He went back and said grace and found a golden dove. Why should it have been just a dove? — Because the community of Israel are compared to a dove, as it is written, *The wings of the dove are covered with silver, and her pinions with the shimmer of gold.*[4] Just as the dove is saved only by her wings, so Israel are saved only by the precepts.

UNTIL WHEN CAN HE SAY THE GRACE. How long does it take to digest a meal? — R. Johanan said: Until he becomes hungry again; Resh Lakish said: As long as one is thirsty on account of the meal. Said R. Yemar b. Shelemia to Mar Zutra, or, according to others R. Yemar b. Shezbi to Mar Zutra: Can Resh Lakish have said this? Has not R. Ammi said in the name of Resh Lakish: How long does it take to digest a meal? Long enough for one to walk four mil? — There is no contradiction: one statement refers to a light meal, the other to a heavy one.[5]

IF WINE IS SERVED etc. This implies, [if] an Israelite [says the grace],[6] even though one has not heard the whole of it he responds [Amen]. But if he has not heard how can he have performed his duty by doing so?[7] Hiyya b. Rab replied: This applies to one who has not joined in the meal. Similarly said R. Nahman in the name of Rabbah b. Abbuha: It refers to one who has not joined in the meal. Said Rab to his son Hiyya: My son, snatch [the cup of wine] and say grace.[8] And so said R. Huna to his son Rabbah: My son, snatch and say grace. This implies that he who says the grace is superior to one who answers, Amen. But it has been taught: 'R. Jose says: Greater is he who answers, Amen than he who says the blessing? — Said R. Nehorai to him: I swear to you by heaven that it is so. The proof is that while the common soldiers advance and open the battle, it is the seasoned warriors who go down to win the victory!' — On this point there is a difference between Tannaim, as it has been taught: Both he who says the blessing and he who answers, Amen are equally implied,[9] only he who says the blessing is more quickly [rewarded] than he who answers, Amen.

---

[1] And returned to the place where he forgot, thus following the stricter rule.
[2] Being in a hurry to go somewhere else.
[3] Which applies only to accidental omission.
[4] Ps. LXVIII, 14.
[5] According to Rashi, it takes the time for walking four mil to digest a heavy meal; according to Tosaf., to digest a light one.
[6] V. supra p. 312 n. 1.
[7] He assumes that he is one of the diners, who too must hear the grace.
[8] I.e., seize every opportunity of saying it on behalf of the company.
[9] In the text of Neh. IX, 5, which speaks of those who 'stand up and bless', and those who respond 'Blessed be Thy glorious name', which is equivalent to Amen, v. infra 63a.

Samuel inquired of Rab: Should one respond Amen after [a blessing said by] schoolchildren? — He replied: We respond Amen after everyone except children in school, because they are merely learning. This is the case only when it is not the time for them to say the haftarah;[1] but when it is the time for them to say the haftarah, we respond Amen after them.

Our Rabbis taught: The absence of oil[2] is a bar to the saying of grace. So said R. Zilai.
R. Ziwai said: It is no bar. R. Aha said: Good oil is indispensable. R. Zuhamai said: Just as a dirty person is unfit for the Temple service, so dirty hands unfit one for saying grace. R. Nahman b. Isaac said: I know nothing either of Zilai or Ziwai or Zuhamai, but I do know the following teaching, viz.: Rab Judah said in the name of Rab: some say it was taught in a Baraitha, Sanctify yourselves:[3] this refers to washing of the hands before the meal;[4] And be ye holy: this refers to washing of the hands after the meal;[5] 'For holy': this refers to the oil; 'Am I the Lord your God': this refers to the grace.

---

[1] The prophetical reading following the public reading of the Pentateuch on Sabbath and festivals and public fasts.
[2] For cleansing the hands after the meal.
[3] Lev. XI, 44.
[4] Lit., 'the first water'.
[5] Lit., 'the latter water'.

Folio 54a

CHAPTER IX

MISHNAH. IF ONE SEES A PLACE WHERE MIRACLES HAVE BEEN WROUGHT FOR ISRAEL, HE SHOULD SAY, BLESSED BE HE WHO WROUGHT MIRACLES FOR OUR ANCESTORS IN THIS PLACE. ON SEEING A PLACE FROM WHICH IDOLATRY HAS BEEN EXTIRPATED, HE SHOULD SAY, BLESSED BE HE WHO EXTIRPATED IDOLATRY FROM OUR LAND. [ON WITNESSING] SHOOTING STARS, EARTHQUAKES, THUNDERCLAPS, STORMS AND LIGHTNINGS ONE SHOULD SAY, BLESSED BE HE WHOSE STRENGTH AND MIGHT FILL THE WORLD. ON SEEING MOUNTAINS, HILLS, SEAS, RIVERS AND DESERTS HE SHOULD SAY, BLESSED BE HE WHO WROUGHT CREATION.[1] R. JUDAH SAYS: IF ONE SEES THE GREAT SEA[2] ONE SHOULD SAY, BLESSED BE HE WHO MADE THE GREAT SEA, [THAT IS] IF HE SEES IT AT [CONSIDERABLE] INTERVALS. FOR RAIN AND FOR GOOD TIDINGS ONE SAYS, BLESSED BE HE THAT IS GOOD AND BESTOWS GOOD. FOR EVIL TIDINGS ONE SAYS, BLESSED BE THE TRUE JUDGE. ONE WHO HAS BUILT A NEW HOUSE OR BOUGHT NEW VESSELS SAYS, BLESSED BE HE WHO HAS KEPT US ALIVE AND PRESERVED US AND BROUGHT US TO THIS SEASON. OVER EVIL A BLESSING IS SAID SIMILAR TO THAT OVER GOOD AND OVER GOOD A BLESSING IS SAID SIMILAR TO THAT OVER EVIL,[3] BUT TO CRY OVER THE PAST IS TO UTTER A VAIN PRAYER. IF A MAN'S WIFE IS PREGNANT AND HE SAYS, [GOD] GRANT THAT MY WIFE BEAR A MALE CHILD, THIS A VAIN PRAYER. IF HE IS COMING HOME FROM A JOURNEY AND HE HEARS CRIES OF DISTRESS IN THE TOWN AND SAYS, [GOD] GRANT THAT THIS IS NOT IN MY HOUSE, THIS IS A VAIN PRAYER. ONE WHO [IN THE COURSE OF A JOURNEY] GOES THROUGH A CAPITAL CITY[4] SHOULD SAY TWO PRAYERS, ONE ON ENTERING AND ONE ON LEAVING. BEN AZZAI SAYS, FOUR,[5] TWO ON ENTERING AND TWO ON LEAVING- HE GIVES THANKS FOR PAST MERCIES AND SUPPLICATES FOR THE FUTURE. IT IS INCUMBENT ON A MAN TO BLESS [GOD] FOR THE EVIL IN THE SAME WAY AS FOR THE GOOD, AS IT SAYS, AND THOU SHALT LOVE THE LORD THY GOD WITH ALL THY HEART ETC.[6] 'WITH ALL THY HEART, MEANS WITH THY TWO IMPULSES, THE EVIL IMPULSE AS WELL AS THE GOOD IMPULSE; 'WITH ALL THY SOUL' MEANS, EVEN THOUGH HE TAKES THY SOUL [LIFE]; 'WITH ALL THY MIGHT' MEANS, WITH ALL THY MONEY. ANOTHER EXPLANATION OF 'WITH ALL THY MIGHT [ME'ODEKA]' IS, WHATEVER TREATMENT[7] HE METES OUT TO THEE.

ONE SHOULD AVOID SHOWING DISRESPECT TO THE EASTERN GATE[8] BECAUSE IT IS IN A DIRECT LINE WITH THE HOLY OF HOLIES.[9] A MAN SHOULD NOT ENTER THE

---

[1] Var. lec.: who fashions the work of creation.
[2] Generally taken to refer to the Mediterranean Sea.
[3] This is explained in the Gemara.
[4] The residence of a governor or ruler.
[5] As explained in the Gemara.
[6] Deut. VI, 5.
[7] Heb. Lit., 'measure'; Heb. middah, a play on me'odeka.
[8] Of the Temple Mount.
[9] I.e., a direct line led from it through the other gates up to the inner shrine.

TEMPLE MOUNT WITH HIS STAFF OR WITH HIS SHOES ON OR WITH HIS WALLET OR WITH HIS FEET DUST-STAINED; NOR SHOULD HE MAKE IT A SHORT CUT [KAPPANDARIA], AND SPITTING [ON IT IS FORBIDDEN] A FORTIORI.

AT THE CONCLUSION OF THE BENEDICTIONS SAID IN THE TEMPLE THEY USED AT FIRST TO SAY SIMPLY, 'FOR EVER'.[1] WHEN THE SADDUCEES PERVERTED THEIR WAYS AND ASSERTED THAT THERE WAS ONLY ONE WORLD, IT WAS ORDAINED THAT THE RESPONSE SHOULD BE, FROM EVERLASTING TO EVERLASTING.[2] IT WAS ALSO LAID DOWN THAT GREETING SHOULD BE GIVEN IN [GOD'S] NAME,[3] IN THE SAME WAY AS IT SAYS, AND BEHOLD BOAZ CAME FROM BETHLEHEM AND SAID UNTO THE REAPERS, THE LORD BE WITH YOU; AND THEY ANSWERED HIM, THE LORD BLESS THEE;[4] AND IT ALSO SAYS, THE LORD IS WITH THEE, THOU MIGHTY MAN OF VALOUR;[5] AND IT ALSO SAYS, AND DESPISE NOT THY MOTHER WHEN SHE IS OLD;[6] AND IT ALSO SAYS, IT IS TIME TO WORK FOR THE LORD; THEY HAVE MADE VOID THY LAW.[7] R. NATHAN SAYS: [THIS MEANS] THEY HAVE MADE VOID THY LAW BECAUSE IT IS TIME TO WORK FOR THE LORD.

GEMARA. Whence is this rule[8] derived? — R. Johanan said: Because Scripture says, And Jethro said, Blessed be the Lord who hath delivered you, etc.[9] And is a blessing said only for a miracle wrought for a large body, but not for one wrought for an individual? What of the case of the man Who was once travelling through Eber Yemina[10] when a lion attacked him, but he was miraculously saved, and when he came before Raba he said to him, Whenever you pass that place say, Blessed be He who wrought for me a miracle in this place? There was the case, too, of Mar the son of Rabina who was once going through the valley of 'Araboth[11] and was suffering from thirst and a well of water was miraculously created for him and he drank, and another time he was going through the manor of Mahoza[12] when a wild camel attacked him and at that moment the wall of a house just by fell in and he escaped inside; and whenever thereafter he came to 'Araboth he used to say, Blessed be He who wrought for me miracles in 'Araboth and with the camel, and when he passed through the manor of Mahoza he used to say, Blessed be He who wrought for me miracles with the camel and in 'Araboth? — The answer [is that] for a miracle done to a large body it is the duty of everyone to say a blessing, for a miracle done to an individual he alone[13] is required to say a blessing.

Our Rabbis taught: If one sees the place of the crossing of the Red Sea, or the fords of the Jordan, or

---

[1] Heb. le'olam, which can also mean 'for the world'.
[2] Or 'from world to world', i.e., two worlds.
[3] I.e., the Tetragrammaton, although this might appear to be breaking the third commandment. The reason of this ordinance is not certain. Marmorstein, The Old Testament Conception of God, etc. I, pp. 24ff conjectures this to have been designed to counteract the Hellenistic teaching that God had no name.
[4] Ruth 11, 4.
[5] Judg. VI, 12.
[6] Prov. XXIII, 22.
[7] In time of emergency the law of God may be set aside. Ps. CXIX, 126. E.V. 'for the Lord to work'. The relevance of these citations is explained in the Gemara.
[8] Of saying a blessing over a miracle.
[9] Ex. XVIII, 10.
[10] Lit., 'the south side'. The southern suburb of Mahoza, v. Obermeyer, p. 181.
[11] Between the river Chabor and the canal of Is.
[12] Rostaka di Mahoza, v. Obermeyer, p. 172.
[13] Alfasi adds, His son and his son's son.

the fords of the streams of Arnon, or hail stones [abne elgabish] in the descent of Beth Horon, or the stone which Og king of Bashan wanted to throw at Israel, or the stone on which Moses sat when Joshua fought with Amalek, or [the pillar of salt of] Lot's wife,[1] or the wall of Jericho which sank into the ground,[2] for all of these he should give thanksgiving and praise to the Almighty. I grant you the passage of the Red Sea, because it is written, And the children of Israel went into the midst of the sea upon the dry ground;[3] also the fords of the Jordan, because it is written, And the priests that bore the ark of the covenant of the Lord stood firm on dry ground in the midst of the Jordan, while all Israel passed over on dry ground, until all the nation were passed clean over the Jordan.[4] But whence is the title derived for the fords of the streams of Arnon? — Because it is written: Wherefore it is said in the book of the Wars of the Lord, Eth and Heb in the rear;[5] [in explanation of which] a Tanna taught: 'Eth and Heb in the rear' were two lepers who followed in the rear of the camp of Israel, and when the Israelites were about to pass through [the valley of Arnon] the Amorites came

---

[1] V. Gen. XIX, 26.
[2] Lit., 'was swallowed in its place'.
[3] Ex. XIV, 22.
[4] Josh. III, 17.
[5] Num. XXI, 14. E.V. 'Vahab in Suphah'.

Berakoth 54b

and made cavities [in the rocks] and hid in them, saying, When Israel pass by here we will kill them. They did not know, however, that the Ark Was advancing in front of Israel and levelling the hills before them. When the Ark arrived there, the mountains closed together and killed them, and their blood flowed down to the streams of Arnon. When Eth and Heb came they saw the blood issuing from between the rocks[1] and they went and told the Israelites, who thereupon broke out into song. And so it is written, And he poured forth the streams[2] [from the mountain] which inclined toward the seat of Ar[3] and leaned upon the border of Moab.[4]

'Hailstones [abne elgabish]'. What are 'abne elgabish'? A Tanna taught: Stones [abanim] which remained suspended for the sake of a man ['al gab ish] and came down for the sake of a man. 'They remained suspended for the sake of a man': this was Moses, of whom it is written, Now the man Moses was very meek,[5] and it is also written, And the soldiers and hail ceased, and the rain poured not upon the earth.[6] 'They came down for the sake of a man': this was Joshua, of whom it is written, Take thee Joshua the son of Nun, a man in whom there is spirit,[7] and it is written, And it came to pass as they fled from before Israel, while they were at the descent of Beth-Horon, that the Lord cast down great stones.[8]

'The stone which Og, king of Bashan wanted to throw at Israel'. This has been handed down by tradition. He said: How large is the camp of Israel? Three parasangs. I will go and uproot a mountain of the size of three parasangs and cast it upon them and kill them. He went and uprooted a mountain of the size of three parasangs and carried it on his head. But the Holy One, blessed be He, sent ants which bored a hole in it, so that it sank around his neck. He tried to pull it off, but his teeth projected on each side, and he could not pull it off. This is referred to in the text, Thou hast broken the teeth of the wicked,[9] as explained by R Simeon b. Lakish. For R. Simeon b. Lakish said: What is the meaning of the text, Thou hast broken the teeth of the wicked? Do not read, shibbarta [Thou hast broken], but shirbabta [Thou hast lengthened]. The height of Moses was ten cubits.[10] He took an axe ten cubits long, leapt ten cubits into the air, and struck him on his ankle and killed him.

'The stone on which Moses sat'. As it is written, But Moses' hands were heavy; and they took a stone and put it under hint and he sat thereon.[11] 'Lot's wife'. As it says, But his wife looked back from behind him and she became a pillar of salt.[12]

---

[1] Lit., 'mountains'. After they had opened out again.
[2] E.V. 'and the slope of the valleys'.
[3] I.e., Moab.
[4] Ibid. 15.
[5] Num. XII, 3.
[6] Ex. IX, 33.
[7] Num. XXVII, 18.
[8] Josh. X, 11.
[9] Ps. III, 8.
[10] About fifteen feet.
[11] Ex. XVII, 12. MS.M adds: 'Had not Moses a cushion or bolster to sit upon? Moses said to himself: Since Israel are suffering, I will suffer with them'; v. Ta'an. 11a.
[12] Gen. XIX, 26.

'And the wall of Jericho which sank into the ground'. As it is written, And the wall fell down flat.[1]

We understand [why this blessing should be said over] all the others, because they are miracles, but the transformation of Lot's wife was a punishment. One should say on seeing it, Blessed be the true Judge,[2] yet [the Baraitha] says: 'Thanksgiving and praise'? — Read: 'For Lot and his wife two blessings are said. For his wife we say, "Blessed be the true Judge", and for Lot we say, "Blessed be He who remembereth the righteous"'. R. Johanan said: Even in the hour of His anger the Holy One, blessed be He, remembers the righteous, as it says, And it came to pass when God destroyed the cities of the Plain, that God remembered Abraham and sent Lot out of the midst of the overthrow.[3]

'And the wall of Jericho which sank [into the ground]'. But did the wall of Jericho sink [into the ground]? Surely it fell, as it says, And it came to pass when the people heard the sound of the horn, that the people shouted with a great shout and the wall fell down flat?[4] — Since its breadth and its height were equal, it must have sunk [into the ground].[5]

Rab Judah said in the name of Rab: There are four [classes of people] who have to offer thanksgiving: those who have crossed the sea, those who have traversed the wilderness, one who has recovered from an illness, and a prisoner who has been set free. Whence do we know this of those who cross the sea? — Because it is written, They that go down to the sea in ships ... these saw the works of the Lord ... He raised the stormy wind ... they mounted up to the heaven, they went down to the deeps ... they reeled to and fro and staggered like a drunken man ... they cried unto the Lord in their trouble, and He brought them out of their distresses. He made the storm a calm ... then were they glad because they were quiet ... Let them give thanks unto the Lord for His mercy, and for His wonderful works to the children of men.[6] Whence for those who traverse the desert? — Because it is written: They wandered in the wilderness in a desert way; they found no city of habitation ... Then they cried unto the Lord ... and He led them by a straight way ... Let them give thanks unto the Lord for His mercy.[7] Whence for one who recovers from an illness? — Because it is written: Crazed because of the way of their transgressions and afflicted because of their iniquities, their soul abhorred all manner of food ... They cried unto the Lord in their trouble. He sent His word unto them ... Let them give thanks unto the Lord for His mercy.[8] Whence for a prisoner who was set free? — Because it is written: Such as sat in darkness and in the shadow of death ... Because they rebelled against the words of God ... Therefore He humbled their heart with travail ... They cried unto the Lord in their trouble ... He brought them out of darkness and the shadow of death ... Let them give thanks unto the Lord for His mercy.[9] What blessing should he say? Rab Judah said: 'Blessed is He who bestows lovingkindnesses'. Abaye said: And he must utter his thanksgiving in the presence of ten, as it is written: Let them exalt Him in the assembly of the people.[10] Mar Zutra said: And two of them must

---

[1] Josh. VI, 20. This sentence is obviously out of place and should be transferred to the next paragraph.
[2] The formula recited on hearing bad news.
[3] Gen. XIX, 29.
[4] Josh. VI, 20.
[5] To enable the people to enter the city. According to Rashi this is also signified by the word translated 'flat', which means literally 'under it' or 'in its place'.
[6] Ps, CVII, 23-31.
[7] Ibid. 4-8.
[8] Ibid. 17-21.
[9] Ibid. 10-15.
[10] Ibid. 32.

be rabbis, as it says, And praise Him in the seat of the elders.[1] R. Ashi demurred to this: You might as well say [he remarked], that all should be rabbis! — Is it written, 'In the assembly of elders'? It is written, 'In the assembly of the people'! — Let us say then, in the presence of ten ordinary people and two rabbis [in addition]? — This is a difficulty.

Rab Judah was ill and recovered. R. Hanna of Bagdad and other rabbis went to visit him. They said to him: 'Blessed be the All Merciful who has given you back to us and has not given you to the dust'. He said to them: 'You have absolved me from the obligation of giving thanks'. But has not Abaye said that he must utter his thanksgiving in the presence of ten! — There were ten present. But he did not utter the thanksgiving? — There was no need, as he answered after them, Amen.

Rab Judah said: Three persons require guarding,[2] namely, a sick person, a bridegroom, and a bride. In a Baraitha it was taught: A sick person, a midwife, a bridegroom and a bride; some add, a mourner, and some add further, scholars at night-time.

Rab Judah said further: There are three things the drawing out of which prolongs a man's days and years; the drawing out of prayer, the drawing out of a meal, and the drawing out of [easing in] a privy. But is the drawing out of prayer a merit? Has not R. Hiyya b. Abba said in the name of R. Johanan:

---

[1] Ibid.
[2] Against evil spirits (Rashi).

Folio 55a

If one draws out his prayer and expects therefore its fulfilment, he will in the end suffer vexation of heart, as it says, Hope deferred maketh the heart sick;[1] and R. Isaac also said: Three things cause a man's sins to be remembered [on high], namely, [passing under] a shaky wall,[2] expectation of [the fulfilment of] prayer, and calling on heaven to punish his neighbour?[3] — There is no contradiction; one statement speaks of a man who expects the fulfilment of his prayer, the other of one who does not count upon it. What then does he do? — He simply utters many supplications. 'He who draws out his meal', because perhaps a poor man will come and he will give him something, as it is written, The altar of wood three cubits high ... and he said to me, This is the table that is before the Lord[4] [Now the verse] opens with 'altar' and finishes with 'table'? R. Johanan and R. Eleazar both explain that as long as the Temple stood, the altar atoned for Israel, but now a man's table atones for him. 'To draw out one's stay in a privy', is this a good thing? Has it not been taught: Ten things bring on piles; eating the leaves of reeds, and the leaves of vines, and the sprouts of vines, and the rough parts of the flesh of an animal,[5] and the backbone of a fish, and salted fish not sufficiently cooked, and drinking wine lees, and wiping oneself with lime, potters' clay or pebbles which have been used by another. Some add, to strain oneself unduly in a privy! — There is no contradiction: one statement refers to one who stays long and strains himself, the other to one who stays long without straining himself. This may be illustrated by what a certain matron said to R. Judah b. R. Ila'i: Your face is [red] like that of pig-breeders and usurers,[6] to which he replied: On my faith, both [occupations] are forbidden me, but there are twenty-four privies between my lodging and the Beth ha-Midrash, and when I go there I test myself in all of them.[7]

Rab Judah also said:[8] Three things shorten a man's days and years: To be given a scroll of the Law to read from and to refuse, to be given a cup of benediction to say grace over and to refuse, and to assume airs of authority. 'To be given a scroll of the Law to read from and to refuse', as it is written: For that is thy life and the length of thy days.[9] 'To be given a cup of benediction to say grace over and to refuse', as it is written: I will bless them that bless thee.[10] 'To assume airs of authority', as R. Hama b. Hanina said: Why did Joseph die before his brethren?[11] Because he assumed airs of authority.

Rab Judah also said in the name of Rab: There are three things for which one should supplicate: a good king, a good year, and a good dream.[12] 'A good king', as it is written: A king's heart is in the hands of the Lord as the water-courses.[13] 'A good year', as it is written: The eyes of the Lord thy God

---

[1] Prov, XIII, 12. Cf. 32b, p. 200.
[2] Which is, as it were, tempting Providence.
[3] Which is a mark of selfrighteousness. Lit., 'surrendering the case against his fellow to heaven'.
[4] Ezek. XLI, 22.
[5] E.g., the palate. Lit., 'threshing-sledge'.
[6] Who were notoriously good livers.
[7] Cf. Ned. 49b.
[8] We should probably add, 'In the name of Rab'.
[9] Deut. XXX, 20.
[10] Gen. XII, 3. The one who says grace blesses his host.
[11] As we learn from Ex. I, 6: 'And Joseph died and (then) all his brethren'.
[12] These things depending directly upon the will of God.
[13] prov. XXI, 1.

are always upon it, from the beginning of the year even unto the end of the year.¹ 'A good dream', as it is written; Wherefore cause Thou me to dream² and make me to live.³

R. Johanan said: There are three things which the Holy One, blessed be He, Himself proclaims, namely, famine, plenty, and a good leader. 'Famine', as it is written: The Lord hath called for a famine.⁴ 'Plenty', as it is written: I will call for the corn and will increase it.⁵ 'A good leader', as it is written: And the Lord spoke unto Moses, saying, See I have called by name Bezalel, the son of Uri.⁶

R. Isaac said: We must not appoint a leader over a Community without first consulting it, as it says: See, the Lord hath called by name Bezalel, the son of Uri.⁷ The Holy One, blessed be He, said to Moses: Do you consider Bezalel suitable? He replied: Sovereign of the Universe, if Thou thinkest him suitable, surely I must also! Said [God] to him: All the same, go and consult them. He went and asked Israel: Do you consider Bezalel suitable? They replied: If the Holy One, blessed be He, and you consider him suitable, surely we must!

R. Samuel b. Nahmani said in the name of R. Johanan: Bezalel was so called on account of his wisdom. At the time when the Holy One, blessed be He, said to Moses; Go and tell Bezalel to make me a tabernacle, an ark and vessels,⁸ Moses went and reversed the order, saying, Make an ark and vessels and a tabernacle. Bezalel said to him: Moses, our Teacher, as a rule a man first builds a house and then brings vessels into it; but you say, Make me an ark and vessels and a tabernacle. Where shall I put the vessels that I am to make? Can it be that the Holy One, blessed be He, said to you, Make a tabernacle, an ark and vessels? Moses replied: Perhaps you were in the shadow of God⁹ and knew!

Rab Judah said in the name of Rab: Bezalel knew how to combine the letters by which the heavens and earth were created.¹⁰ It is written here, And He hath filled him with the spirit of God, in wisdom and in understanding, and in knowledge,¹¹ and it is written elsewhere, The Lord by wisdom founded the earth; by understanding He established the heavens,¹² and it is also written, By His knowledge the depths were broken up.¹³

R. Johanan said: The Holy One, blessed be He, gives wisdom only to one who already has wisdom, as it says, He giveth wisdom unto the wise, and knowledge to them that know understanding.¹⁴ R. Tahlifa from the West¹⁵ heard and repeated it before R. Abbahu. He said to him: You learn it from there, but we learn it from this text, namely, In the hearts of all that are wise-hearted I have put

---

¹ Deut. XI, 12.
² E.V. 'Recover Thou me'. The Talmud, however, connects the word in the text tahalimeni with halom, a dream.
³ Isa. XXXVIII, 16.
⁴ II Kings VIII, 1.
⁵ Ezek. XXXVI, 29.
⁶ Ex. XXXI, 1.
⁷ Ibid. XXXV, 30.
⁸ This is the order in Ex. XXXI, 7.
⁹ Heb. bezel el.
¹⁰ The Kabbalah assigns mystic powers to the letters of the Hebrew alphabet.
¹¹ Ibid. XXXV, 31.
¹² Prov. III, 19.
¹³ Ibid. 20.
¹⁴ Dan. II, 21.
¹⁵ I.e., palestine.

wisdom.[1]

R. Hisda said: Any dream rather than one of a fast.[2] R. Hisda also said: A dream which is not interpreted is like a letter which is not read.[3] R. Hisda also said: Neither a good dream nor a bad dream is ever wholly fulfilled. R. Hisda also said: A bad dream is better than a good dream.[4] R. Hisda also said: The sadness caused by a bad dream is sufficient for it and the joy which a good dream gives is sufficient for it.[5] R. Joseph said: Even for me[6] the joy caused by a good dream nullifies it. R. Hisda also said: A bad dream is worse than scourging, since it says, God hath so made it that men should fear before Him,[7] and Rabbah b. Bar Hanah said in the name of R. Johanan: This refers to a bad dream.

A prophet that hath a dream let him tell a dream: and he that hath My word let him speak My word faithfully. What hath the straw to do with the wheat, saith the Lord.[8] What is the connection of straw and wheat with a dream? The truth is, said R. Johanan in the name of R. Simeon b. Yohai, that just as wheat cannot be without straw, so there cannot be a dream without some nonsense. R. Berekiah said: While a part of a dream may be fulfilled, the whole of it is never fulfilled. Whence do we know this? From Joseph, as it is written, And behold the sun and the moon [and eleven stars bowed down to me,][9] and

---

[1] Ex. XXXI, 6. It was preferable to learn it from a text of the Pentateuch.
[2] I.e., to dream oneself fasting. So Rashi. The Aruch, however, explains: There is reality in every dream save one that comes in a fast.
[3] Compare the dictum infra, 'A dream follows its interpretation
[4] Because it incites one to repentance.
[5] I.e., there is no need for them to be fulfilled.
[6] R. Joseph was blind, and consequently could not derive so much pleasure from a dream.
[7] Eccl. III, 14.
[8] Jer. XXIII, 28.
[9] Gen. XXXVII, 9.

Berakoth 55b

at that time his mother was not living. R. Levi said: A man should await the fulfilment of a good dream for as much as twenty-two years. Whence do we know this? From Joseph. For it is written: These are the generations of Jacob. Joseph being seventeen years old, etc.;[1] and it is further written, And Joseph was thirty years old when he stood before Pharaoh.[2] How many years is it from seventeen to thirty? Thirteen. Add the seven years of plenty and two of famine,[3] and you have twenty-two.

R. Huna said: A good man is not shown a good dream, and a bad man is not shown a bad dream.[4] It has been taught similarly; David, during the whole of his lifetime, never saw a good dream and Ahitophel, during the whole of his lifetime, never saw a bad dream. But it is written, There shall no evil befall thee,[5] and R. Hisda said, in the name of R. Jeremiah: this means that you will not be disturbed either by bad dreams or by evil thoughts, neither shall any plague come nigh thy tent[6] … i.e., thou shalt not find thy wife doubtfully menstruous when thou returnest from a journey? — Though he does not see an evil dream, others see one about him. But if he does not see one, is this considered an advantage? Has not R. Ze'ira said: If a man goes seven days without a dream he is called evil, since it says, He shall abide satisfied, he shall not be visited by evil?[7] — Read not sabe'a [satisfied] but [seven] sheba'.[8] What he means is this: He sees, but he does not remember what he has seen.

R. Huna b. Ammi said in the name of R. Pedath who had it from R. Johanan: If one has a dream which makes him sad he should go and have it interpreted in the presence of three. He should have it interpreted! Has not R. Hisda said: A dream which is not interpreted is like a letter which is not read?[9] — Say rather then, he should have a good turn given to it in the presence of three. Let him bring three and say to them: I have seen a good dream; and they should say to him, Good it is and good may it be. May the All-Merciful turn it to good; seven times may it be decreed from heaven that it should be good and may it be good. They should say three verses with the word hapak [turn], and three with the word padah [redeem] and three with the word shalom [peace]. Three with the word 'turn', namely (i) Thou didst turn for me my mourning into dancing, Thou didst loose my sackcloth and gird me with gladness;[10] (ii) Then shall the virgin rejoice in the dance, and the young men and the old together; for I will turn their mourning into joy and will comfort them and make them rejoice from their sorrow;[11] (iii) Nevertheless the Lord thy God would not hearken unto Balaam; but the Lord

---

[1] Ibid. 2.
[2] Gen. XLI, 46.
[3] After which Joseph saw his brothers.
[4] Rashi reads: A good man is shown a bad dream and a bad man is shown a good dream. The purpose is to turn the good man to repentance and to give the bad man his reward in this world.
[5] Ps. XCI, 10.
[6] Ps. XCI, 10.
[7] Prov. XIX, 23.
[8] And translate: If he abides seven nights without being visited, it is evil.
[9] And therefore what harm can it do?
[10] Ps. XXX, 12.
[11] Jer. XXXI, 13.

thy God turned the curse into a blessing unto thee.[1] Three verses with the word 'redeem', namely, (i) He hath redeemed my soul in peace, so that none came nigh me;[2] (ii) And the redeemed of the Lord shall return and come with singing unto Zion … and sorrow and sighing shall flee away;[3] (iii) And the people said unto Saul, Shall Jonathan die who hath wrought this great salvation in Israel? … So the people redeemed Jonathan that he died not.[4] Three verses with the word 'peace', namely, (i) Peace, peace, to him that is far off and to him that is near, saith the Lord that createth the fruit of the lips; and I will heal him;[5] (ii) Then the spirit clothed Amasai who was chief of the captains: Thine are we, David, and on thy side, thou son of Jesse: Peace, peace, be unto thee and peace be to thy helpers, for thy God helpeth thee;[6] (iii) Thus ye shall say: All hail! and peace be both unto thee, and peace be to thy house, and peace be unto all that thou hast.[7]

Amemar, Mar Zutra and R. Ashi were once sitting together. They said: Let each of us say something which the others have not heard. One of them began: If one has seen a dream and does not remember what he saw, let him stand before the priests at the time when they spread out their hands,[8] and say as follows: 'Sovereign of the Universe, I am Thine and my dreams are Thine. I have dreamt a dream and I do not know what it is. Whether I have dreamt about myself or my companions have dreamt about me, or I have dreamt about others, if they are good dreams, confirm them and reinforce them[9] like the dreams of Joseph, and if they require a remedy, heal them, as the waters of Marah were healed by Moses, our teacher, and as Miriam was healed of her leprosy and Hezekiah of his sickness, and the waters of Jericho by Elisha. As thou didst turn the curse of the wicked Balaam into a blessing, so turn all my dreams into something good for me'.[10] He should conclude his prayer along with the priests, so that the congregation may answer, Amen! If he cannot manage this,[11] he should say: Thou who art majestic on high, who abidest in might, Thou art peace and Thy name is peace. May it be Thy will to bestow peace on us.

The second commenced and said: If a man on going into a town is afraid of the Evil Eye,[12] let him take the thumb of his right hand in his left hand and the thumb of his left hand in his right hand, and say: I, so-and-so, am of the seed of Joseph over which the evil eye has no power, as it says: Joseph is a fruitful vine, a fruitful vine by a fountain.[13] Do not read 'ale 'ayin [by a fountain] but 'ole 'ayin [overcoming the evil eye]. R. Jose b. R. Hanina derived it from here: And let them grow into a multitude [weyidgu] in the midst of the earth;[14] just as the fishes [dagim] in the sea are covered by the waters and the evil eye has no power over them so the evil eye has no power over the seed of Joseph.[15] If he is afraid of his own evil eye, he should look at the side of his left nostril.

---

[1] Deut. XXIII, 6.
[2] Ps, LV, 19.
[3] Isa. XXXV, 10.
[4] I Samuel XIV, 45.
[5] Isa. LVII, 19.
[6] I Chron. XII, 19.
[7] I Sam. XXV, 6.
[8] To say the priestly benediction.
[9] Var. lec. adds here the words: And may they be fulfilled.
[10] This prayer is included in the prayer books and recited in some congregations between each of the three blessings constituting the priestly benediction, whether they have dreamt or not.
[11] I.e., he is unable to finish it together with the priests. Var. lec.: When the priests (at the conclusion of the benediction) turn their faces (to the ark).
[12] I.e., his own sensual passions.
[13] Gen. XLIX, 22.
[14] Ibid. XLVIII, 16.
[15] V. supra p. 120, nn. 9 and 10.

The third commenced and said: If a man falls ill, the first day he should not tell anyone, so that he should not have bad luck; but after that he may tell. So when Raba fell ill, on the first day he did not tell anyone, but after that he said to his attendant: Go and announce that Raba is ill. Whoever loves him, let him pray for him, and whoever hates him, let him rejoice over him; for it is written: Rejoice not when thine enemy falleth, and let not thy heart be glad when he stumbleth, lest the Lord see it and it displease Him and He turn away His wrath from him.[1]

When Samuel had a bad dream, he used to say, The dreams speak falsely.[2] When he had a good dream, he used to say, Do the dreams speak falsely, seeing that it is written, I [God] do speak with him in a dream?[3] Raba pointed out a contradiction. It is written, 'I do speak with him in a dream', and it is written, 'the dreams speak falsely'. — There is no contradiction; in the one case it is through an angel, in the other through a demon.

R. Bizna b. Zabda said in the name of R. Akiba who had it from R. Panda who had it from R. Nahum, who had it from R. Biryam reporting a certain elder — and who was this? R. Bana'ah: There were twenty-four interpreters of dreams in Jerusalem. Once I dreamt a dream and I went round to all of them and they all gave different interpretations, and all were fulfilled, thus confirming that which is said: All dreams follow the mouth.[4] Is the statement that all dreams follow the mouth Scriptural?[5] Yes, as stated by R. Eleazar. For R. Eleazar said: Whence do we know that all dreams follow the mouth? Because it says, and it came to pass, as he interpreted to us, so it was.[6] Raba said: This is only if the interpretation corresponds to the content of the dream: for it says, to each man according to his dream he did interpret.[7] When the chief baker saw that the interpretation was good.[8] How did he know this? R. Eleazar says: This tells us that each of them was shown his own dream and the interpretation of the other one's dream.[9]

R. Johanan said: If one rises early and a Scriptural verse comes to his mouth,[10] this is a kind of minor prophecy. R. Johanan also said: Three kinds of dream are fulfilled: an early morning dream, a dream which a friend has about one, and a dream which is interpreted in the midst of a dream. Some add also, a dream which is repeated, as it says, and for that the dream was doubled unto Pharoah twice, etc.[11]

R. Samuel b. Nahmani said in the name of R. Jonathan: A man is shown in a dream only what is suggested by his own thoughts, as it says, As for thee, Oh King, thy thoughts came into thy mind upon thy bed.[12] Or if you like, I can derive it from here: That thou mayest know the thoughts of the heart.[13] Raba said: This is proved by the fact that a man is never shown in a dream a date palm of

---

[1] Prov. XXIV, 17.
[2] Zech. X, 2.
[3] Num. XII, 6.
[4] 'Mouth' here seems to have the sense of interpretation.
[5] As the formula 'thus confirming' etc., would seem to imply.
[6] Gen. XLI, 13.
[7] Ibid. 12.
[8] Ibid. XL, 16.
[9] R. Eleazar stresses the word 'saw'.
[10] I.e., either he spontaneously utters it, or he hears a child repeating it.
[11] Ibid. XLI, 32.
[12] Dan. II, 29.
[13] Ibid. 30.

gold, or an elephant going through the eye of a needle.[1]

Folio 56a

The Emperor [of Rome][2] said to R. Joshua b. R. Hananyah: You [Jews] profess to be very clever. Tell me what I shall see in my dream. He said to him: You will see the Persians[3] making you do forced labour, and despoiling you and making you feed unclean animals with a golden crook. He thought about it all day, and in the night he saw it in his dream.[4] King Shapor [I] once said to Samuel: You [Jews] profess to be very clever. Tell me what I shall see in my dream. He said to him: You will see the Romans coming and taking you captive and making you grind date-stones in a golden mill. He thought about it the whole day and in the night saw it in a dream.

Bar Hedya was an interpreter of dreams. To one who paid him he used to give a favourable interpretation and to one who did not pay him he gave an unfavourable interpretation. Abaye and Raba each had a dream. Abaye gave him a zuz, and Rab did not give him anything, They said to him: In our dream we had to read the verse, Thine ox shall be slain before thine eyes,[5] etc. To Raba he said: Your business will be a failure, and you will be so grieved that you will have no appetite to eat. To Abaye he said: Your business will prosper, and you will not be able to eat from sheer joy. They then said to him: We had to read in our dream the verse, Thou shalt beget sons and daughters but they shall not be thine,[6] etc. To Raba he interpreted it in its [literal] unfavourable sense. To Abaye he said: You have numerous sons and daughters, and your daughters will be married and go away, and it will seem to you as if they have gone into captivity. [They said to him:] We were made to read the verse: Thy sons and thy daughters shall be given unto another people.[7] To Abaye he said: You have numerous sons and daughters; you will want your daughters to marry your relatives, and your wife will want them to marry her relatives, and she will force you to marry them to her relatives, which will be like giving them to another people. To Raba he said: Your wife will die, and her sons and daughters will come under the sway of another wife. (For Raba said in the name of R. Jeremiah b. Abba, reporting Rab: What is the meaning of the verse: 'Thy sons and thy daughters shall be given to another people'? This refers to a step-mother.) [They further said]: We were made to read in our dream the verse, Go thy way, eat thy bread with joy, etc.[8] To Abaye he said: Your business will prosper, and you will eat and drink, and recite this verse out of the joy of your heart. To Raba he said: Your business will fail, you will slaughter [cattle] and not eat or drink and you will read Scripture to allay your anxiety. [They said to him]: We were made to read the verse, Thou shalt carry much seed out into the field, [and shalt gather little in, for the locusts will consume it].[9] To Abaye he interpreted from the first half of the verse; to Raba from the second half. [They said to him:] We were made to read the verse, Thou shalt have olive trees throughout all thy borders, [but thou shalt not anoint thyself, etc.][10] To Abaye he interpreted from the first half of the verse; to Raba from the second half.

---

[1] Because he never thinks of such things.
[2] Probably Trajan, when he passed through Palestine during his expedition to Persia.
[3] I.e., the Parthians.
[4] Trajan was defeated by the Parthians in 116 C.E.
[5] Deut. XXVIII, 31.
[6] Ibid. 41.
[7] Deut. XXVIII, 32.
[8] Eccl. IX, 7.
[9] Deut. XXVIII, 38.
[10] Ibid. 40.

[They said to him:] We were made to read the verse: And all the peoples of the earth shall see that the name of the Lord is called upon thee, etc.¹ To Abaye he said: Your name will become famous as head of the college, and you will be generally feared. To Raba he said: The King's treasury² will be broken into, and you will be arrested as a thief, and everyone will draw an inference from you.³ The next day the King's treasury was broken into and they came and arrested Raba: They said to him: We saw a lettuce on the mouth of a jar. To Abaye he said: Your business will be doubled like a lettuce. To Raba he said: Your business will be bitter like a lettuce. They said to him: We saw some meat on the mouth of a jar. To Abaye he said: Your wine will be sweet, and everyone will come to buy meat and wine from you. To Raba, he said: Your wine will turn sour, and everyone will come to buy meat to eat with it.⁴ They said: We saw a cask hanging on a palm tree. To Abaye he said: Your business will spring up like a palm tree. To Raba he said: Your goods will be sweet like dates.⁵ They said to him: We saw a pomegranate sprouting on the mouth of a jar. To Abaye he said: Your goods will be high-priced like a pomegranate. To Raba he said: Your goods will be stale like a [dry] pomegranate. They said to him: We saw a cask fall into a pit. To Abaye he said: Your goods will be in demand according to the saying: The pu'ah⁶ has fallen into a well and cannot be found.⁷ To Raba he said: Your goods will be spoilt and they will be thrown into a pit. They said to him: We saw a young ass standing by our pillow and braying. To Abaye he said: You will become a king,⁸ and an Amora⁹ will stand by you. To Raba he said: The words 'The first-born of an ass'¹⁰ have been erased from your tefillin. Raba said to him: I have looked at them and they are there. He replied to him: Certainly the waw of the word hamor [ass] has been erased from your tefillin.¹¹

Subsequently Raba went to him by himself and said to him: I dreamt that the outer door fell. He said to him: Your wife will die. He said to him: I dreamt that my front and back teeth fell out. He said to him: Your sons and your daughters will die. He said: I saw two pigeons flying. He replied: You will divorce two wives.¹² He said to him: I saw two turnip-tops.¹³ He replied: You will receive two blows with a cudgel. On that day Raba went and sat all day in the Beth ha-Midrash. He found two blind men quarrelling with one another. Raba went to separate them and they gave him two blows. They wanted to give him another blow but he said, Enough! I saw in my dream only two.

Finally Raba went and gave him a fee. He said to him: I saw a wall fall down. He replied: You will acquire wealth without end. He said: I dreamt that Abaye's villa fell in and the dust of it covered me. He replied to him: Abaye will die and [the presidency of] his College will be offered to you. He said to him: I saw my own villa fall in, and everyone came and took a brick. He said to him: Your teachings will be disseminated throughout the world. He said to him: I dreamt that my head was split open and my brains fell out. He replied: The stuffing will fall out of your pillow. He said to him: In

---

¹ Ibid. 10.
² Where the tax payments were received.
³ Saying: If Raba is suspect, how much more so are we.
⁴ I.e., to dip in it.
⁵ Rashi explains this to mean: Sweet to the customer because of its cheapness.
⁶ A vegetable dyer's madder, a prophylactic.
⁷ I.e., it is a useless remedy, v. Shab. 66b. MS.M. reads: Your goods will be in demand like something which has fallen into a pit.
⁸ I.e., president of a college.
⁹ An interpreter.
¹⁰ Ex. XIII, 13. This passage is one of the four contained in the tefillin.
¹¹ BaH adds: 'Raba examined and found that the waw of hamor had been erased etc.'.
¹² A wife is compared to a dove in Cant. V, 2.
¹³ Looking like sticks.

my dream I was made to read the Hallel of Egypt.[1] He replied: Miracles will happen to you.

Bar Hedya was once travelling with Raba in a boat. He said to himself: Why should I accompany a man to whom a miracle will happen?[2] As he was disembarking, he let fall a book. Raba found it, and saw written in it: All dreams follow the mouth. He exclaimed: Wretch! It all depended on you and you gave me all this pain! I forgive you everything except [what you said about] the daughter of R. Hisda.[3] May it be God's will that this fellow be delivered up to the Government, and that they have no mercy on him! Bar Hedya said to himself: What am I to do? We have been taught that a curse uttered by a sage, even when undeserved, comes to pass; how much more this of Raba, which was deserved! He said: I will rise up and go into exile. For a Master has said: Exile makes atonement for iniquity. He rose and fled to the Romans. He went and sat at the door of the keeper of the King's wardrobe. The keeper of the wardrobe had a dream, and said to him: I dreamt that a needle pierced my finger. He said to him: Give me a zuz! He refused to give him one, and he would not say a word to him. He again said to him: I dreamt that a worm[4] fell between two of my fingers. He said to him: Give me a zuz. He refused to give him one, and he would not say a word to him. I dreamt that a worm filled the whole of my hand. He said to him: Worms have been spoiling all the silk garments. This became known in the palace, and they brought the keeper of the wardrobe in order to put him to death. He said to them: Why execute me? Bring the man who knew and would not tell. So they brought Bar Hedya, and they said to him: Because of your zuz, the king's silken garments have been ruined.

---

[1] I.e., the Hallel as said on Passover Eve to celebrate the going forth from Egypt, v. Glos. s.v. Hallel.
[2] As much as to say, he will be saved but I will not.
[3] Raba's wife, whose death Bar Hedya had foretold.
[4] Aliter: 'decay'.

Berakoth 56b

They tied two cedars together with a rope, tied one leg to one cedar and the other to the other, and released the rope, so that even his head was split.[1] Each tree rebounded to its place and he was decapitated and his body fell in two.

Ben Dama, the son of R. Ishmael's sister, asked R. Ishmael: I dreamt that both my jaws fell out; [what does it mean]? — He replied to him: Two Roman counsellors[2] have made a plot against you, but they have died.

Bar Kappara said to Rabbi: I dreamt that my nose fell off. He replied to him: Fierce anger[3] has been removed from you. He said to him: I dreamt that both my hands were cut off. He replied: You will not require the labour of your hands. He said to him: I dreamt that both my legs were cut off. He replied: You will ride on horseback.[4] dreamt that they said to me: You will die in Adar and not see Nisan. He replied: You will die in all honour [adrutha], and not be brought into temptation [nisayon].

A certain Min said to R. Ishmael: I saw myself [in a dream] pouring oil on olives. He replied: [This man][5] has outraged his mother. He said to him: I dreamt I plucked a star. He replied: You have stolen an Israelite.[6] He said to him: I dreamt that I swallowed the star. He replied: You have sold an Israelite and consumed the proceeds. He said to him: I dreamt that my eyes were kissing one another. He replied: (This man] has outraged his sister. He said to him: I dreamt that I kissed the moon. He replied: He has outraged the wife of an Israelite. He said to him: I dreamt that I was walking in the shade of a myrtle. He replied: He has outraged a betrothed damsel.[7] He said to him: I dreamt that there was a shade above me, and yet it was beneath me. He replied: It means unnatural intercourse. He said to him: I saw ravens keep on coming to my bed. He replied: Your wife has misconducted herself with many men. He said to him: I saw pigeons keep on coming to my bed. He replied: You have defiled many women. He said to him: I dreamt that I took two doves and they flew away. He replied: You have married two wives and dismissed them without a bill of divorce. He said to him: I dreamt that I was shelling eggs. He replied: You have been stripping the dead. He then said to him: You are right in all of these, except the last! of which I am not guilty. Just then a woman came and said to him: This cloak which you are wearing belonged to So-and-so who is dead, and you have stripped it from him. He said to him: I dreamt that people told me: Your father has left you money in Cappadocia. He said to him: Have you money in Cappadocia? No, he replied. Did your father ever go to Cappadocia? No. In that case, he said, kappa means a beam and dika means ten.[8] Go and examine the beam which is at the head of ten, for it is full of coins. He went, and found it full of coins.

---

[1] Another reading is: 'released the rope till he was split in two. Said Raba: I will not forgive him till his head is split. Each tree, etc.'.
[2] Signified by 'jaws' because of their powers of speech.
[3] The word for 'nose' (af) means also 'anger'.
[4] Another reading is: 'released the rope till he was split in two. Said Raba: I will not forgive him till his head is split. Each tree, etc.'.
[5] In attributing to him such a crime he would not address him in the second person.
[6] The Israelites being compared to stars. Gen. XV, 5.
[7] For whom it is usual to make a canopy of myrtle.
[8] Kappa in the sense of 'beam' is an Aramaic word (Kofa), while dika in the sense of ten is the Greek The Jer. more plausibly explains kappa as the Greek letter equivalent to twenty, and dokia as representing the Greek , a beam.

R. Hanina said: If one sees a well in a dream, he will behold peace, since it says: And Isaac's servants digged in the valley, and found there a well of living water.[1] R. Nathan said: He will find Torah, since it says, Whoso findeth me findeth life[2] and it is written here, a well of living water.[3] Raba said: It means life literally.

Rab Hanan said: There are three (kinds of dreams which signify] peace, namely, about a river, a bird, and a pot. 'A river', for it is written: Behold I will extend peace to her like a river.[4] 'A bird', for it is written: As birds hovering so will the Lord of Hosts protect Jerusalem.[5] 'A Pot' for it is written, Lord, thou wilt establish[6] peace for us.[7] Said R. Hanina: But this has been said of a pot in which there is no meat, [for it says]:[8] They chop them in pieces, as that which is in the pot and as flesh within the cauldron.[9]

R. Joshua b. Levi said: If one sees a river in his dreams, he should rise early and say: Behold I will extend peace to her like a river,[10](11) before another verse occurs to him, viz., for distress will come in like a river.[11] If one dreams of a bird he should rise early and say: As birds hovering, so will the Lord of Hosts protect,[12] before another verse occurs to him, viz., As a bird that wandereth from her nest, so is a man that wandereth from his place.[13] If one sees a pot in his dreams, he should rise early and say, Lord thou will establish [tishpoth] peace for us,[14] before another verse occurs to him, viz., Set [shefoth] on the pot, set it on.[15] If one sees grapes in his dream, he should rise early and say: I found Israel like grapes in the wilderness,[16] before another verse occurs to him, viz., their grapes are grapes of gall.[17] If one dreams of a mountain, he should rise early and say: How beautiful upon the mountains are the feet of the messenger of good tidings,[18] before another verse occurs to him, viz., for the mountains will I take up a weeping and wailing.[19] If one dreams of a horn he should rise early and say: And it shall come to pass in that day that a great horn shall be blown,[20] before another verse occurs to him, viz., Blow ye the horn of Gibeah.[21] If one sees a dog in his dream, he should rise early and say: But against any of the children of Israel shall not a dog whet his tongue,[22] before another

---

[1] Gen. XXVI, 19.
[2] Prov. VIII, 35.
[3] Lit. 'water of life'.
[4] Isa. LXVI, 12.
[5] Ibid. XXXI, 5.
[6] Heb. tishpoth, which is also used for placing a pot on a fire.
[7] Ibid. XXVI, 12.
[8] V. Marginal Gloss.
[9] Micah III, 3.
[10] Prov. XXVII, 8.
[11] Isa. LIX, 19.
[12] Ezek. XXIV, 3.
[13] Prov. XXVII, 8.
[14] Deut. XXXII, 32.
[15] Ezek. XXIV, 3.
[16] Hos. IX, 10.
[17] Deut. XXXII, 32.
[18] Isa. LII, 7.
[19] Jer. IX, 9.
[20] Isa. XXVII, 13.
[21] Hos. V, 8. This introduces a denunciation.
[22] Ex. XI, 7.

verse occurs to him, viz., Yea, the dogs are greedy.[1] If one sees a lion in his dream he should rise early and say: The lion hath roared, who will not fear?[2] before another verse occurs to him, viz., A lion is gone up from his thicket.[3] If one dreams of shaving, he should rise early and say: And Joseph shaved himself and changed his raiment,[4] before another verse occurs to him, viz., If I be shaven, then my strength will go from me.[5] If one sees a well in his dream, he should rise early and say: A well of living waters,[6] before another verse occurs to him, viz., As a cistern welleth with her waters, so she welleth with her wickedness.[7] If one sees a reed, he should rise early and say, A bruised reed shall he not break,[8] before another verse occurs to him, viz., Behold thou trusteth upon the staff of this bruised reed.[9]

Our Rabbis taught: If one sees a reed [kaneh] in a dream, he may hope for wisdom, for it says: Get [keneh] wisdom.[10] If he sees several reeds, he may hope for understanding, since it says: With all thy getting [kinyaneka] get understanding.[11] R. Zera said: A pumpkin [kara], a palm-heart [kora] wax [kira], and a reed [kanya] are all auspicious in a dream.[12] It has been taught: Pumpkins are shown in a dream only to one who fears heaven with all his might.[13] If one sees an ox in a dream, he should rise early and say: His firstling bullock, majesty is his,[14] before another verse occurs to him, viz., If an ox gore a man.[15]

Our Rabbis taught: There are five sayings in connexion with an ox in a dream. If one [dreams that he] eats of its flesh, he will become rich; if that an ox has gored him, he will have sons who will contend together[16] in the study of the Torah; if that an ox bit him, sufferings will come upon him; if that it kicked him, he will have to go on a long journey; if that he rode upon one, he will rise to greatness. But it has been taught: If he dreamt that he rode upon one,[17] he will die? — There is no contradiction. In the one case the dream is that he rides on the ox, in the other that the ox rode upon him.

If one sees an ass in a dream, he may hope for salvation, as it says, Behold thy king cometh unto thee; he is triumphant and victorious, lowly and riding upon an ass.[18] If one sees a cat in a dream, if in a place where they call it shunara, a beautiful song [shirah na'ah] will be composed for him; if in a

---

[1] Isa. LVI, 11.
[2] Amos III, 8.
[3] Jer. IV, 7.
[4] Gen. XLI, 24.
[5] Judg. XVI, 17. Spoken by Samson.
[6] Cant. IV, 15.
[7] Jer. VI, 7.
[8] Isa. XLII, 3.
[9] Ibid. XXXVI, 6.
[10] Prov. IV, 5.
[11] Ibid. 7.
[12] They all resemble in sound the word 'reed' and hence have a favourable significance.
1.39. Despite their large size they do not grow high above the ground, and are plants symbolic of the Godfearing man who, despite his worth, remains lowly and humble.
2.(R. Nissim, Gaon.)
[13] Deut. XXXIII, 17.
[14] Ex. XXI, 28.
[15] Lit., 'gore' (one another).
[16] The original can equally mean 'it rides upon him'.
[17] Zech. IX, 9.
[18] MS.M. reads: If in a place ... shunara he will undergo a change for the worse; if shunara a beautiful song, etc.

place where they call it shinra, he will undergo a change for the worse [shinnui ra'].[19] If one sees grapes in a dream, if they are white, whether in their season or not in their season, they are a good sign; if black, in their season they are a good sign, not in their season a bad sign.[20] If one sees a white horse in a dream, whether walking gently or galloping, it is a good sign, if a red horse, if walking gently it is a good sign, if galloping it is a bad sign. If one sees Ishmael in a dream, his prayer will be heard.[21] And it must be Ishmael, the son of Abraham, but not an ordinary Arab.[22] If one sees a camel in a dream, death has been decreed for him from heaven and he has been delivered from it. R. Hama b. Hanina said: What is the Scriptural text for this? — I will go down with thee into Egypt, and I will also surely bring thee up again.[23] R. Nahman b. Isaac derives it from here: The Lord also hath put away thy sin, thou shalt not die. If one sees Phineas in a dream, a miracle will be wrought for him. If one sees an elephant [pil] in a dream, wonders [pela'oth] will be wrought for him; if several elephants, wonders of wonders will be wrought for him. But it has been taught: All kinds of beasts are of good omen in a dream except the elephant and the ape? — There is no contradiction.

---

[19] MS.M. adds: He should offer supplication. If (he dreamt) that he had eaten these, he can be assured that he is a son of the world to come.
[20] Cf. Gen. XXI, 17.
[21] Who is also called Ishmael.
[22] Gen. XLVI, 4. The last words in the Hebrew are gam 'aloh, which resemble gamal, 'a camel'.
[23] II Sam. XII, 13. The derivation in this case is not clear; perhaps it is from the word gam 'also' which resembles gamal.

Folio 57a

The elephants are of good omen[1] if saddled, of bad omen if not saddled. If one sees the name Huna in a dream, a miracle will be wrought for him.[2] If one sees the name Hanina, Hananiah or Jonathan, miracles will be wrought for him.[3] If one dreams of a funeral oration [hesped] mercy will be vouchsafed to him from heaven and he will be redeemed.[4] This is only if he sees the word in writing.[5] If one [in a dream] answers, 'May His great name be blessed', he may be assured that he has a share in the future world. If one dreams that he is reciting the Shema', he is worthy that the Divine presence should rest upon him, only his generation is not deserving enough. If one dreams he is putting on tefillin, he may look forward to greatness, for it says: And all the peoples of the earth shall see that the name of the Lord is called upon thee, and they shall fear thee;[6] and it has been taught: R. Eliezer the Great says: This refers to the tefillin of the head.[7] If one dreams he is praying, it is a good sign, for him, provided he does not complete the prayer.[8]

If one dreams that he has intercourse with his mother, he may expect to obtain understanding, since it says, Yea, thou wilt call understanding 'mother'.[9] If one dreams he has intercourse with a betrothed maiden, he may expect to obtain knowledge of Torah, since it says, Moses commanded us a law [Torah], an inheritance of the congregation of Jacob.[10] Read not morashah [inheritance], but me'orasah [betrothed]. If one dreams he has had intercourse with his sister, he may expect to obtain wisdom, since it says, Say to wisdom, thou art my sister.[11] If one dreams he has intercourse with a married woman, he can be confident that he is destined for the future world,[12] provided, that is, that he does not know her and did not think of her in the evening.

R. Hiyya b. Abba said: If one sees wheat in a dream, he will see peace, as it says: He maketh thy borders peace; He giveth thee in plenty the fat of wheat.[13] If one sees barley[14] in a dream, his iniquities will depart, as it says: Thine iniquity is taken away, and thy sin expiated.[15] R. Zera said: I did not go up from Babylon to the Land of Israel until I saw barley in a dream.[16] If one sees in a dream a vine laden with fruit, his wife will not have a miscarriage, since it says, thy wife shall be as a fruitful vine.[17] If one sees a choice vine, he may look forward to seeing the Messiah, since it says,

---

[1] Lit., 'this is ... that is'.
[2] The Hebrew for miracle, nes, also contains the letter nun.
[3] These names contain more than one nun.
[4] Heaped is here connected with hus 'to have pity' and padah 'to redeem'.
[5] And similarly the proper names Huna, etc. enumerated above.
[6] Deut. XXVIII, 10.
[7] V. supra 6a.
[8] I.e., wakes up before it is finished.
[9] Prov. II, 3 with a slight change of reading. E.V. Yea, If thou wilt call forunderstanding.
[10] Deut. XXXIII, 4.
[11] Prov. VII, 4.
[12] The signification being that he obtains his own share and that of his neighbour (Rashi).
[13] Ps. CXLVII, 14.
[14] Se'orim (barley) equals sar 'awon, 'iniquity has departed'.
[15] Isa VI, 7.
[16] A visit to the Holy Land was held to bring with it an expiation for sin.
[17] Ps. CXXVIII, 3.

Binding his foal unto the vine and his ass's colt unto the choice vine.¹ If one sees a fig tree in a dream, his learning will be preserved within him, as it says: Whoso keepeth the fig tree shall eat the fruit thereof.² If one sees pomegranates in a dream, if they are little ones, his business will be fruitful like a pomegranate; if big ones, his business will increase like a pomegranate. If they are split open, if he is a scholar, he may hope to learn more Torah, as it says: I would cause thee to drink of spiced wine, of the juice of my pomegranate;³ if he is unlearned, he may hope to perform precepts, as it says: Thy temples are like a pomegranate split open.⁴ What is meant by 'Thy temples' [rakothek]? — Even the illiterate [rekanim]⁵ among thee are full of precepts like a pomegranate. If one sees olives in a dream, if they are little ones his business will go on fructifying and increasing like an olive. This is if he sees the fruit; but if he sees the tree he will have many sons, as it says: Thy children like olive plants, round about thy table.⁶ Some say that if one sees an olive in his dream he will acquire a good name, as it says, The Lord called thy name a leafy olive-tree, fair and goodly fruit.⁷ If one sees olive oil in a dream, he may hope for the light of the Torah, as it says, That they bring unto thee pure olive oil beaten for the light.⁸ If one sees palm-trees in a dream his iniquities will come to an end, as it says, The punishment of thine iniquity is accomplished, O daughter of Zion.⁹

R. Joseph said: If one sees a goat in a dream, he will have a blessed year; if several goats, several blessed years, as it says: And there will be goat's milk enough for thy food.¹⁰ If one sees myrtle in his dream, he will have good luck with his property,¹¹ and if he has no property he will inherit some from elsewhere. 'Ulla said — according to others, it was taught in a Baraitha: this is only if he sees myrtle on its stem.¹² If one sees citron [hadar] in his dream, he is honoured [hadur] in the sight of his Maker, since it says: The fruit of citrons,¹³ branches of palm-trees.¹⁴ If one sees a palm branch in a dream, he is single-hearted in devotion to his Father in Heaven.¹⁵ If one sees a goose in a dream, he may hope for wisdom, since it says: Wisdom crieth aloud it, the street;¹⁶ and he who dreams of being with one will become head of an academy. R. Ashi said: I saw one and was with one, and I was elevated to a high position.¹⁷ If one sees a cock in a dream he may expect a male child; if several cocks, several sons; if a hen, a fine garden and rejoicing.¹⁸ If one sees eggs in a dream, his petition remains in suspense;¹⁹ if they are broken his petition will be granted. The same with nuts and cucumbers and all vessels of glass and all breakable things like these.

---

¹ Gen. XLIX, 11. This verse is supposed to refer to the Messiah.
² Prov. XXVII, 18.
³ Cant. VIII, 2.
⁴ Ibid. IV, 3.
⁵ Lit., 'the empty ones'.
⁶ Ps. CXXVIII, 3.
⁷ Jer. XI, 16.
⁸ Ex. XX VII, 20.
⁹ Lam. IV, 22. Temarin (palm-trees) suggest tammu morin, 'finished are rebels (sins)'.
¹⁰ Prov. XXVII, 27.
¹¹ Like a myrtle which has numerous leaves.
¹² I.e., attached to the soil.
¹³ E.V. 'Goodly trees'.
¹⁴ Lev. XXIII, 40.
¹⁵ The palm branch having no twigs.
¹⁶ Prov. I, 20.
¹⁷ He became the head of the Academy of Matha Mehasia (a suburb of Sura).
¹⁸ The Hebrew word for cock (tarnegol) suggests these interpretations.
¹⁹ Like the contents of the egg, of which one is doubtful as long as the shell is unbroken (Rashi).

If one dreams that he enters a large town, his desire will be fulfilled, as it says, And He led them unto their desired haven.[1] If one dreams that he is shaving his head, it is a good sign for him; if his head and his beard, for him and for all his family. If one dreams that he is sitting in a small boat, he will acquire a good name; if in a large boat, both he and all his family will acquire one; but this is only if it is on the high sea. If one dreams that he is easing himself, it is a good omen for him, as it is said, He that is bent down shall speedily be loosed,[2] but this is only if he did not wipe himself [in his dream]. If one dreams that he goes up to a roof, he will attain a high position; if that he goes down, he will be degraded. Abaye and Raba, however, both say that once he has attained a high position he will remain there. If one dreams he is tearing his garments, his evil decree[3] will be rent. If one dreams that he is standing naked, if in Babylon he will remain sinless,[4] if in the Land of Israel he will be bare of pious deeds.[5] If one dreams that he has been arrested by the police, protection will be offered him; if that he has been placed in neck-chains,[6] additional protection will be afforded him.
This is only [if he dreams] of neck-chains, not a mere rope. If one dreams that he walks into a marsh, he will become the head of an academy;[7] if into a forest he will become the head of the collegiates.[8]

R. Papa and R. Huna the son of Joshua both had dreams. R. Papa dreamt that he went into a marsh and he became head of an academy.[9] R. Huna the son of R. Joshua dreamt that he went into a forest and he became head of the collegiates. Some say that both dreamt they went into a marsh, but R. Papa who was carrying a drum[10] became head of the academy, while R. Huna the son of R. Joshua who did not carry a drum became only the head of the collegiates. R. Ashi said: I dreamt that I went into a marsh and carried a drum and made a loud noise with it.

A Tanna recited in the presence of R. Nahman b. Isaac: If one dreams that he is undergoing blood-letting, his iniquities are forgiven.[11] But it has been taught: His iniquities are recounted? — What is meant by recounted? Recounted so as to be forgiven.

A Tanna recited in the presence of R. Shesheth: If one sees a serpent in a dream, it means that his living is assured;[12] if it bites him it will be doubled; if he kills it he will lose his living. R. Shesheth said to him: [In this case] all the more will his living be doubled! This is not so, however; R. Shesheth [explained thus] because he saw a serpent in his dream and killed it.[13]

A Tanna recited in the presence of R. Johanan: All kinds of drinks are a good sign in a dream except wine; sometimes one may drink it and it turns out well and sometimes one may drink it and it turns

---

[1] Ps. CVII, 30.
[2] Isa. LI, 14.
[3] The evil decreed against him from heaven.
[4] V. Keth. 110b. He who dwells outside the Land of Israel is as though he worshipped idols. To stand naked in a dream in Babylon hence means to be sinless.
[5] V. Keth. 111a. He who dwells in the Land abides sinless. To stand naked in a dream in Palestine hence means to be bare of pious deeds.
[6] With which criminals were strung together to be led to execution.
[7] Short and long reeds in a marsh are figurative of the students of different ages and standards attending the Academy.
[8] The full-grown trees in a forest represent the mature students who meet often for discussion and study. V., however, Rashi.
[9] He became the head of the school in Naresh, near Sura.
[10] Such as was used for announcing the approach of a man of distinction.
[11] Sins are described as crimson, cf. Isa. I, 18.
[12] Because the serpent eats dust of which there is always abundance.
[13] And he wished to give his dream a favourable interpretation.

out ill. 'Sometimes one may drink it and it turns out well', as it says: Wine that maketh glad the heart of man'.[1] 'Sometimes one may drink it and it turns out ill', as it says: Give strong drink unto him that is ready to perish, and wine unto the bitter in soul.'[2] Said R. Johanan unto the Tanna: Teach that for a scholar it is always good, as it says: Come eat of my bread and drink of the wine which I have mingled.[3]

---

[1] Ps. CIV, 15.
[2] Prov. XXXI, 6.
[3] Ibid. IX, 5.

Berakoth 57b

R. Johanan said: If at the moment of rising a text occurs to one, this is a minor kind of prophecy.

Our Rabbis taught there are three kings [who are important for dreams]. If one sees David in a dream, he may hope for piety; if Solomon, he may hope for wisdom; if Ahab, let him fear for punishment. There are three prophets [of significance for dreams]. If one sees the Book of Kings, he may look forward to greatness; if Ezekiel, he may look forward to wisdom; if Isaiah he may look forward to consolation; if Jeremiah, let him fear for punishment. There are three larger books of the Hagiographa [which are significant for dreams]. If one sees the Book of Psalms, he may hope for piety; if the Book of Proverbs, he may hope for wisdom; if the Book of Job, let him fear for punishment. There are three smaller books of the Hagiographa [significant for dreams]. If one sees the Songs of Songs in a dream, he may hope for piety;[1] if Ecclesiastes, he may hope for wisdom; if Lamentations, let him fear for punishment; and one who sees the Scroll of Esther will have a miracle wrought for him. There are three Sages [significant for dreams]. If one sees Rabbi in a dream, he may hope for wisdom; if Eleazar b. Azariah, he may hope for riches;[2] if
R. Ishmael b. Elisha, let him fear for punishment.[3] There are three disciples[4] [significant for dreams]. If one sees Ben 'Azzai in a dream, he may hope for piety; if Ben Zoma, he may hope for wisdom; if Aher,[5] let him fear for punishment.

All kinds of beasts are a good sign in a dream, except the elephant, the monkey and the long-tailed ape. But a Master has said: If one sees an elephant in a dream, a miracle will be wrought for him?[6] — There is no contradiction; in the latter case it is saddled, in the former case it is not saddled. All kinds of metal implements are a good sign in a dream, except a hoe, a mattock, and a hatchet; but this is only if they are seen in their hafts.[7] All kinds of fruit are a good sign in a dream, except unripe dates. All kinds of vegetables are a good sign in a dream, except turnip-tops. But did not Rab say: I did not become rich until I dreamt of turnip-tops? — When he saw them, it was on their stems.[8] All kinds of colours are a good sign in a dream, except blue.[9] All kinds[10] of birds are a good sign in a dream, except the owl, the horned owl and the bat.

(Mnemonic: The body, The body, Reflex, Restore, Self-esteem.) Three things enter the body without benefiting it: melilot,[11] dateberries, and unripe dates. Three things benefit the body without being absorbed by it: washing, anointing, and regular motion. Three things are a reflex of the world to

---

[1] The Song of Songs being calculated to implant in the reader the love of God.
[2] R. Eleazar was very wealthy.
[3] R. Ishmael suffered martyrdom under the Romans, v. Halevi, Doroth I, p. 309.
[4] Who became authorities though they were never ordained as Rabbis.
[5] Elisha b. Abuya, called Aher (lit., 'Another') when he came a renegade, v. Hag. 15a.
[6] V. supra 56b.
[7] Otherwise they portend blows, as stated above.
[8] I.e., attached to the soil.
[9] The colour of sickness.
[10] MS.M. inserts: 'of reptiles are a good sign in a dream except the mole. All kinds'.
[11] A kind of clover.

come: Sabbath, sunlight, and tashmish.[1] Tashmish of what? Shall I say of the bed?[2] This weakens. It must be then tashmish of the orifices. Three things restore a man's good spirits: [beautiful] sounds, sights, and smells. Three things increase a man's self-esteem:[3] a beautiful dwelling, a beautiful wife, and beautiful clothes.

(Mnemonic: Five, Six, Ten.) Five things are a sixtieth part of something else: namely, fire, honey, Sabbath, sleep and a dream. Fire is one-sixtieth part of Gehinnom. Honey is one-sixtieth part of manna. Sabbath is one-sixtieth part of the world to come. Sleep is one-sixtieth part of death. A dream is one-sixtieth part of prophecy.

Six things are a good sign for a sick person, namely, sneezing, perspiration, open bowels, seminal emission, sleep and a dream. Sneezing, as it is written: His sneezings flash forth light.[4] Perspiration, as it is written, In the sweat of thy face shalt thou eat bread.[5]
Open bowels, as it is written: If lie that is bent down hasteneth to be loosed, he shall not go down dying to the pit.[6] Seminal emission, as it is written: Seeing seed, he will prolong his days.[7] Sleep, as it is written: I should have slept, then should I have been at rest.[8] A dream, as it is written: Thou didst cause me to dream and make me to live.[9]

Six things heal a man of his sickness with a complete cure, namely, cabbage, beet, a decoction of dried poley, the maw [of an animal], the womb, and the large lobe of the liver. Some add small fishes, which [not only have this advantage] but also make fruitful and invigorate a man's whole body.

Ten things bring a man's sickness on again in a severe form, namely, to eat beef, fat meat, roast meat, poultry and roasted egg, shaving, and eating cress, milk or cheese, and bathing. Some add, also nuts; and some add further, also cucumbers. It was taught in the school of
R. Ishmael: Why are they called kishshu'im [cucumbers]? Because they are painful [kashim] for the body like swords. Is that so? See, it is written: And the Lord said unto her, Two nations are in thy womb.[10] Read not goyim [nations] but ge'im [lords], and Rab Judah said in the name of Rab: These are Antoninus and Rabbi, whose table never lacked either radish, lettuce or cucumbers either in summer or winter![11] — There is no contradiction; the former statement speaks of large ones, the latter of small ones.

Our Rabbis taught: [If one dreams of] a corpse in the house, it is a sign of peace in the house; if that he was eating and drinking in the house, it is a good sign for the house; if that he took articles from the house, it is a bad sign for the house. R. Papa explained it to refer to a shoe or sandal. Anything that the dead person [is seen in the dream] to take away is a good sign except a shoe and a sandal; anything that it puts down is a good sign except dust and mustard.

---

[1] Lit., 'service'.
[2] I.e., sexual intercourse.
[3] Lit., 'enlarge his spirit'.
[4] Job XLI, 10.
[5] Gen. III, 19.
[6] Isa. LI, 14. E.V. 'He that is bent down shall speedily, etc.'.
[7] Ibid. LIII, 10.
[8] Job. III, 13.
[9] Isa. XXXVIII, 16. V. p. 335, n. 10.
[10] Gen. XXV, 23.
[11] V. A.Z. (Sonc. ed.) p. 50, n. 3.

A PLACE FROM WHICH IDOLATRY HAS BEEN UPROOTED. Our Rabbis taught: If one sees a statue of Hermes,[1] he says, Blessed be He who shows long suffering to those who transgress His will. If he sees a place from which idolatry has been uprooted, he says, Blessed be He who uprooted idolatry from our land; and as it has been uprooted from this place, so may it be uprooted from all places belonging to Israel; and do Thou turn the heart of those that serve them[2] to serve Thee. Outside Palestine it is not necessary to say: Turn the heart of those that serve them to serve Thee, because most of them are idolaters.

R. Simeon b. Eleazar says: Outside Palestine also one should say this, because they will one day become proselytes, as it says, For then will I turn to the peoples a pure language.[3]

R. Hamnuna said in a discourse: If one sees the wicked Babylon, he should say five benedictions: On seeing [the city] Babylon itself he says, Blessed be He who has destroyed the wicked Babylon. On seeing the palace of Nebuchadnezzar, he says, Blessed be He who destroyed the palace of the wicked Nebuchadnezzar. On seeing the lions' den, or the fiery furnace, he says, Blessed be He who wrought miracles for our ancestors[4] in this place. On seeing the statue of Hermes, he says, Blessed be He who shows long suffering to those that transgress His will. On seeing the place from which dust is carried away,[5] he says, Blessed be He who says and does, who decrees and carries out. Rab, when he saw asses carrying dust, used to give them a slap on the back and say, Run, ye righteous ones, to perform the will of your Master. When Mar the son of Rabina came to [the city of] Babylon, he used to put some dust in his kerchief and throw it out, to fulfil the text, I will sweep it with the besom of destruction. R. Ashi said: I had never heard this saying of
R. Hamnuna, but of my own sense I made all these blessings.

---

[1] Heb. Markolis, the Latin Mercurius. This was the commonest of the heathenimages.
[2] I.e., of renegade Israelites.
[3] Zeph. III, 9.
[4] Daniel and Hananiah, Mishael and Azariah.
1.27. The ruins of the city of Babylon from which earth was taken for building elsewhere,
2.v. Obermeyer, p. 303.
[5] Isa. XIV, 23.

Folio 58a

R. Jeremiah b. Eleazar said: When Babylon was cursed, her neighbours were also cursed; but when Samaria was cursed, her neighbours were blessed. 'When Babylon was cursed her neighbours were cursed', as it is written: I will also make it a possession for the bittern and pools of water.[1] 'When Samaria was cursed her neighbours were blessed', as it is written: Therefore I will make Samaria a heap in the field, a place for the planting of vineyards.[2]

R. Hamnuna further said: If one sees a crowd of Israelites, he should say: Blessed is He who discerneth secrets.[3] If he sees a crowd of heathens, he should say: Your mother shall be ashamed, etc.[4]

Our Rabbis taught: If one sees a crowd of Israelites, he says, Blessed is He who discerneth secrets, for the mind of each is different from that of the other, just as the face of each is different from that of the other. Ben Zoma once saw a crowd on one of the steps of the Temple Mount. He said, Blessed is He that discerneth secrets, and blessed is He who has created all these to serve me. [For] he used to say: What labours Adam had to carry out before he obtained bread to eat! He ploughed, he sowed, he reaped, he bound [the sheaves], he threshed and winnowed and selected the ears, he ground [them], and sifted [the flour], he kneaded and baked, and then at last he ate; whereas I get up, and find all these things done for me. And how many labours Adam had to carry out before he obtained a garment to wear! He had to shear, wash [the wool], comb it, spin it and weave it, and then at last he obtained a garment to wear; whereas I get up and find all these things done for me. All kinds of craftsmen[5] come early to the door of my house, and I rise in the morning and find all these before me.

He used to say: What does a good guest say? 'How much trouble my host has taken for me! How much meat he has set before me! How much wine he has set before me! How many cakes he has set before me! And all the trouble he has taken was only for my sake!' But what does a bad guest say? 'How much after all has mine host put himself out? I have eaten one piece of bread, I have eaten one slice of meat, I have drunk one cup of wine! All the trouble which my host has taken was only for the sake of his wife and his children!' What does Scripture say of a good guest? Remember that thou magnify his works, where of men have sung.[6] But of a bad guest it is written: Men do therefore fear him; [he regardeth not any that are wise of heart].[7]

And the man was an old man in the days of Saul, stricken in years among men.[8] Raba (or, as some say, R. Zebid; or again, as some say, R. Oshaia) said: This is Jesse, the father of David, who went out with a crowd and came in with a crowd, and expounded [the Torah] to a crowd. 'Ulla said: We have a

---

[1] Ibid. The whole neighbourhood of Babylon became desolate.
[2] Micah I, 6.
[3] Lit., 'wise in secrets'. Vi., the secrets of each one's heart.
[4] Jer. L, 12.
[5] So Marginal Gloss. Cur. edd. 'peoples'.
[6] Job XXXVI, 24.
[7] Ibid. XXXVII, 24.
[8] I Sam. XVII, 12.

tradition that there is no crowd¹ in Babylon. It was taught: A multitude is not less than sixty myriads.

Our Rabbis taught: On seeing the Sages of Israel one should say: Blessed be He who hath imparted of His wisdom to them that fear Him. On seeing the Sages of other nations, one says, Blessed be He who hath imparted of His wisdom to His creatures. On seeing kings of Israel, one says: Blessed be He who hath imparted of His glory to them that fear Him. On seeing non-Jewish kings, one says: Blessed be He who hath imparted of His glory to His creatures. R. Johanan said: A man should always exert himself and run to meet an Israelitish king; and not only a king of Israel but also a king of any other nation, so that if he is deemed worthy,² he will be able to distinguish between the kings of Israel and the kings of other nations.

R. Shesheth was blind. Once all the people went out to see the king, and R. Shesheth arose and went with them. A certain Sadducean³ came across him and said to him: The whole pitchers go to the river, but where do the broken ones go to?⁴ He replied: I will show you that I know more than you. The first troop passed by and a shout arose. Said the Sadducean: The king is coming. He is not coming, replied R. Shesheth. A second troop passed by and when a shout arose, the Sadducean said: Now the king is coming. R. Shesheth replied: The king is not coming. A third troop passed by and there was silence. Said R. Shesheth: Now indeed the king is coming. The Sadducean said to him: How did you know this? — He replied: Because the earthly royalty is like the heavenly. For it is written: Go forth and stand upon the mount before the Lord. And behold, the Lord passed by and a great and strong wind rent the mountains, and broke in pieces the rocks before the Lord; but the Lord was not in the wind; and after the wind an earthquake; but the Lord was not in the earthquake; and after the earthquake a fire; but the Lord was not in the fire; and after the fire a still small voice.⁵ When the king came, R. Shesheth said the blessing over him. The Sadducean said to him: You, you say a blessing for one whom you do not see? What happened to that Sadducean? Some say that his companions put his eyes out; others say that R. Shesheth cast his eyes upon him and he became a heap of bones.

R. Shila administered lashes to a man who had intercourse with an Egyptian⁶ woman. The man went and informed against him to the Government, saying: There is a man among the Jews who passes judgment without the permission of the Government. An official was sent to [summon] him. When he came he was asked: Why did you flog that man? He replied: Because he had intercourse with a she-ass. They said to him: Have you witnesses? He replied: I have. Elijah thereupon came in the form of a man and gave evidence. They said to him: If that is the case he ought to be put to death! He replied: Since we have been exiled from our land, we have no authority to put to death; do you do with him what you please. While they were considering his case, R. Shila exclaimed, Thine, Oh Lord, is the greatness and the power.⁷ What are you saying? they asked him. He replied: What I am saying is this: Blessed is the All-Merciful Who has made the earthly royalty on the model of the heavenly, and has invested you with dominion, and made you lovers of justice. They said to him: Are you so solicitous for the honour of the Government? They handed him a staff⁸ and said to him: You may act as judge.

---

¹ Of Israelites assembled to hear the Torah.
² Of the Messianic age.
³ MS.M. min (v. Glos.).
⁴ As much as to say: What is the use of a blind man going to see the king.
⁵ 1 Kings XIX, 11f.
⁶ Var. lec. Gentile.
⁷ I Chron. XXIX, 11.
⁸ Or perhaps, 'strap' (J.T.).

When he went out that man said to him: Does the All-Merciful perform miracles for liars? He replied: Wretch! Are they not called asses? For it is written: Whose flesh is as the flesh of asses.[1] He noticed that the man was about to inform them that he had called them asses. He said: This man is a persecutor, and the Torah has said: If a man comes to kill you, rise early and kill him first.[2] So he struck him with the staff and killed him. He then said: Since a miracle has been wrought for me through this verse, I will expound it. 'Thine, Oh Lord, is the greatness': this refers to the work of creation; and so it says: Who doeth great things past finding out.[3] 'And the power': this refers to the Exodus from Egypt, as it says: And Israel saw the great work, etc.[4] 'And the glory': this refers to the sun and moon which stood still for Joshua, as it says: And the sun stood still and the moon stayed.[5] 'And the victory [nezah]': this refers to the fall of Rome,[6] as it says: And their life-blood [nizham] is dashed against my garments.[7] 'And the majesty': this refers to the battle of the valleys of Arnon, as it says, Wherefore it is said in the book of the wars of the Lord: Vaheb in Supah, and the valleys of Arnon.[8] 'For all that is in heaven and earth': this refers to the war of Sisera, as it says: They fought front heaven, the stars in their courses fought against Sisera.[9] 'Thine is the kingdom, O Lord': this refers to the war against Amalek. For so it says: The hand upon the throne of the Lord, the Lord will have war with Amalek from generation to generation.[10] 'And Thou art exalted': this refers to the war of Gog and Magog; and so it says: Behold I am against thee, Oh Gog, chief prince of Meshech and Tubal.[11] 'As head above all': R. Hanan b. Raba said in the name of R. Johanan: Even a waterman[12] is appointed from heaven. It was taught in a Baraitha in the name of R. Akiba: 'Thine, oh Lord, is the greatness': this refers to the cleaving of the Red Sea. 'And the power': this refers to the smiting of the first-born. 'And the glory': this refers to the giving of the Torah. 'And the victory': this refers to Jerusalem. 'And the majesty': this refers to the Temple.

---

[1] Ezek. XXIII, 20.

[2] This lesson is derived by the Rabbis from Ex. XXII, 1 which declares it legitimate to kill a burglar who is prepared to commit murder.

[3] Job. IX, 10.

[4] Ex. XIV, 31.

[5] Josh. X, 13.

[6] MS.M.: The wicked kingdom.

[7] Isa. LXIII, 3.

[8] Num. XXI, 14.

[9] Judg. V, 20.

[10] Ex. XVII, 16.

[11] Ezek. XXXVIII, 3.

[12] A man who looked after the well from which fields were irrigated — quite a menial office.

Berakoth 58b

Our Rabbis taught: On seeing the houses of Israel, when inhabited one says: Blessed be He who sets the boundary of the widow;[1] when uninhabited, Blessed be the judge of truth. On seeing the houses of heathens, when inhabited, one says: The Lord will pluck up the house of the proud;[2] when uninhabited he says: O Lord, thou God, to whom vengeance belongeth, thou God, to whom vengeance belongeth, shine forth.[3]

Once when 'Ulla and R. Hisda Were walking along the road, they came to the door of the house of R. Hana b. Hanilai. R. Hisda broke down and sighed. Said 'Ulla to him: Why are you sighing, seeing that Rab has said that a sigh breaks half a man's body, since it says, Sigh therefore thou son of man, with the breaking of thy loins,[4] etc.; and R. Johanan said that it breaks even the whole of a man's body, as it says: And it shall be, when they say unto thee, wherefore sighest thou? Thou shalt say: Because of the tidings for it cometh; and every heart shall melt, etc.?[5] — He replied: How shall I refrain from sighing on seeing the house in which there used to be sixty[6] cooks by day and sixty cooks by night, who cooked for every one who was in need. Nor did he [R. Hana] ever take his hand away from his purse, thinking that perhaps a respectable poor man might come, and while he was getting his purse he would be put to shame. Moreover it had four doors, opening on different sides, and whoever went in hungry went out full. They used also to throw wheat and barley outside in years of scarcity, so that anyone who was ashamed to take by day used to come and take by night. Now it has fallen in ruins, and shall I not sigh? — He replied to him: Thus said R. Johanan: Since the day when the Temple was destroyed a decree has been issued against the houses of the righteous that they should become desolate, as it says: In mine ears, said the Lord of hosts: Of a truth many houses shall be desolate, even great and fair, without inhabitants.[7] R. Johanan further said: The Holy One, blessed be He, will one day restore them to their inhabited state, as it says: A Song of Ascents. They that trust in the Lord are as Mount Zion.[8] Just as the Holy One, blessed be He, will restore Mount Zion to its inhabited state, so will He restore the houses of the righteous to their inhabited state. Observing that he was still not satisfied, he said to him: Enough for the servant that he should be like his master.[9]

Our Rabbis taught: On seeing Israelitish graves, one should say: Blessed is He who fashioned you in judgments who fed you in judgment and maintained you in judgment, and in judgment gathered you in, and who will one day raise you up again in judgment. Mar, the son of Rabina, concluded thus in the name of R. Nahman: And who knows the number of all of you; and He will one day revive you and establish you. Blessed is He who revives the dead.[10] On seeing the graves of heathens one says:

---

[1] Sc., Jerusalem.
[2] Prov. XV, 25.
[3] Ps. XCIV, 1.
[4] Ezek. XXI, 11.
[5] Ibid. 22.
[6] I.e., a great many.
[7] Isa. V, 9.
[8] Ps. CXXV, 1.
[9] I.e., that R. Hana's house should be like the house of God.
[10] V. P.B. p. 319.

Your mother shall be sore ashamed, etc.

R. Joshua b. Levi said: One who sees a friend after a lapse of thirty days says: Blessed is He who has kept us alive and preserved us and brought us to this season. If after a lapse of twelve months he says: Blessed is He who revives the dead. Rab said: The dead is not forgotten till after twelve months, as it says: I am forgotten as a dead man out of mind; I am like a lost vessel.[1] R. Papa and R. Huna the son of R. Joshua were once going along the road when they met R. Hanina, the son of R. Ika. They said to him: Now that we see you we make two blessings over you: 'Blessed be He who has imparted of His wisdom to them that fear Him', and 'That has kept us alive etc.'. He said to them: I, also, on seeing you counted it as equal to seeing sixty myriads of Israel, and I made three blessings over you, those two, and 'Blessed is He that discerneth secrets'. They said to him: Are you so clever as all that? They cast their eyes on him and he died.[2]

R. Joshua b. Levi said: On seeing pock-marked persons one says: Blessed be He who makes strange creatures. An objection was raised: If one sees a negro, a very red or very white person, a hunchback, a dwarf or a dropsical person, he says: Blessed be He who makes strange creatures. If he sees one with an amputated limb, or blind, or flatheaded, or lame, or smitten with boils, or pock-marked, he says: Blessed be the true Judge! — There is no contradiction; one blessing is said if he is so from birth, the other if he became so afterwards. A proof of this is that he is placed in the same category as one with an amputated limb; this proves it.

Our Rabbis taught: On seeing an elephant, an ape, or a long-tailed ape, one says: Blessed is He who makes strange creatures. If one sees beautiful creatures and beautiful trees, he says: Blessed is He who has such in His world.

OVER SHOOTING-STARS [ZIKIN]. What are ZIKIN? Samuel said: A comet.[3] Samuel also said: I am as familiar with the paths of heaven as with the streets of Nehardea, with the exception of the comet, about which I am ignorant. There is a tradition that it never passes through the constellation of Orion, for if it did, the world would be destroyed. But we have seen it pass through? — Its brightness passed through, which made it appear as if it passed through itself. R. Huna the son of R. Joshua said: Wilon[4] was torn asunder and rolled up,[5] showing the brightness of Rakia.[6] R. Ashi said: A star was removed from one side of Orion and a companion star appeared on the other side, and people were bewildered and thought the star had crossed over.[7]

Samuel contrasted two texts. It is written, Who maketh the Bear, Orion, and the Pleiades.[8] And it is written elsewhere, That maketh Pleiades and Orion.[9] How do we reconcile these? Were it not for the heat of Orion the world could not endure the cold of Pleiades; and were it not for the cold of Pleiades the world could not endure the heat of Orion. There is a tradition that were it not that the tail of the

---

[1] Ps. XXXI, 13. A thing is not given up as lost till after twelve months.
[2] Apparently they thought he was sarcastic.
[3] Kokeba di-Shabi Lit., 'Star that draws'. What exactly is meant is a matter of dispute. Rashi explains as 'shooting-stars'.
[4] The lowest of the seven firmaments, which is a kind of 'Veil' to the others.
[5] Rashi and Tosaf. omit 'and rolled up'.
[6] Lit., 'firmament'. The next of the seven firmaments.
[7] I.e., mere error of perspective, v. on the passage Brodetsky, Jewish Review July, 1909, p. 167 ff.
[8] Job IX, 9.
[9] Amos V, 8. The order is here reversed.

Scorpion has been placed in the Stream of Fire,[1] no one who has ever been stung by a scorpion could live. This is what is referred to in the words of the All-Merciful to Job: Canst thou bind the chains of Pleiades or loose the bands of Orion?[2]

What is meant by Kimah [Pleiades]?[3] Samuel said: About a hundred [ke'me-ah] stars. Some say they are close together; others say that they are scattered. What is meant by "Ash [the Bear]'?[4] — Rab Judah said: Jutha. What is Jutha? — Some say it is the tail of the Ram; others say it is the hand of the Calf.[5] The one who says it is the tail of the Ram is more probably right, since it says: 'Ayish will be comforted for her children.[6] This shows that it lacks something,

---

[1] Mentioned in Dan. VII, 10, denoting probably the Milky Way.
[2] Job. XXXVIII, 31.
[3] Job IX, 9.
[4] Job IX, 9.
[5] This constellation follows that of the Ram.
[6] Ibid. 32. E.V. 'or canst thou guide the Bear with her sons'.

Folio 59a

and in fact it looks like a piece torn off;[1] and the reason why she follows her is because she is saying to her: Give me my children. For at the time when the Holy One, blessed be He, wanted to bring a flood upon the world, He took two stars from Kimah and brought a flood upon the world. And when He wanted to stop it, He took two stars from 'Ayish and stopped it. But why did He not put the other two back? — A pit cannot be filled with its own clods;[2] or another reason is, the accuser cannot become advocate. Then He should have created two other stars for it? — There is nothing new under the sun.[3] R. Nahman said: The Holy one, blessed be He, will one day restore them to her, as it says: and 'Ayish will be comforted for her children.[4]

AND OVER EARTHQUAKES [ZEWA'OTH]. What are ZEWA'OTH? R. Kattina said: A rumbling of the earth. R. Kattina was once going along the road, and when he came to the door of the house of a certain necromancer, there was a rumbling of the earth. He said: Does the necromancer know what this rumbling is? He called after him, Kattina, Kattina, why should I not know? When the Holy One, blessed be He, calls to mind His children, who are plunged in suffering among the nations of the world, He lets fall two tears into the ocean, and the sound is heard from one end of the world to the other, and that is the rumbling. Said R. Kattina: The necromancer is a liar and his words are false. If it was as he says, there should be one rumbling after another! He did not really mean this, however. There really was one rumbling after another, and the reason why he did not admit it was so that people should not go astray after him. R. Kattina, for his own part, said: [God] clasps His hands, as it says: I will also smite my hands together, and I will satisfy my fury.[5] R. Nathan said: [God] emits a sigh, as it is said: I will satisfy my fury upon them and I will be eased.[6] And the Rabbis said: He treads upon the firmament, as it says: He giveth a noise as they that tread grapes against all the inhabitants of the earth.[7] R. Aha b. Jacob says: He presses his feet together beneath the throne of glory, as it says: Thus saith the Lord, the heaven is my throne and the earth is my foot-stool.[8]

AND OVER THUNDERS [RE'AMIM]. What are RE'AMIM? — Clouds in a whirl, as it says: The voice of Thy thunder was in the whirlwind; the lightning lighted up the world, the earth trembled and shook.[9] The Rabbis, however, say: The clouds pouring water into one another, as it says: At the sound of His giving a multitude of waters in the heavens.[10] R. Aha b. Jacob said: A powerful lightning flash that strikes the clouds and breaks off hailstones. R. Ashi said: The clouds are puffed out and a blast of wind comes and blows across the mouth of them and it makes a sound like wind blowing across the mouth of a jar. The most probable view is that of R. Aha b. Jacob; for the lightning flashes and the clouds rumble and then rain falls.

---

[1] And then stuck on artificially.
[2] V. supra, p. 10, n. 1.
[3] Eccl. 1, 9.
[4] Job. XXXVIII, 32. E.V. 'or canst thou guide the Bear with her sons'.
[5] Ezek. XXI, 22.
[6] Ibid. V, 13.
[7] Jer. XXV, 30.
[8] Isa. LXVI, 1.
[9] Ps. LXXVII, 19.
[10] Jer. X, 13.

AND OVER STORMS [RUHOTH]. What are RUHOTH? — Abaye said: A hurricane. Abaye further said: We have a tradition that a hurricane never comes at night. But we see that it does come? — It must have commenced by day. Abaye further said: We have a tradition that a hurricane does not last two hours, to fulfil the words of Scripture, Troubles shall not rise up the second time.[1] But we have seen it lasting as long? — There was an interval in the middle.

OVER LIGHTNINGS [BERAKIM] ONE SAYS, BLESSED IS HE WHOSE STRENGTH AND MIGHT FILL THE WORLD. What are BERAKIM? Raba said: Lightning. Rab also said: A single flash, white lightning, blue lightning, clouds that rise in the west and come from the south, and two clouds that rise facing one another are all [signs of] trouble. What is the practical bearing of this remark? That prayer is needed [to avert the omen]. This is only the case by night; but in the daytime there is no significance in them. R. Samuel b. Isaac said: Those morning clouds have no significance,[2] as it is said: Your goodness is as a morning cloud.[3] Said R. Papa to Abaye: But there is a popular saying: When on opening the door you find rain, ass-driver, put down your sack and go to sleep [on it]?[4]
— There is no contradiction; in the one case the sky is covered with thick clouds, in the other with light clouds.
R. Alexandri said in the name of R. Joshua b. Levi: Thunder was created only to straighten out the crookedness of the heart, as it says: God hath so made it that men should fear before him.[5] R. Alexandri also said in the name of R. Joshua b. Levi: One who sees the rainbow in the clouds should fall on his face, as it says, As the appearance of the bow that is in the cloud, and when I saw it I fell upon my face.[6] In the West [Palestine] they cursed anyone who did this, because it looks as if he was bowing down to the rainbow; but he certainly makes a blessing. What blessing does he say? — 'Blessed is He who remembers the Covenant'. In a Baraitha it was taught: R. Ishmael the son of R. Johanan b. Beroka says: He says: Who is faithful with his Covenant and fulfils his word.

FOR MOUNTAINS AND HILLS, etc. Do all the things we have mentioned hitherto not belong to the work of creation? Is it not written, He maketh lightnings for the rain?[7] — Abaye said: Combine the two statements.[8] Raba said: In the former cases he says two blessings, 'Blessed be He whose strength fills the world and who has wrought the work of creation'; in this case there is ground for saying 'Who has wrought creation' but not for 'Whose strength fills the world'.[9]

R. Joshua b. Levi said: If one sees the sky in all its purity, he says: Blessed is He who has wrought the work of creation. When does he say so? — Abaye said: When there has been rain all the night, and in the morning the north wind comes and clears the heavens. And they differ from Rafram b. Papa quoting R. Hisda. For Rafram b. Papa said in the name of
R. Hisda: Since the day when the Temple was destroyed there has never been a perfectly clear sky, since it says: I clothe the heavens with blackness

---

[1] Nahum I, 9.
[2] I.e., do not portend a good fall of rain.
[3] Hosea VI, 4.
[4] Because corn will be cheap on account of the abundant rain.
[5] Eccl. III, 14.
[6] Ezek. I, 28.
[7] Ps. CXXXV, 7.
[8] I.e., say in all cases the double blessing.
[9] Because the mountains are not all in one place.

Berakoth 59b

and I make a sackcloth their covering.[1]

Our Rabbis taught:[2] He who sees the sun at its turning point,[3] the moon in its power,[4] the planets in their orbits,[5] and the signs of the zodiac in their orderly progress,[6] should say: Blessed be He who has wrought the work of creation. And when [does this happen]?[7] — Abaye said: Every twenty-eight years when the cycle[8] begins again and the Nisan [Spring] equinox falls in Saturn on the evening of Tuesday,[9] going into Wednesday.

---

[1] Isa. L. 3.

1.2. (*) Note 6 [note 3 on this web page] and the notes on the following page are based on material supplied by the late Dr. W. M. Feldman, M.D., B.S., F.R.C.P., F.R.A.S.,
2.F.R.S. (Edin.), shortly before his death on July 1st, 1939.

[2] In its apparent motion in the ecliptic, the sun has four 'turning points' which mark the beginnings of the four respective seasons. These points are generically referred to as the tekufoth (sing. tekufah). They are: the two equinoctial points when the sun crosses the equator at the beginning of spring and autumn respectively, and 'turns' from one side of the equator to the other; and the two solstices, when the sun is at its maximum distance, or declination, from the equator, at one or other side of it, at the beginning of summer and winter respectively, and instead of progressively increasing its declination it 'turns' to decrease it progressively. (It may be mentioned that the term 'tekufah' is also used not only for the beginning of a season but for the whole of the season itself.)

[3] As the sun and moon were created to rule the day and night respectively (Gen. I, 16), they are necessarily endowed with the attribute of power (cf. Sabbath Liturgy) . In this passage, however, 'the moon in its power' may have a special significance, because at the Nisan, or spring equinox, the spring tides are greatest, owing to the combined action of the sun and the moon in conjunction, or new moon. The moon in its power to cause tides (a fact known to Pliny and Aristotle, and referred to by Maimonides (Guide II, 10), although never directly mentioned in the Talmud), is therefore best seen at this time.

[4] The orbits of the planets which are now known to be ellipses, were, on the Ptolemaic system, which prevailed at that time, assumed to be traced out by a most ingenious combination of eccentric circles and epicycles, (v. for instance, the epicyclic theory of the moon in Feldman W.M., Rabbinical Mathematics and Astronomy, London, 1931, pp. 132ff). Hence the contemplation of the planets in their orbits was an adequate reason for pronouncing the blessing.

[5] The vernal or autumnal equinox is not a fixed point in relation to the signs of the zodiac, but keeps on changing its position to the extent of 50.1". (50.1 seconds of arc) per year. This movement which is called 'precession of the equinoxes' is due to the continual shifting of the point of intersection of the ecliptic with the equator, but was believed by the ancients to be due to the progressive movement of the signs of the zodiac. As the result of precession, the equinoctial point which 2,000 years ago was the beginning of the sign Ram (first point of Aries) has since shifted 30" to the sign Pisces, although it is still spoken of as the first point of Aries.

[6] The reference is to the sun at its turning point (Rashi).

[7] This means here the Big or Solar Cycle. Taking a Samuel, or Julian, year to consist of 365 1/4 days or 52 weeks 1/4 days, every tekufah occurs 1 1/4 days later in the week every consecutive year, so that after 4 years it occurs at the same time of the day but (1 1/4 X 4 =) 5 days later in the week. After 28, or 4 X 7 years, the tekufah will recur not only at the same time of the day, but also on the same day of the week. V. Feldman, op. cit. p. 199.

[8] As the sun and moon were created on the 4th day, the beginning of the 28 years cycle is always on a Wednesday which begins at the vernal equinox at 6 p.m. on Tuesday. This, according to computation coincides with the rise of Saturn, v. Rashi.

[9] Because it was supposed that the River Euphrates from that point upwards had never changed its course since

R. JUDAH SAYS: IF ONE SEES THE GREAT SEA etc. How long must the intervals be? Rami b. Abba said in the name of R. Isaac: From thirty days. Rami b. Abba also said in the name of R. Isaac: If one sees the River Euphrates by the Bridge of Babylon, he says: Blessed is He who has wrought the work of creation.[1] Now, however, that the Persians have changed it,[2] only if he sees it from Be Shapor[3] and upwards. R. Joseph says: From Ihi Dekira[4] and upwards. Rami b. Abba also said: If one sees the Tigris by the Bridge of Shabistana,[5] he says: Blessed is He who wrought the work of creation. Why is it [the Tigris] called Hiddekel?[6] — R. Ashi said: Because its waters are sharp [had] and swift [kal]. Why is it [the Euphrates] called Perath? — Because its waters are fruitful [parim] and multiply. Raba also said: The reason why people of Mahoza are so sharp is because they drink the waters of the Tigris; the reason why they have red spots is because they indulge in sexual intercourse in the daytime; the reason why their eyes blink is because they live in dark houses.[7]

FOR THE RAIN etc. Is the benediction for rain 'Who is good and does good'? Has not R. Abbahu said — some say it has been taught in a Baraitha: From when do they say the blessing over rain? From the time when the bridegroom goes out to meet his bride.[8] What blessing do they say? R. Judah said: We give thanks to Thee for every drop which Thou hast caused to fall for us; and R. Johanan concluded thus: 'If our mouths were full of song like the sea ... we could not sufficiently give thanks unto Thee, O Lord our God, etc.' up to 'shall prostrate itself before Thee. Blessed art Thou, O Lord, to whom abundant thanksgivings are due'.[9] (Is it abundant thanksgivings and not all thanksgivings? — Raba said: Say, 'the God to whom thanksgivings are due'. R. Papa said: Therefore let us say both 'to whom abundant thanksgivings are due' and 'God of thanksgivings'.) But after all there is a contradiction? — There is no contradiction; the one blessing[10] is said by one who has heard [that it has been raining]; the other by one who has seen it. But one who hears of it hears good tidings, and we have learnt: For good tidings one says: Blessed is He who is good and does good?[11] In fact both are said by one who sees it, and still there is no contradiction: the one is said if only a little falls, the other, if much falls. Or if you like, I can say that both are said for a heavy fall, and still there is no contradiction: the one is said by a man who has land, the other by one who has no land. Does one who has land say the blessing, 'Who is good and does good'? Has it not been taught: One who has built a new house or bought new clothes says: Blessed is He who has kept us alive and brought us to this season; [if it is] for himself along with others, he says: 'Who is good and does good'?[12] This is no contradiction. The one blessing[13] is said if he has a partnerships the others if he has no partnership. And thus it has been taught: In a word, for his own things he says: Blessed is He who has kept us

---

the days of Adam (Rashi).
[1] By making canals.
[2] Piruz Shabur on the eastern side of the Euphrates at the part where the Nahr Isa Canal branches off from the Euphrates connecting it at Bagdad with the Tigris (Obermeyer P. 57).
[3] The modern Hit.
[4] The bridge on the southern Tigris forming part of the great trading route between Khurzistan and Babylon during the Persian period (Obermeyer pp. 62ff.). For a full discussion and explanation of this whole passage v. Obermeyer pp. 52ff.
[5] Gen. II, 14.
[6] I.e., well-shaded from the sun.
[7] I.e., when the drops commence to rebound from the earth.
[8] V. P.B. p. 125.
[9] I.e., 'Who is good and does good'.
[10] And why should we be taught this again in the case of rain?
[11] And a landowner presumably does not share his land with others.
[12] The blessing, 'Who has kept us alive, etc.'.
[13] And the landowner shares the rain with all other landowners. (V. Rashi and Asheri).

alive and preserved us; for things which belong to him in conjunction with this neighbour, he says: Blessed is He who is good and does good.[1] And if no-one is associated with him in the ownership, does he never say the blessing, Who is good and does good? Has it not been taught: If a man is told that his wife has borne a son, he says: Blessed is He that is good and does good? — In that case, too, his wife is associated with him, because she is glad to have a son. Come and hear: If a man's father dies and he is his heir, first he says: Blessed is the true Judge, and afterwards he says: Blessed is He who is good and does good? — There, too, it is a case where there are brothers who inherit with him. Come and hear: Over a new kind of wine[2] there is no need to make a blessing; but if one goes to another place,[3] he must say a blessing again; and R. Joseph b. Abba said in the name of R. Johanan: Although they said that over a fresh kind of wine there is no need to make a blessing, still he says: Blessed is He who is good and does good? — There, too, It is a case where there are other members of the company who drink with him.

ONE WHO HAS BUILT A NEW HOUSE OR BOUGHT NEW VESSELS etc. R. Huna said: This is the rule only if he does not possess similar things; but if he has similar ones, he need not say the blessing. R. Johanan, however, says: Even if he has similar ones[4] he must make the blessing.

---

[1] I.e., if one drinks a new (and better) kind of wine in the course of a meal.
[2] To finish his meal, and wine is brought to him there.
[3] E.g., from an inheritance.
[4] Because the buying at any rate is fresh.

Folio 60a

We infer from this that if one bought things, and then bought some more, all agree that he need not say a blessing.[1] Some say: R. Huna said, This rule applies only where he does not buy again after already buying; but if he buys again after already buying, he need not say the blessing. R. Johanan, however, says: Even if he buys again after already buying, he must make a blessing. We infer from this that if he buys a kind of thing which he has already,[2] all agree that he has to say a blessing. An objection was raised: If one builds a new house, not having one like it already, he must say a blessing. If he already has any like them, he need not say a blessing. So R. Meir. R. Judah says: In either case he must make a blessing. Now this accords well with the first version, R. Huna following R. Meir and R. Johanan following R. Judah. But if we take the second version, it is true that R. Huna follows R. Judah, but whom does R. Johanan follow? It is neither R. Meir nor R. Judah![3]
— R. Johanan can reply: The truth is that according to R. Judah also If one buys again after already buying, he must make a blessing, and the reason why they join issue over the case of his buying something of a kind which he has already is to show you how far R. Meir is prepared to go, since he says that even if he buys something of a kind which he already has, he need not make a blessing, and all the more so if he buys again after already buying, he need not make a blessing. But should they rather not join issue over the case of buying again after already buying, where there is no need to say a blessing,[4] to show how far he
[R. Judah] is prepared to go?[5] — He prefers that the stronger instance should be a case of permission.[6]

OVER EVIL A BLESSING IS SAID etc. How is this to be understood? — For instance, if a freshet flooded his land. Although it is [eventually] a good thing for him, because his land is covered with alluvium and becomes more fertile, nevertheless for the time being it is evil.[7]

AND OVER GOOD etc. How can we understand this? — If for instance he found something valuable. Although this may [eventually] be bad for him, because if the king hears of it he will take it from him, nevertheless for the time being it is good.

IF A MAN'S WIFE IS PREGNANT AND HE SAYS, MAY [GOD] GRANT THAT MY WIFE BEAR etc. THIS IS A VAIN PRAYER. Are prayers then [in such circumstances] of no avail? R. Joseph cited the following in objection: And afterwards she bore a daughter and called her name Dinah.[8] What is meant by 'afterwards'? Rab said: After Leah had passed judgment on herself, saying, 'Twelve tribes are destined to issue from Jacob. Six have issued from me and four from the handmaids, making ten. If this child will be a male, my sister Rachel will not be equal to one of the

---

[1] Because in this case it is not a fresh buying.
[2] By inheritance or presentation.
[3] Because even R. Judah holds that if he buys again after already buying, he need not make a blessing.
[4] For the second purchase according to R. Meir.
[5] In demanding a blessing for the second purchase.
[6] I.e., a case in which a blessing need not be made.
[7] Because it spoils the produce of this year, and he has to say the blessing, 'Blessed is the true Judge'.
[8] Gen. XXX, 21.

handmaids'. Forthwith the child was turned to a girl, as it says, And she called her name Dinah![1] — We cannot cite a miraculous event [in refutation of the Mishnah]. Alternatively I may reply that the incident of Leah occurred within forty days [after conception], according to what has been taught: Within the first three days a man should pray that the seed should not putrefy; from the third to the fortieth day he should pray that the child should be a male; from the fortieth day to three months he should pray that it should not be a sandal;[2] from three months to six months he should pray that it should not be still-born; from six months to nine months he should pray for a safe delivery. But does such a prayer[3] avail? Has not R. Isaac the son of R. Ammi said: If the man first emits seed, the child will be a girl; if the woman first emits seed, the child will be a boy?[4] — With what case are we dealing here? If, for instance, they both emitted seed at the same time.

IF HE WAS COMING FROM A JOURNEY. Our Rabbis taught: It once happened with Hillel the elder that he was coming from a journey, and he heard a great cry in the city, and he said: I am confident that this does not come from my house. Of him Scripture says: He shall not be afraid of evil tidings; his heart is steadfast, trusting in the Lord.[5] Raba said: Whenever you expound this verse you may make the second clause explain the first, or the first clause explain the second. 'You may make the second clause explain the first', thus: 'He will not fear evil tidings'. Why? Because 'his heart is steadfast, trusting in the Lord'. 'You may explain the second clause by the first', thus: 'His heart is steadfast trusting in the Lord'; therefore, 'he shall not be afraid of evil tidings'. A certain disciple was once following R. Ishmael son of R. Jose in the market place of Zion. The latter noticed that he looked afraid, and said to him: You are a sinner, because it is written: The sinners in Zion are afraid.[6] He replied: But it is written: Happy is the man that feareth alway?[7] — He replied: That verse refers to words of Torah.[8] R. Judah b. Nathan used to follow R. Hamnuna. Once he sighed, and the other said to him: This man wants to bring suffering on himself, since it is written; For the thing which I did fear is come upon me, and that which I was afraid of hath overtaken me.[9] But [he replied] it is written: 'Happy is the man who feareth alway'? — He replied: That is written in connection with words of Torah.

ONE WHO GOES THROUGH A CAPITAL CITY. Our Rabbis taught: What does he say on entering? 'May it be Thy will O Lord, my God, to bring me into this city in peace'. When he is inside he says: 'I give thanks to Thee, O Lord, my God, that Thou hast brought me into this city in peace'. When he is about to leave he says: 'May it be Thy will, O Lord, my God, and God of my fathers, to bring me out of this city in peace'. When he is outside he says: 'I give thanks to Thee, O Lord, my God, that Thou hast brought me out of this city in peace, and as Thou hast brought me out in peace, so mayest Thou guide me in peace and support me in peace and make me proceed in peace and deliver me from the hands of all enemies and liers-in-wait by the way'. R. Mattena said: This applies only to a city where criminals are not tried and sentenced:[10] but in a city where criminals are tried and sentenced, this is unnecessary. Some report: R. Mattena said: Even in a city where criminals are tried

---

[1] Lit., 'judgment'.
[2] A kind of abortion resembling a flat-shaped fish called sandal.
[3] That the child should be a male.
[4] Which shows that it is all fixed beforehand.
[5] Ps CXII, 7.
[6] Isa. XXXIII, 14.
[7] Prov. XXVIII, 14.
[8] A man should always be afraid lest he may forget them.
[9] Job III, 25.
[10] I.e., where the protection of the law can not be relied on

and sentenced, for sometimes he may happen not to find a man who can plead in his defence.

Our Rabbis taught: On entering a bath-house one should say: 'May it be Thy will O Lord, my God, to deliver me from this and from the like of this, and let no humiliation or iniquity befall me; and if I do fall into any perversity or iniquity, may my death be an atonement for all my iniquities'. Abaye said: A man should not speak thus, so as not to open his mouth for the Satan.[1] For Resh Lakish said—and so it was taught in the name of R. Jose: A man should never open his mouth for the Satan. R. Joseph said: What text proves this? Because it is written, We should have been as Sodom, we should have been like unto Gomorrah.[2] What did the prophet answer them? Hear the word of the Lord, ye rulers of Sodom, etc.[3] On leaving the bath-house what does he say? R. Aha said: 'I give thanks unto Thee, O Lord, my God, that Thou hast delivered me from the fire'. R. Abbahu once went into the bathhouse and the floor of the bath-house gave way beneath him, and a miracle was wrought for him, and he stood on a pillar and rescued a hundred and one men with one arm. He said: This is what R. Aha meant.[4]

On[5] going in to be cupped one should say: 'May it be Thy will, O Lord, my God, that this operation may be a cure for me, and mayest Thou heal me, for Thou art a faithful healing God, and Thy healing is sure, since men have no power to heal, but this is a habit with them'.[6] Abaye said: A man should not speak thus, since it was taught in the school of R. Ishmael: [It is written], He shall cause him to be thoroughly healed.[7] From this we learn that permission has been given to the physician to heal. When he gets up [after cupping] what does he say? — R. Aha said: Blessed be He who heals without payment.

---

[1] Cf. supra 190.
[2] Isa. I, 9.
[3] Ibid., 10.
[4] In saying that one should give thanks on emerging.
[5] Cur. edd. introduce this with the words 'for R. Aha said': but this is best left out.
[6] To be cupped.
[7] Ex. XXI, 19.

Berakoth 60b

On entering a privy one should say: 'Be honoured, ye honoured and holy ones[1] that minister to the Most High. Give honour to the God of Israel. Wait for me till I enter and do my needs, and return to you'. Abaye said: A man should not speak thus, lest they should leave him and go. What he should say is: 'Preserve me, preserve me, help me, help me, support me, support me, till I have entered and come forth, for this is the way of human beings'. When he comes out he says: 'Blessed is He who has formed man in wisdom and created in him many orifices and many cavities. It is fully known before the throne of Thy glory that if one of them should be [improperly] opened or one of them closed it would be impossible for a man to stand before Thee'. How does the blessing conclude? Rab said: '[Blessed art Thou] that healest the sick'. Said Samuel: Abba[2] has turned the whole world into invalids! No; what he says is, 'That healest all flesh'. R. Shesheth said: 'Who doest wonderfully'. R. Papa said: Therefore let us say both, 'Who healest all flesh and doest wonderfully'.[3]

On going to bed one says from 'Hear, oh Israel' to 'And it shall come to pass if ye hearken diligently'. Then he says: 'Blessed is He who causes the bands of sleep to fall upon my eyes and slumber on my eyelids, and gives light to the apple of the eye. May it be Thy will, O Lord, my God, to make me lie down in peace, and set my portion in Thy law and accustom me to the performance of religious duties, but do not accustom me to transgression; and bring me not into sin, or into iniquity, or into temptation, or into contempt. And may the good inclination have sway over me and let not the evil inclination have sway over me. And deliver me from evil hap and sore diseases, and let not evil dreams and evil thoughts disturb me, and may my couch be flawless before Thee, and enlighten mine eyes lest I sleep the sleep of death. Blessed art Thou, oh Lord, who givest light to the whole world in Thy glory.'[4]

When he wakes he says: 'My God, the soul which Thou hast placed in me is pure. Thou hast fashioned it in me, Thou didst breathe it into me, and Thou preservest it within me and Thou wilt one day take it from me and restore it to me in the time to come. So long as the soul is within me I give thanks unto Thee, O Lord, my God, and the God of my fathers, Sovereign of all worlds, Lord of all souls. Blessed art Thou, O Lord, who restorest souls to dead corpses'.[5] When he hears the cock crowing he should say: 'Blessed is He who has given to the cock understanding to distinguish between day and night'. When he opens his eyes he should say: 'Blessed is He who opens the eyes of the blind'. When he stretches himself and sits up he should say: 'Blessed is He who looseneth the bound'. When he dresses he should say: 'Blessed is He who clothes the naked'. When he draws himself up he should say: 'Blessed is He who raises the bowed'. When he steps on to the ground he should say: 'Blessed is He who spread the earth on the waters'. When he commences to walk he should say: Blessed is He who makes firm the steps of man'. When he ties his shoes he should say: 'Blessed is He who has supplied all my wants'. When he fastens his girdle, he should say: 'Blessed is He who girds Israel with might'. When he spreads a kerchief over his head he should say: 'Blessed is

---

[1] These words are addressed to the angels who are supposed to accompany a man to the privies, which were regarded as the haunt of evil spirits, v. infra 61a.
[2] Rab.
[3] P.B. p. 4.
[4] Ibid. p. 293.
[5] Ibid. p. 5.

He who crowns Israel with glory'. When he wraps himself with the fringed garment he should say: 'Blessed is He who hast sanctified us with His commandments and commanded us to enwrap ourselves in the fringed garment'. When he puts the tefillin on his arm he should say: 'Blessed is He who has sanctified us with His commandments and commanded us to put on tefillin'. [When he puts it] on his head he should say: 'Blessed is He who has sanctified us with His commandments and commanded us concerning the commandment of tefillin'. When he washes his hands he should say: 'Blessed is He who has sanctified us with His commandments and commanded us concerning the washing of hands'.[1] When he washes his face he should say: 'Blessed is He who has removed the bands of sleep from mine eyes and slumber from mine eyes. And may it be Thy will O Lord, my God, to habituate me to Thy law and make me cleave to Thy commandments, and do not bring me into sin, or into iniquity, or into temptation, or into contempt, and bend my inclination to be subservient unto Thee, and remove me far from a bad man and a bad companion, and make me cleave to the good inclination and to a good companion in Thy world, and let me obtain this day and every day grace, favour, and mercy in Thine eyes, and in the eyes of all that see me, and show lovingkindness unto me. Blessed art Thou, O Lord, who bestowest lovingkindness upon Thy people Israel'.[2]

IT IS INCUMBENT ON A MAN TO BLESS etc. What is meant by being bound to bless for the evil in the same way as for the good? Shall I say that, just as for good one says the benediction 'Who is good and bestows good', so for evil one should say the benediction 'Who is good and bestows good'? But we have learnt: FOR GOOD TIDINGS ONE SAYS, WHO IS GOOD AND BESTOWS GOOD: FOR EVIL TIDINGS ONE SAYS, BLESSED BE THE TRUE JUDGE? — Raba said: What it really means is that one must receive the evil with gladness. R. Aha said in the name of R. Levi: Where do we find this in the Scripture? I will sing of mercy and justice, unto Thee, O Lord, will I sing praises,[3] whether it is 'mercy' I will sing, or whether it is 'justice' I will sing. R. Samuel b. Nahmani said: We learn it from here: In the Lord I will praise His word, in God I will praise His word.[4] 'In the Lord[5] I will praise His word': this refers to good dispensation; 'In God[6] I will praise His word': this refers to the dispensation of suffering. R. Tanhum said: We learn it from here: I will lift up the cup of salvation and call on the name of the Lord;[7] I found trouble and sorrow, but I called upon the name of the Lord.[8] The Rabbis derive it from here: The Lord gave and the Lord hath taken away,' blessed be the name of the Lord.[9]

R. Huna said in the name of Rab citing R. Meir, and so it was taught in the name of R. Akiba: A man should always accustom himself to say, 'Whatever the All-Merciful does is for good', [as exemplified in] the following incident. R. Akiba was once going along the road and he came to a certain town and looked for lodgings but was everywhere refused. He said 'Whatever the All-Merciful does is for good', and he went and spent the night in the open field. He had with him a cock, an ass and a lamp. A gust of wind came and blew out the lamp, a weasel came and ate the cock, a lion came and ate the ass. He said: 'Whatever the All-Merciful does is for good'. The same night some brigands came and

---

[1] For all these blessings v. P.B. P. 5f. These blessings are now no longer said after each act, but are all said together in the morning service.
[2] Ibid. p. 6.
[3] Ps. CI, 1.
[4] Ibid. LVI, 11. in the M.T. the order of the divine names is reserved.
[5] The name of the Attribute of Mercy.
[6] The name of the Attribute of Justice.
[7] Ibid. CXVI, 13.
[8] Ibid. 3.
[9] Job. I, 21.

carried off the inhabitants of the town. He said to them:[1] Did I not say to you, 'Whatever the All-Merciful does

---

[1] Apparently to the men of the town, on a subsequent occasion; or perhaps to his disciples who accompanied him.

Folio 61a

is all for good?[1]

R. Huna further said in the name of R. Meir: A man's words should always be few in addressing the Holy One, blessed be He, since it says, Be not rash with thy mouth and let not thy heart be hasty to utter a word before God,' for God is in heaven and thou upon earth; therefore let thy words be few.[2]

R. Nahman b. R. Hisda expounded: What is meant by the text, Then the Lord God formed [wa-yizer] man?[3] [The word wa-yizer] is written with two yods, to show that God created two inclinations, one good and the other evil. R. Nahman b. Isaac demurred to this. According to this, he said, animals, of which it is not written wa-yizer,[4] should have no evil inclination, yet we see that they injure and bite and kick? In truth [the point of the two yods] is as stated by R. Simeon b. Pazzi; for R. Simeon b. Pazzi said: Woe is me because of my Creator [yozri],[5] woe is me because of my evil inclination [yizri]![6] Or again as explained by R. Jeremiah b. Eleazar; for R. Jeremiah b. Eleazar said: God created two countenances in the first man,[7] as it says, Behind and before hast Thou formed me.[8]

And the rib which the Lord God had taken from man made he a woman.[9] Rab and Samuel explained this differently. One said that [this 'rib'] was a face, the other that it was a tail.[10] No objection can be raised against the one who says it was a face, since so it is written, 'Behind and before hast Thou formed me'. But how does he who says it was a tail explain 'Behind and before hast Thou formed me'? — As stated by R. Ammi; for R. Ammi said: 'Behind' [i.e., last] in the work of creation, and 'before' [i.e., first] for punishment. We grant you he was last in the work of creation, for he was not created till the eve of Sabbath. But when you say 'first for punishment', to what punishment do you refer? Do you mean the punishment in connection with the serpent? Surely it has been taught: Rabbi says, in conferring honour we commence with the greatest, in cursing with the least important. 'In conferring honour we commence with the greatest', as it is written, And Moses spoke to Aaron and to Eleazar and to Ithamar his sons that were left, Take the meal-offering that remaineth etc.[11] 'In cursing we commence with the least'; first the serpent was cursed then Eve and then Adam![12] I must say then that the punishment of the Flood is meant, as it is written, And He blotted out every living substance which was upon the face of the ground, both man and cattle.[13]

---

[1] Because the lamp or the cock or the ass might have disclosed his whereabouts to the brigands.
[2] Eccl. V, 1.
[3] Gen. II, 7.
[4] In Gen. II, 19, And the Lord God formed all the beasts of the field, etc., the word wa-yizer is spelt with one yod.
[5] If I follow my inclination.
[6] If I combat it.
[7] And out of one of them Eve was made.
[8] Ps. CXXXIX, 5. E.V. 'Thou host hemmed me in'.
[9] Gen. II, 22.
[10] I.e., projected like a tail.
[11] Lev. X, 12. Aaron is mentioned first.
[12] V. Gen. III, 14-20.
[13] Ibid. VII, 23. Man is here mentioned before cattle.

No difficulty arises for the one who says that Eve was created from the face, for so it is written, wa-yizer, with two yods. But he who says it was a tail, what does he make of wa-yizer? — As explained by R. Simeon b. Pazzi? For R. Simeon b. Pazzi said: Woe is me because of my Creator [yozri,] woe is me because of my evil inclination [yizri]! No difficulty arises for one who says it was a face, for so it is written, Male and female created He them',[1] But he who says it was a tail, what does he make of 'male and female created He them'? — As explained by R. Abbahu. For R. Abbahu contrasted two texts. It is written, 'Male and female created He them', and it is also written, For in the image of God made He man.[2] How are these statements to be reconciled? At first the intention was to create two, but in the end only one was created. No difficulty arises for him who says it was a face, since so it is written, He closed up the place with flesh instead thereof.[3] But he who says it was a tail, how does he explain, 'he closed up the place with flesh instead thereof'[4] — R. Jeremiah, or as some say R. Zebid, or again as some say, R. Nahman b.
Isaac, replied: These words are meant to apply only to the place of the cut. No difficulty arises for the one who says it was a tail, for so it is written, And God built.[5] But he who says, it was a face, what does he make of the words 'And God built'?[6] As explained by
R. Simeon b. Menasia. For R. Simeon b. Menasia expounded: What is meant by the words, 'And the Lord built the rib'? It teaches that the Holy One, blessed be He, plaited Eve's hair and brought her to Adam; for in the seacoast towns 'plaiting' [keli'atha][7] is called, 'building' [binyatha]. Another explanation: R. Hisda said (some say, it was taught in a Baraitha): It teaches that [God] built Eve after the fashion of a storehouse. Just as a storehouse is narrow at the top and broad at the bottom so as to hold the produce [safely], so a woman is narrower above and broader below so as to hold the embryo. And he brought her to the man.[8] R. Jeremiah b. Eleazar said: This teaches that [God] acted as best man[9] to Adam. Here the Torah teaches a maxim of behaviour, that a man of eminence should associate himself with a lesser man in acting as best man, and he should not take it amiss.

According to the one who says it was a face, which of the two faces went in front? — R. Nahman b. Isaac answered: It is reasonable to suppose that the man's face went in front, since it has been taught: A man should not walk behind a woman on the road,[10] and even if his wife happens to be in front of him on a bridge he should let her pass on one side, and whoever crosses a river behind a woman will have no portion in the future world.[11]

Our Rabbis taught: If a man counts out money from his hand into the hand of a woman so as to have the opportunity of gazing at her, even if he can vie in Torah and good deeds with Moses our teacher, he shall not escape the punishment of Gehinnom, as it says, Hand to hand, he shall not escape from evil,[12] he shall not escape from the punishment of Gehinnom.

---

[1] Ibid. V, 2.
[2] Ibid. IX, 6.
[3] Ibid. II, 22.
[4] Ibid. 22. E.V. 'made'.
[5] Ibid. 22. E.V. 'made'.
[6] The face needed no 'building', since it was already there.
[7] This word in Aramaic also means 'tents'.
[8] Gen. II, 22.
[9] Heb. shoshbin, the man who looks after the wedding arrangements; v. B.B., Sonc. ed., p. 618 n. 10.
[10] To avoid unchaste thoughts.
[11] Because the woman in crossing will naturally lift up her dress.
[12] Prov. XI, 21. E.V. 'My hand upon it! The evil man shall not be unpunished!'

R. Nahman said: Manoah was an 'am ha-arez, since it is written, And Manoah went after his wife.¹ R. Nahman b. Isaac demurred to this. According to this, [he said,] in the case of Elkanah when it says, 'And Elkanah went after his wife',² and in the case of Elisha when it says, And he rose and went after her,³ are we to suppose that this means literally after her? No; it means, after her words and her advice. So here [in the case of Manoah] it means, after her words and her advice! Said R. Ashi: On the view of R. Nahman that Manoah was an 'am ha'arez, he cannot even have known as much of Scripture as a schoolboy;⁴ for it says, And Rebekah arose and her damsels, and they rode upon the cammels and followed the man,⁵ [after the man] and not in front of the man.

R. Johanan said: Better go behind a lion than behind a woman; better go behind a woman than behind an idol; better go behind an idol than behind the synagogue when the congregation are praying.⁶ This, however, is the case only when he is not carrying a load; if he is carrying a load, there is no objection. And also this is the case only when there is no other entrance; but if there is another entrance there is no objection. And again this is the case only when he is not riding on an ass, but if he is riding on an ass, there is no objection. And again this is the case only when he is not wearing tefillin; but if he is wearing tefillin there is no objection.
Rab said: The evil inclination resembles a fly⁷ and dwells between the two entrances of the heart, as it says, Dead flies make the ointment of the perfumers fetid and putrid.⁸ Samuel said: It is a like a kind of wheat [hittah], as it says, Sin [hattath] coucheth at the door.⁹

Our Rabbis taught: Man has two kidneys, one of which prompts him to good, the other to evil; and it is natural to suppose that the good one is on his right side and the bad one on his left, as it is written, A wise man's understanding is at his right hand, but a fool's understanding is at his left.¹⁰

Our Rabbis taught: The kidneys prompt, the heart discerns, the tongue shapes [the words], the mouth articulates, the gullet takes in and lets out all kinds of food, the wind-pipe produces the voice,

---

¹ Judg. XIII, 11.
² This text is not found in the Scripture, and Tosaf. deletes the mention of Elkanah here; v. Rashal and Maharsha.
³ II Kings IV, 30.
⁴ Lit., 'he did not read Scripture in a schoolhouse'.
⁵ Gen. XXIV, 61.
⁶ V. supra 8b.
⁷ V. Suk. 52b.
⁸ Eccl. X, 1.
⁹ Gen. IV, 7. This is probably connected with the view that the forbidden fruit of which Adam ate was wheat; v. supra 40a (Maharsha).
¹⁰ Eccl. X, 2.

Berakoth 61b

the lungs absorb all kinds of liquids,[1] the liver is the seat of anger, the gall lets a drop fall into it and allays it, the milt produces laughter, the large intestine grinds [the food], the maw brings sleep and the nose awakens. If the awakener sleeps or the sleeper rouses,[2] a man pines away. A Tanna taught: If both induce sleep or both awaken, a man dies forthwith.

It has been taught: R. Jose the Galilean says, The righteous are swayed[3] by their good inclination, as it says, My heart[4] is slain within me.[5] The wicked are swayed by their evil inclination, as it says, Transgression speaketh to the wicked, methinks, there is no fear of God before his eyes.[6] Average people are swayed by both inclinations, as it says, Because He standeth at the right hand of the needy,[7] to save him from them that judge his soul.[8] Raba said: People such as we are of the average. Said Abaye to him: The Master gives no one a chance to live![9] Raba further said: The world was created only for either the totally wicked or the totally righteous.[10] Raba said: Let a man know concerning himself whether he is completely righteous or not! Rab said: The world was created only for Ahab son of Omri and for R. Hanina b. Dosa; for Ahab son of Omri this world, and for R. Hanina b. Dosa the future world.

And thou shalt love the Lord thy God etc.[11] It has been taught: R. Eliezer says: If it says 'with all thy soul', why should it also say, 'with all thy might',[12] and if it says 'with all thy might', why should it also say 'with all thy soul'? Should there be a man who values his life more than his money, for him it says; 'with all thy soul'; and should there be a man who values his money more than his life, for him it says, 'with all thy might'. R. Akiba says: With all thy soul': even if He takes away thy soul![13]

Our Rabbis taught: Once the wicked Government[14] issued a decree forbidding the Jews to study and practise the Torah. Pappus b. Judah came and found R. Akiba publicly bringing gatherings together and occupying himself with the Torah. He said to him: Akiba, are you not afraid of the Government? He replied: I will explain to you with a parable. A fox was once walking alongside of a river, and he saw fishes going in swarms from one place to another. He said to them: From what are you fleeing? They replied: From the nets cast for us by men. He said to them: Would you like to come up on to the dry land so that you and I can live together in the way that my ancestors lived with your ancestors?

---

[1] I.e., they absorb some moisture from the stomach.
[2] I.e., if the nose induces sleep or the maw waking.
[3] Lit., 'judged'.
[4] I.e., evil promptings
[5] Ps CIX, 22. E.V. 'wounded'.
[6] Ibid. XXXVI, 2.
[7] I.e., in good deeds.
[8] I.e., his two inclinations. Ibid. CIX, 31.
[9] If Raba is only average, what must other people be?
[10] I.e., this world for the wicked and the next for the righteous.
[11] Deut. VI, 5.
[12] This word is interpreted by the Rabbis to mean money.
[13] I.e., thy very self, thy life.
[14] I.e., Roman.

They replied: Art thou the one that they call the cleverest of animals? Thou art not clever but foolish. If we are afraid in the element in which we live, how much more in the element in which we would die! So it is with us. If such is our condition when we sit and study the Torah, of which it is written, For that is thy life and the length of thy days,[1] if we go and neglect it how much worse off we shall be! It is related that soon afterwards R. Akiba was arrested and thrown into prison, and Pappus b. Judah was also arrested and imprisoned next to him. He said to him: Pappus, who brought you here? He replied: Happy are you, R. Akiba, that you have been seized for busying yourself with the Torah! Alas for Pappus who has been seized for busying himself with idle things! When R. Akiba was taken out for execution, it was the hour for the recital of the Shema', and while they combed his flesh with iron combs, he was accepting upon himself the kingship of heaven.[2] His disciples said to him: Our teacher, even to this point? He said to them: All my days I have been troubled by this verse, 'with all thy soul', [which I interpret,] 'even if He takes thy soul'. I said: When shall I have the opportunity of[3] fulfilling this? Now that I have the opportunity shall I not fulfil it? He prolonged the word ehad[4] until he expired while saying it. A bath kol[5] went forth and proclaimed: Happy art thou, Akiba, that thy soul has departed with the word ehad! The ministering angels said before the Holy One, blessed be He: Such Torah, and such a reward? [He should have been] from them that die by Thy hand, O Lord.[6] He replied to them: Their portion is in life.[7] A bath kol went forth and proclaimed, Happy art thou, R. Akiba, that thou art destined for the life of the world to come.

ONE SHOULD AVOID SHOWING DISRESPECT TO THE EASTERN GATE BECAUSE IT IS IN A DIRECT LINE WITH THE HOLY OF HOLIES, etc. Rab Judah said in the name of Rab: These rules apply only to this side of Mount Scopus[8] and to one who can see the Temple.[9] It has also been recorded: R. Abba the son of R. Hiyya b. Abba said: Thus said R. Johanan: These rules apply only to this side of Scopus and to one who can see [Jerusalem], and when there is no fence intervening, and at the time when the Divine Presence rests on it.[10]

Our Rabbis taught: One who consults nature in Judea should not do so east and west[11] but north and south. In Galilee he should do so only east and west.[12] R. Jose, however, allows it, since R. Jose said: The prohibition was meant to apply only to one in sight of the Temple and in a place where there is no fence intervening and at the time when the Divine Presence rests there. The Sages, however, forbid it. The Sages say the same as the First Tanna? — They differ with regard to the sides.[13] It has been taught elsewhere: One who consults nature in Judea should not do so east and west but south and north, and in Galilee north and south is forbidden, east and west is permitted. R. Jose, however, permits it, since

---

[1] Deut. XXX, 20.
[2] I.e., recited the Shema'. V. supra 130.
[3] Lit., 'when will it come to my hands'.
[4] 'One' in Hear, O Israel etc.
[5] V. Glos.
[6] Ps. XVII, 14. E.V. 'From men by thy hand, O Lord'.
[7] Ibid.
[8] From the other side of Mount Scopus the Temple was no longer visible.
[9] Even from this side of Scopus, not being in a hollow.
[10] I.e., when the Temple is in existence.
[11] So as not to turn his back to Jerusalem.
[12] Galilee being north of Jerusalem.
[13] I.e., those parts of Judea and Galilee which were not due east or due north of Jerusalem. The first Tanna prohibits even in these parts, since they speak of the whole of Judea, whereas the Sages permit, referring as they do only to R. Jose's statement.

R. Jose used to say: This prohibition was meant to apply only to one who is in sight [of Jerusalem]. R. Judah says: When the Temple is in existence it is forbidden, when the Temple is not in existence it is permitted. R. Akiba forbids it in all places. R. Akiba says the same as the First Tanna? — They differ in the matter of outside of Palestine. Rabbah had bricks placed for him east and west.[1] Abaye went and changed them round to north and south. Rabbah went in and readjusted them. He said, Who is this that is annoying me? I take the view of R. Akiba, who said that it is forbidden in every place.

---

[1] So that he should not turn his back on Palestine.

Folio 62a

It has been taught: R. Akiba said: Once I went in after R. Joshua to a privy, and I learnt from him three things. I learnt that one does not sit east and west but north and south; I learnt that one evacuates not standing but sitting; and I learnt that it is proper to wipe with the left hand and not with the right. Said Ben Azzai to him: Did you dare to take such liberties with your master? He replied: It was a matter of Torah, and I required to learn. It has been taught: Ben 'Azzai said: Once I went in after R. Akiba to a privy, and I learnt from him three things. I learnt that one does not evacuate east and west but north and south. I also learnt that one evacuates sitting and not standing. I also learnt it is proper to wipe with the left hand and not with the right. Said R. Judah to him: Did you dare to take such liberties with your master? — He replied: It was a matter of Torah, and I required to learn.
R. Kahana once went in and hid under Rab's bed. He heard him chatting [with his wife] and joking and doing what he required. He said to him: One would think that Abba's mouth had never sipped the dish before! He said to him: Kahana, are you here? Go out, because it is rude.[1] He replied: It is a matter of Torah, and I require to learn.

Why should one wipe with the left hand and not with the right? — Raba said: Because the Torah was given with the right hand, as it says, At His right hand was a fiery law unto them.[2] Rabbah b. Hanah said: Because it is brought to the mouth.[3] R. Simeon b. Lakish said: Because one binds the tefillin [on the left arm] with it. R. Nahman b. Isaac said: Because he points to the accents in the scroll with it.[4] A similar difference of opinion is found among Tannaim. R. Eliezer says, because one eats with it; R. Joshua says, because one writes with it; R. Akiba says, because one points with it to the accents in the scroll.

R. Tanhum b. Hanilai said: Whoever behaves modestly in a privy is delivered from three things: from snakes, from scorpions, and from evil spirits. Some say also that he will not have disturbing dreams.[5] There was a certain privy in Tiberias which if two persons entered together even by day, they came to harm. R. Ammi and R. Assi used to enter it separately, and they suffered no harm. The Rabbis said to them, Are you not afraid? They replied: We have learnt a certain tradition.[6] The tradition for [avoiding harm in] the privy is modesty and silence; the tradition relating to sufferings is silence[7] and prayer. The mother of Abaye trained for him a lamb to go with him into the privy.[8] She should rather have trained for him a goat?[9](9) A satyr might be changed into a goat.[10] Before Raba became head of

---

[1] Lit., 'it is not the way of the world'.
[2] Deut. XXXIII, 2.
[3] It was usual to bring food to the mouth with the right hand and not with the left.
[4] Rashi explains: Because in chanting he makes corresponding movements with the right hand, this having been the custom of Palestinians in his day.
[5] Lit., 'his dreams will be settled on him'.
[6] Jastrow, with a slight change of reading (kible), renders 'charm'.
[7] I.e., resignation.
[8] As a protection against evil spirits.
[9] Goats were associated by the ancients with evil spirits.
[10] The Hebrew word sa'ir means both 'he-goat' and 'satyr'.

the Academy, the daughter of R. Hisda[1] used to rattle a nut in a brass dish.[2] After he became head, she made a window for him,[3] and put her hand on his head.[4]

'Ulla said: Behind a fence one may ease himself immediately; in an open field, so long as he can break wind without anyone hearing it. Issi b. Nathan reported thus: Behind a fence, as long as he can break wind without anyone hearing it; in a open field, as long as he cannot be seen by anyone. An objection was raised: [The watchers][5] may go out by the door of the olive press and ease themselves behind a fence [immediately] and they [the olives] remain clean! — For the sake of ritual purity they made a concession. Come and hear: How far can one go without affecting the cleanness [of the olive press]? Any distance as long as he can still see it![6] — The case of food-stuffs prepared in purity is different, as the Rabbis made a concession for them. R. Ashi said: What is meant by the words 'as long as he cannot be seen by anyone' used by Issi b. Nathan? As long as the exposed part of his body cannot be seen; but the man himself may be seen.

A certain funeral orator went down in the presence of R. Nahman [to deliver an address] and said: This man was modest in all his ways. Said R. Nahman to him: Did you ever follow him into a privy so that you should know whether he was modest or not? For it has been taught: A man is called modest only if he is such in the privy. And why was R. Nahman so much concerned about it? Because it has been taught: Just as the dead are punished,[7] so the funeral orators are punished[8] and those who answer [Amen] after them.

Our Rabbis taught: Who is a modest man? One who eases himself by night in the place where he eased himself by day.[9] Is that so? Has not Rab Judah said in the name of Rab: A man should always accustom himself [to consult nature] in the early morning and in the evening[10] so that he may have no need to go a long distance? And again, in the day-time Raba used to go as far as a mile, but at night he said to his attendant, Clear me a spot in the street of the town, and so too R. Zera said to his attendant, See if there is anyone behind the Seminary as I wish to ease myself? — Do not read 'in the place', but read, 'in the same way as he eases himself by day'.[11] R. Ashi said, You may even retain the reading 'place', the reference being to a private corner.[12]

The [above] text [states:] 'Rab Judah said in the name of Rab: A man should always accustom himself to consult nature morning and evening so that he may have no need to go a long distance'. It has been taught similarly, Ben 'Azzai said: Go forth before dawn and after dark, so that you should not have to go far. Feel yourself before sitting, but do not sit and then feel yourself, for if one sits and then feels himself, should witchcraft be used against him even as far away as Aspamia,[13] he will not be immune from it. And if he forgets and does sit and then feels, what is his remedy? — When he rises he should

---

[1] His wife.
[2] To frighten away the evil spirits.
[3] In the wall of the house, through which she could put her hand.
[4] As a protection. After becoming head of the Academy, he was more exposed to danger from the evil spirits.
[5] Men who watched the olive-oil press to see that no unclean person entered.
[6] But not further, so that he would himself still be visible. This refutes Issi.
[7] If they were sinners.
[8] For uttering false eulogies.
[9] I.e., a long way off.
[10] I.e., before daylight and after dark.
[11] I.e., modestly; v. supra, p. 389.
[12] To be used by night as well as by day.
[13] A name given to several far-distant places, including Spain.

say, thus: Not for me, not for me; not tahim nor tahtim;[1] not these nor any part of these;[2] neither the sorceries of sorcerers nor the sorceries of sorceresses!

---

[1] Words apparently used in incantations
[2] Aliter: 'Let not avail against me either the sorceries etc.'.

Berakoth 62b

. It has been taught: Ben 'Azzai says: Lie on anything but not on the ground;[1] sit on anything but not on a beam.[2]

Samuel said: Sleep[3] at dawn is like a steel edge to iron; evacuation at dawn is like a steel edge to iron. Bar Kappara used to sell sayings for denarii. 'While thou art still hungry, eat; while thou art still thirsty, drink; while thy pot is still hot, empty it out.[4] When the horn is sounded in [the market of] Rome, do you, O son of the fig-seller, sell thy father's figs'.[5] Abaye said to the Rabbis: When you go through the lanes of Mahoza to get to the fields, do not look to this side or to that, for perhaps women[6] are sitting there, and it is not proper to gaze at them.

R. Safra entered a privy. R. Abba came and cleared his throat at the entrance.[7] He said to him: Let the master enter. When he came out, he [R. Abba] said to him: You have not yet been turned into a satyr,[8] but you have learnt the manners of a satyr.[9] Have we not learnt as follows: There was a fire there,[10] and a superior privy. Its superiority lay in this: if one found it locked, he could be sure that someone was in there, but if he found it open, he could be sure that there was no one there. We see therefore, that it is not proper [for two to be in a privy].[11] He [R. Safra], however, was of opinion that it was dangerous [to keep him waiting], as it has been taught:[12] R. Simeon b. Gamaliel says: To keep back the fecal discharge causes dropsy; to keep back the urinary discharge causes jaundice.

R. Eleazar once entered a privy, and a Persian[13] came and thrust him away. R. Eleazar got up and went out, and a serpent came and tore out the other's gut.[14] R. Eleazar applied to him the verse, Therefore will I give a man for thee.[15] Read not adam [a man] but edom [an Edomite].

And he bade to kill thee, but he spared thee.[16] 'And he bade'! It should be, 'And I bade'![17] 'And he spared'! It should be, 'And I spared'! R. Eleazar said: David said to Saul: According to the law, you

---

[1] For fear of serpents.
[2] Lest it may break.
[3] The Aruch renders the word shinah here 'Making water'.
[4] The proverb is applied to relieving oneself.
[5] And do not wait for thy father to come; an admonition against procrastination.
[6] MS.M. 'men'.
[7] To find out if anyone was within.
[8] Lit., 'goat' v. supra p. 389, n. 6.
[9] Inviting me to come in, not in accordance with the rules of propriety. The meaning is not clear, Rashi seems to read (Seir), thus rendering: You have not yet entered Seir (Edom) and you have learnt the manners of (the people of) Seir, v. Maharsha.
[10] In the Temple court, to keep the priests warm.
[11] V. Strashun Glosses.
[12] V. supra 25a.
[13] This is obviously a censor's correction for 'Roman', v. MS.M.
[14] Jast. renders 'his gut dropped', from fright.
[15] Isa. XLIII, 4.
[16] I Sam. XXIV, 11.
[17] Since David is reporting his own action.

deserve to be slain, since you are a pursuer, and the Torah has said, If one comes to kill your rise and kill him first.[1] But the modesty which you have shown has caused you to be spared. What is this? As it is written: And he came to the fences[2] by the way, where was a cave; and Saul went in le-hasek [to cover his feet].[3] It has been taught: There was a fence within a fence, and a cave within a cave. R. Eleazar says: It [the word le-hasek] teaches that he covered himself like a booth [sukkah].

Then David arose and cut off the skirt of Saul's robe privily.[4] R. Jose son of R. Hanina said: Whoever treats garments contemptuously will in the end derive no benefit from them; for it says, Now King David was old and stricken in years; and they covered him with clothes, but he could get no heat.[5]

If it be the Lord that hath stirred thee up against me, let Him accept an offering.[6] R. Eleazar said: Said the Holy One blessed be He, to David: Thou callest me a 'stirrer-up'. Behold, I will make thee stumble over a thing which even school-children know, namely, that which is written, When thou takest the sum of the children of Israel according to their number, then shall they give every man a ransom for his soul into the Lord... [that there be no plague among them] etc.[7] Forthwith, Satan stood up against Israel;[8] and it is further written, He stirred up David against them saying, Go, number Israel.[9] And when he did number them, he took no ransom from them and it is written, So the Lord sent a pestilence upon Israel from the morning even to the time appointed.[10] What is meant by 'the time appointed'? Samuel the elder, the son-in-law of R. Hanina, answered in the name of R. Hanina: From the time of slaughtering the continual offering until the time of sprinkling the blood. R. Johanan said: Right up precisely to midday.

And He said to the Angel that destroyed the people, It is enough[11] [rab]. R. Eleazar said: The Holy One, blessed be He, said to the Angel: Take a great man [rab] among them, through whose death many sins can be expiated for them.[12] At that time there died Abishai son of Zeruiah, who was [singly] equal in worth to the greater part of the Sanhedrin.

And as he was about to destroy, the Lord beheld, and He repented Him.[13] What did He behold? — Rab said: He beheld Jacob our ancestor, as it is written, And Jacob said when he beheld them.[14] Samuel said: He beheld the ashes of [the ram of] Isaac, as it says, God will see[15] for Himself the lamb.[16] R. Isaac Nappaha said: He saw the money of the atonement, as it says, And thou shalt take the atonement money from the children of Israel, and it shall be a memorial[17] etc. R. Johanan said: He

---

[1] V. supra 58a.
[2] E.V. 'sheepcotes'.
[3] Ibid. 4.
[4] Ibid. 5.
[5] I Kings I, 1.
[6] I Sam. XXVI, 19.
[7] Ex. XXX, 12.
[8] I Chron. XXI, 1.
[9] II Sam. XXIV, 1.
[10] Ibid. 15.
[11] Ibid. 16.
[12] According to the dictum that the death of the righteous is an atonement.
[13] I Chron. XXI, 15.
[14] Gen. XXXII, 3.
[15] So lit., E.V. 'provide'.
[16] Ibid. XXII, 8.
[17] Ex. XXX, 16.

saw the Temple, as it is written, In the mount where the Lord is seen.[1] R. Jacob b. Iddi and R. Samuel b. Nahmani differed on the matter. One said that He saw the atonement money, the other that He saw the Temple. The more likely view is that of him who says that He saw the Temple, since it is written, As it will be said on that day, in the mount where the Lord is seen.

A MAN SHOULD NOT ENTER THE TEMPLE MOUNT WITH HIS STAFF etc. What is the meaning of kappandaria? Raba said: A short cut, as its name implies.[2] R. Hanah b. Adda said in the name of R. Sama the son of R. Meri: It is as if a man said, instead of going round the blocks [makkifna adari], I will go in here. R. Nahman said in the name of Rabbah: If one enters a synagogue not intending to use it as a short cut, he may use it as a short cut. R. Abbahu said: If there was a path there originally,[3] it is permitted. R. Helbo said in the name of R. Huna: If one entered a synagogue to pray, he may use it as a short cut, as it says, But when the people of the land shall come before the Lord in the appointed seasons [he that entereth by the north gate shall go forth by the south gate, etc.].[4]

AND SPITTING [ON IT IS FORBIDDEN] A FORTIORI. R. Bibi said in the name of R. Simeon b. Lakish: If one spits in these times[5] on the Temple mount, it is as if he spat into the pupil of His eye, since it says: And Mine eyes and My heart shall be there perpetually.[6] Raba said: It is permitted to expectorate in the synagogue, this being on the same footing as wearing a shoe. Just as wearing a shoe is forbidden on the Temple mount but permitted in the synagogue, so spitting is forbidden in the Temple mount but permitted in the synagogue. Said R. Papa to Raba — according to others, Rabina said to Raba, while others again report that R. Adda b. Mattena said it to Raba, Instead of learning the rule from the analogy of a shoe, why not learn it from that of a short cut?[7] — He replied: The Tanna derives it from a shoe, and you want to derive it from a short cut! What is this [reference]? As it has been taught: 'A man should not enter the Temple mount either with his staff in his hand or his shoe on his foot, or with his money tied up in his cloth, or with his money bag slung over his shoulder, and he should not make it a short cut, and spitting [on it is forbidden] a fortiori from the case of the shoe: seeing that regarding a shoe, the wearing of which does not show contempt, the Torah has said, Put off thy shoes from off thy feet,[8] must not the rule all the more apply to spitting, which does show contempt? R. Jose b. Judah said: This reasoning is not necessary. For see, it says, For none might enter within the king's gate clothed in sackcloth.[9] Now have we not here an argument a fortiori: if such is the case with sackcloth which is not in itself disgusting, and before an earthly king, how much more so with spitting which is in itself disgusting, and before the supreme King of Kings!'[10] He [R. Papa] replied to him [Raba]: What I mean is this. Let us be stringent in both cases,[11] and reason thus:

---

[1] Adverting to the name of the mountain which is 'The Lord shall see'. Gen. XXII, 14.
[2] Representing as it does the Latin compendiaria via. Raba seems to imply that there is no need to try to interpret it as an Aramaic expression.
[3] Before the synagogue was built.
[4] Ezek. XLVI, 9.
[5] When the Temple is no longer there.
[6] I Kings IX, 3.
[7] A synagogue may not be used as a short cut, v. Meg. 28a.
[8] Ex. III, 5.
[9] Esth. IV, 2.
[10] Thus we see that the Tanna derives the rule regarding spitting from the analogy of a shoe.
[11] Of spitting on the Temple mount and in the synagogue.

Folio 63a

The rule [about spitting] for the Temple mount where the shoe is forbidden we may derive from the analogy of the shoe, but in the case of the synagogue where the shoe is permitted, instead of deriving the rule from the shoe and permitting it, let us rather derive it from the short cut and forbid it? — Rather, said Raba: [The synagogue is] on the same footing as a man's house. Just as a man objects to his house being made a short cut but does not object to the wearing of shoes or to spitting there, so in the case of the synagogue, the using it as a short cut is forbidden, but wearing the shoe and spitting in it is not forbidden.

AT THE CONCLUSION OF THE BENEDICTIONS SAID IN THE TEMPLE [THEY USED TO SAY, FOR EVER etc.]. Why all this? — Because the Amen response is not given in the Sanctuary. And whence do we know that the Amen response was not made in the Sanctuary? — Because it says, Stand up and bless the Lord your God from everlasting to everlasting,[1] and it goes on, And let them say,[2] Blessed be Thy glorious name that is exalted above every[3] blessing and praise. I might think that one praise would suffice for all the blessings.[4] It therefore says, 'Above every blessing and praise', implying, for every blessing assign to Him praise.[5]

IT WAS LAID DOWN THAT GREETING SHOULD BE GIVEN IN [GOD'S] NAME etc. Why the further citation? — You might think that Boaz spoke thus on his own accord;[6] come and hear, therefore, [the other text] 'THE LORD IS WITH THEE, THOU MIGHTY MAN OF VALOUR'. You might still say that it was an angel who spoke thus to Gideon;[7] come and hear, therefore, the other text, 'DESPISE NOT THY MOTHER WHEN SHE IS OLD';[8] and it says, 'IT IS TIME TO WORK FOR THE LORD, THEY HAVE MADE VOID THY LAW.[9] Raba said: The first clause of this verse can be taken as explaining the second, and the second can be taken as explaining the first. 'The first clause may be taken as explaining the second', thus: It is time to work for the Lord.[10] Why? Because they have made void Thy law.'The second clause may be taken as explaining the first', thus: They have made void Thy law.[11] Why? Because it is time to work for the Lord.

It was taught: Hillel the Elder said: When the scholars keep in [the teaching of] the Torah, do thou disseminate it,[12] and when they disseminate it do thou keep it in.[13] If thou seest a generation which is eager for the knowledge of the Torah, spread it abroad,[14] as it says, There is that scattereth and yet

---

[1] Neh. IX, 5.
[2] Those who made the response.
[3] E.V. 'all'.
[4] I.e., that one response should be made at the end of all the blessings (Rashi).
[5] V. Sot. (Sonc. ed.) p. 198, n. 2.
[6] And his action need not be taken as a precedent.
[7] Simply transmitting his message.
[8] I.e., despise not the example of Boaz.
[9] V. p. 329, n. 4.
[10] As much as to say, Boaz had good warrant for what he did. This rule apparently was cavilled at in certain quarters, and the Rabbis felt that some very strong justification was needed for it.
[11] Like Elijah in sacrificing on Mount Carmel.
[12] So that it should not be forgotten. Lit., 'scatter', like a sower scattering.
[13] So as not to compete with them.
[14] Lit., 'scatter'. Cf. n. 7.

increaseth.¹ But if thou seest a generation which takes no interest in the Torah, keep it in to thyself, as it says, When it is time to work for the Lord,² they make void Thy law. Bar Kappara expounded: When goods are cheap, collect³ [money] and buy. In a place where there is no man, there be a man. Abaye said: You may infer from this that in a place where there is a man [to teach the Torah], there you should not be a man. This is obvious? — It required to be stated for the case where the two are equal.⁴

Bar Kappara expounded: What short text is there upon which all the essential principles of the Torah depend? In all thy ways acknowledge Him and He will direct thy paths.⁵ Raba remarked: Even for a matter of transgression.⁶ Bar Kappara [further] expounded: A man should always teach his son a clean and not laborious trade. What, for example? R. Hisda said: Needle-stitching.⁷

It has been taught: Rabbi says, A man should not invite too many friends to his house, as it says, There are friends that one hath to his own hurt.⁸ It has been taught: Rabbi says, A man should not appoint a steward over his house, for had not Potiphar appointed Joseph as steward over his house, he would not have fallen into such trouble as he did. It has been taught: Rabbi says, Why does the section of the Nazirite⁹ follow immediately on that of the unfaithful wife?¹⁰ To teach you that anyone who sees an unfaithful wife in her evil ways should completely abstain from wine. Hezekiah the son of R. Parnak said in the name of R. Johanan: Why does the section of the unfaithful wife follow immediately on one dealing with terumoth¹¹ and tithes?¹² To teach you that if one has terumoth and tithes and does not give them to the priest, in the end he will require the priest's services to deal with his wife. For so it says, Every man's hallowed things shall be his,¹³ and immediately afterwards it says, If any man's wife go aside,¹⁴ and later is it written, And the man shall bring his wife, etc.¹⁵ Nay more, in the end he shall be in need of them,¹⁶ as it says, 'Every man's hallowed things shall be his'.¹⁷ R. Nahman b. Isaac said: If he does give, he will eventually become rich, as it says, Whatever a man giveth the priest, he shall have¹⁸ — he shall have much wealth.

R. Huna b. Berekiah said in the name of R. Eleazar ha-Kappar: Whoever associates the name of heaven with his suffering¹⁹ will have his sustenance doubled, as it says, And the Almighty shall be in

---

¹ Prov. XI, 24.
² I.e., when disseminating the Torah would bring it into contempt.
³ The Aruch reads, 'make haste'.
⁴ For there is no question that a superior may displace an inferior.
⁵ Prov. III, 6.
⁶ Weigh the pros and cons of it. This must be linked with the foregoing principle which permits the violation of the law when the exigencies of the time demand it.
⁷ Lit., 'the stitching of furrows'.
⁸ Prov. XVIII, 24.
⁹ Num. VI.
¹⁰ Ibid. V, 11-31.
¹¹ Plural of terumah, v. Glos.
¹² Ibid. V, 5-10.
¹³ Ibid. 10.
¹⁴ Ibid. 12. The juxtaposition implies: 'If a man keeps his hallowed things to himself and does not give them to the priest, then this wife, etc.'.
¹⁵ Ibid. 15.
¹⁶ Since he will lose his money.
¹⁷ In the form of poor man's tithe.
¹⁸ Ibid. 10. E.V. 'it shall be his'.
¹⁹ By blessing God for the evil, or praying.

thy distress, and thou shalt have double silver.[1] R. Samuel b. Nahmani said: His sustenance shall fly to him like a bird, as it says, And silver shall fly to thee.[2]

R. Tabi said in the name of R. Josiah: Whoso is faint[3] in the study of the Torah will have no strength to stand in the day of trouble, as it says, If thou art faint [in the study of the Torah] in the day of adversity thy strength will be small.[4] R. Ammi b. Mattenah said in the name of Samuel: Even if only in the performance of a single precept, as it says, 'If thou faint', in any case.

R. Safra said: R. Abbahu used to relate that when Hananiah the son of R. Joshua's brother went down to the Diaspora,[5] he began to intercalate the years and fix new moons outside Palestine. So they [the Beth din] sent after him two scholars, R. Jose b. Kippar and the grandson of R. Zechariah b. Kebutal. When he saw them, he said to them: Why have you come? — They replied: We have come to learn Torah [from you]. He thereupon proclaimed: These men are among the most eminent of the generation. They and their ancestors have ministered in the Sanctuary (as we have learnt: Zechariah b. Kebutal said: Several times I read to him[6] out of the book of Daniel). Soon they began to declare clean what he declared unclean and to permit what he forbade. Thereupon he proclaimed: These men are worthless, they are good for nothing. They said to him: You have already built and you cannot overthrow, you have made a fence and you cannot break it down.[7] He said to them: Why do you declare clean when I declare unclean, why do you permit when I forbid? — They replied: Because you intercalate years and fix new moons outside of Palestine. He said to them: Did not Akiba son of Joseph intercalate years and fix new moons outside of Palestine?[8] — They replied: Don't cite R. Akiba, who left not his equal in the Land of Israel. He said to them: I also left not my equal in the Land of Israel. They said to him: The kids which you left behind have become goats with horns, and they have sent us to you, bidding us, 'Go and tell him in our name. If he listens, well and good; if not, he will be excommunicated.

---

[1] Job XXII, 25. E.V. 'And the Almighty shall be thy treasure, and thou shalt have precious silver. The word to'afoth (precious) is connected by the Rabbis with the Aramaic word 'af, to double.
[2] Here the word to'afoth is connected with the Hebrew 'uf, to fly.
[3] I.e., is negligent.
[4] Prov. XXIV, 10. E.V. 'If thou art faint in the day of adversity, thy strength shall be small indeed'.
[5] Golah, Babylon. Here the reference is to Pumbeditha. This was during the Hadrianic persecution following the Bar Kochebah Wars. V. J.E. VI, p. 207.
[6] The High Priest. V. Yoma 18b.
[7] I.e., you cannot take away from us the name you have conferred on us.
[8] Yeb. 122a.

Berakoth 63b

Tell also our brethren in the Diaspora [not to listen to him]. If they listen to you, well and good; if not, let them go up to the mountain, let Ahia[1] build an altar and let Hananiah play the harp,[2] and let them all become renegades and say that they have no portion in the God of Israel'. Straightway all the people broke out into weeping and cried, Heaven forbid, we have a portion in the God of Israel. Why all this to-do? — Because it says, For out of Zion shall go forth the law, and the word of the Lord from Jerusalem.[3] We can understand that if he declared clean they should declare unclean, because this would be more stringent. But how was it possible that they should declare clean what he declared unclean, seeing that it has been taught: If a Sage has declared unclean, his colleague is not permitted to declare clean? — They thought proper to act thus so that the people should not be drawn after him.

Our Rabbis have taught: When our teachers entered the vineyard at Jabneh,[4] there were among them R. Judah and R. Jose and R. Nehemiah and R. Eliezer the son of R. Jose the Galilean. They all spoke in honour of hospitality and expounded texts [for that purpose]. R. Judah, the head of the speakers in every place,[5] spoke in honour of the Torah and expounded the text, Now Moses used to take the tent and pitch it without the camp.[6] Have we not here, he said, an argument a fortiori? Seeing that the Ark of the Lord was never more than twelve mil distant[7] and yet the Torah says, Everyone that sought the Lord went out unto the tent of meeting,[8] how much more [is this title[9] applicable to] the disciples of the wise who go from city to city and from province to province to learn Torah!

And the Lord spoke unto Moses face to face.[10] R. Isaac said: The Holy One, blessed be He, said to Moses, Moses, I and thou will propound views[11] on the halachah. Some say that the Holy One, blessed be He, said thus to Moses: Just as I have turned upon thee a cheerful face, so do thou turn upon Israel a cheerful face and restore the tent to its place. And he would return to the camp.[12] R. Abbahu said: The Holy One, blessed be He, said to Moses: Now they will say, The Master[13] is angry and the disciple[14] is angry, what will happen to Israel? If thou wilt restore the tent to its place, well and goods but if not, Joshua son of Nun, the disciple, will minister in thy place. Therefore it is written, 'And he would return to the camp'. Raba said: All the same [God's] word was not uttered in vain, since it says, But his minister Joshua, the son of Nun, a young man, departed not out of the

---

[1] The head of the community.
[2] Hananiah was a Levite.
[3] Isa. II, 3.
[4] The Academy at Jabneh, so called either because it actually was in a vineyard, or because the disciples sat in rows like the vines in a vineyard. The incident is related in a somewhat different form in the Midrash Rabbah on Cant. II, 5.
[5] V. Shab. 33b.
[6] Ex. XXXIII, 7.
[7] This being the extent of the Israelitish camp.
[8] Ex. XXXIII, 7.
[9] Of 'one who seeks the Lord'.
[10] Ibid. 11.
[11] Lit., 'faces'.
[12] Ibid.
[13] God.
[14] Moses.

tent.[1]

R. Judah spoke further in honour of the Torah, expounding the text, Attend [hasket] and hear, O Israel: this day thou art become a people unto the Lord thy God.[2] Now was it on that day that the Torah was given to Israel? Was not that day the end of the forty years [of the wandering]? It is, however, to teach thee that the Torah is as beloved every day to those that study it as on the day when it was given from Mount Sinai. R. Tanhum the son of R. Hiyya, a man of Kefar Acco[3] said: The proof is that if a man recites the Shema' every morning and evening and misses one evening, it is as if[4] he had never recited the Shema'. The word 'hasket' implies: Make yourselves into groups [kittoth] to study the Torah, since the knowledge of the Torah can be acquired only in association with others, as stated by R. Jose b. Hanina; for R. Jose b. Hanina said: What is the meaning of the text, A sword is upon the boasters [baddim] and they shall become fools?[5] A sword is upon the enemies of the disciples of the wise[6] who sit separately [bad bebad] and study the Torah. What is more, they become stupid. It is written here, 'and they shall become fools', and it is written elsewhere, For that we have done foolishly.[7] What is more, they are sinners, as it says, and we have sinned.[8] If you prefer, I can learn the meaning from here: The princes of Zoan are become fools [no'alu].[9] Another explanation of 'Attend [hasket] and hear, Israel'. Cut yourselves to pieces [kattetu] for words of Torah, as was said by Resh Lakish. For Resh Lakish said: Whence do we learn that words of Torah are firmly held by one who kills himself for it? Because it says, This is the Torah, when a man shall die in the tent.[10] Another explanation of 'Attend and hear, O Israel': Be silent [has] and then analyse [katteth],[11] as stated by Raba; for Raba said: A man should always first learn Torah and then scrutinize it.

They said in the school of R. Jannai: What is meant by the verse, For the churning of milk bringeth forth curd, and the wringing of the nose bringeth forth blood; so the forcing of wrath bringeth forth strife?[12] With whom do you find the cream of the Torah? With him who spits out upon it the milk which he has sucked from the breasts of his mother.[13] 'The wringing of the nose[14] bringeth forth blood'. Every student who is silent when his teacher is angry with him the first time will become worthy to distinguish between clean blood and unclean. 'The forcing of wrath[15] bringeth forth strife': Every student who is silent when his teacher is angry with him a first and a second time will be worthy to distinguish between money cases and capital cases,[16] as we have learnt: R. Ishmael says, One who desires to be wise should occupy himself with money judgments, since no branch of the Torah surpasses them, for they are like a perpetual fountain [of instruction]. R. Samuel b. Nahmani said: What is meant by the verse, If thou hast done foolishly [nobaltah] in lifting up thyself, or if thou

---

[1] Ibid. This is taken to mean that he succeeded Moses.
[2] Deut. XXVII, 9. .
[3] In Lower Galilee.
[4] I.e., he feels as if.
[5] Jer. L, 36.
[6] Euphemism for the disciples themselves.
[7] Num. XII, 11. In both texts the Hebrew word is no'alu.
[8] Ibid.
[9] Isa. XIX, 13.
[10] Num. XIX, 14. 'Tent' is taken to mean a place of study.
[11] I.e., first listen to the teacher, and then discuss what he has said.
[12] Prov. XXX, 33.
[13] I.e., who commences to learn in his earliest childhood.
[14] Heb. af, which also means anger.
[15] Heb. appayim, lit., 'two angers'.
[16] I.e., to decide to which category an intricate case belongs.

hast planned devices [zammotah], lay thy hand upon thy mouth?¹ Whoever abases [menabbel] himself for words of Torah² will in the end be exalted, but if one muzzles [zamam] himself, his hand will be upon his mouth.³

R. Nehemiah began to speak in praise of hospitality, expounding the text, And Saul said unto the Kenites, Go, depart, get you down from among the Amalekites, lest I destroy you with them; for ye showed kindness to all the children of Israel when they came up out of Egypt.⁴ Have we not here an argument a fortiori: if such was the reward of Jethro⁵ who befriended Moses only for his own benefit, how much more will it be for one who entertains a scholar in his house and gives him to eat and drink and allows him the use of his possessions!

R. Jose began to speak in praise of hospitality, expounding the verse, Thou shalt not abhor an Edomite, for he is thy brother; thou shalt not abhor an Egyptian, because thou wast a stranger in his land.⁶ Have we not here an argument a fortiori? If such was the reward of the Egyptians who befriended the Israelites only for their own purposes, as it says, And if thou knowest any able men among them, then make them rulers over my cattle,⁷ how much more will it be for one who entertains a scholar in his house and gives him to eat and drink and allows him the use of his possessions!

R. Eliezer the son of R. Jose the Galilean began to speak in praise of hospitality, expounding the verse, And the Lord blessed Obed-Edom and all his house … because of the Ark of God.⁸ Have we not here an argument a fortiori? If such was the reward for attending to the ark which did not eat or drink, but before which he merely swept and laid the dust, how much more will it be for one who entertains a scholar in his house and gives him to eat and drink and allows him the use of his possessions! What was the blessing with which God blessed him [Obed-Edom]? — R. Judah b. Zebida says: This refers to Hamoth⁹ and her eight daughters-in-law who each bore six children at a birth,

---

¹ Prov. XXX, 32
² I.e., is not ashamed to ask questions which may at first sound foolish.
³ He will be unable to answer questions put to him.
⁴ I Sam. XV, 6.
⁵ Who is called the Kenite, Judg. I, 16.
⁶ Deut. XXIII, 8.
⁷ Gen. XLVII, 6.
⁸ II Sam. VI, 12.
⁹ The wife of Obed-Edom.

Folio 64a

as it says, Peullethai the eighth son[1] for God blessed him,[2] and it is written, All these were of the sons of Obed-Edom, they and their sons and their brethren, able men in the strength for the service, threescore and two of Obed-Edom.[3]

R. Abin the Levite said: Whoever tries to force his [good] fortune will be dogged by [ill] fortune,[4] and whoever forgoes his [good] fortune will postpone his [ill] fortune.[5] This we can illustrate from the case of Rabbah and R. Joseph. For R. Joseph was 'Sinai'[6] and Rabbah was 'an uprooter of mountains'.[7] The time came when they were required [to be head of the Academy].[8] They [the collegiates] sent there [to Palestine] to ask, As between 'Sinai' and an 'uprooter of mountains', which should have the preference? They sent answer: Sinai, because all require the owner of wheat.[9] Nevertheless, R. Joseph would not accept the post, because the astrologers had told him that he would be head for only two years. Rabbah thereupon remained head for twenty-two years, and R. Joseph after him for two years and a half.[10] During all the time that Rabbah was head, R. Joseph did not so much as summon a cupper to come to his house.[11]

R. Abin the Levite further said: What is the point of the verse, The Lord answer thee in the day of trouble, the name of the God of Jacob set thee up on high?[12] The God of Jacob and not the God of Abraham and Isaac? This teaches that the owner of the beam should go in with the thickest part of it.[13]

R. Abin the Levite also said: If one partakes of a meal at which a scholar is present, it is as if he feasted on the effulgence of the Divine Presence, since it says, And Aaron came and all the elders of Israel, to eat bread with Moses' father-in-law before God.[14] Was it before God that they ate? Did not they eat before Moses? This tells you, however, that if one partakes of a meal at which a scholar is present, it is as if he feasted on the effulgence of the Divine Presence.

R. Abin the Levite also said: When a man takes leave of his fellow, he should not say to him, 'Go in peace'. but 'Go to peace'. For Moses, to whom Jethro said, Go to peace,[15] went up and prospered,

---

[1] Omitting with BaH: 'and it is written' inserted in cur. edd.
[2] I Chron. XXVI, 5. This shows that he had eight sons.
[3] Ibid. 8. The sixty-two are made up of the eight sons mentioned, six more to his wife at one birth, and six to each of his eight daughters-in-law.
[4] Lit., 'whoever pushes his hour will be pushed by his hour'.
[5] Lit., 'if one is pushed away from before his hour, his hour is pushed away from before him'.
[6] I.e., possessed an encyclopaedic knowledge of the traditions.
[7] I.e., exceptionally skillful in dialectic.
[8] Sc. of Pumbeditha.
[9] I.e., to know the authentic traditions.
[10] Rabbah was head 309-330. R. Joseph who succeeded him died in 333.
[11] But went instead to him, like any ordinary individual. On the whole passage v. Hor. (Sonc. ed.) p. 105 notes.
[12] Ps. XX, 2.
[13] He should put the thicker end in the ground so as to give better support. So the name of Jacob would be more efficacious in prayer because he was the more immediate ancestor of the Jewish people.
[14] Ex. XVIII, 12.
[15] Ibid. IV, 18.

whereas Absalom to whom David said, Go in peace,[16] went away and was hung.

R. Abin the Levite also said: One who takes leave of the dead[3] should not say to him 'Go to peace', but 'Go in peace', as it says, But thou shalt go to thy fathers in peace.[4]

R. Levi b. Hiyya said: One who on leaving the synagogue goes into the House of Study and studies the Torah is deemed worthy to welcome the Divine Presence, as it says, They go from strength to strength, every one of them appeareth before God in Zion.[5]

R. Hiyya b. Ashi said in the name of Rab: The disciples of the wise have no rest either in this world or in the world to come,[6] as it says, They go from strength to strength, every one of them appeareth before God in Zion'.

R. Eleazar said in the name of R. Hanina: The disciples of the wise increase peace in the world, as it says, And all thy children shall be taught of the Lord, and great shall be the peace of thy children.[7] Read not banayik [thy children] but bonayik [thy builders].[8] Great peace have they that love Thy law, and there is no stumbling for them.[9] Peace be within thy walls and prosperity within thy palaces.[10] For my brethren and companions' sake I will now say, Peace be within thee.[11] For the sake of the house of the Lord our God I will seek thy good.[12] The Lord will give strength unto His people, the Lord will bless His people with peace.[13]

---

[16] II Sam. XV, 9.
[3] On leaving the funeral procession.
[4] Gen. XV, 15.
[5] Ps. LXXXIV, 8.
[6] Because they are always progressing in their spiritual strivings.
[7] Isa. LIV, 13.
[8] I.e., learned men.
[9] Ps. CXIX, 165.
[10] Ibid. CXXII, 7.
[11] Ibid. 8.
[12] Ibid. 9.
[13] Ibid. XXIX, 11.

BN Publishing

www.bnpublishing.com

We have Book Recommendations for you

Automatic Wealth: The Secrets of the Millionaire Mind--Including: Acres of Diamonds, As a Man Thinketh, I Dare you!, The Science of Getting Rich, The Way to Wealth, and Think and Grow Rich [UNABRIDGED]
by Napoleon Hill, et al (CD-ROM - February 23, 2005)

Think and Grow Rich [MP3 AUDIO] [UNABRIDGED]
by Napoleon Hill, Jason McCoy (Narrator) (Audio CD - January 30, 2006)

As a Man Thinketh [UNABRIDGED]
by James Allen, Jason McCoy (Narrator) (Audio CD - May 1, 2005)

Your Invisible Power: How to Attain Your Desires by Letting Your Subconscious Mind Work for You [MP3 AUDIO] [UNABRIDGED]
by Genevieve Behrend, Jason McCoy (Narrator) (Audio CD - February 9, 2006)

Thought Vibration or the Law of Attraction in the Thought World [MP3 AUDIO] [UNABRIDGED]
by William Walker Atkinson, Jason McCoy (Narrator) (Audio CD - July 1, 2005)

Automatic Wealth, The Secrets of the Millionaire Mind-Including:As a Man Thinketh, The Science of Getting Rich, The Way to Wealth and Think and Grow Rich (Paperback)

BN Publishing

www.bnpublishing.com

BN Publishing

www.bnpublishing.com

BN Publishing

www.bnpublishing.com

BN Publishing

www.bnpublishing.com

BN Publishing

www.bnpublishing.com

BN Publishing

www.bnpublishing.com

BN Publishing

www.bnpublishing.com

BN Publishing

www.bnpublishing.com

BN Publishing

www.bnpublishing.com

BN Publishing

www.bnpublishing.com

BN Publishing

www.bnpublishing.com

BN Publishing

www.bnpublishing.com

BN Publishing

www.bnpublishing.com

www.ingramcontent.com/pod-product-compliance
Lightning Source LLC
Chambersburg PA
CBHW080331170426
43194CB00014B/2525